SYSTEMS SHIFT: CREATING AND NAVIGATING CHANGE IN RHETORIC AND COMPOSITION ADMINISTRATION

PERSPECTIVES ON WRITING

Series Editors: Rich Rice, Heather MacNeill Falconer, and J. Michael Rifenburg
Consulting Editor: Susan H. McLeod | Associate Editor: Olivia Johnson

The Perspectives on Writing series addresses writing studies in a broad sense. Consistent with the wide ranging approaches characteristic of teaching and scholarship in writing across the curriculum, the series presents works that take divergent perspectives on working as a writer, teaching writing, administering writing programs, and studying writing in its various forms.

The WAC Clearinghouse and University Press of Colorado are collaborating so that these books will be widely available through free digital distribution and low-cost print editions. The publishers and the series editors are committed to the principle that knowledge should freely circulate and have embraced the use of technology to support open access to scholarly work.

Recent Books in the Series

Michael J. Michaud, *A Writer Reforms (the Teaching of) Writing: Donald Murray and the Writing Process Movement, 1963–1987* (2023)

Michelle LaFrance and Melissa Nicolas (Eds.), *Institutional Ethnography as Writing Studies Practice* (2023)

Phoebe Jackson and Christopher Weaver (Eds.), *Rethinking Peer Review: Critical Reflections on a Pedagogical Practice* (2023)

Megan J. Kelly, Heather M. Falconer, Caleb L. González, and Jill Dahlman (Eds.), *Adapting the Past to Reimagine Possible Futures: Celebrating and Critiquing WAC at 50* (2023)

William J. Macauley, Jr. et al. (Eds.), *Threshold Conscripts: Rhetoric and Composition Teaching Assistantships* (2023)

Jennifer Grouling, *Adapting VALUEs: Tracing the Life of a Rubric through Institutional Ethnography* (2022)

Chris M. Anson and Pamela Flash (Eds.), *Writing-Enriched Curricula: Models of Faculty-Driven and Departmental Transformation* (2021)

Asao B. Inoue, *Above the Well: An Antiracist Argument From a Boy of Color* (2021)

Alexandria L. Lockett, Iris D. Ruiz, James Chase Sanchez, and Christopher Carter (Eds.), *Race, Rhetoric, and Research Methods* (2021)

Kristopher M. Lotier, *Postprocess Postmortem* (2021)

Ryan J. Dippre and Talinn Phillips (Eds.), *Approaches to Lifespan Writing Research: Generating an Actionable Coherence* (2020)

SYSTEMS SHIFT: CREATING AND NAVIGATING CHANGE IN RHETORIC AND COMPOSITION ADMINISTRATION

Edited by Genesea M. Carter and Aurora Matzkel

The WAC Clearinghouse
wac.colostate.edu
Fort Collins, Colorado

University Press of Colorado
upcolorado.com
Denver, Colorado

The WAC Clearinghouse, Fort Collins, Colorado 80523

University Press of Colorado, Denver, Colorado 80203

© 2023 by Genesea M. Carter and Aurora Matzke. This work is licensed under a Creative Commons Attribution-NonCommercial-NoDerivatives 4.0 International License.

ISBN 978-1-64215-184-8 (PDF) | 978-1-64215-185-5 (ePub) | 978-1-64642-498-6 (pbk.)

DOI 10.37514/PER-B.2023.1848

Produced in the United States of America

Library of Congress Cataloging-in-Publication Data

Names: Carter, Genesea M. (Genesea Mackenzie), 1979– editor. | Matzke, Aurora, 1981– editor.
Title: Systems Shift: Creating and Navigating Change in Rhetoric and Composition Administration / Edited by Genesea M. Carter and Aurora Matzke.
Description: Perspectives on writing. | Fort Collins, Colorado : The WAC Clearinghouse ; Louisville, Colorado : University of Colorado Press, 2023.
Identifiers: LCCN 2023040105 (print) | LCCN 2023040106 (ebook) | ISBN 9781646424986 (paperback) | ISBN 9781642151848 (adobe pdf) | ISBN 9781642151855 (epub)
Subjects: LCSH: English language—Composition and exercises—Study and teaching (Higher) | English language—Rhetoric—Study and teaching (Higher) | Social justice and education. | Educational technology. | Information literacy. | LCGFT: Essays.
Classification: LCC PE1404 .N384 2023 (print) | LCC PE1404 (ebook) | DDC 808.0071/1—dc23/eng/20231103
LC record available at https://lccn.loc.gov/2023040105
LC ebook record available at https://lccn.loc.gov/2023040106

Copyeditor: Annie Halseth
Designer: Mike Palmquist
Cover Photo: Malcolm G. Childers, "In the Wake of the Ice River, Johns Hopkins Straits, Alaska." Used with permission.
Series Editors: Rich Rice, Heather MacNeill Falconer, and J. Michael Rifenburg
Consulting Editor: Susan H. McLeod

The WAC Clearinghouse supports teachers of writing across the disciplines. Hosted by Colorado State University, it brings together scholarly journals and book series as well as resources for teachers who use writing in their courses. This book is available in digital formats for free download at wac.colostate.edu.

Founded in 1965, the University Press of Colorado is a nonprofit cooperative publishing enterprise supported, in part, by Adams State University, Colorado State University, Fort Lewis College, Metropolitan State University of Denver, University of Alaska Fairbanks, University of Colorado, University of Denver, University of Northern Colorado, University of Wyoming, Utah State University, and Western Colorado University. For more information, visit upcolorado.com.

Land Acknowledgment. The Colorado State University Land Acknowledgment can be found at landacknowledgment.colostate.edu.

CONTENTS

Acknowledgments vii

Foreword ix
    Eric C. Camarillo

Introduction 3
    Aurora Matzke and Genesea M. Carter

SECTION 1. DISCIPLINARY AND PUBLIC NETWORKS: EXISTING AS A
PROFESSION 23

Chapter 1. Purposeful Access: Reinventing Supersystems through
Rhetorical Action 27
    Bre Garrett and Matt Dowell

Chapter 2. At a Crossroads: The Committee for Change and the
Voices of CCCC 51
    Bernice Olivas, Janelle Jennings-Alexander, Mara Lee Grayson,
    Tamara Issak, Lana Oweidat, Christina V. Cedillo,
    Ashanka Kumari, Caitlyn Rudolph-Schram, and Trent M. Kays

Chapter 3. "Help I Posted": Race, Power, Disciplinary Shifts, and
the #WPAListserv-FeministRevolution 73
    Iris Ruiz, Latina Oculta, Brian Hendrickson, Mara Lee Grayson,
    Holly Hassel, Mike Palmquist, and Mandy Olejnik

Chapter 4. Critiquing the "Networked Subject" of Anti-racism: Toward a
More Empowered and Inclusive "We" in Rhetoric and Composition 99
    Erec Smith

SECTION 2. INTRA-CAMPUS AND INSTITUTIONAL NETWORKS:
EXISTING AS A PROGRAM 117

Chapter 5. Basic Writing's Interoffice, Intercampus Actor-Network:
Assembling Our History through Dolmagean Analysis 121
    John Paul Tassoni

Chapter 6. Outsiders Looking In: Discursive Constructions of
Remediation beyond the Academy 141
    Lynn Reid

Contents

Chapter 7. Working Within the Rhetorical Constraints: Renovation and Resistance in a First-Year Writing Program 165
    Mara Lee Grayson

Chapter 8. Negotiating Dominance in Writing Program Administration: A Case Study 189
    Emily R. Johnston

Chapter 9. Networking Across the Curriculum: Challenges, Contradictions, and Changes 203
    Kelly Bradbury, Sue Doe, and Mike Palmquist

Chapter 10. The Writing Center as Border Processing Station 235
    Eric C. Camarillo

Chapter 11. Voice, Silence, and Invocation: The Perilous and Playful Possibilities of Negotiating Identity in Writing Centers 249
    Lucien Darjeun Meadows

SECTION 3. PERSONAL AND RELATIONAL NETWORKS: EXISTING AS AN ADMINISTRATOR 269

Chapter 12. Is Resistance Futile? Struggling against Systematic Assimilation of Administrative Work 271
    Genesea M. Carter

Chapter 13. "It's Complicated": Scheduling as an Intellectual, Networked Social Justice Issue for WPAs 293
    Julia Voss and Kathryn Bruchmann

Chapter 14. Flexible Framing, Open Spaces, and Adaptive Resources: A Networked Approach to Writing Program Administration 321
    Jenna Morton-Aiken

Conclusion. A Tool Kit 345
    Genesea M. Carter and Aurora Matzke

Afterwords 357
    Lucien Darjeun Meadows

Contributors 359

ACKNOWLEDGMENTS

The nascent idea of this collection, and indeed the collection introduction, come from a talk given in 2017 at the Sixteenth Annual Conversation on the Liberal Arts by Elmar Hashimov, Aurora Matzke, and Christine Watson. We thank Elmar, Christine, and our panel attendees for drawing attention to how our own networks and communities participate in and influence change over time. We are incredibly grateful for the hard work, feedback, and editing expertise Bonnie brought to this project. We also thank the attendees of our 2018 CCCC panel for their ideas, feedback, and suggestions. In addition, we profusely thank Mike Palmquist for his support, ideas, mentorship, and help finalizing this collection. We are grateful as well as for the series editors' thoughtful feedback. Mike and the editors' editorial support and expertise strengthened this collection. Perhaps most importantly, we thank the collection authors, without whom this collection would not exist, for bringing their wisdom and telling their stories.

FOREWORD

Eric C. Camarillo
Tarrant County College, Northwest

As I progress in writing center work, I have become more attuned to the ways in which that work is delimited by structural systems and network forces. Trying to see how these systems bend the arc of our work is akin to making out something just at the edge of your vision: when you look head-on, they vanish; they only make themselves known in the periphery.

Part of deploying systems and network theories as frameworks for understanding our work means being willing to examine what lies peripherally just out of sight. This level of work might be unsettling for some because it basically means examining elements and factors that lie outside our control—I mean that both locally in terms of institutional context and as a field in terms of what we in writing centers, writing programs, and other areas of writing studies are willing and able to engage with.

Yet, I personally find theories around systems and networks to be oddly comforting. They help me to articulate more concretely the issues I face when working with students, faculty, staff, and administration at various institutions. These theories help me to visualize students from diverse backgrounds and not rely on whatever imaginary ideal version of a student I might want to cling to as I engage in this work. And being more aware of the systems at play wherever I'm at helps me to be proactive when it comes to supporting students rather than reactive. I think this last piece is where this collection is most powerful as I and each of my fellow contributors has strived to provide strategies and recommendations to better see and navigate these invisible networks.

This collection, at this time, is highly kairotic. Never before has the field had to contend so explicitly with systems and networks than we have during the pandemic, especially those material networks of various technologies and technological platforms that mediate much of our work. In the introduction to this collection, Genesea and Aurora highlight how the lens of networks and systems theories allows us to see technology as an ecological framework, one that can support or thwart an institution's larger efforts. From a network perspective, technology becomes an agent that can be influenced rather than an immutable force beyond our control.

While you can find more detailed information about the chapters in the introduction, I'd be remiss without celebrating my wonderful co-contributors

DOI: https://doi.org/10.37514/PER-B.2023.1848.1.2

who continued the process of writing and revising even in the face of a global pandemic, the editors who remained hopeful and optimistic during unprecedented times, and you, dear reader, as you read through this collection, the product of pandemic times.

I first began my work with networks and systems around the same time that Aurora and Genesea sent out the CFP. The (literal and metaphorical) borders of my writing center at that time were becoming clearer and clearer to me, but I didn't have the language to articulate how and why I felt encroached upon by exterior forces. You may be reading this collection because you have similar concerns with how your work is being shaped or with how your work is being delimited—and with how to resist these invisible systems and networks in productive ways. This collection is for you.

Because of the breadth of areas covered, anyone in rhetoric and composition should be able to find a chapter that speaks either to their experience or provides a strategy that can be implemented or modified for different contexts. As much as the individual chapters may be working with the theoretical concepts of systems and networks, the collection as a whole exists at the junction of theory and practice and can be an invaluable resource no matter where you are in the work or at what level you're performing this work.

Thank you for reading.

SYSTEMS SHIFT: CREATING AND NAVIGATING CHANGE IN RHETORIC AND COMPOSITION ADMINISTRATION

INTRODUCTION

Aurora Matzke
Chapman University

Genesea M. Carter
Colorado State University

The seeds of this collection were planted in 2017, when we (Genesea and Aurora), along with several of our friends, started having conversations with our colleagues about how systems and networks affect, shape, or prevent the institutional and programmatic change-making efforts in our profession—everything from academic labor issues and workplace boundaries to inclusive assessment benchmarks and equitable service requirements. These conversations culminated in our Conference on College Composition and Communication's (CCCC) 2018 panel, "Seeking Justice for Basic Writing and English Language Administration through Networked Theories." Simply put, our goal of that panel was this: acknowledging that citing best practice was not cutting it when we tried to work toward equity and inclusion within our administrative roles. But what was working? Openly talking about, applying, and working through various program issues within the context of system and network theories. At our panel, we suggested that rhetoric and composition administrators—who we define as any faculty, staff, or students engaged in writing program, writing center, writing and language, and/or writing across curriculum/communities administrative work—pivot their focus from the individual (themselves and their expertise) to the system and networks shaping their work. During the panel, one of the attendees said, "You all really need to publish something on this. I don't think there's anything quite like it out there."

Leaving CCCC 2018, we continued to apply system and network theories to better understand and navigate our own institutional contexts. We began closely examining the systems and networks impeding or confining the disciplinary best practices and change-making efforts we wanted to enact. We focused on the systems and networks stalling the equitable hiring practices we wanted to adopt; we examined the systems and networks prohibiting the inclusive and diverse curriculum redesigns we wanted to make; we tried to shift the systems and networks stopping our efforts at reducing overwork and burnout; we studied the systems and networks prolonging our efforts to update assessment practices to honor students' positionalities and intersectionalities. As writing program administration,

DOI: https://doi.org/10.37514/PER-B.2023.1848.1.3

writing center administration, and writing across curriculum/communities scholarship has shown, it is downright challenging—and sometimes impossible—to do meaningful work, sometimes *because of* the existing systems and networks that define the parameters of our jobs, our spheres of influence, our resources, and our agency. It is with these passions, commitments, and frustrations we were determined to have "naming and changing conversations" with our colleagues and stakeholders to define and work through university systems and networks that impacted or impeded efforts toward meaningful change. Since 2018, we have kept coming back to networks and systems frameworks to help us unpack, expose, and demystify the roadblocks getting in the way of our work: the disciplinary and institutional conversations and efforts, the intra-campus initiatives, and the personal and relational changes (and boundaries) in which we invested.

Networks and systems impose agency or act like agentive beings in that they may shape how rhetoric and composition administrators work, impose deficit-based pedagogies or approaches, stifle emotional and physical well-being, and/or perpetuate problematic labor practices (Boylan & Bonham, 2014; Otte & Mlynarczyk, 2010; Poe et al., 2018). This collection compiles and presents efforts that have led rhetoric and composition program administrators to confront and respond to networks and systems that problematically affect administrative work, disciplinary best practices, curriculum design, working conditions, and change-making efforts.[1] We do not offer a one-size-fits-all approach, as institutions, networks, and systems are organic and ecosocial. However, one feature of this collection is that contributors have included specific recommendations for readers to try out within their own contexts to further contextualize and mobilize the work outside of local contexts. As a result of our own administrative experiences being shaped by networks and systems (and the intra-campus and disciplinary conversations we were having), we wrote the call for this collection.

This collection is itself a rhizomic system. Within these pages, we intend to show diverse networks existing from macro (national conversations in the field) to micro (the internal well-being of the administrator). The sections and chapters are pieces of the of the academic supersystem and, as such, offer different rhetorical roots: some chapters are research-based case studies, some chapters utilize narrative, some chapters are hybrid genres of multiple authors' conversations. The hope is that the collection gives readers both a taste of the familiar and something that is different from their own normative expectations—be it genre, voice, or argument.

---

1   Within the collection, we use the umbrella term "rhetoric and composition administrators/administration" to encapsulate the different administrative work the collection authors wrote about, including WPA work, Writing Center work, Basic Writing work, WAC work, among other roles. We encourage readers to read each chapter with eyes towards the possibilities of what each chapter might offer their particular contexts and roles.

The collection contains experts and researchers of and from various gender identities, socioeconomic statuses, races, religions, and professional levels. Because of the purposeful inclusion of diverse experts, voices, and academic backgrounds—and because this collection is an exercise in pushing against established systems that stifle our work, our identities, and our values—we encouraged the collection authors to rhetorically use mediums of writing that incorporate, bend, or push back against historically normative expectations of academic writing. We intentionally showcase various ways to interpret, experience, and resist networks and systems. Try to enjoy this. Allow yourself to notice and make note of any homecoming or resistance you may feel as a reader, and ask yourself: is this not the very nature of systems?

SYSTEMS, NETWORKS, AND ADMINISTRATIVE WORK

Systems and network theories offer us lenses for problem-solving because they allow us to zoom both out of and into the complexities within our work. In a salient article, Patricia Ericsson et al. (2016) cited ecosocial systems theory as going "beyond a linguistic or a language-based approach and demands that community (and communication) be viewed in its complexity" (para. 8; see also Inoue, 2015, and Carter et al., 2023). At the same time, in the past decade or so, different liberal arts, particularly rhetoric, writing, and language studies, have been making a turn toward object-orientation and materiality within the social, including applications of Bruno Latour's phenomenological framework (see, for instance, Lynch & Rivers, 2015). For example, to understand how new programs and initiatives focused on equity-based practices might find traction in increasingly tight budgetary situations, we believe systems and network theories in particular—which consider time, place, culture, actors, agentive beings (both human and non) to name just a few—might be deployed by rhetoric and composition administrators as they act as change agents to strategically maximize educational opportunity.

As networks and systems collapse, are built, and collapse again under differing leadership structures, power-dynamics, and availabilities, rhetoric and composition administrators frequently step into the gaps. These are the spaces between, alongside, and absent from the (often) hegemonically-mapped, complex ecosocial systems comprised of smaller-scale systems and networks within our colleges and universities. These include, but are not limited to, academic departments, administrative offices, student-support programs, co-curricular committees, university facilities, students, faculty, and staff. Many of the groups make decisions that influence, support, and/or downright consternate rhetoric and composition administrative work, such as where classes are held, course caps, when courses are offered; how much money will be budgeted toward ongoing teaching and professional development initiatives; if student success initiatives will feature sound writing pedagogies and practices; whether or not there is a university-wide interest in supporting anti-racist or decolonizing pedagogies; how textbook selection or open access materials are or are not supported; and the list goes on. Writing program administrative (WPA) work, for example, plugs directly into campus-wide conversations in ways not easily felt or understood by all faculty or administrators. That is one of the reasons why some institutions struggle to fully fund WPA work and why the field has spent a considerable amount of time and research energy connecting itself to industry, retention, and academic promotion. This "everywhere but nowhere" problem, we would suggest, is connected to a lack of systemic thinking, rhetorical listening, and networked doings beyond the scope of the discipline.

Rhetoric and composition administrators step into the gaps to (re)build, collapse, interrogate, and problematize programs. We develop curricula, positions, policies, and practices based on educational home point standards, best practices in language acquisition and writing, and on current educational research at large. We may embed this work in English departments, alongside freestanding writing programs, in our writing centers, or our local and national organizations. We work to include and reach out toward key university ecosystems and networks (in addition to the ones in which we are immediately nested): linguistics, modern languages, communication studies, global student development, and their attendant professional organizations; admissions, advising, registrar, marketing, student support services, and several stakeholder academic programs; upper administrators, including deans, vice provosts, and the provost and senior vice presidents; and community partners, businesses, and local action groups.

Our administrative work naturally moves us in these directions, as we persist in forming connections in concert with our communities. As Aurora has stated elsewhere with our contributor Bre Garrett (2018), this is why after a year of being on the campuses of their respective first WPA positions, they knew more campus stakeholders than many of their colleagues. In this collection and elsewhere, we actively encourage WPAs to put out the welcome mat as much as possible. For example, it is a lot harder to get those course caps raised on you at the 11th hour if your enrollment and marketing leader knows the research: you are going to lose students at a higher rate once you pass certain capacities. They do not want to waste their recruitment efforts any more than you want to waste student time or burn out your faculty. Sure, it is best practice, and sure we should be listened to about that. But really, institutions have many competing interests, and a successful administrator will create connections among the systems to make the most nuanced argument possible at any given time.

When we examine this work as part of larger systems, as guided by ecosocial and networked systems frameworks, the stakeholder constituencies understand each other not just as related entities, inorganic rooms that touch impermeable walls within buildings; but rather they understand each other as vital, dynamic ecosystems within the eco-supersystem with knowledge growing and interchanging not through rigid hierarchies but rather organically, *rhizomatically*. Therein lies the power of ecosocial systems and network language.

Let's look at an example. Administrators spend an enormous amount of time interacting with others through technology. We know that almost all systems-based change for academic administrators involves mediation through technological tools. Consequently, understanding these actions as ones that are mediated by non-human agents (technology) through the work of Victor Kaptelinin and Bonnie Nardi (2009, 2018) could be particularly useful for those looking to understand how campus efforts toward change are supported or thwarted by learning management systems (LMS) or scheduling software—say, whether or not the LMS supports individual choice in the use of personal pronouns. In many cases, this is a function that must be "turned on" and integrated within student records. In addition, an emphasis on mediation, when examined from further distance, shows a complex matrix that is nourished or depleted by the human agents and/or actors that exist within, alongside, and outside these technologies and their systems. Essentially, it shows an ecological framework (Kaptelinin & Nardi, 2009). In the example, can your registration and records folx support, with time and energy, the integration of the LMS function, and even if they do, who will explain it to the faculty and the students?

Yet, given that we know humans interact with technology and that actions are mediated, it might be more useful to move to a type of non-human participant that is not as concretely realized in the day-to-day. For example, how might an administrator understand and utilize the concept of "attention" within a system—at what points does the organization and movement of the data require human interaction or use? Nathaniel Rivers (2016) argued, "Attention isn't simply an *a priori* human possession, but is instead a contingent attunement tightly bound to material relations across bodies, environments, media, and other nonhumans" (2016, para. 5). This should sound familiar to the reader, as Rivers is describing an ecosocial system bound by *kairos*. It is an attempt to note when actors are present in particular systems in particular ways via discussion of Latour's conception of "things." Things are the nonhuman actors that shape the conversations, actions, politics, and events within networks and systems (Latour, 2005). Things often "no longer have the clarity, transparency, obviousness of matters-of-fact; they are not made of clearly delineated, discrete objects" (Latour, 2005, p. 13). By placing "thing" in the open context of the environment, Rivers connects conceptions of "things" to the ecosystem in which they manifest. He posited, "As a Latourian thing, attention is not what's brought to bear on, given, distracted or captured, but rather what is always at stake in any interaction—it is an assembly, and it is one that emerges kairotically" (Rivers, 2016, para. 5). This is the very *thing* the editors of the collection have poignantly observed in our (re)design work. How do we make space for the kairotic interaction that is both mediated and/or denied by both human and non-human actors or agents?

In our analyses, many of the reasons that diversity, equity, inclusion, belonging, and social justice (DEIBSJ) efforts fail is that many parties involved—the program leadership, the instructors, the community or campus stakeholders—are not only functioning in isolation but are also paying little attention to what is happening outside of their immediate ecosystem. For us, attention, and rhetorical listening particularly focused on the inside, alongside, and outside of the given supersystems, is a crucial element in any consensus-based efforts to deconstruct harmful systems. Let us give an example. At one of the many California Hispanic-serving institutions (HSIs), there are four different offices, reporting to four different vice presidents, that manage affinity and financial support for students who self-identify as Hispanic, first-generation students. On the one hand, the commitment that each area has to support Hispanic, first-generation students is commendable, and they do provide a myriad of support opportunities. On the other, splitting up the supports under different vice presidents has actually worked to reinforce hegemonic, systematized higher-educational structures because the differing offices are not required to work together or actively share information, strategies, or analytics around effectiveness. The *system as thing*, as assemblage, prevents the very real desire of the agents within the system, because it does not require nor encourage accountability for decision-making and subject positionality awareness beyond the immediate. The DEIBSJ efforts of the people within these offices become constricted by the disconnected networks—the offices and their respective vice presidents—within the larger university system.

Often, rhetoric and composition administrators do not approach higher educational supersystems as a series of internetworked systems and networks. To give another example: one of us once worked for four years to take the word "basic" out of a course. First, they needed department approval; two deans and a year later, they had it. Then, they needed curricular committee approval; one year later, they had it. But wait, there was another curricular committee. Uninvolved with the oversight of this particular course, but with a fairly large interest in controlling entrance "gatekeeping" courses, this committee convinced the registrar to hold the request, so the proposal languished a year—neither approved nor denied. Then, the leadership in both of the previous curricular committees changed over, and those chairs were happy to support the request in session. Low and behold, four years later, the catalog no longer listed the course as "basic." The story above is not uncommon. It is, however, more than a frustrating glimpse at bureaucracy. To a certain extent, the WPA approached the change of the name as a fairly straight-forward filling out of forms without considering how all of the differing bodies (both organic and inorganic) were a series of internetworked webs. Did the system cause the lag in change, did the WPA (in their ignorance) cause the lag in change, did the chairs cause the lag in change? We could go on, but we think you get our point: they all did and none of them did. Each of these nodes represent a microsystem connected to differing macrosystems that continue to cycle and connect outward. After all, why did one of us want to take "basic" out of the name of the course in the first place? Because of national, disciplinary research.

When we view our administrative work through the lenses of systems and networks, we can initiate an ongoing systems-based analysis of the supersystem we are working within. Let us be clear, we are not arguing disciplinary expertise should be thrown out the window or that carefully crafted research never will work or that subject positionality does not shift the discourse in demonstrable ways. Rather, once we gather the information we need to better understand the moving pieces of the supersystem, such as how the intra-campus and institution move together or how the personal and relational networks move together, we can make better choices about how to move forward, pivot, or resist. With this information, we can build practical tools and strategies that ensure long-term sustainable change. While many aspects of these analytical and experiential processes involve different types of materiality (e. g., program and course proposals; funding streams; social media advocacy; sample syllabi and assignments; classroom spaces; and other tangible or observable artifacts), some of the most pivotal "things" are immaterial. It is not enough to design an educationally and administratively sound program if we're not also considering the network and systems the program will exist within.

WHERE DOES DEIBSJ FIT IN?

In much of the rhetoric and composition administration literature, higher educational change efforts are examined as a complex, fluid network of communities of practice composed of people with competing or similar purposes and values (Inoue, 2015; Kinney et al., 2010; Perryman-Clark & Craig, 2019; Rhodes & Alexander, 2014; Ruiz, 2016; Wenger, 1999), and these are indeed helpful frameworks. As a framework, diversity, equity, inclusion, belonging, and social justice (DEIBSJ) are broadly understood to be the active work put toward the examination and advocacy for change in relation to the fair and equitable distribution of goods, services, access, and opportunity across an identified populace. We draw our broad conception of DEIBSJ from Michael Reisch's definition of social justice in the *Routledge International Handbook of Social Justice*. According to Reisch, enacting social justice "involves envisioning what a just society would look like . . ." and "address[ing] fundamental questions about human nature and social relationships; about the distribution of resources, power, status, rights, access, and opportunities; and about how decisions regarding this distribution are made" (2014, p. 1). These broad definitions, both within the field and beyond, are helpful (but not exhaustive) in situating the different positionalities and approaches taken by the collection authors. Each author highlights the changes (or not) afforded by the systems they work within. As the reader, you also bring frameworks and definitions into your reading, and we encourage you to do so. Collectively, we all take part in moving the discipline toward more equitable practices for all.

This collection extends the discourse on change efforts within the field by drawing connections among the rhetoric and composition administrative work we do, the DEIBSJ values (sometimes competing, developing, or changing) we have, and applying the systems and network theories to examine their impact and how they shape us. Rhetoric and composition administrators' change-making efforts may include, but are not limited to, equitable labor and working conditions, student and/or faculty retention, persistence, promotion and/or successes, tenure or contracted labor requirements, collaborations between and across programs and offices, curriculum development and redesign, program assessment, community outreach, professional development support, mental and/or physical well-being, and responding to current events. These interactions and developments are embodied acts that interact with and participate in potentially sexist, racist, ableist systems and networks that remain unacknowledged even as the actors within these systems and networks want to actively work against oppression. Therefore, the collection is motivated by our sense that rhetoric and composition administrators, and the field at large, would benefit from continuing to work toward understanding and untangling how networks and systems at times supersede administrator, faculty, and student consensus for change (Hayles, 1999; Lemke, 1995; Rickert, 2013).

Furthermore, we deliberately sought authors with a diverse range of administrative experiences, positionalities, intersectionalities, and perspectives in response to calls from Asao Inoue (2015), CCCC (2020; 2021), April Baker-Bell (2020), and others to develop more collections and articles that prioritize anti-racist writing styles and genre conventions. Two of our priorities, as editors, was to not only follow the anti-racist, inclusive frameworks for editing outlined by the WAC Clearinghouse, *Peitho*, *Composition Studies*, and others, but also to make space for linguistic and genre justice, so we welcomed authors' writing styles and genre hybridity. As a result, this collection includes memoir, narrative, research, theory, vignettes, reflection, and action items, among other genres. The authors and their chapters intentionally represent the unique human sides within a complex supersystem. People cannot be systematized, regardless of how hard neoliberal proponents might try.

We also believe administrators, faculty, staff, and graduate students in the field of rhetoric and composition need tangible recommendations to confront and push back against the networks and systems that seek to constrict equity-based, inclusive education. That said, our and the authors' definitions and applications of DEIBSJ are not singular. And the collection could never claim it to be. The authors in this collection define it broadly and through a situated lens that tells their stories. In an effort to critically consider inequities, many problem-solve by relying on theory to aid their perspective. For example, Erec Smith uses Miguel Castells' network theory to consider our professional networks while John Tassoni relies on Jay Dolmage's "steep steps" theory to analyze the intercampus networks related to basic writing. Additionally, authors offer perspectives from the lens of decolonial theory, critical systems thinking, network analysis, cultural-historical activity theory, neoliberalism, among others. Yet, while you will find heavy theory in some chapters, the collection also makes room for voices and vignettes that reflect historical moments within our field. We embrace these varied approaches because it illuminates the humanness of our administrative work.

The Collection as a Network

To aid in the application and understanding of the systems and network theories, we have three key features meant to demonstrate the human experience of working within systems and networks: (1) we encouraged authors to include vignettes in their chapters, if they believed vignettes would help them tell their stories; (2) we invited authors to play with genre conventions and writing style that honor their intersectionalities and positionalities while also challenging White supremacist writing conventions of the field; and (3) we asked authors to include tangible recommendations at the end of their chapters so readers would have ideas and things to try.

We believe a collection of authors who adopt similar but different genre conventions, theories, and approaches toward change mirrors the complex, dynamic, and diverse strategies taken when working within institutional systems and networks. Some strategies may feel familiar to some readers; others may feel unfamiliar. Our authors' different strategies are meant to help readers connect with their experiences, and/or acknowledge where experiences and/or insights are disparate, as well as to provide a personal outlet for contributors to express their experiences working in and across systems and networks in ways that best reflect their perspectives.

Additionally, in welcoming authors' diverse approaches to sharing their research and experiences, we are, as some of us have noted elsewhere, naming and claiming the embodied experience when working within systems and networks. As Bre Garrett et al. (2019) wrote:

> By placing embodiment and delivery side-by-side, we compel ourselves and others to remain critically aware of how bodies interplay in communication situations. Imagine the implications for work environments, for community development, if leadership strategies accounted for bodied interactions. In a feminist tradition, embodied delivery invites and celebrates the personal, regarding people as living beings susceptible to health and harm, pain and pleasure. Embodied delivery's focus on difference enables a more careful understanding of bodies as situated in time and place. (p. 275)

At times, embodiment takes center stage. In other chapters, explicit attention to bodies might not be so readily found. However, in all chapters, bodies are there. Bodies are working, whether they are human bodies, bodies of knowledge, systems as bodies, or other kinds of bodies.

Organizationally, we have structured the collection from a macro perspective (our profession at the national level) to a micro perspective (the managerial tasks of the individual administrator). If read from cover to cover, the scope begins broadly with conversations about our national conferences, historical moments in the field, and the closing of the Writing Program Administrators listserv. Next, Section 2 narrows to campus-based work, covering basic writing, FYC, WAC, and the Writing Center. Last, in Section 3, the individual administrator's work—of self-care, scheduling, and archiving—becomes the final focus.

Wayfinding Through the Collection

In this next part of our introduction, we include strategies and approaches for reading the collection and offer author-written abstracts. Additionally, to guide readers through the collection themes, we have developed section introductions with thematic through-lines, more developed chapter overviews, and reflection and discussion questions. One through-line in this collection that you will find—by whatever wayfinding you do to arrive at the chapters you read—is an emphasis on problem-solving and navigating the existing systems and networks our authors find themselves within. We see our emphasis on our solutions to working within systems and networks as timely, especially as our nation confronts networks and systems relating to COVID-19, systemic oppression, and educational access concerns.

There are three approaches readers might take through the collection: the first approach is to start at the beginning (and here you are!) and work towards the end, as the collection works as a funnel, moving readers from the larger profession to the smaller program to the individual. Reading the collection from start to finish will provide discussions of framing that continue to gain in complexity as the individual subject is progressively addressed in greater detail throughout the chapters.

The second approach is through five thematic road maps, directly below. We know the nature of a collection is that readers most often do not read collections from cover to cover and may be interested in reading the collection like a hypertext. Each section includes an introduction with thematic through-lines and more descriptive chapter overviews to guide readers.

THEMATIC ROAD MAPS

Reading Map 1: Who Has the Power and What Do They Do with It?

- Kelly Bradbury, Sue Doe, and Mike Palmquist
- John Paul Tassoni
- Lynn Reid

Reading Map 2: Dominance and Resistance

- Bre Garrett and Matt Dowell
- Mara Lee Grayson
- Emily R. Johnston

Reading Map 3: Historical Events in our Profession

- Committee for Change
- Iris Ruiz, Latina Oculta, Brian Hendrickson, Mara Lee Grayson, Holly Hassel, Mike Palmquist, and Mandy Olejnik
- Erec Smith

Reading 4: Map: Re-seeing the Commonplace

- Eric C. Camarillo

- Julia Voss and Kathryn Bruchmann
- Jenna Morton-Aiken

Reading Map 5: Identity and Positionality in the System

- Lucien Darjeun Meadows
- Genesea M. Carter

The third reading approach is a "Choose Your Own Adventure," where readers start anywhere they like based on their interests. This approach works well for readers coming to the collection from the WAC Clearinghouse website or other open sources. We invite you to begin by skimming the abstracts that follow.

With these possible reading strategies in mind, feel free to start your journey. Know that however you decide to make your way through the collection, the chapters are pathways for you: a pathway through the national to the regional discourse, for example, or a pathway from institutional power to personal power, as another example. We hope that however you experience the collection, you take with you the practical application of the systems theories which are discussed therein, try on or play with the recommendations in each chapter, and reflect on your own experiences as administrators and humans living within a world of systems and networks.

CHAPTER ABSTRACTS

Chapter 1. "Purposeful Access: Reinventing Supersystems through Rhetorical Action" by Bre Garrett and Matt Dowell

Drawing on six years of work by the Council of Writing Program Administrators (CWPA) Disability and Accessibility Committee, accessibility planning for and challenges related to the 2019 CWPA Conference, and public artifacts related to accessibility claims at the Conference on College Composition and Communication 2019, Bre Garrett and Matt Dowell examine the barriers to full-bodied access at academic conferences. In questioning why conference accessibility, both rhetorically and in action, often functions as a retrofit or afterthought, the authors demonstrate how the interconnected supersystems of higher education and hyperableism make the task of increasing conference accessibility difficult. Inaccess to academic conferences, like the CWPA Conference, both prevents those who experience inaccess from full participation in shaping the discipline and detaches the WPA's local work from the larger national systems and networks related to that work. The authors, therefore, conclude by offering specific interventions that position invention, access, and delivery as interrelated rhetorical acts.

Introduction

Chapter 2. "At a Crossroads: The Committee for Change and the Voices of CCCC" by the CCCC Committee for Change: Bernice Olivas, Janelle Jennings-Alexander, Mara Lee Grayson, Tamara Issak, Lana Oweidat, Christina V. Cedillo, Ashanka Kumari, Caitlyn Rudolph-Schram, and Trent M. Kays

This chapter blends ten counternarratives from diverse members of the Conference on College Composition and Communication (CCCC) Committee for Change focusing specifically on CCCC 2019 and the Writing Program Administrators listserv (WPA-L) to illustrate how the discipline's structure acts as a limiting, stifling supersystem. The authors interweave their positionalities, intersectionalities, and experiences to expose deeply held racism and biases that do harm in our classrooms, to our students, and to our profession. Rather than a single, individualized narrative, this collective narrative illuminates how personal experiences are a network across spaces, places, and people. As a call to action, the authors demand a shift to antiracist and inclusive practices at all levels within one of the foremost professional spaces in our field.

Chapter 3. "'Help I Posted': Race, Power, Disciplinary Shifts, and the #WPAListservFeministRevolution" by Iris Ruiz, Latina Oculta, Brian Hendrickson, Mara Lee Grayson, Holly Hassel, Mike Palmquist, and Mandy Olejnik

To many members of the discipline of rhetoric, composition, and writing studies (RCWS), the #WPAListservFeministRevolution, so named for the hashtag that circulated as the disciplinary authority of the Writing Program Administrators listserv (WPA-L) was challenged, represented a pivotal moment of resistance and a veritable paradigm shift in the recent history of the field. In this chapter, a collective of co-authors, who take a multi-theoretical and polyvocal approach to reflection and analysis, examine a series of significant events—incidents of racist and sexist rhetoric on WPA-L—that led to this intersectional, antiracist, online (both through the listserv and Twitter), network-based disciplinary movement. Drawing upon actor-network theory and decolonial theory, the co-authors suggest that the White supremacy, misogyny, and inequity that catalyzed the revolution are representative of a longstanding disciplinary paradigm. As well, they consider what those dynamics and the resistance to them tell RCWS professionals about disciplinary history, present, and future.

Chapter 4. "Critiquing the 'Networked Subject' of Anti-racism: Toward a More Empowered and Inclusive 'We' in Rhetoric and Composition" by Erec Smith

By referencing contentious threads in the now-defunct Writing Program Administrators listserv, Erec Smith seeks to prove that the field of rhetoric and composition has not taken a turn toward social justice so much as social justice—in its manifestations as "identity politics"—has usurped the field, hijacking academic discourse for a monological agenda and a clear willingness to silence others rather than engage them. Smith attributes this to a dire need for a secure base among social justice-oriented teachers and scholars and, as a corollary, the need to censor and censure those they see as threats to that secure base.

Chapter 5. "Basic Writing's Interoffice, Intercampus Actor-Network: Assembling Our History through Dolmagean Analysis" by John Paul Tassoni

Drawing from Jay Dolmage's (2017) legend of steep steps, retrofits, and universal design, John Paul Tassoni charts basic writing (BW) networks at the author's university. The Dolmagean analysis traces competing and aligned interests and activities across the school's history as they relate to "traditional" undergraduate students, diverse constituencies, and the teaching of writing. This history indicates the system of offices, initiatives, and personnel who have (had) a stake in the goals of access, retention, and institutional transformation that can drive BW missions. The author argues that WPAs can use Dolmage's legend to bolster their own interoffice, intercampus networks, to find allies and align missions to better articulate BW's concerns at the center of university business.

Chapter 6. "Outsiders Looking In: Discursive Constructions of Remediation beyond the Academy" by Lynn Reid

Lynn Reid focuses on perspectives about basic writing (BW) from an actor-network beyond the institution, including Complete College America, the popular press, and state legislation. The discourse constructed by these actors about BW emphasizes its implications for impeding student success and has led to widespread efforts toward remediation reform. This chapter examines that discourse and argues that writing program administrators who are responsible for BW courses must be attuned to the nuances of this extra-institutional conversation to advocate successfully for their programs, as the wholesale elimination of BW courses may not provide an inherently equitable option for students in all institutional contexts.

Chapter 7. "Working Within the Rhetorical Constraints: Renovation and Resistance in a First-Year Writing Program" by Mara Lee Grayson

Mara Lee Grayson's chapter explores the intersecting networks and systems at play during a wholescale revision of a first-year writing program. Using critical systems thinking to examine anecdotal and empirical data, Grayson examines how existing systems posed both opportunities and constraints, describes how individuals worked across formal and informal networks to effect change, and highlights the saliency of ideology as a systematic, structuring force on the program and those who labor within it. Ultimately, this chapter underscores the limitations of programmatic revision without accompanying institutional critique.

Chapter 8. "Negotiating Dominance in Writing Program Administration: A Case Study" by Emily R. Johnston

This chapter documents how the structure of University of California, San Diego (UCSD) compounds what this collection calls the "everywhere but nowhere" problem in writing program administration. Case studying a first-year composition (FYC) program that teaches writing as a tool for interrogating power, UCSD's Dimensions of Culture Program (DOC), Emily R. Johnston reveals how DOC both resists and contributes to dominance as the program's administrators must function within the converging systems of institutional bureaucracies, academic elitism, the capitalist structure of higher education in the United States, and White supremacy. Johnston draws from intersectionality (Crenshaw, 1989) to identify DOC's agency and subordination within these converging systems and cultural-historical activity theory (Prior et. al., 2007) to situate DOC in its particular historical, cultural context.

Chapter 9. "Networking Across the Curriculum: Challenges, Contradictions, and Changes" by Kelly Bradbury, Sue Doe, and Mike Palmquist

In this chapter, Kelly Bradbury, Sue Doe, and Mike Palmquist share the story of Colorado State University's gtPathways Writing Integration Project through a lens of activity theory, highlighting the ways in which each of us, over the course of fifteen years, has met with institutional networks that have and continue to inform, shape, and challenge the goals and the work of the project. Readers can glean from their story insights about the complexities involved in undertaking, developing, and maintaining a socially just writing across the curriculum program amidst an array of changing institutional players and forces. While it is in many ways a story of missed opportunities, it is also a story of localized triumphs, perseverance, and long-term dedication to supporting meaningful work happening from the bottom up.

Chapter 10. "The Writing Center as Border Processing Station" by Eric C. Camarillo

Eric C. Camarillo's chapter expands activity theory's application to writing centers and the activity systems in which they exist. The border processing station, especially as it functions in a United States context, is applied as a metaphor to visualize the hegemonic function of the traditional writing center. To resist this model of writing center practice, Yrjö Engeström's (2015) concept of third generation activity theory is deployed alongside a direct application of this theory to a writing center context. Camarillo argues that applying an activity-theoretical lens can help writing center practitioners to engage with apparent contradictions in their work and to make systemic activities of exclusion or oppression more visible, which better enables writing centers to mitigate the potential for harm. A systems-theoretical lens allows for more efficient problem solving, letting us see the complexities of writing center or, more broadly, writing program work. This chapter also positions writing center work as a part of a larger milieu of writing programmatic work, all of which is ultimately delimited by institutional systems and networks.

Chapter 11. "Voice, Silence, and Invocation: The Perilous and Playful Possibilities of Negotiating Identity in Writing Centers" by Lucien Darjeun Meadows

Focusing on the relational and holistic dimensions of systems theory as relevant to the intra-campus network of the writing center, this chapter considers what happens, and what could happen, when writers or consultants disclose personal identities in the tutoring session. By discussing current conversations on navigating identity in writing centers, offering lived scenarios and resulting reflections on coming out and remaining silent, and introducing the concept of invocation as a generative alternative to self-disclosure, Lucien Darjeun Meadows extends scholarship on social systems and queer theories. This chapter closes with scalable takeaways for writing center administrators and consultants, as well as writing program administrators, who seek to promote positive change through practices of identity-based invocation.

Chapter 12. "Is Resistance Futile?: Struggling against Systematic Assimilation of Administrative Work" by Genesea M. Carter

In this chapter, Genesea M. Carter uses social science and business administration scholarship to highlight how the neoliberal system creates a culture of auditing, workaholism and overwork, and professional identity fragmentation to keep the system running. Using Star Trek's the Borg as a metaphor for neoliberal systematic assimilation, Carter explains why the neoliberal system is hard to resist for rhetoric and composition administrators. However, resistance is not futile. Carter offers readers what she calls a "workplace mindfulness mindset" with specific reflective and boundary strategies that are based in neuroscience, psychology, and mindfulness to help readers identify the ways they need to reclaim their professional and personal agency, first, before taking on the system at the program, department, college, and/or university level.

Chapter 13. "'It's Complicated': Scheduling as an Intellectual, Networked Social Justice Issue for WPAs" by Julia Voss and Kathryn Bruchmann

Scheduling courses and assigning classrooms are common program administrative tasks, ones that, despite their difficulty and labor-intensiveness, have not been widely discussed in the rhetoric and composition literature. This chapter applies a network theory lens to scheduling to deepen understanding of the challenges program administrators face, especially how logics and priorities motivate stakeholders within the scheduling process. Drawing from survey data of directors of 120 North American writing programs, including doctoral-, masters-, bachelors-, and associates-granting institutions, Julia Voss and Kathryn Bruchmann identify seven major scheduling stakeholders: WPAs, department chairs, office administrators, non-teaching offices, upper administrators, software, and instructors that can help or hinder scheduling and classroom assignment equity. Voss and Bruchmann's findings point to the necessity of including program administrators and department chairs in the scheduling process. Additionally, they illuminate the problematic outcomes associated with involving both non-teaching stakeholders and individual instructors in making scheduling decisions. Troublingly, their findings indicate institutional-student characteristics and resources impact scheduling classroom types with inequality manifesting even in the scheduling process.

Chapter 14. "Flexible Framing, Open Spaces, and Adaptive Resources: A Networked Approach to Writing Program Administration" by Jenna Morton-Aiken

Intentionally playing with genre and writing style, Jenna Morton-Aiken uses systems theory, relational architecture, and archival theory to assert that digital and physical archives shape access, agency, and arrangement at all levels of administrative work. Morton-Aiken opens her chapter explaining how she created a self-generated archival network built to survive graduate school and exams while pregnant, which inspired her to rethink the value of archival theory as important to all writing program administrators, even those who don't consider themselves archivists. Namely, archival theory, as a network and system, can (and should be) used as thoughtful conversation about the ways administrators organize institutional history, values, and processes. Answering the editors' call to think about how systems and networks impact equity and can affect positive change in rhetoric and composition programs, Morton-Aiken concludes with tangible recommendations for how administrators might use analog and digital archival approaches to further equity and inclusion.

CONCLUSION

In the years we've been graduate teaching assistants, part-time and full-time instructors or faculty, writing program administrators, writing center directors, English language acquisition program directors, and under/upper administrators, we continue to think about how the systems and networks we work within, alongside, and against affect equity and positive change for our students, our non-tenure-track faculty, our graduate teaching assistants, our staff, our curriculum, our programs, our communities, and our workloads. We struggle to do our jobs without compromising ourselves and/or others ethically, economically, and/or professionally. We intend for the chapters in this collection to posit new frameworks within 21st century rhetoric and composition administrative conditions that can work toward progress and justice for all of us, including our departments, our universities, and our professional communities. We are convinced our contributors' examinations of the disciplinary and public networks, the intra-campus and institutional networks, and the personal and relational networks does not just benefit rhetoric and composition administrators, but benefit people involved in and impacted by higher education writ large. Ultimately, the collection authors work together to create a tapestry of application, both large and small, so that others might, too, find solidarity, education, and encouragement in their administrative change-making efforts.

REFERENCES

Baker-Bell, A. (2020). *Linguistic justice: Black language, literacy, identity, and pedagogy.* Routledge.

Boylan, H. R. & Bonham, B. S. (2014). *Developmental education: readings on its past, present, and future.* Bedford/St. Martin.

Carter, G. M., Matzke, A. & Vidrine-Isbell, B. (2023). Navigating networks and systems: Practicing care, clarifying boundaries, and reclaiming self in higher education administration. In R. Hentschell & C. E. Thomas (Eds.), *Transforming leadership pathways for humanities professionals in higher education* (pp. 81–104). Purdue University Press.

Conference on College Composition and Communication. (2020). *This ain't another statement! This is a DEMAND for Black Linguistic Justice!* National Council of Teachers of English. https://cccc.ncte.org/cccc/demand-for-black-linguistic-justice

Conference on College Composition and Communication. (2021). *Statement on White language supremacy.* National Council of Teachers of English. https://cccc.ncte.org/cccc/white-language-supremacy.

Ericsson, P., Downing Hunter, L., Macklin, T. M. & Edwards, E. S. (2016). Composition at Washington State University: Building a multimodal bricolage. *Composition Forum, 33.* https://compositionforum.com/issue/33/wsu.php.

Garrett, B., Matzke, A. & Rankins-Robertson, S. (2017). Reembodying the positionality of MiddleMAN administrators in higher education. In K. Cole & H. Hassel (Eds.), *Surviving sexism in academia: Strategies for feminist leadership*. Routledge.

Hayles, N. K. (1999). *How we became posthuman: Virtual bodies in cybernetics, literature, and informatics*. The University of Chicago Press.

Inoue, A. B. (2015). *Antiracist writing assessment ecologies: Teaching and assessing writing for a socially just future*. The WAC Clearinghouse; Parlor Press. https://doi.org/10.37514/per-b.2015.0698.

Kaptelinin, V. & Nardi, B. (2009). *Acting with technology: Activity theory and interaction design*. MIT Press.

Kaptelinin, V. & Nardi, B. (2018). Activity theory as a framework for human-technology interaction research. *Mind, Culture, and Activity, 25*(1), 3–5.

Kinney, K., Girshin, T. & Bowlin, B. (2010). The third turn toward the social: Nancy Welch's living room, Tony Scott's dangerous writing, and rhetoric and composition's turn toward grass roots political activism. *Composition Forum, 21*.

Latour, B. (2005). From realpolitik to dingpolitik or how to make things public. In B. Latour & P. Weibel (Eds.), *Making things public: Atmospheres of democracy* (pp. 4–31). MIT Press.

Lemke, J. L. (1995). *Textual politics: Discourse and social dynamics*. Taylor and Francis.

Lynch, P. & Rivers, N. (Eds.). (2015). *Thinking with Bruno Latour in rhetoric and composition*. Southern Illinois University Press.

Matzke, A. & Garrett, B. (2018). Studio bricolage: Inventing writing studio pedagogy for local contexts. In M. Sutton & S. Chandler (Eds.), *The writing studio sampler: Stories about change* (pp. 43–59). The WAC Clearinghouse; University Press of Colorado. https://doi.org/10.37514/per-b.2018.0179.2.03.

Matzke, A., Rankins-Robertson, S. & Garrett, B. (2019). Nevertheless, she persisted: Strategies to counteract the time, place, and structure for academic bullying of WPAs. In C. L. Elder & B. Davila (Eds.), *Defining, locating, addressing bullying in the WPA workplace* (pp. 49–68). Utah State University Press.

Otte, G. & Mlynarczyk, R. W. (2010). *Basic writing*. Parlor Press; The WAC Clearinghouse. https://wac.colostate.edu/books/referenceguides/basicwriting/.

Perryman-Clark, S. & Craig, C. (2019). *Black perspectives in writing program administration: From the margins to the center*. National Council of Teachers of English.

Poe, M., Inoue, A. B. & Elliot, N. (Eds.). (2018). *Writing assessment social justice, and the advancement of opportunity*. The WAC Clearinghouse, University Press of Colorado. https://doi.org/10.37514/per-b.2018.0155.

Ratcliffe, K. (2005). *Rhetorical listening: Identification, gender, Whiteness*. Southern Illinois University Press.

Reisch, M. (2014). *The Routledge international handbook of social justice*. Routledge.

Rickert, T. (2013). *Ambient rhetoric: The attunement of rhetorical being*. University of Pittsburgh Press.

Rivers, N. A. (2016). Paying attention with cache. *Enculturation, 23*. http://enculturation.net/paying-attention.

Rhodes, J. & Alexander, J. (2014). Reimagining the social turn: New work from the field. *College English, 76*(6), 481–487.
Ruiz, I. D. (2016). *Reclaiming composition for Chicano/as and other ethnic minorities: A critical history and pedagogy*. Palgrave Macmillan.
Wenger, E. (1999). *Communities of practice: Learning, meaning, and identity*. Cambridge University Press.

SECTION 1.
DISCIPLINARY AND PUBLIC NETWORKS: EXISTING AS A PROFESSION

Committees

Disability and Accessibility

Chapter 1. "Purposeful Access: Reinventing Supersystems through Rhetorical Action" by Bre Garrett and Matt Dowell

Committee for Change

Chapter 2. "At a Crossroads: The Committee for Change and the Voices of CCCC" by the CCCC Committee for Change: Bernice Olivas, Janelle Jennings-Alexander, Mara Lee Grayson, Tamara Issak, Lana Oweidat, Christina V. Cedillo, Ashanka Kumari, Caitlyn Rudolph-Schram, and Trent M. Kays

WPA-Listserv

Chapter 3. "'Help I Posted': Race, Power, Disciplinary Shifts, and the #WPAListservFeministRevolution" by Iris Ruiz, Latina Oculta, Brian Hendrickson, Mara Lee Grayson, Holly Hassel, Mike Palmquist, and Mandy Olejnik

Chapter 4. "Critiquing the 'Networked Subject' of Anti-racism: Toward a More Empowered and Inclusive 'We' in Rhetoric and Composition" by Erec Smith

The first section opens the collection with chapters centered on DEIBSJ work in our national organizations and communication venues. The authors in this section provide a multiplicity of voices, allowing readers to attend to the diverse manner in which change making is understood and pursued. As readers consider, incorporate, and respond to different points of view, they will have the opportunity to develop their own lines of thought, and better name their stance within existing systems.

In the first chapter, Bre Garrett and Matt Dowell share just some of their experiences with the Council for Writing Program Administrators (CWPA) Disability and Accessibility Committee. They use the planning and participation of the committee at the 2019 CWPA conference to highlight ongoing issues of (in)access and hyperableism before concluding with specific interventions that "position invention, access, and delivery [as] interrelated rhetorical acts" that must be reflexively addressed in all organizational planning.

The second chapter begins by centering the experience of the Conference on College Composition and Communication's (CCCC) Committee for Change. The chapter investigates the professional narrative of the field of composition and rhetoric as inclusive and participatory with the lived experiences of several scholars at the CCCC 2019 annual convention. With a focus on the experiential, the authors poignantly note, "If we are ever to tell a story of our field that we can all live with, we must center our conversation on the people who cannot live within the fiction we are telling now." With this goal in mind, the authors share the impetus behind the formation of the Committee for Change and argue that "despite ample scholarship on equitable education and antiracism in composition and rhetoric, our discipline's scholarly and professional networks continue to center Whiteness and perpetuate discrimination and marginalization." The chapter, then, provides both an introduction to the active DEIBSJ work in the field of Composition and Rhetoric, and creates an opening by which the rest of the collection can be viewed.

Chapter 3, written by seven Writing Program Administrators listserv members (Iris Ruiz, Latina Oculta, Brian Hendrickson, Mara Lee Grayson, Holly Hassel, Mike Palmquist, and Mandy Olejnik), and Chapter 4, written by Erec Smith, address what Ruiz et al. call the "rhetorical rupture that led to the [WPA] listserv revolution." While Ruiz et al. utilize actor-network theory (ANT) and decolonial theory as a dialogic approach to examining issues of power and contention present on the listserv, Smith argues that the creation of a "secure base" within these areas create "insular networks working together across organizations and social media platforms that fortify [the base] at the expense of generative dialogue." When read alone, they provide unique perspectives on how a grouping and an individual experienced the same networked rupture. When read together, they highlight that social justice efforts are not value free and that these values shape our understandings of community action.

Committees and public networks within the profession of rhet/comp exemplify complex systems, in which groups of people with different perspectives and backgrounds remain silent or speak out about their concerns. Limits of time and/or word count often leave a perspective from being fully explained or given due consideration. This section provides space for authors to both broaden the sphere of their identity and give readers more insight into their pathways of thought. We hope that this section encourages those at all professional levels to consider the rhetorical power of these public, disciplinary spaces, noting the tensions inherent in our professional networks.

As we close this interchapter, we offer you a few reflection and/or discussion questions, should you want to journal about your reading or use the book for a faculty book club or professional development. In particular, we encourage you to think about what you might take away or try from this section:

- Where might you identify hyperabelism in your own committee work, program work, or institution? How do you or might you, as Garrett and Dowell wrote, "position invention, access, and delivery [as] interrelated rhetorical acts" in your workplace, homelife, and community?
- How do you or might you center the conversation on the colleagues, students, and staff (and others) who need to be centered? What does that look like in your classroom, your program, your department, and your community? How and what kinds of research play a part in these decisions?
- What modes of communication do you use in a professional capacity (social media, listservs, etc.) that centers, decenters, undermines, or supports your values? How might your values align more closely with certain modes of communication?

CHAPTER 1.

PURPOSEFUL ACCESS: REINVENTING SUPERSYSTEMS THROUGH RHETORICAL ACTION

Bre Garrett
University of West Florida

Matt Dowell
Towson University

> Method begins in embodiment.
> – Byron Hawk, *A Counter-History of Composition*

> She has thought about what could have been the intellectual history of any academic discipline if it had not insisted upon, or been forced into, the waste of time and life that rationalizations for and representations of dominance required—lethal discourses of exclusion blocking access . . . for both the excluder and the excluded
> – Toni Morrison, 2001

I [Matt] stand at the conference accessibility table, when a presenter approaches to ask about having a table placed in their presentation room on which they could place a laptop. Of all the details reviewed for accessibility, the room setup for presenters slipped through the cracks. The hotel's default room layout assumes presenters stand for the duration of their presentations, which privileges normative embodiment. After retrofitting the room to "accommodate" alternatives by lugging in a rather ill-fitting table a few minutes before the session, I turn my attention to "planning" for the panel, "Rooting for Radical Inclusion in Writing Programs and Writing Program Administration," presented by members of the Council of Writing Program Administrators (CWPA) Disability and Accessibility (D&A) Committee. As a result of unexpected life events and funding gaps, four of the five session speakers were not able to physically attend the conference. I offer my assistance to Jessi Ulmer, the only panel participant present, and we carry out a hybrid, synchronous delivery in which two speakers participated via video, and I presented Bre's materials. Although not ideal, the group created a doable, alternative path that enables participation. Later

DOI: https://doi.org/10.37514/PER-B.2023.1848.2.01

Saturday evening, I attend the conference outing at the American Visionary Art Museum. I'd been nervous about the outing since visiting the museum when preparing the conference access guide. During this visit, I quickly noticed lacking accessibility. Entering into the museum during that visit, I immediately encountered an ascending ramp. Beyond that ramp are most of the museum's exhibits, the elevators, and the accessible restrooms. On this Saturday evening, I walk around the different physical spaces CWPA has rented and it appears that everyone is having a good time. But I also know that some conference attendees may have chosen to not attend the outing because of how the access guide described the museum's access limitations.

The conference "experience" described above captures in/access-in-action and reveals the felt realities that in/access both imposes and makes possible for living bodies. In/access, configured with a slash that separates the preposition "in" and the noun "access," reveals inaccessibility—a lack of or barriers to access—and accessibility, the fullest capabilities of participation for all bodies. The liminal space between performs a necessary pause, an intrusion, that urges readers to recognize what Brenda Brueggemann et al. (2001) articulated, ableism and ability exist as fluid, ever-changing states of being. Ability performs as an unstable privilege located in time and place, according to situated embodiment (Brueggemann et al., 2001, p. 369). Together, the two words conjoin and create new meaning, suggesting a deliberate movement inward, into access, and a vital stance to reside within access rather than resist and push back against access. Through in/access, we name and resist barriers, but we also design, with intention, realities that carve space for disability.

The exclusion of disability, Jay Dolmage (2017) argued, results from privileging able-bodiedness and able-mindedness, as well as the erasure of disability from language, physical spaces, and places (p. 6–7). Ableism, Dolmage defines, "has to be seen as a series of entrenched structures," such that "we have to understand that because of these pervasive structures, we live in a society that resists efforts to ameliorate or get rid of ableism" (2017, p. 53). Higher education exists within this system of exclusion and forwards such overt exclusion through explicit barriers and unconscious biases. Dolmage (2008) uses physical-spatial metaphors to show how the system of in/access affects and excludes, in particular, those with disabilities. The "steep steps," which keep certain bodies out, and "retrofits," which Dolmage describes as "adding ramps at the sides of buildings and making accommodations to the standard curriculum," continue to shape the experiences of disabled members of the university (2008, p. 15). Retrofits characterize added components or structures that serve "as a correction" after production or construction is complete (Dolmage, 2008, p. 20). Teachers, scholars, and conference organizers "react" to embodied differences instead of making spaces that include, through deliberate invention—or purposeful access—spaces, places, and pedagogies for multiple bodies (Dolmage, 2008, p. 21). In/access in its various forms materializes the expected norms of higher education and is buttressed by interventions, such as "reasonable accommodations" and accommodation request processes, that are inadequate in their very design (Dolmage, 2017, pp. 79–80). Continuing inadequacies secure the supersystem of hyper-ableism, which in turn cycles across and makes pervasive the system of inaccessibility in higher education—and more specifically WPA work. Central to our work in this chapter is an urgency to re-imagine and enact access in higher education, in home institutions and programs, and in disciplinary spaces such as academic conferences.

Composition and writing programs across the nation suffer from the overarching system of inaccessibility, an offshoot of the supersystem of hyper-ableism. Stephanie Kerschbaum (2015) argued "disability is not often at the forefront of classroom planning or pedagogical practice," which reveals that disability is not an explicit priority of WPAs (p. 9). In her 2019 CWPA conference presentation, Ashanka Kumari concurs that most higher education academic spaces are "inherently inaccessible," which echoes Dolmage's 2008 summary of composition's history: "Composition is not always an accessible space" (p. 14). Composition's governing force—writing program administration—perpetuates and feeds the supersystem of hyper-ableism. Conference settings as well as many of our home writing programs (un)intentionally reproduce in/access and exclusionary practices. For example, presentation delivery tends to reinforce one mode, the linguistic, and speakers too often neglect to include captions when images or videos accompany written text and oral speech. Speakers often fail to provide alternative methods for accessing materials—even larger font handout requests symbolize an extra "burden" for presenters. Despite the best intentions, access as an afterthought and add-on never prioritizes the lives and participation of disabled peoples and others with multiple corporealities (Kuppers, 2014; McRuer, 2006, 2018). Consequently, access becomes realized through retrofits. Disabled people encounter roadblocks that prevent participation and presence (Dolmage, 2008, 2017). As the members of the CCCC Committee for Change demonstrated in this collection, such exclusion often intersects with race and "other areas of difference like ethnicity, class, and gender." Through a collection of counterstories, the authors assemble a chorus of voices to speak against hegemonic practices, to resist systems and supersystems that block participation. Our particular story focuses on the possibilities for resisting such exclusion when serving in official positions and on official committees created to increase inclusion. Our story, then, captures our experiences working within hegemonic structures and voices what this work has accomplished, still must accomplish, and can't accomplish in its current form. In alignment with the CCCC Committee for Change, we call for a counterstory that subverts or inverts the supersystem of hyper-ableism.

In this chapter, two members of the CWPA Disability and Accessibility (D&A) committee argue for a revisionary, re-corporealization of in/access and call for purposeful access as an embodied positionality for CWPA and for its constituents in writing program administration. Framing this discussion, we question, what are the barriers to full-bodied access, and why does access continuously perform, rhetorically or in action, as a retrofit or afterthought? Why does access feel synonymous with traversing cracks in the road? We argue the responses to such questions reveal both the interconnected supersystems of higher education and inaccessibility that shape professional academic organizations and academic institutions as well as the language practices intricately tied to both disability and ableism.

We draw from six years of D&A committee research and continued occurrences of inaccessibility at academic conferences to theorize a radical rearrangement that foregrounds access as an integral part of the conference organization process—moving access from a latter delivery concern, most often discovered through missteps, to an early and recursive invention concern. Moving access earlier as a rhetorical invention process foregrounds equity as a critical component of project design. In this case, projects represent conferences, curricula, and program design. As much of academia moves from a culture of bureaucratic isolation to a more grassroots and agile organizational model that prioritizes universal design, we argue that accessibility must move from the outside of rhetoric to the inner-ions and particles of invention (Dolmage, 2008, 2017; Garrett, 2018; Price, 2011; Vidali, 2015; Yergeau, 2016). Such a shift is necessary because of the force the supersystem of hyper-ableism exerts on both academia and socio-material gatherings such as academic conferences. Short of purposeful action in the form of reinvention, accessibility will remain an afterthought, one that occurs in the form of response and not invention, such that accessible interventions will not have lasting effect on larger structures.

We would like to pause and account for the significant shifts that conferences have undergone since our 2019 experience due to the COVID-19 pandemic. Disruptions to the very systems people use to attend—to access—in-person conferences created necessary changes to conference infrastructures and modalities. Given great differences in the size, budget, staffing, purposes, and lead time for pandemic conferences, these professional meetings have likely existed on a continuum of in/accessibility, just as conferences did before the pandemic. We recognize that many conferences during this time privileged purposeful access, but such access was, at times, in the service of re-establishing "conferencing," not accounting for the supersystem of hyper-ableism. We also worry that access gains made by retrofitting conferences online and remotely will be lost going forward and that similar gains will not be applied to what are seen to be "traditional" in-person conferences.[1] Our argument that access links invention and delivery, then, can operate as a useful heuristic for all conferences, as many people continue to discuss what the future of academic conferences will be.

The remobilization we propose places the first and last rhetorical canons of invention and delivery in a bi-directional relationship as a re-embodied supersystem that both disables access and critically re-examines the retrofits that pervade the networks and systems of writing program administration—and the supersystem of hyper-ableism. Thus far, a disconnect between discourse and action demonstrates that access functions as an abstract requirement—a polite gesture or, worse, what Dolmage (2017) calls "the ableist apologia"—rather than a foundational, concrete value and action (pp. 35–36). In pushing back against accessibility as retrofit, in conversation with Margaret Price (2009), we identify the academic conferences as a "kairotic professional space," and forward Ada Hubrig and Ruth Osorio's (2020) claim that "access can be world making" (Price, 2009, para. 5; Hubrig & Osorio, 2020, p. 95). We see such "world making" as functioning as a central tenet of this section in this edited collection, especially as demonstrated in the ongoing work to make a professional organization a more inclusive space described by members of the CCCC Committee for a Change (in this volume) and by those doing related work to changing the Writing Program Administrators listserv as to create a more supportive, accountable space (Ruiz et al., this volume).

In the 2019 CWPA conference narrative we shared to open the chapter, the conference organizers—and the hotel conference set-up staff who must abide by The American with Disabilities Act (ADA) standards—deemed proper conference staging as inclusive of those who stand and deliver. Such a limited, ableist view erases individuals who may have fatigue, injuries, and illnesses, and excludes those who move in wheelchairs. Stand and deliver as an embodied rhetorical device marks a deep physical entrenchment that secures the performativity of hyper-ableism by signifying, as Debra Hawhee (2004) argued, "fit," "agile" bodies as those able to fully participate (p. 97). In this chapter, we pay special attention to the academic conference and the CWPA summer conference because of the always-present relations among space, bodies, access, and discourse. Whether held on or off academic campuses, online or off, situated participation in a disciplinary conference, including one's ability to engage in knowledge production and circulation as well as the development of an organization's professional priorities, requires access to physical, digital, and social spaces that replicate the hyper-ableism of higher education and society at large.

---

1   We do not intend to overgeneralize or speak about online conferences as non-existent or in/accessible prior to the pandemic. Our central focus is the intersections between hyper-ableism and the normate academic conference.

In conversation with Dolmage (2008; 2017), Hubrig and Osorio (2020), Robert McRuer (2006), Price (2009; 2011), and Remi Yergeau (2016), as well as others in disability studies, we identify hyper-ableism as a super-system, a discursive structure at the very center of how academic institutions, and by extension, academic conferences function. Hyper-ableism exerts bodies as super-able and physically "robust" (McRuer, 2006, p. 7). As long as accessibility unfolds through retrofits—and access remains stigmatized by normative embodiment and identity—hyper-ableism will maintain its status and performance as a supersystem. Our examination of retrofits, similar to John Tassoni's analysis, in this collection, of Dolmage's schema of the actor-network surrounding basic writing at Miami University, extends questions of how accessibility "persists, pushes, and perishes at a variety of . . . sites" (this volume). For writing program administration, only by "disabling" the CWPA academic conference (Vidali, 2015), can the full(er) accessibility pronounced as valued within writing program administration scholarship materialize within the physical-spatial-digital locations in which we gather.

Accessibility, the word, carries empty weight when actions result in inaccessibility and exclusion. Declaring a state of accessibility when material reality is in/access, as we will demonstrate, forces those needing accessibility to confirm for themselves a lack of that which is needed and to communicate this lack to those who have constructed a fiction as (their) reality. Said differently, it is an act of gaslighting. Access, most often through the supersystem of hyper-ableism and the system or network of language, defines itself and becomes known through interaction with in/access. Although ripe with capacious potentials, language tends to restrict discourse based on economy networks and contexts that reinforce language as a system of cultural production (McRuer, 2006, 2018). In her 1993 Nobel Prize acceptance speech, Toni Morrison argued that it is the users of language who distort or "forego" the "nuanced" potential in language to promote inclusivity; therefore, only through revisionary and purposeful use will language return to its life-sustaining potential (Morrison, 2001, p. 418). In institutional contexts, policy and curricular design, and governing bodies, the systemic uses of language erect barriers between the material environment and action, which results in in/access experienced by living bodies.

Those in privileged or normative embodiments remain unaffected by in/access's disruption and harm—unless or until a body, as Kristin Lindgren (2008) urges, "demands acknowledgement" (p. 146). Within higher education, the acknowledgment of disabilities is bound up in legalities. As Dolmage (2017) reminds us, the granting of an accommodation makes disability visible; short of accommodations being granted, disabilities, from the institution's perspective, remain unknown and "invisible" (p. 9). The privilege of ignoring or remaining unaware and complacent with one's own able-bodiedness, however temporary to echo Brueggemann et al. (2001), marks the exact ideology that oils the grind of hyper-ableism as a supersystem. Such evasiveness of in/access and dis/ability enables the supersystem of hyper-ableism to remain the dominant structure of academic spaces, particularly conferences, which epitomize scholastic exclusion in terms of budgetary expense, physical capabilities for attendance and participation, indications of hierarchies such as keynote speakers, and a number of additional time and space-based actions that hinder or promote participation and community-belonging. Until a body demands attention, bodies remain unobserved, hidden by the supersystem of hyper-ableism and made obsolete by the system of inaccessibility.

IN/ACCESS IN WRITING PROGRAMS AND ACADEMIC CONFERENCES

In their 2016 keynote address, Yergeau appealed to the CWPA community, the three-hundred plus room of WPAs and writing specialists, to harness rhetorical prowess toward radical reinvention: we must respond to "the crises" that perpetuate hyper-ableism by both naming and responding to the "structures that are . . . woefully problemed" (p. 155). Yergeau urges the organization to re-build "a culture of access," a call that the CWPA D&A committee and the executive board (EB) strives, continually anew, to prioritize, although not without fault and shortcomings. The supersystem of hyper-ableism, an ideology within the very framework, or "design," of how writing studies functions, remains insidiously—and always—at work, Yergeau attests (2016, p. 155). As Petra Kuppers (2014) explained, "[D]isability culture is not a thing, but a process. . . . disability cultural environments have to safeguard against perpetuating or erecting other exclusions (based on racial stereotypes, class, gender, economic access, internalized ableism, etc.)" (p. 4), a charge that mirrors the "intersections of difference" highlighted by Olivas and co-authors in this collection. In conversation together, Yergeau's (2016) call for a culture of access, Kuppers' (2014) warning about the complications of building a culture of disability, and CCCC Committee for Change (this volume) illuminate the supersystems and systems that work in unison to create exclusion and power struggles—such constraints as budgets, top-down privilege and ableism, or "internalized ableism" (Kuppers, 2014, p. 4). The places and spaces, and infrastructure, to name a few, remove responsibility from humans—those with the power to make and enforce decisions—by replacing agency in the systems themselves.

As in the example at the start of the chapter, where a presentation was able to continue despite speakers' unanticipated absence, at the same time that the spaces for presenters in other rooms were in/accessible, CWPA demonstrated accessibility and in/accessibility-in-action. In/access here relates to fuller options for participation. Virtual attendance and participation in academic conferences is an expanding practice at the Conference on College Composition and Communication (CCCC) as well. Individuals unable to attend the physical convention participate through social media such as Twitter, with hashtag following and even a robust and intentional review thread, and through an online archive of posted presentation materials initiated by the Committee on Disability Issues in College Composition (CDICC). Yet, more must be done to foreground accessibility-in-action as a micro-practice of rhetorical invention.

Yergeau's argument, that the immovable ideology of hyper-ability shapes the language of WPAs and imparts an agency only available to the fittest few, identifies a supersystem that necessitates cautious yet forceful restructuring. They lament, "Without inaccessibility, would we even know ourselves as a discipline?" (2016, p. 159). The D&A committee emerged in the summer of 2012, through a think-tank conversation at the closing of the summer CWPA workshop, a space that convenes newly appointed WPAs and is facilitated by advanced, experienced WPAs. The CWPA EB then charged the committee with developing more inclusive practices for the organization. The development of a particular committee, one focused explicitly on making the conference more inclusive, provides a discursive and structural priority that holds the power to re-shape the conference experience. However, for action to move from the realm of discourse to the experiential, felt-sense of conference attendees and to make the experience more accessible to disabled members—and all members—the impetus must extend beyond the system of language by materializing into renovations of space and place, eradications of budgetary constraints, and removal of inaccessible presentation practices, just to name a few surface issues.

While a rising subject discussed in WPA scholarship, as evidenced by publications in the WPA journal, access and disability have only recently taken root as cornerstones from which to proceed with program creation, pedagogical and conference design, and, as a counter-system to the supersystem of hyper-ableism. Scholastic conversation coincided with the 1990 passing of national legislature that aimed to bring disability rights to political attention (Lewiecki-Wilson & Brueggemann, 2008). James Wilson and Cynthia Lewiecki-Wilson (2001) explained that disability rights and issues became a prominent political topic with the passing of the 1990 ADA signed into action by President George Bush, which resulted in "a start of the reversal of legal exclusion" for disabled individuals (p. 4). One year prior to the ADA Act, in 1989, Susan McLeod, a WPA, and Kathy Jane Garretson, an ADA expert (1989), collaborated to develop and implement faculty training that included access as a core component in classroom and pedagogical design. Twenty-six years later—and one year prior to the CWPA conference in which Yergeau delivered their keynote on inaccessibility—Amy Vidali (2015) published "Disabling Writing Program Administration," advocating for a programmatic methodology that disrupts the conventional supersystem(s) of writing program administration by foregrounding the voices and stories of disabled WPAs. Vidali's article received the Kenneth Bruffee Award, a prestigious acclaim that testifies to not only Vidali's research and writing esteem but also the communal reception of the subject as timely and of utmost importance. A close examination of WPA article titles from 1990–2012 reveal not one title with the terms "access," "disability," or "inclusion." Then, in the Fall 2013 issue, Fernando Sánchez (2013) published "Creating Accessible Spaces for ESL Students Online," the first article title to explicitly name "access" as a core WPA topic since McLeod and Garretson's 1989 publication. Vidali's (2015) article moves beyond arguing for disability's place in WPA scholastic conversation and positions disabling as a methodology for WPA work. The almost complete lack of WPA scholarship on disability and access in the discipline's own journal, across more than twenty years following the passing of the 1990 ADA legislation, further makes explicit the power of hyper-ableism and the larger system of inaccess that defines WPA work.

Then, in 2017, *WPA: Writing Program Administrators* journal released a special issue, "Ability and Accessibility," edited by Kathleen Hunzer. In this issue, Melissa Nicolas (2017) examined the failure of writing program policies to capture "the embodied, material realities of our students' lives" and, in doing so, challenged WPAs to develop policies that center difference and make space for difference (p. 11). In the same issue, Sushil Oswal and Lisa Melonçon (2017) highlighted the limitations of checklist implementation for centering inclusion in online writing instruction, while Kelly Shea (2017) reminded WPAs that effective design of inclusive classrooms benefits all students, not just those with recognized disabilities. In 2019, with the articulation of the annual CWPA conference theme, "More Seats at the Table: Radical Inclusion in Writing Programs," the conference membership united to scholastically examine access and make conscious, collective efforts to become more inclusive. Through 11 consecutive sessions, consisting of several presentations and round-table discussions on topics ranging from giving greater voice to contingent faculty within writing program leadership, to modifying campus writing support for shifting student populations, to enacting anti-racist writing assessment, to metacognitive reflecting on the conference space itself—as well as a plenary address by Holly Hassel and Joanne Baird Giordano—the 2019 conference interrogated numerous constraints to access in WPA work, and in doing so acknowledged as Yergeau (2016) insisted, the true lack of diversity and exclusion that infiltrates the organization and WPA practices more broadly.

Despite the most altruistic intentions of CWPA members, the supersystem of hyper-ableism engines forward, disrupting the system of access through the co-operating systems of language/discourse/policies/budgets, to echo Nicholas (2017) and others who point out the numerous constraints that impede access-in-action. To use the words of Cynthia Selfe (1999), WPAs need "*small potent gestures* [emphasis added]" (p. 412). We need to see articles on disability and access in more issues, as special topics and integrated and prioritized as daily experience that informs all areas of WPA work. Through the mangled arrangement that (dis)places access as a latter, delivery concern, in/access emerges through the presence of retrofits. Rather than beginning with access as part of project, program, curricular, and conference invention, too often, WPAs and other academics/scholars discover in/access once delivery occurs. The resulting, "oops," requires a significant rehaul of rhetorical action that engages delivery, audience, and disability as core pieces of invention, or design.

I put the finishing touches on the conference's accessibility guide. Though proud of my work, the final product feels more like an appendage to the conference and not central to the conference itself. While I've provided information that will allow all conference participants to experience greater access while at the conference, I can't help but feel that the document reflects a checklist, not a text that centers access as the organization's identity and mission.

Tara Wood et al. (2014) asked, "Now that disabled students and teachers are accepted as belonging in our classrooms, and we affirm that their presence is an asset rather than a deficiency, what should we be doing?" (p. 147). Similar questions of "what should we be doing?" have been asked by Yergeau (2016) and Vidali (2015) about writing program administration. These authors argue that greater attention be given to the roles played by disability and accessibility within writing program administration, specifically. Yergeau (2016) challenged CWPA to "consider, as many of our colleagues have claimed about whiteness and heteronormativity, whether . . . the act of administering or teaching can ever be anything but ableist" (p. 159). Vidali (2015) resisted the normative tradition within writing program administration by introducing "disabling" as an operative term to name a "process of bridging the insights of disabled people and perspectives in order to innovate, include, and transgress expected and exclusionary norms" (p. 33). Similarly, Yergeau submitted that "a culture of access" is not simply one of participation but also "of redesign" (2016, p. 155). Redesign carries connotations of building anew, revising, and reinventing. Such conceptions and actions apply to physical architecture as much as ideologies, pedagogies, and theories. Redesign means composing with a new, or different, system of language to disrupt the cycle of hyper-ableism.

Language functions as a system that informs the supersystem of hyperableism, and together, both reproduce a system of in/access. According to Morrison (2001), "both the excluded and the excluder" suffer the damages of "the lethal discourse of exclusion" (pp. 419–420). Uses of lethal language are fueled, Morrison said, by the motivation to "preserve privilege," and such discursive moves of exclusion result in the deliberate "blocking [of] access" (2001, p. 420). This systematic process often occurs without recognition or awareness. When access functions as an afterthought, and, consequently, as a retrofit, the word itself performs as "evacuated language," often the outcome of policing and official language use (Morrison, 2001, p. 419). In such use contexts, the word access loses its intention for inclusion and full participation, fulfilling, instead, the outcome of exclusion, and even violence. Speaking before the elite Nobel Prize in Literature audience, Morrison exclaimed, "Oppressive language does more than represent violence; it is violence" (2001, p. 419). How do we revive language; how do we avoid violence and microaggressions that inflict harm and perpetuate lethal practices? Such microaggressions, though perhaps not micro at all but instead aggressions that fully perpetuate the ableist hyper system, include, for example, proclamations by instructors that a course is already accessible. Such statements disregard differences and dissuade students from seeking the specific accommodations they need. Morrison suggests, "the proud but calcified language of the academy" is "salvageable only by an effort of the will . . . it must be rejected, altered and exposed" (2001, pp. 418–19). As we move through different scholastic recommendations for how to heal and improve, we extrapolate actions that inform purposeful access as a renewed system. From Yergeau, we bring forth re-design as we embark on building a culture of access; from Dolmage, we explicitly include disability as an embodied identity; from Morrison, we listen to language as a powerful mechanism, a living organism that shapes supersystems.

In examining how diversity within organizations is communicated, Sarah Ahmed (2012) offers that "diversity can be used as an adjective, as a way of describing the organization, a quality, or an attribute of an organization" (p. 52). It can also be used, she argued, "normatively, as an expression of the priorities, values, or commitments of an organization." Why this duality matters are in how a description of diversity "also indicates the values of that organization" (Ahmed, 2012, p. 52). The same, we argue, can be said of accessibility. Such use of and the consequences of such use emerged in March 2019 at CCCC, where a large, red sign reading "The CCCC Convention is accessible!" greeted conference attendees at check-in. Under this statement were a list of bullet points identifying accessibility features, including accessibility guides; quiet, lactation, and family rooms; childcare grants; gender-neutral bathrooms; and interpreters.

As Osorio (2019a) described on her accessibility website, "Turns out, folks had very different experiences than this sign presumed. Anonymous CCCC members used post-it notes to decorate the large, standing sign with specific access issues they've encountered." Along with capturing these different experiences—even going as far as posting transcriptions to her website of the post-its conference attendees plastered to this sign—Osorio (2019a) questioned, "if #4c19 is applauding itself for achieving accessibility, will it stop trying to expand accessibility?" With a worrisome tone, she wondered, "is this the end of the road for Cs?"[2] In thinking about and sharing our own experiences with in/access at the CWPA summer conference, we raise similar questions and offer purposeful access as a starting point for situating explicit, intentional (re)design to resist "the end of the road."

In 2006, the CDICC submitted an official policy statement on "Disability in CCCC" (Conference on College Composition and Communication, 2020).[3] The policy, once approved, became instituted, agreed-upon language. Despite the official language, thirteen years following the policy approval, at CCCC 2019 (4C19), conference attendees spoke back, noting nearly fifty specific instances of in/access. Osorio (2019b), a current member of the CDICC, documented the 4C19 happening as "collective direct action." In her email to the DS_Rhet-Comp listserv (Discussions in the field of Disability Studies and Rhetoric and Composition), Osorio "Thanks . . . the people who resisted the erasure of disabled folks and inaccessibility at CCCC" (Osorio, 2019b). This particular conference occurrence and Osorio's analysis demonstrate the real risk about which Ahmed wrote. In the case of this conference, the act of making equivalent a description of an event as accessible with the priorities, values, or commitments of the organization putting on the event operated as an attempt for accessibility to be accepted and agreed upon apart from any questioning of the priorities, values, or commitments of the hosting organization itself. One point of contention that arose was who actually authorized the sign, as no one from the CDICC, the organizational committee devoted to access and disability, was informed or consulted. This lack of consultation represents what Dolmage (2017) referred to as a "defeat device," an act intended to pronounce decision makers as "more expert than [disabled] students or disability officers" (p. 74). Announcing that the conference "is accessible," and doing so while

---

2   Osorio's (2019a) fuller account of the event and a photo of the original sign with transcriptions of the post-it notes is included on her website: http://www.ruthosorio.com/accessibility-at-4c19/.

3   The statement was passed in 2006 and reaffirmed in 2011. In March 2020, the statement was replaced with a new statement, "Disability Studies in Composition: Position Statement on Policy and Best Practices."

excluding the CDICC, creates a constructed "reality" in which inaccessibility will continue regardless of the actual events of the conference, as demonstrated by the post-it note protest. The "self-congratulation" of achieving "accessibility" defeats the possibility of continued work occurring within the organization itself (Dolmage, 2017, p. 74). We share this story about 4C19 as an imperative for how we all want to move forward. As Osorio (2019b) said, "Access is complex, ongoing." To name access as complete and packaged for delivery renders the multitude of situated experiences static. The list of access issues present at 4C19 reveals the extent to which hyper-ableism instills barriers despite the best intentions.

Here, then, is a foundational point to our argument: accessibility operates both linguistically and materially. That a claim can be made that a conference is accessible undermines the innovation, inclusion, transgression, and redesign that Vidali and Yergeau argued must be central to creating accessible spaces, ones that are made "disabled" and not merely retrofitted. Noting audience as a "treasured rhetorical concept" central to WPA work, Yergeau (2016) nonetheless "remain[s] unconvinced that audience-as-concept is meant to include the so-called cripples and the feeble-minded among its ranks" (p. 159). For all the talk there is about conference accessibility, has any of this talk centrally changed the "non-disabled default" that has traditionally shaped how academic conferences are conceived of and held (Yergeau, 2016, p. 159)? We argue that, at best, the standard adjustments made to academic conferences to create greater accessibility operate primarily as retrofits that don't disrupt the hyper-ableist supersystem present in the discursive-materiality of academic conferences. Disabling, to borrow Vidali's term, provides a linguistic-material framework that goes beyond how access has been used as a retrofit to hyper-ableism by transgressing "expected and exclusionary norms." Disabling, therefore, gets to the "priorities, values, [and] commitments of an organization" (Ahmed, 2012, p. 52; Vidali, 2015, p. 33). As academic conferences operate simultaneously as rhetorical, physical, and disciplinary spaces, working toward disabling the academic conference is also an act of resistance to the hyper-ableism that circulates in higher education. Yet, the centrality of ableism in higher education also makes such interventions difficult.

In 2013, the D&A committee[4] formed as a result of a conversation that took place at the 2012 CWPA pre-conference workshop. At the end of the week, workshop facilitators, Shirley Rose, Dominic DelliCarpini, and guest speaker Duane Roen, opened a discussion about what was missing in CWPA: what

---

4 The committee launched as the Disability Committee, but one of the inaugural committee's first actions changed the name to include access: Disability and Accessibility Committee. Thus, one of the committee's first actions was, itself, a retrofit.

new committees would help serve and extend the mission of CWPA and the work of WPAs? Workshop attendees Bre Garrett and Tracy Morse suggested that the conference and CWPA community needed a committee to emphasize and implement access, providing a more explicit conversation about and charges on inclusion and disability issues. Since its inception, Kathleen Hunzer, Tracy Morse, and Bre Garrett have chaired the committee, and attention has focused on drafting new policies, spreading the visibility and necessity of access and inclusion, and creating practices for making CWPA's annual conference more accessible and inclusive. Re-positioning access as an integral part of the conference's infrastructure has been a process of renovation and revision, one filled with continuously discovering faults and cracks in light of maintaining the most important goal: fostering a community of belonging by removing barriers that inhibit participation. Prior to 2013, no official committee, policies, or language existed that foregrounded inclusion, access, disability and disabled people in the CWPA organization—an absence that likely influenced the omission of scholarship on such topics in the WPA journal.

The D&A Committee has focused a great deal on working to establish an infrastructure for making the conference more accessible and inclusive.[5] The following list names short- and long-term actions the committee has accomplished, most of which occur annually:

- The development of an annual access guide.
- The recommendation and use of captioning services (CART) for plenary and large auditorium talks.
- The creation, publication, and circulation of guidelines for creating accessible presentations.
- The allocation of a quiet room and a lactation room at the conference site.
- The request for gender-neutral bathrooms at the conference site
- The implementation of an access table.
- The recommendation to include mics in all session rooms.
- The implementation of a site visit to evaluate access at the conference venue.

Many of the committee's efforts borrow directly from the CCCC's initiatives developed by the CDICC, from whom we've aligned our discourse and praxis.

---

5   This list represents the annual actions and activities that enhanced access and inclusion at the CWPA's face-to-face, physical convention, pre-COVID-19. We acknowledge that this list needs rethinking and updating as a result of shifts in conferencing practices due to the pandemic. With conferences taking place either solely online or in a hybrid modality, the actions to ensure access must shift to account for more varied modes of participation.

Yet, even given this discourse and praxis, the creation of the D&A committee itself operated as a retrofit, one intended to extend the mission of CWPA but not explicitly intended to disable and disrupt in the ways Yergeau and Vidali intend. As we know, language falls short, and the system of budget constraints restricts action and institutes access as retrofits. Site visits often occur after venues are selected, and cancellations or budget reallocations are typically out of the question when schedules and calendar time hold authority and agency over individual bodies. What this means, long term, for changing the system of inaccessibility is that access must become a central and forefront part of the rhetorical action of conference design. Furthermore, the work of access must no longer occur in isolation. Each year, the annual conference design process begins anew, with access falling to a collaboration between the D&A committee and the local host committee. Rather, access should become a priority of the EB and should be situated as an annual budget item. The conference access materials, such as guidelines for creating accessible presentations, should be housed on the main CWPA website rather than the individually designed conference website that changes each year. Redesign in this regard relates to digital, virtual spaces as much as physical, concrete spaces.

In their 2016 address, Yergeau highlighted the conference space itself as evidence of the needed redesign in writing program administration. Noting that spatial design "makes particular statements about the bodies it values," Yergeau described:

> . . . the arrangement of tables and chairs, the lack of aisle space, the positioning and placements of screens and speakers, the way in which our bodies are packed into this space, the line setup of our food stations, the proximity of our exhibition tables to the walls, the un-ease or uneasiness or sheer mortal peril in which certain groups of people can or cannot access restrooms, [and] the absence (or presence) of prepared materials and handouts during sessions. (p. 158)

Yergeau's list overlaps with the concerns raised at 4C19 and points of priority for the D&A committee. While CWPA and the D&A committee have delivered successes that have improved conference inclusion, much more continual work must occur. To resound the words of Kuppers (2014), "disability culture is . . . a process" (p. 4). For example, the 2019 CWPA conference included CART captioning services for the large auditorium talks, making the presentation more accessible to all attendees. However, the method used by the CART specialist was such that readability was difficult to follow, and transcripts of the talk were an additional service and thus an additional cost; therefore, not something that the conference committed to this time around.[6] In addition, while guidelines for presenters to create accessible materials exist and are posted to the conference website, the official email often goes out too close to the start of the conference, which promotes the treatment of access as a delivery concern rather than an invention, pre-planning part of project design. Finally, speaking to the point about the creation and role of the D&A Committee—and further reflecting on the role of the CDICC—the work often happens as middle negotiations, among individuals who have no real budgetary authority. The D&A chair makes recommendations and the committee relays suggestions back to the EB through annual reports, but most correspondence occurs through emails and often requires time for awaiting responses. At the pivotal moment of action, as when securing CART services, for example, the D&A chair is not able to negotiate costs, and therefore, the charge moves ahead to someone on the EB. Major charges and suggestions are documented in reports that circulate up to the board. To make access and disability issues a prominent part of the conference organization would necessitate representation from the committee on the EB to ensure issues remain a core part of conference design.

While many of these successes—gender-neutral restrooms, quiet and lactation rooms, the production and distribution of the conference accessibility guide—may be assumed to be standard operations for many academic conferences, their material existence must be made into each annual conference as part of the conference planning process. To assume accessible continuation apart from the labor that brings access into being is to imagine accessibility apart from a conference's embodied and material realities. Up until the point accessibility becomes material within the conference design, it merely operates as a checklist of features desired at an "inclusive" conference. Further, much of the local work, including the access guide, materializes through the local host committee rather than the D&A committee, which is another layer of dissonance between the work and the implementation of purposeful action.

Each academic conference, then, faces its own accessibility challenges, ranging from state laws regarding gender-neutral restrooms, to the conference site's geography, topography, and weather, to the funds available to underwrite accessibility. The conference snapshot that introduces this chapter offers a small glimpse at the successes, challenges, and oversights that occurred at the 2019 CWPA conference. For example, the conference featured real-time captioning for keynote addresses for the first time, but microphones were only available in larger breakout rooms. The accessibility guide circulated via multiple media, but

---

6   Funding for the CART services was provided by Towson University's College of Liberal Arts and not taken from conference registration fees such that the funding itself was a retrofit to the conference's financial plan.

large-print copies were not available at the conference's outset due to miscommunication among organizers. To continue in this "good-bad" structure would give the incorrect impression that accessibility results from correctly applying a checklist of desired features. Our purposes here are to speak to the larger system(s) that results in a continuation of in/access and hyper-ableism at academic conferences and in writing program administration. Extending from the previous point that the D&A committee operated as a retrofit, the same can be said of accessibility at an academic conference and accessible considerations within conference planning.

In closing this chapter, we explore the collaborations and relationships WPAs might leverage to produce a system of purposeful access that counters the supersystem of hyper-ableism. The question posed at CWPA 2019, "what does radical inclusion look like in practice?" deserves pedagogical attention as well as exploration of the daily activities that comprise WPA work—in teacher-training, curricular design, campus and community out/in-reach, budget management, and assessment. How do local institutional contexts shape the work of creating access? What do we need to know about our institutions and who do we need to know to sustain a culture of access? Through what discourse(s) and methodologies can we advocate for accessibility practices that will result in purposeful action? We offer readers actionable steps, resources and tools, as well as starting places to begin the work of radical inclusion—whatever position they hold in the institution for both programmatic and institutional change. We also call for more voices to respond to these critical questions. We call for more work in the WPA journal and more sessions at the annual CWPA conference to grapple with these questions.

PURPOSEFUL ACCESS AS EMBODIED POSITIONALITY: PRACTICAL APPLICATION, IMPLEMENTATION, AND RECOMMENDATIONS

The title of this chapter, Purposeful Access, asks composers, presenters, conference organizers, teachers, and WPAs to approach design as a deliberate act that foregrounds difference and explicitly invites disability and multiple corporealities into scholastic conversation "in order to innovate, include, and transgress expected and exclusionary norms in writing program administration" (Vidali, 2015, p. 33). As an embodied positionality, purposeful access acknowledges situated bodies as inextricable from delivery, or, how, through what available means, different bodies are able to respond. Feminist philosopher Elizabeth Grosz (1994) defined bodies as "the very condition of our access to and conception of space" (p. 91). Ability, therefore, cannot separate from theories and practices of delivery; delivery must always prompt, how is one able to respond, and that question must pose early in project/conference design if it is to have real action for lived, concrete experience.

To engage in purpose-driven action, access and delivery require careful consideration and pre-thought—invention—about/of space, place, and materials, and about/of the numerous different bodies: people with disabilities, illnesses, and other conditions that challenge normative activities that are, as Susan Wendell (1996) defined, "necessary for survival . . . or necessary to participate" in an "environment or society" (p. 4). The following list provides extended definitions of purposeful access, showing how language can shift to help move forward a system of access that counters hyper-ableism. Purposeful access:

- Experiences the rhetorical canons as interdependent.
- Casts bodies as rhetorical means and sites of invention and delivery and actively considers the situated embodiment of audiences, aiming to cast the widest net possible for human involvement.
- Positions bodies as points of access, the physical means by which humans make contact with other materials and spaces and with other humans.

In many ways, purposeful access is about membership, participation, and valorization. On the Composing Access website, produced by CDICC members, each page opens, top center, with a quote by Aimi Hamraie that reads, "Meaningful access requires us to ask not only, 'Who belongs?' but also, 'How do we know?' The power of such questions demands attention to bodies and requires an imperative and deliberate reflexivity. Whose knowledge and leadership is foregrounded? Whose labors are employed in creating access, and how are labors compensated?" The emphasis on belonging as a tangible outcome means we advocate for more than systematic, official language and the failures that words, divorced from purpose, employ. Purposeful access opens otherwise closed-off and exclusive spaces "to people with different forms of embodiment," including disability (Kuppers, 2014, p. 1). In many ways, the normative conversation about access in regard to conference design is already diminished when it begins.

As a material take-away from this chapter, we present a diagram Bre designed as a pedagogical heuristic to guide accessible classroom design. The diagram displays a traditional rhetorical triangle with vertices marked by author, subject, and audience. Within the traditional triangle, four circles reside. In the center, the phrase "embodied delivery" makes explicit the place of bodies and access in rhetorical situations. Embodied delivery performs as a method for rhetorical invention, resituating the abstract terms of author, audience, and subject with "situated bodies," "composing materials and technologies," and "wider context," which includes spaces, places, and time. The word "access" touches every aspect of the situation: purposeful access, a framework for how we can foreground access as a system that forges an inter-animate relationship. We can apply this heuristic to conference design and, in doing so, disable the supersystem of hyper-ableism.

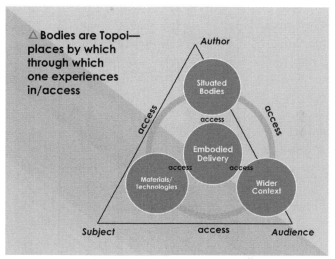

Figure 1.1 Bodies are Topoi by Bre Garrett.

We conclude with actions that readers can employ as central to reinvention. In offering these recommendations, we acknowledge the sustaining power of hyper-ableism that necessitates we go further than the retrofit "revisions" that have been made to the CWPA summer conference and to other academic conferences. As Dolmage (2017) explained:

> It is worth remembering that at the contemporary college or university, ableism is everywhere: not that it overwhelms all the good schooling can do, not that it invalidates your teaching or your research, but that we are all responsible for looking for it, recognizing our roles in its circulation, and seeking change. (p. 33)

Therefore, members of professional organizations in our field who often double as conference attendees, can:

- Become better informed of how academia systematically excludes those with disabilities such that conversations about accessibility at

conferences and in professional organizations already largely exclude those with disabilities.
- Reflect on, if able-bodied, how ableness is central to full participation in many, and likely most, academic conferences and how one's ableist biases inform the continuation of practices of in/access at conferences.
- Acknowledge the material means required to retrofit accessibility into conferences and conference spaces and to be informed by this knowledge when participating in conversations about conference costs and future designs of academic conferences.
- Reform one's language practices about accessibility including discontinuing the use of the "ableist apologia" such as "we are doing all we can do" and dismissals that state accessibility can't be that important so as to not disrupt traditional conference features and traditions. And avoid using budget constraints as a justification for inaccess.
- Interrogate academic ableism at/on one's own campus so to better understand how in/access operates within educational institutions.

Additionally, those who have power in/over decisions about conference design and in the operations of professional organizations, can:

- Create a workflow that links conferences across space(s) and time(s) instead of treating them as isolated, singular events, so that "purposeful access" can operate more fully and outside the confines created by just-in-time retrofits.
- Place conference accessibility at the center of conference decisions and designs such that no decision that will later require a retrofit or produce inaccess for some "participants" will be made.
- Situate accessibility funding as being central to budgetary decisions instead of treating accessibility as being funded, at least in part, by fundraising executed by disabled members of the organization.
- Resist self-congratulation that announces accessibility as a fixed accomplishment and not labor that must be engaged in a continuous, sustained, recursive manner.
- Center "disabling" by shifting matters of accessibility from being primarily the work of "retrofit" supplementary committees to being the work of the entire organization extending from the executive board, across all committees, and to all members.

That last item is both broad and essential. Shifting accessibility work away from being primarily the isolated work of specialized subcommittees risks deprioritizing the "insights of disabled people," but not making such a shift creates the likelihood that inaccess remains the norm, characterized by retrofits that are inadequate both for the purposes of creating sustained access and for radically changing cultural institutions such as professional organizations and academic conferences (Vidali, 2015, p. 33). Citing Dolmage (2017, p. 77), Tassoni, in this collection, highlighted how retrofitting creates "abeyance structures" that are "perhaps allowing for access, but disallowing the possibility of action for change" (this volume). Our hope is that purposeful access can work in the direction of disabling the academic conference so "to not only remove problematic and dysfunctional practices" but to also "innovate in the ways that disability invites" (Vidali, 2015, p. 48). Such purposeful access matters because as Christina Cedillo, one of the members of the CCCC Committee for Change, stated in the collection: "The bodies we inhabit determine the experiences we have in the world." "Except," Cedillo wrote, "that's not the whole story. The rest of the story is this—how people interpret our bodies determines what experiences we have in the world." Supersystems, such as hyper-ableism, which we extensively discuss, and racism, interrogated in the next chapter, limit existence in a profession because they reinscribe values that privilege exclusion. We must create, with purpose, conditions that are not simply retrofits to the supersystem of hyper-ableism or the experiences of disabled academics will continue to be largely that of, if not full exclusion, limited, begrudging access.

REFERENCES

Ahmed, S. (2012). *On being included: Racism and diversity in institutional life*. Duke University Press.

Brueggeman, B. J., White, L. F., Dunn, P.A., Heifferon, B. A. & Johnson, C. (2001). Becoming visible: Lessons in disability. *College Composition and Communication*, 52(3), 368–398.

Committee on Disability Issues in College Composition & Computers & Composition Digital Press. (n.d.). Composing Access. Retrieved April 4, 2023, from https://u.osu.edu/composingaccess/.

Community on Disability Issues in College Composition & Computers and Composition Digital Press. (n.d.). For conference organizers. Composing access: An invitation to creating accessible events. Retrieved June 30, 2021, from https://u.osu.edu/composingaccess/for-organizers/.

Conference on College Composition and Communication. (2020). Disability studies in composition: Position statement on policy and best practices. https://cccc.ncte.org/cccc/resources/positions/disabilitypolicy.

Dolmage, J. (2008). Mapping composition: Inviting disability in the front door. In C. Lewiecki-Wilson & B. J. Brueggemann (Eds.), *Disability and the teaching of writing: A critical sourcebook* (pp. 14–27). Bedford/St. Martin's.

Dolmage, J. (2017). *Academic ableism: Disability and higher education*. University of Michigan Press.

Garrett, B. (2018). Hacking the curriculum, disabling composition pedagogy: The affordances of writing studio design. *Composition Forum, 39*. https://compositionforum.com/issue/39/hacking.php.

Grosz, E. (1994). *Volatile bodies: Towards a corporeal feminism*. Indiana University Press.

Hassel, H. & Baird Giordano, J. (2019, July 25). *Intersections of privilege and access: Writing programs, disciplinary knowledge, and the shape of a field* [Keynote address]. CWPA 2019 Summer Conference, Baltimore, MD, United States.

Hawhee, D. (2004). *Bodily arts: Rhetoric and athletics in ancient Greece*. University of Texas Press.

Hawk, B. (2007). *A counter-history of composition: Toward methodologies of complexity*. University of Pittsburgh Press.

Hubrig, A. & Osorio, R. (2020). Symposium: Enacting a culture of access in our conference spaces. *College Composition and Communication, 72*(1), 87–96.

Hunzer, K. (Ed.) (2017). Ability and accessibility [Special Issue]. *WPA: Writing Program Administration, 41*(3).

Kerschbaum, S. (2015). Anecdotal relations: On orienting to disability in the composition classroom. *Composition Forum, 32*. http://www.compositionforum.com/issue/32/anecdotal-relations.php.

Kumari, A. (2019, July 27). *Rooting for radical inclusion in writing programs AND writing program administration* [Conference session]. CWPA 2019 Summer Conference, Baltimore, MD, United States.

Kuppers, P. (2014). *Studying disability arts and culture: An introduction*. Palgrave Macmillan.

Lewiecki-Wilson, C. & Brueggemann, B. J. (2008). *Disability and the teaching of writing: A critical sourcebook*. Bedford/St. Martin's.

Lindgren, K. (2008). Body language: Disability narratives and the act of writing. In C. Lewiecki-Wilson & B. J. Brueggemann (Eds.), *Disability and the teaching of writing: A critical sourcebook* (pp. 96–108). Bedford/St. Martin's.

McLeod, S. & Garretson, K. J. (1989). The disabled student and the writing program: A guide for administrators. *WPA: Writing Program Administration, 13*(1–2), 45–51.

McRuer, R. (2006). *Crip theory: Cultural signs of queerness and disability*. NYU Press.

McRuer, R. (2018). *Crip times: Disability, globalization, and resistance*. NYU Press.

Morrison, T. (2001). The Nobel lecture in literature. In J. Ritchie & K. Ronald (Eds.), *Available means: Anthology of women's rhetoric(s)* (pp. 416–423). University of Pittsburgh Press.

Nicolas, M. (2017). Ma(r)king a difference: Challenging ableist assumptions in writing program policies. *WPA: Writing Program Administration, 40*(3), 10–22.

Osorio, R. (2019a, March 16). Accessibility at #4C19. www.ruthosorio.com. http://www.ruthosorio.com/accessibility-at-4c19/.

Osorio, R. (2019b, March 16*). Some collective direct action at CCCC discussion in the field of disability studies and rhetoric and composition* [Listserv post]. DS_Rhet-Comp@Lists.UCDenver.edu.

Oswal, S. K. & Meloncon, L. (2017). Saying no to the checklist: Shifting from an ideology of normalcy to an ideology of inclusion in online writing instruction. *WPA: Writing Program Administration, 40*(3), 61–77.

Price, M. (2009). Access imagined: The construction of disability in conference policy documents. *Disability Studies Quarterly, 29*(1). https://doi.org/10.18061/dsq.v29i1.174

Price, M. (2011). *Mad at school: Rhetorics of disability and academic life*. University of Michigan Press.

Sánchez, F. (2013). Creating accessible spaces for ESL students online. *WPA: Writing Program Administration, 37*(1), 161–185.

Selfe, C. L. (1999). Technology and literacy: A story about the perils of not paying attention. *College Composition and Communication, 50*(3), 411–436.

Shea, K. A. (2017). Kindness in the writing classroom: Accommodations for all students. *WPA: Writing Program Administration, 40*(3), 78–93.

Vidali, A. (2015). Disabling writing program administration. *WPA: Writing Program Administration, 38*(2), 32–55.

Wendell, S. (1996). *The rejected body: Feminist philosophical reflections on disability*. Routledge.

Wilson, J. C. & Lewiecki-Wilson, C. (2001). *Embodied rhetorics: Disability in language and culture*. Southern Illinois University Press.

Wood, T., Dolmage, J., Price, M. & Lewiecki-Wilson, C. (2014). Where we are: Disability and accessibility: Moving beyond disability 2.0 in composition studies. *Composition Studies, 42*(2), 147–150.

Yergeau, R. (2016). Saturday plenary address: Creating a culture of access in writing program administration. *WPA: Writing Program Administration, 40*(1), 155–165.

CHAPTER 2.

AT A CROSSROADS: THE COMMITTEE FOR CHANGE AND THE VOICES OF CCCC

Bernice Olivas
Salt Lake Community College

Janelle Jennings-Alexander
Saint Augustine's University

Mara Lee Grayson
California State University, Dominguez Hills

Tamara Issak
St. John's University

Lana Oweidat
Goucher College

Christina V. Cedillo
University of Houston—Clear Lake

Ashanka Kumari
Texas A&M University—Commerce

Caitlyn Rudolph-Schram
Indiana University—Kokomo

Trent M. Kays
Augusta University

Scholars and administrators of composition and rhetoric long have called for changes that would make the field's policies and its practices more equitable and make its practitioners more cognizant of the deeply held racism and biases

DOI: https://doi.org/10.37514/PER-B.2023.1848.2.02

that do harm in our classrooms, to our students, and to each other. These voices have been powerful but often lonely ones, sparsely distributed across an academic landscape that often has not heard or acknowledged them. Many of us and our readers know all too well that working alone leads to burnout and that individual voices of dissent may be systematically silenced by the very same institutions and practices they seek to reform (Baca, 2021; Kynard, 2015).

However, if we believe that shifting discourse itself is part of effecting change within the system and discipline, we can recognize how, as calls for action continue to rise and as connections between these voices continue to strengthen, individual activist scholarship begins to cohere to create collective action.

This scholarship (e.g., Gloria Anzaldúa, bell hooks, Audre Lorde, Malea Powell, Jacqueline Jones Royster) often bends genre conventions of structure and formality, bringing greater awareness to dominant paradigms that may be resistance to change—the kind of change that posits that languages are meant to be fluid, molded, and responsive to time, social groups, and culture. These recent efforts have ranged from collaborative change-work and resistance at individual institutions to the formation of new networks to resist the disciplinary histories and epistemologies that maintain white cultural hegemony in virtual spaces within composition and rhetoric (see Ruiz et al. in this collection).

We explore another such disciplinary and administrative space: the Conference on College Composition and Communication (CCCC). Arguably our discipline's foremost professional organization, CCCC historically has celebrated the "heteroglossic" nature of the profession (Lunsford, 1990), while simultaneously silencing other voices (Grayson, 2023; Holdstein, 2008; Inoue, 2019; Ruiz, 2021). Recognizing that anti-racist work, like any effort at systemic change, requires collaboration and coalition (Jones et al., 2021), and knowing that sharing the counternarratives and testimonials of the educators and administrators whose voices and stories have been marginalized and misrepresented is itself a form of resistance (Garcia et al., 2021; Martinez, 2020), this essay highlights, through intersecting co-author counternarratives, another example of how individual diverse voices, responding to a single kairotic, networked moment, have come together to amplify the calls that, for decades, have demanded a shift to antiracist and inclusive practices at all system- and network-levels within one of the foremost professional spaces in our field. This positioning—moving singular activism to collective, systematic action—highlights the need for recognition of the individual and the story, as well as how those stories create connections across hegemonic systems in order for change to take root and flourish.

JANELLE JENNINGS-ALEXANDER'S COUNTERNARRATIVE

At the opening address for the CCCC Annual Convention in Pittsburgh, Pennsylvania, the 2019 Conference Chair Asao Inoue offered something that we rarely hear at these kinds of meetings—a deliberate and unwavering calling out of white supremacy. His remarks began with an acknowledgment of the colonization of the Indigenous lands on which we gathered and a direct address to scholars of color in the room, fully decentering whiteness in a space—and a profession—fully dominated by it. As he pointedly told the white scholars in the hall:

> Because I love you, I will be honest with you, and it may hurt. But I promise you; it hurts not because I've done something wrong, but because I'm exposing your racial wounds.... I also ask many of you to be patient as I first address my colleagues of color, but the fact that I must ask for your patience to do this is evidence of the White supremacy that even we, conscientious teachers of writing, are saturated in. (Inoue, 2019)

While Inoue's remarks were rooted in compassion, not everyone in the audience felt the love that morning. This moment of truth-telling, based on the reaction of some of the audience, felt like an act of aggression, of subversion, of insurrection. And, despite the hundreds of people in the room, it was silent. Perhaps the silence was due to the early hour or the general formality that distinguishes a keynote. Or, perhaps, the quiet was due to a brutal truth: calling out white supremacy can be dangerous work, a danger often marked by public silence and private condemnation.

Indeed, there are and have been many others who recognize the persistence of structural inequality within the field of rhetoric and composition studies and the structures of professional organizations like CCCC. Still, many see such discussions as addressing one-off incidents and not significant trends. Race and racism are not discussed or, at times, not even acknowledged as foundational and institutional, "leaving us with no means to confront the racialized atmosphere of the university and no way to account for the impact of the persistence of prejudice on writers and texts" (Prendergast, 2003, p. 36). The silence that filled the room at the CCCC keynote galvanized many who care deeply about the future of language education. It revealed how silence related to racism—but extended to other areas of difference like ethnicity, class, ability, and gender—can undermine attempts to achieve equity in our classrooms, professional organizations, scholarship, leadership, and relationships with one another.

After the address, members engaged in general civil debates via the Writing Program Administrators listserv (WPA-L) and Twitter (see Iris Ruiz et al.'s chapter and Erec Smith's chapter in this collection). That civility, however, was punctured by an anonymous user who dismissed the value of equity work done in composition studies and signed their post "Grand Scholar Wizard," an overt reference to the KKK and dog whistle to white supremacy. In that one post, the user revealed the organization's extreme divisiveness and re-emphasized the need for individual actors to collectively step forward to address the silent and pervasive nature of white supremacy and structural inequality within the CCCC in a fight to save the soul of the field.

The individuals in this chapter responded to that call by sharing their experiences at the 2019 convention, on the WPA-L, and on social media sites. These scholars, who have professionally and personally dedicated their time to researching and addressing silence on white supremacy within writing studies, connected through social media to share their commitment to bringing about change. Individual activism against powerful structures can be difficult, but networks like the ones formed in social spaces like the WPA-L help bind individual actors to each other, granting them social capital and giving them the kind of power needed to shape organizational practice. "Social network theory and analysis can provide helpful insights and strategies . . . to understand the social structure underlying patterns of social injustice as well as efforts to resist social injustice" (Hansen, 2009, p. 5). In this case, social network theory helps explain how individual voices built binding connections to amplify the call to action begun by individual practitioners.

In the months after the WPA-L meltdown, voices that spoke up and spoke back have used the collective power of the social network to amplify this debate and lobby for counter-structures to defy systems of oppression. To that end, the Executive Committee of CCCC established the Committee for Change (CFC). The CFC brought together scholar-educator-activists—from graduate students to emeritus professors, from faculty at major research universities to adjunct instructors at two-year colleges—who share an understanding that a field like ours has the ability to bring diverse voices together to chart new pathways for the future to create a unified call for action. The group engages in an "insurgent intellectual cultural practice" to advocate for long-term, systematic change at administrative levels that will allow for equity and celebrations of difference as a foundational part of the CCCC (hooks, 2015, p. 8).

In this collaborative essay, we committee members engage in a "self-conscious interrogation of how dominant, hegemonic, rhetorics circulate and inform our understanding of authority, entitlement, exclusion, and erasure" within the systems that frame the CCCC (Baca et al., 2019, p. 2). We bear witness to the need for systemic change and offer our counter-narratives as a "community of scholars and teachers who share your concerns about important issues influencing the teaching of composition and rhetoric" (Conference on College Composition and Communication, 2023, para. 2). These stories intend to be illustrative rather than exhaustive, and we know that, even as we give voice to our own stories of marginalization, many other stories remain untold. We see this essay as continuing decades-long efforts to build a more inclusive professional organization of writing studies teachers and scholars.

MARA LEE GRAYSON'S COUNTERNARRATIVE

Jesus still loves you, read the scrawl on the little yellow Post-it.

It was March 2019. I was in Pittsburgh, between sessions at the annual CCCC convention.

For ten minutes, I'd slowly circled the metal installation honoring the victims of the mass shooting at the Tree of Life synagogue, scanning the notes and wishes tacked to its thin mesh walls. Most were messages of hope and perseverance: love trumps hate. Resist. There were a few prayers, a few quotes from scholars and activists, a few condemnations of racism and gun violence—and now this.

I felt like someone had punched me in the stomach. But I'm a researcher, right? I had to make sense of the statement. I had to figure out what it meant.

Who does Jesus still love? I asked myself. Does Jesus still love the Jewish heretics who don't worship him? I'd heard that before, usually followed by a warning that, should I not accept Jesus as my personal savior, I'd be destined to spend eternity in Hell. Or does Jesus still love the man who killed eleven Jewish people in Squirrel Hill just months earlier? At best, the statement was narrow-minded and discriminatory in its attempts to deny Jewish people a belief system; at worst, it celebrated the coldblooded hate-motivated murder of more innocent people than I could count on my hands, which were cold and shaking.

In many ways, CCCC 2019 had felt like a turning point in our discipline, a climax to so much that had built up in recent years. I felt it in Vershawn Ashanti Young's Black English call for proposals and Asao B. Inoue's Chair's Speech denouncing white language supremacy and challenging us, especially those of us who are white, to reflect upon our complicity in maintaining racism through pedagogy. I felt it during presentations and hallway conversations. Though many of us, especially my colleagues of color, had been doing antiracist work for decades, in Pittsburgh it wasn't only happening in caucus meetings, edited collections, and the occasional guest edited issue of a mainstream scholarly journal. The gaze of our organization was unwaveringly focused on publicly unearthing the deep-seated ideologies and practices that maintain inequity in our field and for our students.

Yet even as we emphasized equity, racism was inescapable. During and after Inoue's speech, amid nods of agreement and rounds of applause, I noticed attendees shaking their heads and conspicuously sitting on their hands. These symbolic gestures of resistance made clear that we were not a unified community of teachers and scholars standing strong against inequity but instead an organization divided. While some of us believed ourselves to be pushing back in solidarity against systems of injustice and rhetorical violence, others used body language to identify themselves as part of another system, one defined by the very injustices we sought to illuminate, a system threatened by the very existence of ours.

Racist ideology runs deep, and racism has always thrived alongside antisemitism. As a white, ethnically Jewish woman whose body of work focuses on antiracism, identifying as marginalized in academia often feels strange to me: how can one be marginalized yet overrepresented simultaneously? While some white Jewish people see this as a reason to keep their heads down, I and other members of the NCTE/CCCC Jewish Caucus believe that our ample representation puts us in a unique position to challenge the innate white supremacy of U.S. higher education.

As both ethnicity and religion (with many Jewish people identifying with one more than the other), Jewish identity is complex and complicated. Some U.S. Jews identify as having no religion, and some are multiethnic or multiracial. Although there may be up to 200,000 Black U.S. Jews, and though some Jewish people have dark skin, in the prevailing racial binary, Jewish people are generally categorized as white, even by antiracist authors and activists (see, for example, Bonilla-Silva et al., 2006; Coates, 2009). This reductive framing obscures the intersectional marginalization many of us who are Jewish experience in society and in our professional lives.

Unfortunately, the structures of our scholarly spaces perpetuate reductive conceptions of identity: at CCCC, Caucus and Special Interest Group meetings are scheduled simultaneously, forcing members to choose one identity to nurture in any given year. Only rarely do the caucuses, SIGs, or group chairpersons meet together, which makes challenging the structures that marginalize all of us, albeit in different ways, considerably more difficult. Working with the CFC (and other formal and informal professional groups, including the WPA-L Reimagining Working Group) has provided me an invaluable opportunity to work alongside colleagues, some I've known and some I'm grateful to have met through this work, who are committed to equity. The culturally and socially situated perspectives we each bring to this work better prepares us to attend to the nuances of our work together.

We are stronger when we work together. We, especially we who benefit from the privileges afforded us by white hegemony, must challenge and combat the racism, antisemitism, misogyny, homophobia, Islamophobia, ableism, and numerous other injustices white supremacy promulgates within the academy. Those critiques must extend beyond the bounds of scholarship, administration, and pedagogy: we need to look within our own disciplinary spaces to examine the ingrained ideologies, epistemologies, and practices, blatant or covert, that serve to exclude so many of our members.

TAMARA ISSAK AND LANA OWEIDAT'S COUNTERNARRATIVE

In 2019, the fourth meeting of the Arab/Muslim Special Interest Group (SIG) took place at CCCC. The group hosted a meet and greet session with an author, and the agenda also included tackling issues that the attendees wished to discuss related to Arab/Muslim identity and Arab-Islamic rhetorical studies.

During this meeting, we had a mix of attendees, some identifying as Arab or Muslim and others not, and all were welcome. During an open discussion, one attendee shared her frustrations with teaching Arab and/or Muslim students at her university. She stated that her Arab and/or Muslim students would often self-segregate, and they refused to discuss their culture and religion with the class when prompted. She suggested that the Arab and/or Muslim students should go back to where they came from if they were not willing to engage. She presented herself as an ally who wanted to help. Although her intentions in being a good professor seemed sincere, she voiced racist and troubling views about her students. Attendees politely disagreed with her analysis of the students' behavior. The more we responded, the more she spoke her mind, and in the end the conversation took up the time we had allotted (60 minutes). The meeting ended, the professor left, and we looked around at each other overwhelmed and upset by the conversation.

Should we have asked her to leave? Did we have the authority to do so? How should we have handled this situation differently?

This experience is not random; it speaks to a larger problem in academia and, on a smaller scale, in the field of rhetoric and composition. As a field invested in addressing issues of cross-cultural engagement, equity, and social justice, some may fall into the trap of empty multiculturalism without questioning systems and networks that perpetuate injustices. For example, faculty may voice support for the value of cultures and diversity in their classrooms, programs, and administrative work, but in practice they may view those unwilling or unable to conform as deficient or uncooperative.

Many teachers in our field are trained to honor and respect students' different Englishes. However, fewer teachers have the skills or training to implement an anti-racist pedagogy which enacts this ideal. In the case of the students in the aforementioned class, the students were not only multilingual, but they were also from countries typically derided by the West as uncivilized and anti-American. We think many teachers are not ready to address the complexities of Arab and Muslim students' identities as they manifest themselves in the classroom, and this certainly seemed to be the case here. The combination of implicit bias against Arabs, Muslims, and people of color coupled with a general lack of knowledge and expertise about how to teach multilingual students create a violent and hostile environment for these students.

The creation of our SIG was an attempt to create systemic change in the field by making visible the experiences of Arabs and Muslims and highlighting scholarship on Arab and Muslim issues and identities. As the co-chairs of the SIG, we welcome political discussions while rejecting an apolitical approach that perpetuates systems of privilege, whiteness, American exceptionalism, and monolingualism. These systems ignore the complexities of identity, diversity, and difference.

This was not the first time that we encountered racism and acts of aggression at CCCC. One year, an attendee made a statement during a large group discussion that there was truth to the stereotype that Arab men are hypersexualized and predatory. This comment took the group by surprise and was unrelated to the conversation at hand. Another year, a veiled Muslim woman shared her story of narrowly escaping physical assault after the Muslim Ban, and another attendee responded by downplaying her experience explaining to the white people in the room that the situation was not so bad for us Muslims. Though these examples could be written off as isolated incidents, we see a pattern. Underlying these actions is a view of Arabs and Muslims as a peculiar group of people, Other. Their foreignness is usually exaggerated, corresponding to a stereotypical view of Arabs and Muslims as barbaric, less civilized, and anti-American.

As CCCC members, we ask:

- What does it mean to be an ally?
- How can we raise the visibility and issues impacting SIGs and caucuses?
- What can be done about the hierarchical arrangement of various groups within the organization?

- How can we simplify procedures to make the organization more inclusive and increase participation among members?

These questions are critical especially at a conference like CCCC whose members are committed to equity and inclusion.

The microaggressions we describe are symptomatic of larger racist structures that manifest themselves in our behaviors and practices. Sara Ahmed (2012) explained that organizations deal with diversity by delegating diversity issues to one or two people within the organization leaving a monumental structural issue to be dealt with by a team that could never possibly address the systemic issue alone. Thus, organizations deal with diversity by not actually dealing with it. At CCCC, SIG meetings are side events; they are not sponsored by CCCC, and they do not influence the structural inequities in the organization as a whole. In other words, they provide CCCC with the appearance of diversity even as the organization remains largely white and monolingual. Ahmed further wrote, "[B]odies of color provide organizations with tools, ways of turning action points into outcomes." Therefore, people of color are "ticks in the boxes" (p. 153). This performativity of empty multiculturalism that CCCC engages in reproduces racial oppressive structures through progressive practices. We hope that, through this work, we will be able to contribute to structural change at CCCC that disrupts racism and engages ethically with difference. We believe that we cannot solve these challenges individually and that the power is in networked exchange and collaboration.

CHRISTINA V. CEDILLO'S COUNTERNARRATIVE

In 2012, I attended CCCC and listened to the Chair give her address. Malea Powell (2012) spoke about stories that liberate and stories that paper over others' histories (I mean literally, as in the *letteraturizzazione* explained by Mignolo, 2003). She is a Native scholar, and she began with a land acknowledgment and explained that the talk was a communal text, not a singular story. Then she said something that made me feel like I could finally relax: "When I say 'story,' I don't mean for you to think 'easy.' Stories are anything but easy. When I say story, I mean an event in which I try to hold some of the complex shimmering strands of a constellative, epistemological space long enough to share them with you" (2012, p. 384). I wanted to yell, "*RIGHT?*" As someone from my community/ies, a Latinx of Indigenous descent, a Chicanx, it was always hard for me to "write with authority" as my professors expected. It felt like trying to lay an epistemic claim over Reality. Back home, that behavior earns you a much deserved, "Oye oye, quién te crees?"

Listening to Powell speak about stories, I tried to not get obviously emotional, because I was thinking of swinging on my grandparents' front porch with my grandmother as she told me about things she learned as a girl in Mexico. She told me that she'd wanted so much to go to college, but those were different times, especially for smart Indigenous women. I was thinking about my women students who deal with colonialist misogyny today, only to be told overtly and through microaggressions that they do not belong in college. We all have stories but some are de-legitimized; the ivory tower is built not with bricks but with silence.

Bodies matter. The bodies we inhabit determine the experiences we have in the world. As educators, we know learning and life never happen in a vacuum. We advocate for critical pedagogies that center marginalized identities and would like to think our colleagues appreciate that our students' identities matter and that our identities matter. Yet we keep having to repeat similar arguments from different angles using different approaches because many colleagues refuse to understand. Those of us from marginalized communities, students, teachers, and administrators, continue to contend with what Asao Inoue (2019) called "the steel bars of racism and White language supremacy" (p. 356). I'll say it again: *the bodies we inhabit determine the experiences we have in the world.*

Except, that's not the whole story. The rest of the story is this—how people interpret our bodies determines what experiences we have in the world. Right now, the world is on fire and actual neo-fascist, white supremacists march for their right to terrorize anyone who isn't white, male, cis, straight, able-bodied, European/American. I often hear that it feels like we've slipped into some dystopian parallel universe, and I am always compelled to say, "Welcome to our world." This isn't *schadenfreude* but truth, because some of us have lived with this violence every single day of our lives. I don't wish this on anyone, not even those who enable these violences through their inaction or indifference. But I do wish our colleagues with the most privilege would help stop the burning.

At this point in my career, I have attended a lot of conferences where I feel like the cliché sore thumb, the one brown face at a panel and one of the few in the whole space. This setup proves especially interesting when you're there to hear people discuss issues of race or disability and the progress "we've" made as a discipline. These narratives—replete with self-congratulatory pats on the back—prove we inhabit different chronotopes.

You know what happens to your body outside of your own time/space? It's not really yours. Suddenly, everything you do seems conspicuous; you're the clumsiest person in the room; you let people know through your awkwardness that you really don't belong. Everyone seems so relaxed and refined, and you can't help but notice that the only other non-white folks around are the staff, whom many of these grand scholars don't even see. Inevitably, the staff (who are people, you know) act like they expect you to ignore them too, and they look surprised when you smile back. This tells me that they're used to being invisible. In contrast, I am hypervisible. But we are all unwelcome in these spaces.

Years later after attending my first CCCC, I still get emotional because I dare to have hope. My tears are not sadness but rage that those who already have to work so hard have to work harder still, only to be dismissed because their identities and struggles don't fit whitestream rubrics. Written off by "important scholars" who stand at the podium to say they regard all students as equal, no matter their race or ethnicity; respect their disabled students enough to give them no "special treatment" when accommodations are a bare minimum and required by law; deem their students' queer identities none of their business. To these "important people who benefit from and perpetuate the white supremacy of our disciplinary spaces, I want to say, "We are not on the same team just because we teach or attend Cs if we argue for different measures of our supposed shared humanity." Needless to say, there were evident grumbles after Powell's address and after Inoue's, too.

Dear grumblers, your marginalized colleagues notice when you react negatively if we are centered for once, when you dare prioritize the discomfort of a day or two over another's lifetime of injury. Far beyond the conference space, your umbrage reinforces your privilege and intensifies our vulnerability. Bodies matter but words enmatter bodies. It's that simple. So like Inoue, I ask you to consider, "Does your dominant, White set of linguistic habits of language kill people?"

ASHANKA KUMARI'S COUNTERNARRATIVE

I left CCCC 2018 frustrated. Yet again, I attended a conference for which I worked hard on my presentation to only be slotted in a last-day session time with only four people in attendance–three of whom attended because they would join my carpool back to our home city immediately after my session. I remember tossing a stack of printed access copies of my presentation in a nearby recycling bin on my way out of the room. Why do I invest so much time and money into conferences to receive little to no engagement on my work?

To be fair, the days leading up to this unfortunate presentation were among the best Cs conference experiences I had ever had. A recipient of the Scholars for the Dream award that year—an annual award that sponsors conference participation from members of historically underrepresented groups—I was happily inundated and enthralled to finally get to be a part of a community where I felt I belonged in the field, a community filled with people who looked more like me than those in most academic spaces I've occupied. I spent much of my time at this Cs conference in the Scholars for the Dream lounge space, where I met and networked with incredible (mostly senior) scholars that made me feel welcomed, valued, and offered feedback on my ideas.

In addition to the networking opportunity, I got a peek at the CCCC 2019 CFP, which focused on "Performance-Rhetoric, Performance-Composition." I wondered how I might take some of my dissertation work and submit a proposal for the following year, but I digress. After my poorly attended presentation at CCCC 2018, I was left wondering if I should bother to apply for the next conference. The ever-present imposter syndrome flared, and I decided to focus on other endeavors.

Until I couldn't. I couldn't ignore the racist, classist, sexist, ableist and other issues that dominated the WPA-L in response to the 2019 C's call. I couldn't ignore the ways graduate student- and junior scholar-friend/colleagues were quickly berated for talking back to the incredibly hostile listserv conversations. I wondered, again, whether I belonged in this discipline.

In this WPA-L moment, graduate students were immediately disempowered by the words of senior scholars. While this continued to unfold, many graduate students, junior and senior scholars back-channeled the listserv conversations to Twitter to discuss this clear shaming that continued to take place in WPA-L posts. During this backchanneling, then graduate students Kyle Larson and Lucy Johnson responded to junior scholar Estee Beck's tweet about the need for a safer space for graduate students to dialogue about issues in the field. Specifically, Estee tweeted about what was going on the WPA-L and recognized this need, which Kyle and Lucy further agreed and began a conversation on. And thus, the nextGEN listserv began to take shape. Ten of us engaged in this labor, administrative, emotional, and cognitive, on top of our existing commitments, the majority of which are severely underpaid graduate-stipends during the end of a school year, a time that we all know is particularly hectic for all schedules. I, alongside Kyle Larson and Sweta Baniya became one of the three initiating moderators.

In less than a year, nextGEN began to foster "an advocacy space for graduate students centering around principles of justice, equity, and community" (Kumari, et al., 2020, para. 1). With more than 500 listserv subscribers engaging in weekly discussions on a variety of rhetoric and writing topics, including the systems and networks underpinning teaching, research, and administration, we made numerous professional strides to be proud of including a collaboratively co-authored listserv-to-listserv response to the problematic decorum of the WPA-L, calling for a code of conduct and moderators in that space.

In his Chair's Program Address, 2019 CCCC Chair Vershawn Ashanti Young highlighted the role of nextGEN as a "group of multiracial graduate students talkin' bout: we at the C's and in dis profession, y'all better recognize." This statement was accompanied with a physical space in the form of an Action Hub table and a SIG session time for nextGEN listserv members to physically connect.

As I begin life on the tenure track, I wonder how we can not only make space for new and underrepresented voices in the field, but also create long-term structures of support beyond one-and-done conference presentation scholarships or tables. For instance, existing writing and rhetoric listservs such as WPA-L and nextGEN offer opportunities for networking and connecting about topics about our praxis. Or, in another example, existing disciplinary SIGs and Committees, like the Committee for Change, offer opportunities to create systematic, administrative, and disciplinary change. I want to paraphrase Marian Vasser, the Director of Diversity Education and Inclusive Excellence at the University of Louisville, who taught me through our conversations together that "diversity is what it looks like; inclusion is what it feels like" (Vasser, 2018). While CCCC might be considered diverse in the sense of its membership, caucus spaces offering sites for shared identity communities, and a range of topics present in its annual program, it is not inclusive.

Inclusion means working to reduce triple-digit conference rates, especially for those in precarious positions. Inclusion means that when promoting conference events that include alcohol or non-diet friendly foods, consider food preparation practices and those who cannot be around alcohol for personal, religious, or any reason. Inclusion means attending the presentations of voices beyond our colleagues: consider purposefully attending at least one presentation with new-to-you voices. Inclusion means making spaces as accessible as possible to all: consider not only asking presenters to print access copies but providing the means to do so; offering stim objects, such as fidget spinners and pop-its, in presentation rooms; and providing multiple quiet room locations throughout the massive venue for participants to escape what is immensely overstimulating.

We must do better to actively model, encourage, and practice inclusion in ways that support both the present and new generation of scholars, teachers, and voices to come. To echo Inoue (2019), this effort requires all members of this discipline to act: "And I stand up here today asking everyone to listen, to see, to know you as you are, to stop saying *shit* about injustice while doing *jack shit* about it. We are all needed in this project, this fight, this work, these labors [emphasis in the original]" (p. 355).

CAITLYN RUDOLPH-SCHRAM COUNTERNARRATIVE

I'm not even supposed to be in this space. This is a professional space. There are scholars in this space who have authored the books I'm reading as part of my MA work. I'm following the WPA-L to fulfill the professional development component of my WPA class. I am the only student in my cohort following. It has been made very clear that the listserv is for the "big dogs"—my professor does not even feel comfortable posting. Thus, as a graduate student, my role is to be an observer only. They don't respond kindly to graduate students in their space.

I catch Vershawn Ashanti Young's CCCC's Call for Proposals. I don't read much past the initial responses but begin cataloguing the conversation—I can't keep up. I'm not used to the way the listserv functions. I do not see the problems arising until several months later when I revisit the catalogued conversations.

In the first semester of my second year of my MA, my WPA asks if I've seen the listserv. No? I need to check it out, immediately. I return to my office and spend the next several hours reading the thread started by Michelle LaFrance, "Request for Rubrics." This is important. For the first time I'm witnessing senior scholars being called out for problematic behavior.

I begin cataloguing again. I find the #WPAListservFeministRevolution hashtag on Twitter. I do the thing I'm not supposed to, I respond to the listserv. I have to. I can't not. Other graduate students are already putting themselves on the line and I want them to know that they are not alone and that this feeling of risking everything just to speak to injustice is shared, but also oh so worth it. We are not supposed to be here. Some senior scholars cheer us on, some try to silence us. We push back, and this resistance extends beyond the life of the thread itself.

Those brave voices were emboldening, but not nearly as inspiring as those speaking truth to life on the backchannels, on Twitter. If it weren't for the #WPAListservFeministRevolution I would not be here writing this.

My research has always tried to involve social media and the communities we build. The Twitter community that emerged from the listserv, especially this particular thread, is community in action. We share our stories of discomfort and exclusion from the very space that is supposed to be for all of us and from the field itself. Those excluded range, not unexpectedly, from graduate students, non-tenure-track faculty, adjuncts, people of color, women, LGBT folx, and disabled folx—at every intersection and in-between. The listserv, undoubtedly, mirrors the same oppression and marginalization we experience every day from the public sector and the very institutions that claim to need our diversity.

I attend CCCC for the first time in 2019. I make it a point to only attend sessions that directly address institutional issues of racism, sexism, colonialism. I spend my first day in an Indigenous Rhetorics retreat, trying to understand my own white privileged, mixed blood positionality and how to fight institutional systems and structures of colonialism. I write down everything, trying to absorb these stories into muscle memory. I listen to Asao Inoue passionately call for a fight against institutional white supremacy in our classrooms. I am asked to acknowledge how my very presence in the classroom, as a white person, reinforces this supremacy. I am able to sit in this discomfort; it's a discomfort I have been actively engaging with for a while in order to try to do better and be better.

Leaving Inoue's speech, I read a response from a scholar I admire about how white people are not a monolith. My heart sinks. I keep going to sessions trying to learn as much as I can about doing this work, this oh-so-necessary, radically important work that I want to do. I listen as Sherita Roundtree shares the experiences of Black women GTAs, I listen as Neisha-Anne Green (Faison et al., 2019) passionately shares her frustration with a culture that coddles white people and expects continuous labor from people of color. I abandon ideas of allyship in favor of being an accomplice. I leave CCCC with so much to integrate into my own practices and so much reflection. There is so much work to do.

It's not long until another listserv breakdown. This time, nothing is veiled—the racism is blatant. It is anonymous. It is not handled quietly. There are very few of us still too scared to speak up. The community we've developed has emboldened us. Because that's really what this has become. This isn't about the listserv—this is about marginalized folx and their accomplices combating the intrinsically exclusionary nature of our field and our institution through a radically inclusive community.

So much of what we do in academia is shaped by violent institutional structures—structures that are designed to exclude and oppress the very people it depends on when they fall outside of the white, straight, cis, able-bodied "norm." The work that we have the opportunity to do on the CFC is to radically transform the dominant structures of the field, to call out and condemn acts of violence committed against marginalized folx, and to set a precedent in how to move forward.

The listserv will not change until the field does.

So many of my colleagues here have touched on the problems that permeate the discipline so well. They are serious and numerous and even more reflective of the society and culture we live and exist in. My experience as an academic in rhetoric and composition has been almost entirely shaped by my interactions with the listserv and the community formed on Twitter as a response. Some may say that's an awful way to get into the discipline—I disagree. While problems abound, the community is full of some of the best people doing groundbreaking work and research. I'm lucky to be here.

TRENT M. KAYS' COUNTERNARRATIVE

I'm a queer Buddhist first-generation college writing professor from a working- and middle-class background. I'm a lot of things, but, of course, I'm not only those things. Indeed, I chafe at the form of an academic. My first two years of college were at a community college, and I am proud of my community college experience. But I have been in rooms where a community college background is treated with contempt.

The stench of elitism is hard to wash off. I have seen it creep into discussions of first-year writing, especially where non-rhetoric and composition scholars are "forced" to teach first-year writing students. How we *talk* about first-year writing (and writing in general) is as vital as what we *do* in first-year writing. Carolyn Calhoon-Dillahunt articulated this in her 2018 CCCC Chair's Address. She remarked, "When I refer to first-year writing in this talk, I am not talking about a particular content, but rather a space in academia" (p. 276). In this case, a space within an established system. Undeniably, it is critical to treat first-year writing as something special, where narratives and identities are formed, bounce into each other, and meld into something else. Like my component identities, students are more than students. They are other things. They are living human beings with wants, desires, fears, and struggles.

As a discipline, writing studies presents a problem. The discipline that is dependent on the narratives and identities of students must also continue to articulate its own narratives and identities. Those who work within the discipline must regularly draft a narrative that considers the vagaries and hostilities of constituent identities both inside and outside the academic and administrative environment. Certainly, how we locate and understand those narratives and identities becomes crucial to our work and in challenging systemic norms.

As an outgrowth of NCTE, CCCC is not independent in the same way as other disciplinary organizations, such as Rhetoric Society of America. This contributes to the chafing of my role as an academic. I understand CCCC as a space meant to be welcoming, compassionate, and collaborative; however, this is not always the case. Our discipline and our conferences are not composed of only those people who are trained in the teaching of writing and administration of writing and language programs. As a scholar of rhetoric and writing studies, my role as a writing professor is still treated with derision in certain departments (e.g., English literature) and disciplines. I am a necessary evil for some who consider their disciplines as more learned. I am a professor in the back of the room who is "just a writing teacher." Our discipline continues to struggle with this identity crisis.

In attending CCCC, I have found those of similar thought and action, and an important element of that has been the caucuses and SIGs. But it is not enough to sequester our narratives and identities in small spaces and then push them aside when we must re-enter the larger disciplinary conversation. Despite the binding goal of higher education, the identity crisis of our discipline has forced us to contend with the idea that we must choose one face to wear in our specialties, one face to wear at conferences, and one face to wear in our departments. The opportunity presented to the CFC is to challenge the idea that our narratives and identities must be sequestered from the larger conversation of disciplinarity and the antiquated notions still governing our work. The governing system we find ourselves in is the same system in need of reform or in need of destruction.

The ruling elitism must be eliminated, and the causes for racism, antisemitism, homophobia, unfair labor practices, and other issues need to be identified, examined, and removed. We can construct a new disciplinary identity by recognizing that we are capable of moving in a new and compassionate direction. We should not be afraid of our discomfort; rather, we should use it to learn and grow and change. In constructing this future, we will experience "the troubling and exhilarating feeling that things *could be different*, or at least that *they could still fail*—a feeling never so deep when faced with the final product, no matter how beautiful or impressive it may be" (Latour, 2005, p. 89).

The work of our discipline is daunting. We need look no further than posts on the WPA-L to see our discipline still has issues to confront and work to complete. Writing instructors and WPAs are in the trenches of higher education. Every other discipline depends on our ability to help students become better writers and better thinkers. This amount of pressure is suffocating. The formation of the CFC shows we can no longer wait: we must change—now.

I'm not just a queer Buddhist first-generation college writing professor. I'm a brother, a friend, a colleague, a volunteer. As we consider the CFC's mandate, we must ask ourselves: what do we want our discipline to be known for? What narratives do we want identified with our work? And who do we want to be?

Our urgency for change requires a willingness for discomfort and a willingness to confront failure. It requires a willingness to stand together and push forward as the habits of the past attempt to pull us backward. We can no longer tolerate the derision of our work or our colleagues. This change requires bravery.

Let's be brave.

BERNICE OLIVAS' COUNTERNARRATIVE

CCCC 2019 provided clear examples of how exclusionary actions take place in our professional spaces. This reality isn't easy to hear, partly because the rhetoric and composition self-narrative is a fiction of inclusion and equity. When we tell our histories and self-narratives, we are what Jim Corder (1985) called "fiction-makers/historians" (p. 16). The human in us crafts our narratives into something we can live with.

Unfortunately, crafting a story about how far we've come, about good intentions, about being the progressive branch of the academic tree, does not make it true. Systems of inequity are embedded in our discipline. People of color, LGBTQ+, and disabled folx are still woefully underrepresented in tenure track positions, publications, and seats of power. Our students become more diverse while the faces at the front of the room stay the same. White supremacy never left our field, it just changed. White supremacy crawls into tiniest spaces and takes root.

This truth shouldn't paralyze us with guilt or frustration—it should compel us to action. As a field we need to commit to building up diverse faculty, to celebrating diverse scholars and administrators, and to writing policy that is equitable and just. This work can only begin if the discipline of composition and rhetoric, the WPA, and CCCC stop telling a fiction of our discipline and open ourselves up to listening to the stories we *don't* want to hear.

To change our story, we must "painfully reconcile our habits of judgment, and that means painfully reconciling the paradox between ourselves and our actions" so that we can change "the structures, [cut] the steel bars, [alter] the ecology [to] change the way power moves through White racial biases" (Inoue, 2019, p. 364).

The CFC is charged to make "structural changes to CCCC that address white supremacy and . . . develop a set of guidelines for ethical engagement at CCCC annual convention." This will not be the work of a year or three, a single committee or a series of them. This work needs to be persistent and present every year as we move forward.

As Ashanka Kumari tells us in her narrative above, inclusion means we must be willing to address the issues without fear. We, as a field, must commit to reframing our conversations about white supremacy, inclusion, and equity into a language of action—not a language of intention. We must be willing to discuss racist actions and structures and their consequences without centering on the intentions of the action or the structure. Centering on how being named racist, instead of how being treated with racism, affects individuals, communities, and organizations is one of white supremacy's greatest tricks. If we are ever to tell a story of our field that we can all live with, we must center our conversation on the people who *cannot live* within the fiction we are telling now.

IMPLICATIONS FOR READERS AND CONCLUSION

As demonstrated by the CFC members, seizing kairotic moments and getting to work are key components of systemic change. Below is a compilation of just a few of the actions curated by CFC members throughout the chapter. These actions are meant to highlight anti-racist, inclusionary work currently taking place, as well as challenge individual narratives that may continue to, even unwittingly, support heteronormative, white supremacist ableism.

- Involve yourself in your institution's larger committees and structures with the express purpose of simplifying bureaucracy, increasing access, and calling out exclusionary behaviors.
- On the committees and in the groups in which you are currently a member, ask for and push toward collaborative meetings of leaders and members across committee boundaries, to increase awareness of and breakdown siloing within the system.
- When taking part in conferences—either through attendance, presentation, and/or scholarship—as editor, writer, or reviewer—or community spaces—leading or lurking, moderating or writing—pay attention. Who is speaking? Who has room? What is embodied within the space? What are your patterns of "attendance" across these spaces?
- When taking part in administrative work—either through committee work, curriculum design, program assessment, etc.—pay attention to who is speaking and who has the room. How might you shape which voices are respected and prioritized? How might you create administrative processes and practices that prioritize equity and inclusion?
- What dominant narratives frame your own experiences and actions? What administrative work are you committed to doing, personally, to center the need for change?
- Before closing your exercises with the authors, enact purposeful attention to this chapter's genre bending of the academic, peer-reviewed chapter. What do stories continue to teach us?

The voices of this chapter speak through stories, arguably one of the most systematically integrative genres of our field. Stories serve the rhetorical purposes of sharing identity, creating a network of support and action, an interwoven system that can affect real change. The stories offered here are a networked rhizome of experiences, perspectives, and counternarratives. They are shared within this collection to make the field's policies and its practices more equitable and make its practitioners more cognizant of systems of racism and biases that harm our field. We urge the readers, break the fiction—be with CFC members. Do the work.

REFERENCES

Ahmed, S. (2012). *On being included: Racism and diversity in institutional life.* Duke University Press.

Baca, D., Cushman, E., and Osborne, J. (2019). *Landmark essays on rhetorics of difference.* Routledge.

Baca, I. (2021). Hispanic-serving or not: La lucha sigue in academia; the struggle continues in academia. *Composition Studies, 49*(2), 70–78.

Bonilla-Silva, E., Goar, C. & Embrick, D. G. (2006). When Whites flock together: The social psychology of White habitus. *Critical Sociology, 32*(2–3), 229–253. https://doi.org/10.1163/156916306777835268.

Calhoon-Dillahunt, C. (2018). 2018 CCCC chair's address. *College Composition and Communication, 70*(2), 273–293.

Coates, T. (2009). On Jewish racism. *The Atlantic.* https://www.theatlantic.com/entertainment/archive/2009/06/on-jewish-racism/18840/.

Conference on College Composition and Communication. (2023). What is CCCC? National Council of Teachers of English. https://cccc.ncte.org/cccc/newcomers.

Corder, J. W. (1985). Argument as emergence, rhetoric as love. *Rhetoric Review, 4*(1), 16–32.

Faison, W., Green, N.-A. & Trevino, W. (2019, March 13). *Shut up and listen! Speaking truth to power* [Workshop]. 2019 Conference on College Composition & Communication Annual Convention, Pittsburgh, PA, United States.

Garcia, C., Campos, L. H., Garcia de Mueller, G. & Cedillo, C. V. (2021). "It's not you. You belong here." A Latinx conversation on mentorship and belonging in the academy. *Composition Studies, 49*(2), 53–69.

Grayson, M. L. (2023). *Antisemitism and the White supremacist imaginary: Conflations and contradictions in composition and rhetoric.* Peter Lang.

Hansen, T. (2009). Applying social network theory and analysis in the struggle for social justice. *Peace Research, 41*(1), 5–43.

Holdstein, D. H. (2008). The religious ideology of composition studies. In A. Greenbaum & D. H. Holdstein (Eds.), *Judaic perspectives in rhetoric and composition* (pp. 13–21). Hampton Press.

hooks, b. (2015). *Outlaw culture: Resisting representations.* Taylor & Francis/Routledge.

Inoue, A. (2019). 2019 chair's address: How do we language so people stop killing each other, or what do we do about White language supremacy? *College Composition and Communication, 71*(2), 352–369.

Jones, N. N., Gonzales, L. & Haas, A. M. (2021). So you think you're ready to build new social justice initiatives?: Intentional and coalitional pro-Black programmatic and organizational leadership in writing studies. *WPA: Writing Program Administration, 44*(3), 29–35.

Kumari, A., Baniya, S. & Larson, K. (2020). The necessity of genre disruption in organizing an advocacy space for and by graduate students. *Xchanges: An interdisciplinary journal of technical communication, rhetoric, and writing across the curriculum, 15*(1). https://xchanges.org/the-necessity-of-genre-disruption-15-1.

Kynard, C. (2015). Teaching while Black: Witnessing and countering disciplinary Whiteness, racial violence, and university race-management. *Literacy in Composition Studies, 3*(1), 1–20.

Latour, B. (2005). *Reassembling the social: An introduction to actor-network theory.* Oxford University Press.

Lunsford, A. (1990). Composing ourselves: Politics, commitment, and the teaching of writing. *College Composition and Communication, 41,* 71–82.

Martinez, A. Y. (2020). *Counterstory: The rhetoric and writing of critical race theory.* National Council of Teachers of English.

Mignolo, W. (2003). *The darker side of the Renaissance: Literacy, territoriality, and colonization.* University of Michigan Press.

Powell, M. (2012). 2012 CCCC chair's address: Stories take place: A performance in one act. *College Composition and Communication, 64*(2), 383–406.

Prendergast, C. (2003). *Literacy and racial justice: The politics of learning after Brown v. Board of Education.* Southern Illinois University Press.

Ruiz, I. D. (2021). Critiquing the critical: The politics of race and coloniality in rhetoric, composition, and writing studies research traditions. In A. L. Lockett, I. D. Ruiz, J. Chase Sanchez & C. Carter (Eds.), *Race, rhetoric, and research methods* (pp. 39–79). The WAC Clearinghouse; University Press of Colorado. https://doi.org/10.37514/per-b.2021.1206.

Vasser, M. (2018, September 17). *Engaging Difficult Dialogue in the Classroom* [PowerPoint slides]. University of Louisville. https://louisville.edu/english/composition/DiversityandInclusionintheClassroomEnglishComp.pdf.

Young, V. (2019). *Greetings from the 2019 program chair* [Pre-conference communication]. 2019 Conference on College Composition & Communication Annual Convention, Pittsburgh, PA, United States. http://cccc.ncte.org/wp-content/uploads/2019/03/Front-Matter-Wednesday.pdf.

Young, V. (n.d.). *Call for program proposals 2019: Performance-rhetoric, performance composition* [Pre-conference communication]. 2019 Conference on College Composition & Communication Annual Convention, Pittsburgh, PA, United States. Retrieved April 4, 2023, from https://cccc.ncte.org/cccc/conv/call-2019.

CHAPTER 3.

"HELP I POSTED": RACE, POWER, DISCIPLINARY SHIFTS, AND THE #WPALISTSERV-FEMINISTREVOLUTION

Iris Ruiz
University of California, Merced

Latina Oculta[1]
Anonymous

Brian Hendrickson
Roger Williams University

Mara Lee Grayson
California State University, Dominguez Hills

Holly Hassel
Michigan Technological University

Mike Palmquist
Colorado State University

Mandy Olejnik
Miami University

Iris: WPA-L has never been a space for me let alone a "safe-space." While my colleagues engaged in a Twitter debate about the communicative drawbacks of an "outdated network technology," in my eyes, this myopic debate created a gaping blindspot that I do not intend to contribute to in this chapter. This blindspot is the lack of attention paid to collecting data about the politics of listserv participation and the accompanying trends of women and scholars of color on the WPA-L, which has arguably functioned as a White, heteronormative, patriarchal digital space since its inception. Today, this arguably hostile space has finally been met with so

---

1   This author's name is a pseudonym.

DOI: https://doi.org/10.37514/PER-B.2023.1848.2.03

much revolutionary disruption by both women and people of color that it has reached a tipping point of having to be "rebooted." For many Rhet-Comp professionals impacted by this revolution, this space has lost its utility, novelty, innocence, and charm, and for those who looked to this digital network as a prime authority of the field, but were silenced, this revolution was long overdue.

– Iris

One thing that has concerned me during the conflicts we've seen over the past year or two has been that some of the younger and more vulnerable subscribers said some pretty harsh things, perhaps imagining that WPA-L was becoming a "safe" place. I'm not sure any discourse that's recorded and searchable is ever safe from examination, reinterpretation, and judgment. I worry that some of the things that were written might come back to haunt people. My take on this is that, even if we fundamentally reshape discourse in a positive way on the list, even if we tell people that this list is a safe place—and take action to advance that, we're still working within a larger hierarchical professional/institutional structure, with provosts, deans, chairs, senior faculty members, and so on. All it takes to derail a potential hire is one of these folks remembering an intemperate post or taking the time to search WPA-L's archives. In other words, the problem is not restricted to how we talk to each other on the list. It's baked into what we do on a daily basis, into how we hire and retain people, into how we reward them.

– Mike

Figure 3.1. One of many tweets to use the #WPAListservFeministRevolution hashtag.

According to the May 2021 farewell posts of many prominent writing studies scholars, the Writing Program Administrators Listserv (WPA-L) had tremendous influence on the discipline and on many individuals' professional development. However, it certainly was not seen by the entire community as a safe, supportive, professional networking space. Pre-dating the Council of Writing Program Administrators (CWPA), WPA-L began in 1993 as an informal network of writing program administrators (WPAs) and teachers, never officially affiliated with CWPA, and thus operated for decades without rules or moderation, eventually gaining around 4,000 followers by 2019 before finally shutting down in May 2021, following longtime WPA-L administrator Barry Maid's retirement from WPA-L's host institution, Arizona State University.[2] That lack of connection to and accountability from a specific organization or sponsoring institution for anything beyond mechanical management—what might be described as a lack of intentional *disciplining* of an increasingly "chaotic super-system" (Massumi, 1997, p. 54)—produced a subsequent *disciplinary disruption*, or paradigm shift (Baca, 2010; Kuhn, 2012; Mueller, 2012; Ruiz, 2017), in the form of the #WPAListservFeministRevolution and associated formation of the nextGEN graduate student listserv (nextGEN) and WPA-L Reimagining Working Group (Working Group).[3]

This chapter's authors were concerned witnesses to the numerous racist, misogynist, and classist micro- and macro-aggressions that made WPA-L unsafe for many, for many years. Some of us spoke out against the significant racist, misogynist, and classist actions that catalyzed the #WPAListservFeministRevolution, which this chapter analyzes in detail. Some were and continue to be members of the Working Group. This chapter's nontraditional approach of academic engagement—multi-theoretical and polyvocal—allows us to consider the competing and complementary ways in which we interrogate what we have identified as at least three waves of *kairotic momentum* that animated discussions among and about WPA-L's marginalized members, contributing to efforts to dismantle an arguably racist, misogynist, and classist network.[4] As in this chapter's first paragraphs, individual members' reflections are italicized and signal attempts at dialogue with our larger arguments in this chapter about the three

---

2   Despite never being officially affiliated with CWPA, one could find as late as the summer of 2019 WPA-L listed under the "Support" heading on the CWPA website. Since that time the CWPA website has been reconstructed and neither the "Support" link nor the information on and link to WPA-L are available there.

3   nextGEN was established in April 2018 to provide "a space to network, collaborate, share knowledge, and engage in critical, supportive, and thought-provoking interdisciplinary writing and rhetoric studies conversations on both a national and international level," one that is specifically "moderated by, and produced for, graduate students" (6 November 2018).

4   In this case, *kairotic momentum* refers to the moments in which a certain WPA-L post or response provided an opportunity for others to take the time to weigh in on a previously moot point such as the phenomenon of "mansplaining." The scale and number of responses to an initial post also builds up momentum in that each post becomes more nuanced and provides further opportunity for others to rhetorically engage the topic.

waves identified herein: the 2019 Conference on College Composition and Communication (CCCC) call for papers (CFP), the beginning of the WPA-L Feminist Revolution in 2018, and the 2019 CCCC's Chair's Address.

Throughout the writing process, we found ourselves contending with similarities and differences in our experiences of the #WPAListservFeministRevolution—which we view as an intersectional, antiracist, online, network-based disciplinary movement emerging over several years but escalating in 2018 and 2019—and how we made sense of and theorized them, and so present two theories—actor-network theory (ANT) and decolonial theory—in dialogue here. It was, after all, only through dialogue that we were able to analyze posts from the #WPAListservFeministRevolution and arrive at a shared understanding of WPA-L as a mechanism through which writing studies quasi-informally extends its network of influence, colonizing digital-discursive space in ways that more formal disciplinary spaces might have obscured through official policies and protocols.

As we demonstrate, WPA-L was initially theorized as a space without policy or protocol beyond an assumedly shared community identity based on assumedly shared underlying values and practices, chief among them free speech and civil discourse. These foundational assumptions rendered WPA-L particularly adept at reflecting and reifying settler-colonial, White supremacist, heteronormative, patriarchal values and practices. In the threads we explore in this chapter, it is apparent how oppressive participation on WPA-L could be, with posters sharing their perceptions of being "mansplained" to, "silenced," "ignored," "belittled," "afraid to respond," "discriminated" against, and even "abused." We contend that as a digital-discursive extension of the disciplinary network of writing studies, WPA-L is a manifestation of inequities within the discipline at large, and that by rebooting WPA-L, we can contribute to efforts to reboot writing studies into a more social justice-oriented and equity-minded space of teaching, learning, being, and becoming. There are lessons to be learned for program administrators from our narrative and analysis of the catalyzing events that led to the revamping of the list—and not just because the original list centered on writing program administration. Any work that aims to administer a discursive space (online, face-to-face, institutional, organizational) will navigate tensions that escalate and ebb.

Efforts to reboot writing studies began in 2019, when the Working Group established by vote on WPA-L a moderation board and set of participation guidelines that it would struggle to enforce due to WPA-L's inherent technical constraints, which did not allow for pre-post moderation.[5] Now in 2021, the

---

5   See Appendix A for the June 3, 2019, draft and the most recent version of these guidelines.

Working Group has successfully migrated WPA-L and its archives to the North Dakota University System, and is currently discussing how to apply the lessons learned from WPA-L in moderating its next iteration, WritingStudies-L. This chapter is an effort to discuss, distill, and distribute those lessons toward cultivating a more just and equitable future for digital networking in our discipline.

"JUST" NETWORK?: ACTOR-NETWORK THEORY, DECOLONIALITY, AND WPA-L

> Witnessing inequity on WPA-L deepened my awareness of my own privilege and complicity as a White man and tenure-track faculty member, as well as my commitment to accompliceship, which involves taking risks (Green, 2018). For me, reimagining WPA-L wasn't a big risk. If you are of the opinion that WPA-L is a reflection and reification of inequities in our discipline and society at large, then at worst, moderation boards and community guidelines continue to do the same. For my colleagues of color who already endure having their ideas and experiences questioned and undervalued, though, it is risky to reimagine a WPA-L premised on racial equity and social justice. However, reimagining WPA-L might actually be most risky for White folks who always experienced it as their community. And that is a good thing. Given WPA-L has never actually been the community they thought it was, White folks now have an opportunity to participate in a more democratic reimagining of what a writing studies community might look like, and just maybe start to scrutinize how writing studies' prepositional key of civility undermines its professed commitments to racial equity and social justice.
>
> – Brian

As Brian indicates, spaces like WPA-L operate as extensions of larger disciplinary networks, at once enacting and informing disciplinary networks' underlying values and practices. Because WPA-L existed as an undisciplined network of the discipline, it served the function of orienting some "networked" graduate students and new professionals to the field. Because there are various approaches to mapping the discipline of writing studies[6] and because writing teachers interacted in varying ways with WPA-L (digest format, archives, instant email notifications), it can be challenging to define exactly how WPA-L existed as a disciplinary network. Derek Mueller (2017) explained that "semantic, bibliographic, and geolocative patterns surfaceable from materials and activities describe and

---

6   See WritingStudiesTree.org, a "genealogical" influence network. Other "big data" efforts like Dylan Dryer (2019) and Mueller (2012) analyze bibliographic data or keyword clusters to identify disciplinary themes and values.

in effect set up ways of knowing and participating in an emerging disciplinary future" (p. 8). Mueller's work provides a precedent for drawing inferences about disciplinary networks, and a precedent has also been established for analyzing our discipline via the discourse of WPA-L (Borrowman, 2005; Chen, 2018; Dobrin, 2011; Horner, 2007; Miles, 2007; Pantelides, 2015).

Indeed, WPA-L was (and remains in archive format[7]) a rich site for research into the discursive and ideological structures and tensions within writing studies, including how it oriented those new to the discipline. Unlike scholarship, however, it existed as a dialogic space with immediacy and at least a superficial informality, despite being a place where many members only lurked because of the perceived high stakes of engaging in conversations that could impact one's professional and academic career, as members of the Committee for Change discuss in this volume. Across the various episodes associated with the #WPA-listservFeministRevolution on WPA-L, we observed how that space perpetuated inequities in our discipline, but in ways that were unique to WPA-L as a digital-discursive extension of our disciplinary network.

Turning toward a complementarity of theoretical framing through actor-network theory (ANT) and decoloniality has helped us examine how WPA-L's discursive patterns reflected and reified hegemonic dispositions in writing studies. Rooted in his observation that, rather than making individuals freer from social and natural constraints, modernity had exacerbated the oppressive dimensions of our relationships to one another and the world, Bruno Latour (2013) proposed that modern institutions, e.g., academic disciplines, should identify the prepositional keys, or dispositions, by which they discursively arrive at their own social facts, as therein lies the ontological foundation upon which rests modern Western civilization's self-conceptualization.

While some writing studies scholars have criticized ANT for failing to account for human agency and oppression as historical, material, and embodied (Bazerman, 1999; Russell, 1997; Scott & Welch, 2014), we see ANT as integral to our examination of how modern institutions and their associated discourses and epistemologies have formed around the need to establish and defend particular modes of being, including White supremacy.

Proponents of decolonial theory are also skeptical of claims to human progress in the name of modernism (Anzaldúa, 2012; Dussel, 2003; Lugones, 2010; Mignolo, 2009; Quijano, 2003; Smith, 2012). Decolonial theory exposes the ways that disciplinary network extensions like WPA-L function as colonialist discursive and epistemological structures, resulting in the dehumanization of

---

7 The WritingStudies-L archives can be found at https://lists.asu.edu/cgi-bin/wa?A0=WPA-L. In this chapter, we include selections of emails, with author names and email dates, which readers can find the full emails in the archives above.

Indigenous and African American peoples (Fanon, 2008; Mignolo, 2009). Decolonial theory can help writing studies scholars and administrators analyze how colonized populations are subjected in networked spaces like WPA-L not only to exploitation of their own resources but also to dehumanization and racism (Ruiz & Baca, 2017). It also allows us to think through Anglo- and Eurocentric structures of representation that continue to dominate the field's governing gazes, such as those exposed on WPA-L by the "Grand Scholar Wizard" (22 March 2019), whose post, which we have chosen not to amplify here, once again brought White-supremacist, patriarchal discourse to the fore. (For a contemporaneous response to this post, see Grayson, 2019.) As such, it was necessary for us to take a decolonial methodological approach when considering how scholars of color navigated WPA-L's colonized disciplinary network, and how WPA-L as a network perpetuated, extended, and produced new iterations of epistemes tied to colonial pasts. Decolonial praxis also informs our reimagining work in that it performs "epistemic disobedience" (Mignolo, 2009): a metacognitive break from Eurocentrically minded epistemes, facilitating perspectival shifts from colonized epistemologies that might otherwise continue to silence colonized beings.

"PERSPECTIVES FROM THE FIELD": ESCALATING TENSIONS AND CALLS FOR CHANGE

> Typically, I tried not to put myself out there too much on WPA-L. However, I decided to send a quick response to someone asking for information regarding qualifications for faculty who are teaching general education writing courses. I answered the query with my experience and understanding as an accreditation peer reviewer and former chair of general education. I was soon disappointed when an aggressive White female academic responded by quoting an irrelevant page on my accreditation agency's website and calling my credibility into question. She was not the person asking the original question; she was not asking for clarification of what I posted; she was publicly trying to humiliate me.
> I left WPA-L feeling some despair since it had been a disciplinary resource for me for so many years. When I got involved with the Working Group, my hope in the future of the discipline was renewed. I felt validated in reading the thoughtful policies and procedures and respected when my voice was heard. Many of the problematic behaviors I had encountered on WPA-L struck me as aggressive and coercive. But through this "reimagining" project, I acquired a better understanding of their racial and gendered nature, which makes them seem even more insidious. The project is now more important to my own development and mobility as a minority female in writing studies.
>
> – Latina Oculta

Figure 3.2. Tweet referencing incidents on a co-occurring WPA-L thread.

The coercion Latina Oculta refers to took place on WPA-L in a number of forms, from threatening tones to Man/Race/Able/Other/splaining, highlighting the manner in which discourse on our own disciplinary network reflects and reifies longstanding racism, misogyny, and classism within higher education more broadly. Analyzing how these larger structural inequities manifested within and across individual posts is difficult work that required the very kinds of discussions among coauthors of this chapter that we designed the WPA-L moderation board to facilitate. This work also requires explicating that our intent here is not to label the authors of posts we cite as racist, misogynist, or classist; instead, by tracing how racism, misogyny, and classism operate discursively within and across individual posts, we hope to draw attention to the manner in which all of us are coerced by these hegemonic forces, even as each of us has a different set of positionalities and associated responsibilities to interrogate and transform structural inequities. Although much of the analysis that follows resulted from deliberation by various actants on various networks mentioned here, effectively interpreting the sometimes subtle and often complicated textual and contextual nuances of each WPA-L discussion thread required foregrounding the insights that the women of color among us were able to bring to the task by drawing upon their own lived, embodied experiences.

Indeed, race played a not-so-subtle yet significantly complicated role in the series of WPA-L threads arising from Drew Loewe's March 18, 2018, post, "2019 CFP for CCCC: Is this the first CFP for a major/'flagship' conference to use AAVE extensively?" That initial post garnered 42 responses in one thread, plus over 100 other posts on other, offshoot threads. With a few exceptions, most of those posts did not address the question reflected in the title of the original post. Instead, the brunt of the conversation centered around the second post in the thread, in which Erec Smith (18 March 2018) responded:

> I am not aware of AAVE [African American Vernacular English] being used in a call. What's more, I am not very happy about it. I presented at C's on the inefficacy of code-meshing as a pedagogy and its utter negligence of kairos. What's more, as a black man, I find the use of code-meshing in the conference a bit gimmicky, cosmetic (as opposed to semantically or rhetorically relevant), and a little offensive. I appreciate code-meshed language in interpersonal communication and as a kind of genre, but the whole code-meshing movement is beginning to feel contrived. The term "blaxploitation" comes to mind.

Smith's critique of the 2019 CCCC CFP was multilayered. He began by criticizing code-meshing as a pedagogy before establishing his position "as a black man" and criticizing Young's—another Black scholar's—language as "gimmicky, cosmetic . . . and a little offensive." Then, after acknowledging appreciation for code-meshing in practice, Smith again criticized code-meshing "as a movement," presumably a scholarly and/or pedagogical one, by referencing "blaxploitation."

Smith was not just being provocative by criticizing code-meshing. There is serious discussion within writing studies and associated disciplines regarding the exoticization and reductive conceptualization of code-meshing as a communicative practice and pedagogical intervention (Guerra, 2016; Lee, 2017; Matsuda, 2014; Schreiber & Watson, 2018). Two of the first respondents to Smith's post, established scholars of African American and Latinx language and literacy, affirmed Smith's criticism of code-meshing as a pedagogy (Balester, 20 March 2018; Barajas, 19 March 2018). Smith (19 March 2018), however, followed up the first response by observing,

> Basically, many in rhet/comp, specifically proponents of code-meshing as a pedagogy, have "fallen in love" with themselves. They are so proud of how "woke" they are that they've forgotten that the rest of the world—professional environments, namely—do not yet appreciated (sic) meshed codes like they do.

At this point, Smith's (20 March 2018) comments were becoming increasingly more personal in their attacks on Young, pointing out in a subsequent message that there was a history of personal insult between them:

> Does [the CFP] imply that Black people who do not code-mesh are performing against their own authenticity to placate White people? (This, by the way, is a charge hurled against me, personally, by Young on several occasions. To his defense, he hasn't done it in a few years.

A disciplinary listserv may not be the appropriate place for personal attacks but separating the personal from the political is complicated partly because Smith was interrogating more than the authenticity of Young's performance of his Black identity: he was also interrogating the conference and professional organization as well as an entire theoretical and pedagogical movement. This messy conflation fed into two concurrent and often entangled discussions—of code-meshing as pedagogy and code-meshing as practiced in the CFP—and to entangled criticisms of the appropriateness of Smith's criticisms of both (see Smith [2020] for additional discussion of these tensions and his chapter in this volume).

As arguments for and against Smith's criticisms piled up, Smith continued to engage with posters by asking questions, complementing, elaborating, qualifying, and making concessions, all the while defending his own position in post after post (Smith makes at least 25 posts across the various threads) that the CFP and code-meshing in general were gimmicks in the way that they caricatured Black authenticity, and that Black students needed to learn Standard American English (SAE) in first-year composition to be successful in later coursework and in their careers (20 March 2018). Those who are literacy program coordinators would recognize this rhetorical move as a common point of debate that plays out in writing programs, in writing centers, and across campuses.

Meanwhile, in the predominantly White space of WPA-L, the conversation began to give way to more racially problematic posts that missed the complexity of race involved in Young's CFP, Smith's criticisms of it, and the fact that these criticisms were being directed by one Black scholar at another Black scholar. In one case, a scholar glossed over that important latter nuance in declaring the CFP

> . . . annoying to read. It grated on me as performance—a choice that annoys me as much when a writer from the South I know adopts a "Southern Accent" she has never had as long as I've known her. It's playing to an audience. (Wyatt, 22 March 2018)

One scholar fanned the flames by describing criticism of the CFP as "vitriol" (Knoblauch, 23 Mar 2018). Another scholar oversimplified the theoretical and pedagogical implications of the debate by pointing out that their children code-meshed when they used slang (McLeod, 23 March 2018). And still another oversimplified the racial tension posed by the CFP in remarking, "I mean a little snark about a conference theme is pretty regular fare (not just for C's but in general), but this has seemed to go beyond the typical" (Reid, 23 March 2018). The mounting hostility to Smith's criticism ultimately led Smith to reiterate that he was a Black scholar responding to an issue that would most greatly affect Black students: "I think my understanding of all of this as a Black academic—which, again, I thought I explained—gives me a different take on the matter, if you'd allow for that" (Smith, 23 March 2018). The rising tension across these various threads was connected in part to the way WPA-L's format was ill-equipped to accommodate the debate's complexities.

As mounting criticisms of the CFP continued to ignore or oversimplify its nuances and those of the broader argument for code-meshing—not uncoincidentally via public attacks on a Black scholar's use of AAVE in a CFP—a graduate student eventually called out what they observed to be "a whole bunch of rhetorical gymnastics based on investment in and alignment with white supremacist discourses."[8] That criticism was quickly followed by a more established scholar accusing the graduate student of shaming people and recommending they watch conservative, anti-social justice YouTube videos (Goldstein, 23 March 2018), then by another established scholar confronting the graduate student by asking, "Are you implying then that I'm a white supremacist? Are you suggesting I'm not self-reflective or self-critical? Please, feel free to educate me on this matter" (Krause, 23 March 2018). The quickness with which scholars chastised this graduate student highlights that in addition to race, classism was always at play within WPA-L's discourse, surfacing when graduate students dared to peel back that discourse's veneer of respectability. In her post, Bernice Olivas (22 March 2018) connected critiquing the CFP's use of code-meshing to how the conversation itself performed a certain respectability politics:

> After reading through this thread, I wonder if there is a second conversation to be had here? If we are going to critique code-meshing as an acceptable language for a CCCC's CFP, then I think we also need to be talking about the performance of respectability politics and the ways academic writing and SAE perform respectability. I think the response to the CPF

---

8   To protect their identities against professional discrimination, we have intentionally chosen not to cite by name and date of post-graduate students whose posts we include in this chapter.

> indicates that the topic of code meshing is very timely—clearly our field is less comfortable with diverse linguistics at the academic table than many would like to think.

A pattern emerges across these threads that speaks to what many of the posts gloss over. In post-after-post, scholars of color announced their racial positionality, but the absence of this rhetorical positioning in the vast majority of posts illustrates the conversation was not adequately accounting for its own racial complexities, let alone the racial identities of Smith and Young. Observing this phenomenon, Iris Ruiz (23 March 2018) commented,

> I've never witnessed so many curve balls thrown in one conversation. There is a clear discomfort with the content and tenor of the CFP and the criticism being made, and let's be clear, there is discomfort with who is making those criticisms. Race is a complex code of metaphors, principles, contradictions, ideologies, and corporeal, and social circumstances/realities. I think we are witnessing that on this thread. This is the most honest representation of integration in practice . . . inclusivity in practice. On the stage, for all to see, we see the difficulty in talking back to the establishment as a racial minority, as one who struggles to claim a space within the world of academia, while also trying to claim that same space for others.
>
> I, for one, am happy to see this discomfort on display, for it is only through them that true progress can be made. Let's work through our discomforts. These conversations have to go beyond the all member event. They have to.

Ruiz's post reveals some subscribers' inability to listen to scholars of color as they problematize race as it relates to the teaching of writing and to their own lived and embodied experiences as people of color. The first of several caustic WPA-L conversations that became commonplace, it was nevertheless acknowledged by Ruiz as necessary; better to "see this discomfort on display" and collectively interrogate where it comes from and how we want to work through it as a discipline than to pretend it doesn't exist. What these threads evidence is an illusion of civility that ultimately falls prey to Smith's critique of proponents of code-meshing: writing studies wants to be "proud of how 'woke' [we] are," yet we cannot step outside of our own discursive habitus in order to examine the manner in which it is encoded by White supremacy, because we are embedded within a discipline that is from-the-start mired in White, heteronormative, patriarchal discourse (García de Müeller & Ruiz, 2017).

"Help I Posted"

#WPALISTSERVFEMINISTREVOLUTION: SEXISM, NEXTGEN, AND VIEWPOINT DIVERSITY

> I tried to engage with WPA-L. I used it to find participants for research projects I was doing. I shared suggestions for antiracist faculty development. I posted about the significance of positionality. I called out the championing of racist and conservative talking points. Though teachers and scholars contacted me off-list, most of my attempts to engage in debate on WPA-L were met with strawman fallacies that misrepresented my statements and ignored their explicitly antiracist content. While I never wish to stay silent in the face of injustice, I have no interest in engaging with those whose approach resembles demagoguery more than deliberation (Roberts-Miller, 2017). WPA-L is as entrenched in Whiteness and patriarchy as is the history of our discipline. It is a symptom of the exclusionary disciplinary epistemologies that have made it a mainstay in our field, but I don't think it is who we currently are. The folklore of WPA-L works the same way as the myth of a standard English: it convinces us that it confers access and opportunity where it does not. In the face of progress, people and institutions whose power is threatened will always try to pull us backward. We can better direct our energy toward teaching equitably and producing scholarship that moves our field forward.
>
> – Mara Lee

Other actants in this particular network revolution are graduate students and emerging scholars, some of whom have seriously questioned the parameters of network participation on WPA-L. After all, the dynamics Mara Lee describes were not uncommon on WPA-L. One such burst of activity occurred in October 2018 in response to the "Rubrics to Assess Writing Assignments" query from Michelle LaFrance; after several responses from frequent WPA-L discussants (questioning or imputing assumptions about LaFrance's initial post), LaFrance (22 October 2018) responded (we abridge some of the comments):

> BUT WOW, I'm feeling just a little "mansplained" here.
>
> So, I'd just like to note that 1) I hold a PHD in the field and I have a pretty noteworthy academic appointment.
>
> Also, 2) I asked for examples—that doesn't mean I've broken any sort of ideological code around our assessment norms.
>
> I'd sure like to have taken all of your classes when I was still a grad student and new to our field, but since I'm just crossing off an item on my long to do list so that I can have a conversation that includes everyone at our current assessment table (including those who don't share our values), I'll say that it's

exactly this sort of behavior that keeps many of us from ever posting to this list . . . there's no actual conversation starter here and no benefit of the doubt. Your responses suggest that I don't know what I'm doing and . . . frankly, it's insulting.

Apologies if this makes me come off as—well, any of the things women who "talk back" are accused of. (And see, look at that—I'm apologizing for setting a boundary, if that's not gendered communication . . .) I really do appreciate each of your voices (at the right time) and pretty major contributions to the field, but, I'm done with the pile on.

The resulting discussion produced 162 messages, many of which replicated the very same "mansplaining" LaFrance called out in the above post, as men struggled to come to grips with their perpetuation of misogyny, suggesting how deeply encoded it is in our disciplinary network. This conversation is closely correlated with a corresponding Twitter conversation in which the hashtag #WPAListservFeministRevolution eventually became the "go-to" hashtag.

The #WPAListservFeministRevolution led to a collective response by next-GEN in November of 2018, in which they "recognize that the recent conversations on WPA-L are yet another manifestation of an oppressive discourse that created the exigence for nextGEN's founding in April 2018," then further note how "the culture cultivated on WPA-L directly impacts and, at times, even restricts the culture that is allowed to be cultivated on nextGEN due to the realities and consequences of misused professional power and privilege."[9]

Again, we see those who have not felt safe on WPA-L highlighting the need for serious attention to its dynamics and culture, ultimately inspiring the formation of the Working Group.[10] Furthermore, the nextGEN statement observes that the two digital-discursive disciplinary networks of nextGEN and WPA-L are, for better or worse, entangled in such a way that the culture of one impacts the other. While we might view the efforts of nextGEN, the Working Group, and the #WPAListservFeministRevolution through a decolonialist lens as acts of epistemic disobedience intended to transform our discipline's prepositional key through the formation of new, more intentionally crafted and explicitly antiracist and feminist digital-discursive networked spaces and practices, we must also recognize that such efforts were insufficient to the task of neutralizing WPA-L's toxic culture. Indeed, these two opposing epistemes entered into a kind of dialectical tension resulting in further incidents similar to those already analyzed.

---

9   See more context about the nextGEN listserv at https://nextgenlistserv.wordpress.com/listserv-to-listserv/.
10 For a dialogue between nextGEN and the Working Group, see Baniya, et al. (2019).

RACE/POWER/DISCIPLINARY OWNERSHIP: THE "DUMPSTER FIRE" EXPLODES

> Like many graduate students, I joined WPA-L during my studies to stay abreast of developments in the discipline. During the first of several contentious discussions in the 2018–2019 school year, I was moved to point toward the privilege inherent in some of the posters' responses as they mansplained other accomplished scholars and dominated discussions in unproductive ways. As a first-year doctoral student at the time with zero standing, I faced a certain risk in stating how unacceptable that behavior was but did so anyway.
>
> For me, the resulting #WPAListservFeministRevolution on social media was a central hub of feminist mentoring practices I hadn't experienced on WPA-L. The community of people on social media embraced the conversations happening on the list, acknowledging hurt while also challenging us to be better, especially in terms of who we speak out for—White women in the discipline, and also our colleagues of color who have long suffered mistreatment.
>
> Graduate students like myself are aware of and are influenced by the behaviors happening on WPA-L and in surrounding social media networks. We are the future of this discipline, as we are told again and again, and we are learning who to be, how to act, and what to do with each of these movements and networks.
>
> – Mandy

In March 2019, a post entitled "The C's Chair's Address" started a flurry of 113 email responses in less than a week, reflecting a pattern of hostility and competition, rather than collegiality or support, similar to that in the aforementioned threads. The parent post of this discussion, written by Erec Smith, sparked everything from inflammatory retorts to genuine thoughtfulness. In that post, Smith noted that many activists "prioritized performance and expression of identity over concrete steps for social change" (19 March 2019). Smith explained an assignment in which he asked students to apply Jonathan Smucker (2017) to analyze part of Asao Inoue's (2019) CCCC Chair's Address, which Smith said accomplishes some goals (student empowerment and making societal changes toward respect for minorities) while failing to accomplish more activist goals. As with the previously discussed exchanges, this thread has object lessons for administrators who hope to adopt anti-racist approaches to their programs.

Some scholars of color were quick to enter the discussion to defend the address, which confronted issues of race and social justice related to teaching writing. One response by a graduate student expressed frustration with the initial post:

> What are you asking to sacrifice in our material/visceral/oppressed bodies when you reduce learning the tools that oppress as a necessary evil (that is basically your argument) to navigate "contexts"? . . . You seemingly want to ignore the power dynamics embedded in the work we do. No one is equating the severity of the industrial prison complex and police brutality to FYC [first-year composition]; but they are related because we carry these relations in our bodies in our classrooms, in our academic communities. . . . How do you have more white fragility than some of my white colleagues?

The level of angst the initial post caused this graduate student is communicated in the tone of this message. But also present in the questions the graduate student posed is a desire to better understand the reasoning of the initial post. However, as Mandy mentioned, such an engagement is not easily immune from backlash by the profession. Still, a response from Myrna Nurse (19 March 2019), another scholar of color, got more directly to the point in expressing frustration:

> I take exception to the patronizing perspective disguised as "good intentions" . . . The assumption that people of color don't have the necessary tools to hold forth . . . is already fallacious of who and what the people labeled "of color" are and have.

Figure 3.3. Tweet commenting on the reaction to the "Grand Scholar Wizard" post.

"Help I Posted"

Many of the responses (most written by White academics) that followed this second response to the initial inflammatory post seemed to defend Smith's initial post. For example, one response thanked Smith and chided the others who did not respond in kind: "I also think we owe it to our profession to avoid ad hominem attacks and taking quotations out of context . . . Silencing this perspective (as opposed to giving it a fair hearing) is also silencing people of color" (Wolfe, 20 March 2019). The irony of this response is that it attempts to accomplish what it derides—silencing people of color—and is a perfect example of race-splaining: a White academic's voice taking up the issue of race between two people of color on their behalf. Other comments struck a similar chord and recast the initial response by the graduate student of color by saying he came "out rhetorical/exegetical guns ablazing" (Dickson, 21 March 2019). These comments in support of Smith's initial post were made to subsequent responses by scholars of color, sparking further discussion and serving as an ideal illustration of how WPA-L reached the limits of what could be worked out through "civil discourse." The network fell apart into sub threads and off list in spaces like Twitter, because of WPA-L's lack of systematic constraints.

One response applauded the graduate student's post and the courage it took to submit it to WPA-L:

> What the graduate student did in his long response as I see it is activism. In fighting for social justice publicly, as a marginalized body of a graduate student, he put himself at risk and he might have to pay a high cost professionally in how he will be perceived in academia, for example on the job market. (Diab, 21 March 2019)

Another response supported the graduate student and Smith's views on the difficult but important subject of identity politics and racism in writing studies:

> Both forms of critique from both men are valid and thought provoking. I'm a bit resentful that one is a man of color and that the other is a graduate student because that brings to this debate another set of circumstances and unwritten and unseen exigencies for further elaboration and discussion. Why won't our white, tenured colleagues come out with critiques? Sustained critiques or exegetics? Solutions? What do they or how do they respond to the address? What will they do about the biases in the field? How will they continue to be allies and/or accomplices in helping this field to move forward in a way that calls out the politics of citation, the inherent biases in the work

we do, the exclusivity of the hiring processes, the exclusivity of the definition of rhetoric, the narrow conception of the field's genesis, the ways that POC constantly have to be the forerunners for social justice, etc? (Ruiz, 21 March 2019)

The high level of tension caused by the difficult race-centered conversation also presented an opportunity for scholars of color to foist the underlying unanswered questions of inequality in the discipline back onto their White counterparts. This rhetorical move serves as another example of epistemic disobedience employed to illuminate and disrupt the discipline's prepositional key as reflected and reified on WPA-L. It does not come without consequence, however, as over the next month longtime subscribers began to express both on and off list their dismay with WPA-L and proceeded to unsubscribe, Latina Oculta included. Others, like Mandy and Jennifer, chose to remain.

> **Jennifer:** As the First-Year Writing Coordinator and sole compositionist at my institution, I joined the WPA-L as a much needed, free resource. I was your average WPA-Ler—posting rarely, reading a lot but deleting more. I didn't give the listserv any kind of critical thought until that one evening when I read an email to the listserv that began, "Okay. Look fellas . . . ," and it changed my relationship to and feelings about the field.
>
> While the exchanges that took place on the listserv often horrified me, they also (not to be cliché) woke me up to the deeply embedded racism and patriarchy in our field that I knew were there (of course, how could we be immune?) but had never truly been named, called out, or responded to. Regardless of how ugly the discussions got, I always felt they were crucial ones to be having. I closely followed along with and participated in the #WPAListservFeministRevolution backchannel discussion, from which I learned a lot. I also never stopped believing in the potential of the WPA-L as a (in)valuable resource. I tried to be a strong proponent of keeping the list (behind the scenes—I read all the materials put together by the WPA Reimagining Working Group, answered the surveys, cast my votes, etc.), but with a moderation board and clear guidelines for posting. I still feel this way and have deep gratitude toward the group who voluntarily took on the work of keeping this listserv alive but in a more sustainable, inclusive, and respectful way.

Holly: Because I did not train exclusively in writing studies as a graduate student, I did not come to WPA-L until a few years after I was in my first faculty position at a two-year college, where my English department had no WPA, Composition Committee, or any specific structure of managing the first-year writing program, I struggled the first few years to figure out how to meet the needs of the students in my classrooms and to support new writing instructors.

As our own program developed, and as I became more involved in disciplinary organizations, I began to understand the "networked" space of WPA-L more clearly—the relationships that people had with each other, and that the list focused on writing classes and writing programs in ways that were not specific to "administration." Over time, I also noted how WPA-L did not really meet the needs of two-year college English instructors (hence the TYCA listserv). And the posturing and combativeness of WPA-L became more obvious to me, and more disturbing. I saw the strong and ugly reaction to Vershawn Young's CFP for 2019 CCCC, and the ways some voices were silent, and others tried to intervene. The exit of many junior scholars and graduate students in the form of nextGEN struck me—as did, frankly, the tepid response from WPA-L subscribers and the voices who had often been loudest when the announcement emerged.

I have mixed feelings about the levels of contribution I have made to try to add accountability and community standards to the list. Even as people subscribed and unsubscribed, the hegemony of the list within the field continued to filter into publications, into presentation opportunities, into academic positions—but it seems to have been largely a space that privileged White male scholars in secure tenured positions at selective or elite institutions.

WPA-L REIMAGINING WORKING GROUP AND THE FUTURE OF WRITINGSTUDIES-L

Through our dual framework of ANT and decoloniality, it becomes evident that the WPA-L functioned as an extension of broader systems and supersystems, the ideologies and practices of which the WPA-L reproduced. At the same time, this framework elucidates the ways in which those of us who participated in the Reimagining Working Group have also connected as a system of resistance, one that is itself connected with other systems of resistance. Though we authors, individually, come at this work from our uniquely situated experiences and positionalities, as well as distinctive and even seemingly competing epistemologies, our work, collectively, serves as a reminder of the power of coalition in the face of injustice.

The Working Group was a "loose collection" because it emerged in part from what became known as the "Grand Scholar Wizard" post, which clearly alluded to the Ku Klux Klan, and the lack of a clear mechanism for halting communications. Through a series of email exchanges between Ruiz, Maid, and Hassel, we began an effort to call for a mechanism that would not just enable intervention in extreme cases but establish clear, reasonable boundaries for participation. Ruiz's creation of a document to crowdsource volunteers to moderate and draft principles for engagement began a longer process now informing the establishment of WritingStudies-L.

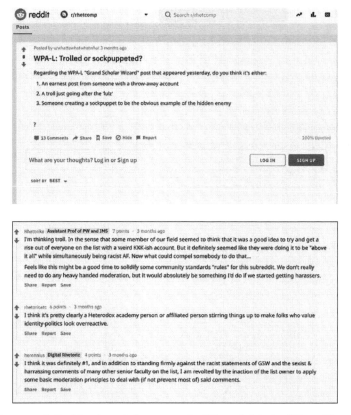

Figure 3.4. Reddit thread discussing the "Grand Scholar Wizard" post.

"Help I Posted"

In this chapter, we have attempted to grapple with the complex and necessary work of adopting a multiple-theoretical and metacognitive lens to study the function of heteronormative networks and colonial spaces such as WPA-L. While we all agree WPA-L served for many as a valuable professional resource, our purpose has not been to recount its utility but instead to reflect upon it through an anti-singular disciplinary and theoretical framework to explore the complex creation and interaction of networks and the interplay of race, gender, power, and disciplinary transformation. We hope to have provided a "thin description" (Färber, 2014) of various events that led to a revolutionary disruption causing major changes in how WPA-L as an extension of the disciplinary network of writing studies proceeded with business as usual. We chose thin over thick description in that we focused "on tracing the elements creating connections, the forms of links and transformations, as well as the materiality involved" (Färber, 2014, p. 354).

We also chose at times to look beyond the limits of WPA-L to account for contours of this disruption as it occurred in various online network spaces, and to consider how such an exploration can accommodate theoretical complementarity. Through both content and structure, we blended both the collective view of our group with some of the individual positions and perspectives we have brought to the work of "disciplining" WPA-L. We hope that the interludes of our "WPA-L stories" have illustrated our motivations to participate in the transformative work.

What we can collectively say is that this desire for change led us to reimagine WPA-L, to transform our understanding and practice of leadership in day-to-day conversations, to act with respect for and appreciation of our differences. The frameworks we draw upon throughout this chapter, ANT and decoloniality, through their possibilities for self-reflection and epistemic exposure, have helped us with our administrative work in the Working Group and as chapter coauthors to press for an epistemic shift in our discipline. Much work, however, remains. We know, for example, that decolonial pursuits are still functioning on the margins of writing studies. We know that rhetoric and composition administrators do not always make space within their programs and departments for anti-racist conversations and programmatic changes or may grapple with resistance to such efforts. We continue to struggle with the difficulty of legitimizing decolonial research methods in a discipline deeply entrenched in Eurocentric hegemonic history (Ruiz & Arellano, 2019). We continue to be pulled, in good faith or otherwise, into debates over the legitimacy and necessity of antiracist research, scholarship, pedagogy, and activism. We continue to struggle, and rightly so, with the ways even those practices we assume to be equitable reinforce the entrenched Whiteness of our discipline and of academia writ large (Grayson, 2020).

Disciplinary identity has been a goal for writing studies for some time (Yancey, 2018). History shows that shifts occur according to transpositions in collective consciousness and political climate as well as through advances in knowledge and technology, as is the case with WPA-L. However, disciplines also embody the collective consciousness of networked professionals and scholars (Foucault, 1969; Mignolo, 2009) and disciplinary change substantive enough to be considered a true shift in paradigm requires not only methodological, pedagogical, and representational movement but also ideological and epistemic reorientation and expansion.

We may not transform the entire field with these actions, but we have started the process. Reimagining WPA-L might provide an opportunity for all of us in writing studies to collectively interrogate and transform our discipline's White supremacist disposition, or, drawing upon the work of Latour (2013), its prepositional key. Resistance to demands for more just and equitable discourse on WPA-L via appeals to civil discourse evidences that writing studies' prepositional key is still—despite our discipline's "social turn" and advocacy for students' right to their own language—the modern, liberal, Western, White supremacist conception of civility, which involves a principal commitment to engaging in a free exchange of ideas through reasoned discourse with those who express opposing views, or at least tolerating others' discourse and views. While we're not arguing that toleration and reasoned discourse are bad, it is bad to value them over justice and equity, because doing so presumes that one doesn't need to actively strive toward the latter in order to make room for the former; that there exists an equal playing field upon which to engage in reasoned discourse and express opposing views; that toleration isn't literally dangerous because certain reasoned discourse isn't literally harmful to others; that civility is always the best way to work toward a more civil society, overlooking the ways in which civility as enacted in an unjust and inequitable disciplinary network is itself inherently uncivil.

In the absence of a clearly identified and maintained framework for interaction, all disciplinary spaces, even those as supposedly unofficial and undisciplined as the WPA-L, will default to the discourses that emerge from and reinforce the status quo. Whatever shape WritingStudies-L takes, and whatever the digital networking mechanism by which writing studies seeks to extend, enrich, or define its disciplinary identity, it must do more to explicate its values, beliefs, and practices in opposition to the tacit assumption that undefined values invite tolerance and civility. A reimagined listserv that is not explicitly decolonial cannot help but to function as a networked extension of colonialism.

IMPLICATIONS FOR EPISTEMOLOGICAL NETWORKS AND COALITIONS

If there is one thing that our collective network has learned from exposing the divisive exchanges on the now defunct WPA-L it is that exposing borders between seemingly disparate theories is the same as exposing possibilities for coalitional epistemics and environmental justice. Breaking down and overcoming epistemological borders presents possibilities for creating coalitional knowledges and teaches people to think and act differently, administrate differently, think differently, write differently and even read differently. Within the scope of this collection, some of the epistemic coalitional possibilities rhetoric and composition administrators may take on in their programs and elsewhere include bridging gaps between critical race theory and decolonial theory, decolonial theory and ANT, postmodernism and modernism, rhetorical theories and decolonial theory. These types of knowledge coalitions are important for rhetoric and composition administrators to build within their programs—for example, in course curriculum, program assessment, program listservs, graduate student training, and professional development—given current demographic shifts in today's state and national demographics along with mandates for diversity, equity, and inclusion measures meant to accommodate these shifts. We have demonstrated these possibilities in both theory and practice in this chapter both figuratively and literally and the ways that they provide possibilities for direct justice in the areas of knowledge ecological futures for epistemic innovation and recovery through continued coalitional building.

REFERENCES

Anzaldúa, G. (2012). *Borderlands/La frontera: The new mestiza* (4th ed.). Aunt Lute Books.

Baca, D. (2010). *Mestizo scripts, digital migrations, and the territories of writing*. Palgrave MacMillan.

Baniya, S., Doan, S., Johnson, G. P., Kumari, A., Larson, K., Schwarz, V. M., Diab, K., Grayson, M. L., Grijalva, R. M., Hassel, H., Hendrickson, B., Hubrig, A., Messina, C. M. & Ruiz, I. (2019). Where we are: Dialogue and disciplinary space. A brief dialogue with members of the WPA-L working group and nextGEN listserv. *Composition Studies, 47*(2), 203–210. https://compositionstudiesjournal.files.wordpress.com/2020/01/whereweare_47.2.pdf.

Bazerman, C. (1999). *The languages of Edison's light*. MIT Press.

Borrowman, S. (2005). We have common cause against the night: Voices from the WPA-L, September 11–12, 2001. In S. Borrowman (Ed.), *Trauma and the teaching of writing* (pp. 201–230). State University of New York Press.

Chen, C. (2018). *Enacting a networked disciplinarity of rhetoric and composition across disciplinary social spaces* [Unpublished doctoral dissertation], North Carolina State University. http://www.lib.ncsu.edu/resolver/1840.20/35240.

Dobrin, S. I. (2011). *Postcomposition*. Southern Illinois University Press.

Dryer, D. B. (2019). Divided by primes: Competing meanings among writing studies' keywords. *College English, 81*(3), 214–255.

Dussel, E. (2003). *Philosophy of liberation*. Wipf and Stock.

Fanon, F. (2008). *Black skin, White masks*. Grove Press.

Färber, A. (2014). Urban ethnicity, world city, and the hookah: The potential of thick-thin descriptions in urban anthropology. In D. Brantz, S. Disko & G. Wagner-Kyora (Eds.), *Thick space: Approaches to metropolitanism* (pp. 333–356). Transcript Verlag.

Foucault, M. (1969). *The archaeology of knowledge*. Éditions Gallamard.

García de Müeller, G. & Ruiz, I. D. (2017). Race, silence, and writing program administration: A qualitative study of US college writing programs. *WPA: Writing Program Administration, 40*(2), 19–39.

Grayson, M. L. (2019). Response to rhetorics of White supremacy on the WPA-L: A statement from the NCTE/CCCC Jewish Caucus. https://mailchi.mp/5f38a8a0f0f7/response-to-rhetorics-of-white-supremacy-on-the-wpa-l.

Grayson, M. L. (2020). *Race talk in the age of the trigger warning: Recognizing and challenging classroom cultures of silence*. Rowman and Littlefield.

Green, N. (2018). Moving beyond alright: And the emotional toll of this, my life matters too, in the writing center work. *The Writing Center Journal, 37*(1), 15–34. https://www.jstor.org/stable/26537361.

Guerra, J. C. (2016). Cultivating a rhetorical sensibility in the translingual writing classroom. *College English, 78*(3), 228–233.

Horner, B. (2007). Redefining work and value for writing program administration. *JAC, 21*, 163–84. https://www.jstor.org/stable/20866772.

Inoue, A. B. (2016). Friday plenary address: Racism in writing programs and the CWPA. *WPA: Writing Program Administration, 40*(1), 134–154. http://association database.co/archives/40n1/40n1inoue.pdf.

Inoue, A.B. (2019). Friday plenary address: How do we language so people stop killing each other, or what do we do about white language supremacy?. *College Composition and Communication, 70*(2), 352–369.

Kuhn, T. (2012). *The structure of scientific revolutions* (5th ed.). University of Chicago Press.

Latour, B. (2013). *An inquiry into modes of existence* (C. Porter, Trans.). Harvard University Press.

Lee, J. W. (2017). *The politics of translingualism: After Englishes*. Routledge.

Lugones, M. (2010). Toward a decolonial feminism. *Hypatia, 25*(4), 742–760.

Massumi, B. (1997). Requiem for our prospective dead (Toward a participatory critique of capitalist power). In E. Kaufman & K. J. Heller (Eds.), *Deleuze & Guattari: New mappings in politics, philosophy, and culture* (pp. 40–64). University of Minnesota Press.

Matsuda, P. K. (2014). The lure of translingual writing. *PMLA, 129*(3), 478–483. https://doi.org/10.1632/pmla.2014.129.3.478.

Mignolo, W. D. (2009). Epistemic disobedience, independent thought and de-colonial freedom. *Theory, Culture, and Society, 26*(7–8), 1–23.

Miles, L. (2007). Rhetorical work: Social materiality, kairos, and changing the terms. *JAC, 27* (3–4), 743–758. https://www.jstor.org/stable/20866810.

Mueller, D. (2012). Grasping rhetoric and composition by its long tail: What graphs can tell us about the field's changing shape. *College Composition and Communication, 42*(1), 195–223.

Mueller, D. (2017). *Network sense: Methods for visualizing a discipline.* The WAC Clearinghouse; University Press of Colorado. https://doi.org/10.37514/wri-b.2017.0124.

nextGen Listserv. (2018, November 18). Re: Listserv to Listserv: A Response from nextGen. https://lists.asu.edu/cgi-bin/wa?A2=ind1811&L=WPA-L&P=R144325&1=WPA-L&9=A&J=on&d=No+Match%3BMatch%3BMatches&z=4.

Pantelides, K. (2015). Metagenre on the WPA-L: Transitional threads as nexus for micro/macro-level discourse on the dissertation. *Composition Forum, 31.* https://compositionforum.com/issue/31/metagenre.php.

Quijano, A. (2003). Coloniality of power, eurocentrism, and Latin America. *Nepantla: Views from South, 1*(3), 533–580.

Roberts-Miller, P. (2017). *Demagoguery and democracy.* The Experiment.

Ruiz, I. D. (2017, March 29). *A decolonial conference review: Meditations on inclusivity.* Latino Rebels. https://www.latinorebels.com/2017/03/29/a-decolonial-conference-review-meditations-on-inclusivity-and-4-cs-17-in-portland-oregon/.

Ruiz, I. D. & Arellano, S. C. (2019). *La cultural nos cura*: Reclaiming decolonial epistemologies through medicinal history. In D. Baca & R. Garcia (Eds.), *Rhetorics elsewhere and otherwise: Contested modernities, decolonial visions* (pp. 141–168). National Council of Teachers of English.

Ruiz, I. D. & Baca, D. (2017). Decolonial options and writing studies. *Composition Studies, 45*(2), 226–229.

Russell, D. R. (1997). Rethinking genre in school and society: An activity theory analysis. *Written Communication, 14*(4), 504–554. https://doi.org/10.1177/0741088397014004004.

Schreiber, B. R. & Watson, M. (2018). Translingualism ≠ code-meshing: A response to Gevers' "Translingualism revisited." *Journal of Second Language Writing, 42,* 94–97.

Scott, T. & Welch, N. (2014). One train can hide another: Critical materialism for public composition. *College English, 76*(6), 562–579. https://www.jstor.org/stable/24238203.

Smith, E. (2020). *A Critique of anti-racism in rhetoric and composition: The semblance of empowerment.* Lexington.

Smith, L. T. (2012). *Decolonizing methodologies: Research and Indigenous peoples* (2nd ed.). Zed Books.

Smucker, J. (2017). *Hegemony how-to: A roadmap for radicals.* AK Press.

WPA-L Archives. (2018, April 5). *Announcing nextGEN graduate student listserv!* WPA-L Archives. https://lists.asu.edu/cgi-bin/wa?A2=ind1804&L=WPA-L&P=R249040&1=WPA-L&9=A&J=on&d=No+Match%3BMatch%3BMatches&z=4.

Yancey, K. B. (2018). Mapping the turn to disciplinarity: A historical analysis of composition's trajectory and its current moment. In R. Malencyzk, S. Miller-Cochran, E. Wardle & K. B. Yancey (Eds.), *Composition, rhetoric, and disciplinarity* (pp. 15–35). Utah State University Press.

Young, V. (n.d.). *Call for program proposals 2019: Performance-rhetoric, performance composition* [Pre-Conference Communication]. 2019 Conference on College Composition & Communication Annual Convention, Pittsburgh, PA, United States. Retrieved April 4, 2023, from https://cccc.ncte.org/cccc/conv/call-2019.

APPENDIX A: WPA-L PARTICIPATION GUIDELINES JUNE 3, 2019, DRAFT

The guidelines can be viewed at https://sites.google.com/view/wpa-l-change-work/home.

The proposal was adopted by list subscribers through a vote in July 2019, though not without pushback by certain "regulars" on the list.

CHAPTER 4.
CRITIQUING THE "NETWORKED SUBJECT" OF ANTI-RACISM: TOWARD A MORE EMPOWERED AND INCLUSIVE "WE" IN RHETORIC AND COMPOSITION

Erec Smith
York College of Pennsylvania

In *Care to Dare: Unleashing Astonishing Potential through Secure Base Leadership*, George Kohlrieser defines a secure base as "a person, place, goal or object that provides a sense of protection, safety and caring *and* offers a source of inspiration and energy for daring, exploration, risk taking and seeking challenge [emphasis added]" (2012, p. 8). This concept correlates to the emotional intelligence competencies of emotional self-control (Kohlrieser, 2017b), conflict management (Kohlrieser, 2017c), and mentoring (Kohlrieser, 2017a) and may be an implicit goal in most, if not all, intersectional social justice initiatives. Research showed that all involved in academia, especially students, need to "develop a sense of belonging" while on campus (Carter, 2021, p. 20). Acquiring a secure base for the historically downtrodden may be a more arduous task. So, once such a secure base is acquired, groups may try to protect and fortify it at all costs.

Marginalized and precarious populations throughout general society may tacitly seek this secure base while an apparently unaccepting hegemony looms. Academia is no different. This can explain the vitriolic backlash to perceived White supremacy in online spaces like the Writing Program Administrators Listserv (WPA-L)—now defunct—that served as an online community for administrators and scholars of rhetoric and composition. Many saw threads started by people who wanted to discuss the merits of viewpoint diversity or the efficacy of current anti-racism initiatives as "toxic," and "harmful" to marginalized people (Baniya et al., 2019, pp. 206–209). Yet, if you were to talk to one of the most vocal of the "toxic" and "harmful" voices on this listserv, he would tell you that he was not supporting White supremacy but critiquing what he saw as a flawed methodology for anti-racism, one he felt embraced a disempowered

DOI: https://doi.org/10.37514/PER-B.2023.1848.2.04

and anti-intellectual stance. (I know this because that voice was mine: an African American man invested in both academic integrity and the empowerment of people of color.) Disagreement with such a critique was not the issue. The problem was that the critique was treated as an attack on a hard-fought but precarious "secure base."

What does it mean that experts in language, literacy, and rhetoric handle critique as they would a threat to their very safety? What does it mean when communication experts cannot communicate, resorting to fallacious reasoning, personal attacks, and misinformation to protect their ideas? What does it mean for rhetoric and composition administrators and their programs, their curriculum, and their initiatives? I believe it means that academia has not taken a turn toward social justice so much as social justice—in its manifestations as "identity politics"—has usurped academia, hijacking academic discourse for a monological agenda and a clear willingness to silence others rather than engage them. The one-sided nature Sweta Baniya et al.'s (2019) attempts to chronicle the events of the WPA-L without identifying the allegedly racist statements, exemplifies this.[1]

I think cross-ideological communication in the anti-racism movement has failed because this movement is looking for a "secure base" more than a collaborative understanding of what can be done to actually create an anti-racist infrastructure within programs, within departments, and within the discipline. If such an infrastructure were the goal, dialogue would be welcomed, strategies would be discussed, and a broader "listening rhetoric" (Booth, 2004, pp. 46–50) would be a salient tool. This is not the case. I am not sure if a desire to feel safe has overtaken desires to be understood and productive or if a secure base is being mistaken for understanding and productivity. According to Kohlrieser, "A secure base simultaneously shuts down the brain's focus on fear, threat and even survival *and* encourages curiosity and risk taking while inspiring exploration" (2012, p. 9). One can understand why such a condition is defended at the slightest provocation.

In *The lure of disempowerment*, I present a confluence of empowerment theory and emotional intelligence as a kind of treatment for the apparent insecurity of anti-racist networks in rhetoric and composition (Smith & Abraham, 2022). Empowerment theory concludes that the fulfillment of three components

---

[1] I believe Baniya et al.'s (2019) is not an accurate assessment of the goings-on on the WPA-L. Along with a neglect to mention that the primary "dissenter" was a Black man, a substantial number of voices, essentialized as racist, were left out. The necessary conversation, the one attempted on the listserv, seemed to be met with dismissal, not a desire to interact and converse. This information, if acknowledged, would change the narrative substantially. Please see the WPA-L archives for March 2019, specifically the thread with the subject heading "The Cs Chairs Address," which can be found at https://lists.asu.edu/cgi-bin/wa?A1=ind1903&L=WPA-L.

comprises empowerment. Psychologist Marc Zimmerman, one of the more prominent empowerment theorists, wrote

> These three components of [empowerment] merge to form a picture of a person who believes that he or she has the capability to influence a given context (intrapersonal component) understand how the system works in that context (interactional component), and engages in behaviors to exert control in the context (behavioral component). . . . All three components must be measured to fully capture [psychological empowerment. (1995, p. 590)

Each component contains corresponding aspects of emotional intelligence necessary to its fulfillment. The intrapersonal necessitates self-awareness and self-management. The interactional necessitates social awareness and empathy. The behavioral component necessitates teamwork, listening skills, and conflict management. One can conclude, then, that to be empowered in this way is to enjoy an existential secure base. A secure base can be felt in several ways (e.g., it can be a person, a place, or even an object). So, shaping a space to obsequiously prioritize the marginalized, or creating a social machinery that necessarily lauds the marginalized while downplaying anyone deemed hegemonic, is not imperative; the base can be widened with empowerment theory and the emotional intelligence competencies therein.

If the foundation for anti-racist initiatives is one of empowerment, initiatives based on empowerment may go a long way in affecting societal change in ways that align with progressive social justice. Unfortunately, many group-based social justice initiatives are notorious for preferring to shut down, deplatform, or "cancel" those who say the wrong thing or hold differing viewpoints, instead of engaging in generative dialogue toward a better understanding of circumstances and effective strategies for progress. I believe this is because that potential dialogue is considered less likely to create and/or perpetuate the secure base sought by social justice advocates in the student body, the faculty, or the administration.

People pine so direly for this secure base that they have created a "Networked Subject," a collective persona, who is ready to strike if threatened. Ultimately, I believe that anti-racism cannot be achieved with an exclusive and insular network dutifully intolerant of anything that does not present the Networked Subject as a victim upon which genuflection is the only acceptable treatment. The network has to be opened and cognizant of the innovative powers of dialectic in addressing several progressive viewpoints. That is, one person's anti-racism may be different from another's, but their confluence may produce ideas and present opportunities that, otherwise, may have gone undiscovered.

Empowerment theory is not meant to erase the realities of racism. It is meant to help us adequately address racism in productive ways. Throughout this essay, I will identify the network of anti-racism in rhetoric and composition, its dynamics, and its determinants before discussing how the confluence of network theory and empowerment theory can move us toward a broader and more generative network of social justice. I close this chapter with reflective questions that rhetoric and composition administrators might want to reflect upon and discuss in disciplinary spaces, program committees, and elsewhere.

THE POWER OF NETWORKS

One may wonder how an ideological minority, even if loud, is able to acquire enough power to present itself as a formidable presence. The answer to that question can be found by looking at that ideological minority through the lens of network theory, specifically as delineated by Miguel Castells. Castells (2011) defines a network as a multidimensional domain in which particular agents wield power. Networks are discourse communities made up of the material and immaterial agents that produce and reproduce them. Networks can be inclusive or exclusive, but exclusivity *seems* to enhance the structural integrity of a network, perpetuating a lifeworld built and utilized by particular agents. It is believed that social power "is primarily exercised by and through networks" (Castells, 2011, p. 774). Taking his cue from Castells, economist C. Otto Scharmer (2016) wrote of "the darker side of the networked society," meaning "those who are not equipped with the *right kind of knowledge*, skills, and networks are socially excluded and polarized [emphasis added]" (p. 85). Networks create discourse which, in turn, legitimizes some ways of looking at the world while delegitimizing—sometimes quite purposefully—other ways. What is often called "deplatforming" or "cancelling" is an example of the social exclusion and polarization of which Scharmer speaks. People who have been deplatformed and cancelled did not have "the right kind of knowledge," according to a particular network, even if they considered themselves allies and proponents of that network. It is in networking that paradigm shifting (or perpetuating) power is realized. But what is a networked society? We can come to an understanding of it through Castells (2011), who distinguishes four major concepts in network theory.

First, "Networking Power" is "the power of actors and organizations included in the networks," such as the power wielded by those privileged enough to be included in the network (Castells, 2011, p. 774). Of course, these "actors and organizations" have dominion over those who want to be included or be in contact with the empowered network. Regarding anti-racism in rhetoric and composition, examples of these "actors and organizations" include the following:

WPA-L Reimagining Working Group tasked with making the WPA-L a more secure base; the nextGen Start-Up Team responsible for starting a separate listserv geared toward creating a secure base for graduate students (Baniya et al., 2019); the burgeoning Institute of Race, Rhetoric, and Literacy (Beavers et al., 2021); and Conference on College Composition and Communication (CCCC) Committee for Change (CCCC, Committee for Change, 2022b) and The Committee on Accessing Whiteness for Equity, Understanding, and Change within CCCC/NCTE (CCCC, Committee on Accessing Whiteness, 2022a), the Social Justice At The Convention Committee (CCCC, Social Justice, 2022d) charged with eradicating apparent White supremacy and unethical behavior at the conference; and the CCCC Officers & Executive Committee Members, specifically from 2018–2023 (CCCC, Officers and Executive Committee, 2022c). These "actors and organizations" interlink to create a "Networked Subject."

Second, "Network Power" is "the power of the standards of the network over its components" (Castells, 2011, p. 775). That is, the power of discourse to define and interpellate identity, define activities, and project value. Network power "ultimately favors the interests of both a specific set of social actors at the source of network formation and also of the establishment of the standards (protocols of communication)" (Castells, 2011, p. 775). Those social actors are imperative in establishing standards—easily construed as the components of a narrative—that veritably cast people in particular roles.

Third, "Networked Power" is the "relational capacity to impose an actor's will over another actor's will on the basis of the structural capacity of domination embedded in the institutions of society" (Castells, 2011, p. 775). Networked Power is given by the social machinery that empowers some actors over others and gives some actors "Networking Power" while denying it to others. Put metaphorically, these are the casting directors that give roles to players based on their fit in the discourse community. Again, that social machinery, the standards and components of the narrative, will determine who is and who is not worthy of wielding or benefiting from power.

Last, "Network-Making Power" consists of two subcategories of power: "the ability to constitute network(s) and to program/reprogram the network(s) in terms of the goals assigned to the network"; and "the ability to connect and ensure the cooperation of different networks by sharing common goals and combining resources while fending off competition from other networks by setting up strategic cooperation" (Castells, 2011, p. 776). The ability to make networks is the ability to gain power through numbers. Although these forms of power are relevant to explaining the concept of networks and its importance in empowering ideological movements, "network-making power" may be the most salient form for the purposes of this essay. This salience is gleaned from what

Castells calls the "holders" of the aforementioned subcategories of power. The holders of the first subcategory, the ability to constitute and program/reprogram networks, are called, appropriately enough, "programmers" (Castells, 2011, p. 775). Holders of the second category, the ability to connect and influence cooperation of various other networks based on common aspirations and resources, are called "switchers" (Castells, 2011, p. 775).

Programmers set up the goals of a network (e.g., anti-racism and decolonialism) and the social machinery—network and networked power—to perpetuate it. According to Castells (2011), a network society mostly embeds the "ideas, visions, projects, frames" in particularly electronic processes of communication, to better ensure input from a variety of origins (p. 776). Controlling networks of communication, then, is an important act of programmers. They can identify the processes of communication to which potentially useful constituents are most exposed and disseminate ideas, visions, etc. Social media, listservs, and backchannel email correspondences are ideal. The CCCC Committee for Change, for example, was put together, "programmed," by such programmers and used the WPA-L and, presumably, other virtual and non-virtual spaces to gather committee members and disseminate information.

Switchers have the power of connecting relatively disparate networks in ways that will prove strategic to each. Switchers see the potential "power in numbers" of collaboration and work to identify modes of communication and synthesize interests to create coalitions stronger than the previously separated entities. These networks, through the switching process, must be able "to communicate with each other, inducing synergy and limiting contradiction" (Castells, 2011, p. 777). The WPA-L Reimagining Working Group and nextGen Start-Up Team are good examples of Switchers and exemplify this relationship in Baniya et al. in which both groups' dialogue about their common interpretations of dissenting voices and their common desire to counteract them (2019). This is what Scharmer, referencing Henry Mintzberg, referred to as "adhocracy": a "mutual adjustment in networked relationships" which depends "on the quality of the relationships among key players" (2016, p. 300) and *not the quality of empirical justifications for policy changes.*

Here is where Castells (2011) sees potential for danger. After explaining switchers and their power, he wrote,

> This is why it is so important that media tycoons do not become political leaders, or that governments do not have total control over the media. The more that switchers become crude expressions of single purpose domination, the more that power relationships in the network society suffocate the dynamism and initiative of its multiple sources of social structuration and change. (p. 777)

Castells' warning suggests that viewpoint diversity is imperative. Even if connections are made to achieve certain common goals, the diversity of viewpoints each network has can stay intact, suggesting that people dedicated to anti-racism while supporting different ideologies of anti-racism can co-exist. Working together can be a synergy, not necessarily a synthesis.

I believe that the danger of current academic networks of racial justice is the possibility of significant overlap between the programmers and the switchers, which can be gleaned from visiting the websites of the aforementioned organizations. Programmers and switchers, as Castells (2011) wrote, "are not single actors . . . as the exercise of power in the network society requires a complex set of joint action that goes beyond alliances to become a new form of subject—a networked subject" (p. 776). The programmers of anti-racist networks and the switchers that connect networks with comparable goals comingle to create "The Networked Subject"—the same people, saying the same things, are co-writing, editing essay collections, and administrating ad hoc committees for change. The programmers and the switchers, who collectively constitute "The Networked Subject," are working to revise modes of communication in spaces within the field of rhetoric and composition, such as through WPA-L and CCCC. For this to truly succeed—that is, for the programmers' and switchers' narrative and ideology to become executive—insularity is imperative. Those who sing a different tune but still want in (i.e., those who care about anti-racism but do not approve of the favored methodologies) may be seen as threats that can weaken the network and, therefore, the power derived from the network. "The Networked Subject" may become relatively one-dimensional.

THE DETRIMENTS OF A SECURE BASE NETWORK

In "Whom do Activists of Color Speak For," Eboo Patel (2019) gives a hypothetical account of a person of color expressing disdain over anti-racist leadership:

> [A]n activist will find him or herself in a classroom or at a conference using the well-worn formulation, "People of color feel . . ." Perhaps a group of well-meaning liberal White people will lean in to listen more closely. But this time some person of color in the audience will decide that she has had enough. She will interrupt the activist who is claiming to speak for her and say, "Please don't pretend that what you are about to say represents me. I am perfectly capable of forming my own thoughts and representing myself." (para. 14)

Patel ends the hypothetical situation there, but I have a good idea of how the rest of the story would pan out. Our dissenter of color would be seen as a threat to the anti-racism network from which the activists speak. The "well-meaning liberal White people" will side with the activists, joining them in an erasure of the dissenter's voice. If initial erasures do not work, all involved will work to demonize, mob, and ignore the explanations of the dissenter. Rumors will be spread, words will be misrepresented, ad hominem insults toward the dissenter will be considered "solid arguments." The necessary "framing of individual and collective minds" that ensures successful intimidation and silencing tactics are established in this network (Castells, 2011, p. 779). This may sound like a decidedly negative speculation on my part, but I am speaking from experience. I was such a dissenter in a rhetoric and composition listserv in the Spring of 2019.

On the WPA-L, a debate about the methodologies of anti-racist tactics and initiatives had been taking place since the 2019 CCCC call for papers in March of 2018 (Young, n.d.), which involved a heated discussion about the use of codemeshed English as either triumph or, in my words, rhetorical "Blaxploitation." To speak for myself, I expected and welcomed pushback. Academia is a field driven by polemic and dialectic; I thought conversation could shed light on different viewpoints and bring everybody to a more thorough understanding of the issues that arise in anti-racist activism, especially the idea that one person or one group of people can speak for an entire race or ethnicity.

In early 2019, a spirited discussion began about the place of viewpoint diversity in the field of rhetoric and composition. Many people took the term "viewpoint diversity" to be a "dog whistle" for extreme right wing and racist opinions, which is not an uncommon conclusion within social justice circles (Murray, 2019, p. 135). Personally, I saw this as a genetic fallacy; people associated the term with unsavory characters who had used it in the past; few seemed to be open to discussing the actual meaning of viewpoint diversity as it was being used in the present context of WPA-L. Many, as can be gleaned from the content of Baniya et al. (2019), saw viewpoint diversity as a toxic and harmful concept for reasons never fully explained in the essay.

Then, in March 2019, Asao Inoue gave a keynote speech at the 2019 CCCC titled How Do We Language so People Stop Killing Each Other, or What Do We Do about White Language Supremacy? In the speech, Inoue discusses the intricacies of racism in the field and insists that White people decenter themselves not only to make room for minority voices, but to best handle the fact that White people embody racism, that their very presence is inherently oppressive to people of color (p. 362).

For many reasons, I will not rehash the intricacies of the WPA-L thread that followed, but I do invite people to visit the archives of March 2019, especially the thread titled, "The Cs Chairs Address," on the 19th of that month (Writing Program Administrators Listserv, 2019), which Baniya et al. wrote "disproportionately harmed marginalized people" (2019, pp. 203–204). Within this thread, dissenting voices, especially mine, were considered bullies. This label was decidedly erroneous for reasons put forth by Aurora Matzke et al. (2019) who distinguish academic bullying from general disagreement in their chapter within *Defining, Locating, and Addressing Bullying in the WPA Workplace*:

> Academic bullying relies on intention, severity, scope, and the ways power is present in the interaction, whereas dissonance and conflict may occur sporadically or be part of the larger rhythms present in the cultural web. . . . While disagreements and conflicts might include unprofessional behavior, they are not synonymous with academic bullying—even though the behavior may seem uncomfortable, unfair, or unwarranted (p. 52).

One can see from this description of bullying that it is not synonymous with mere contention.

I believe bullying took place on a larger scale from the Networked Subject, itself.

From activity on WPA-L and Twitter regarding Inoue's speech,[2] one can see what theorists Brian Martin and Florencia Peña Saint Martin (2014) call "mobbing." According to their research, mobbing

> can be defined as a group systematically attacking a person's reputation for a long period of time, using negative communication as a weapon. The intention is to destroy the target's value as a reliable individual, initially causing them to lose power and prestige, with the long-term goal of achieving their dismissal, resignation or general ostracism. (2014, para 1)

---

2   While scrolling through Twitter, a platform networked to WPA-L, I saw more interpretations of my initial email that did not align with my own understanding, and the unquestioning praise of the graduate student's speech; my response to the graduate student's email was still going unacknowledged and false descriptions of my words and me continued to be used. (I no longer have direct citations of these tweets, but they are referenced in the "Cs Chair's Address" thread on WPA-L in the March 2019 archives.) I decided to try and address this by engaging in conversation. Using a handle that doesn't have my actual name was, in hindsight, a mistake. At the time, I was on Twitter about one month out of the year for the annual College Composition and Communication Conference and did not really think about the importance of a Twitter handle.

I was slandered as a troll, a stalker, a fascist, a coward, and anti-Black racist to eliminate me as a threat to the secure base fortified by the programmers and switcher of this network.[3]

Martin and Saint Martin go on to explain the typical kind of context most conducive to the phenomenon of mobbing. Given the extensive existing research on workplace mobbing, it seems sensible to see whether the same sorts of frameworks can be applied to mobbing in the public sphere, including social media. Martin and Saint Martin, strongly referencing Kenneth Westhues work, break mobbing into component parts and give the following characteristic features. These chronological features may define the Networked Subject's behavior as defender of the network and bringer of a secure base. According to Martin and Saint Martin (2014), mobbing includes:

- Groups with shared interests.
- Individuals (possible targets) who threaten those groups in some way.
- The group with shared interests ganging up against that person. The group thus becomes the mobbing perpetrator team.
- Usually a main instigator or a small group of instigators among the perpetrator team.
- A shift of focus from what targets said or did that threaten the group, to devaluing targets as persons as a strategy to suppress them, taking away their power.
- An aim to discredit and/or destroy the target's reputation, often persistently monitoring them to find ever more information for this purpose.
- Coordination of the group's activities against targets.
- Persistent attacks by the perpetrator team against targets to continually devalue them.

One can see clear parallels between Martin and Saint Martin's description of mobbing and what took place on the WPA-L listserv. The anti-racist network in rhetoric and composition, with its Networked Power, is surely a group with shared interests. When their achieved or sought-after secure base was threatened, the network transformed from academics engaged in discussion to "mobbing perpetrator teams" determined to "change the focus from the issues to the people expressing contrary views, transforming routine interpersonal interactions

---

3   Hate speech can be defined as an "'incitement to hatred'—primarily against a group of persons defined in terms of race, ethnicity, national origin, gender, religion, sexual orientation and the like" (Fisch, 2002, p. 463) or more generally "any form of expression through which speakers primarily intend to vilify, humiliate, or incite hatred against other targets" (Ward, 1998). I think the operative word in each definition, unsurprisingly, is hatred.

into damaging forms of attack" (Martin & Saint Martin, 2014, para. 12). (This is apparent in the "Cs Chair Address" thread of the listserv, in which references to the Twitter interaction can be found.) An aim to "denounce and/or destroy" reputations is clear.

In the anti-racism network in rhetoric and composition, what constitutes violence and injury has broadened to include general critical inquiry toward and disagreement with the victim-based, us-against-them narrative. Ideologies that present the marginalized student or scholar as one who always feels "suffocated" by the presence of White people (Inoue, 2019a, p. 361) are favored; thoughts and inquiries that counter this narrative are demonized or silenced. (Many people of color do not feel suffocated by the presence of White people.) Personally, my words and inquiries, even if mercurial at times—for the same reasons Inoue puts forth to justify his purposefully agitating rhetoric (Corrigan, 2019)—were not examples of hate speech, but were clearly taken as such. My critiques of anti-racist methodologies were critiques, not hateful, violent attacks. Also, my target was not individual personalities, but a set of ideas and behaviors I deemed detrimental and disempowering to real progress in anti-racism. Nevertheless, within the network's logic, my critique was seen as a kind of violence or, at best, a slippery slope toward violence.

GRAND SCHOLAR WIZARD

Perhaps the biggest catalyst for adhocracy and publications by Baniya et al. (2019) was the following email, sent, anonymously, to WPA-L:

> Listers, think about this:
>
> The stakes in this field aren't that high in the big scheme of things.
>
> Sit with this for a moment.
>
> The stakes in this field aren't that high.
>
> Just a moment longer.
>
> Composition and writing studies—and the great experiment of higher education more generally—are on the down tick. We all know that we feel it. Look around. Be real. Don't kid yourself.
>
> When each are finished and gone, you'll still be able to passionately talk about, or bitch and moan about, or mentally masturbate all over others' ideas, their shitty analyses, embodiment, identity politics, and any other thing your heart desires.

> But there will be nobody there to listen to you.
>
> Be kind to each other in the meantime.
>
> Each of you are all that we have.
>
> Peace.
>
> Grand Scholar Wizard (Writing Program Administrators listserv, 2019).

The content of this person's email was not at issue. What was at issue was the writer's sign-off: Grand Scholar Wizard. To most people on WPA-L, this was a purposeful allusion to "Grand Wizard," the moniker given to the leader of a Klu Klux Klan chapter. In anti-racist networks, otherwise innocuous incidents are manipulated to fit a grand narrative. This is not to say that the Grand Scholar Wizard email was nothing to ponder, but within this particular network, it was tantamount to a declaration of war against the secure base. It sparked an adhocracy indicative of a space managed by ideologically homogenous programmers and switchers.

The Grand Scholar Wizard email served as a prompt to create guidelines for communication and behavior for both WPA-L and the CCCC. But besides the sign-off of the Grand Scholar Wizard email—one email sent anonymously—what language etiquette was violated, and what behaviors were beyond the pale? Again, words got heated, but did they constitute hate speech? In the context of this anti-racist network, it would seem so. Through the terministic screen of the Networked Subject who served as the collective protagonist against White supremacy, mere critical inquiry was seen as an attack. Any resulting codes of conduct within rhetoric and composition spaces, such as listservs and conferences, will likely shun critical inquiry and the verbalizing of any stance that counters the preferred one. These revised guidelines could simply be the banning of anything that comes close to threatening the secure base of this field's anti-racist network. Outside of the network, this would look like censorship and the squelching of academic discourse and freedom; within the network, this would look like justice.

TOWARD A WIDER SECURE BASE NETWORK

The network of anti-racism has been established as a secure base that abides by a discourse intolerant of dissenting views, even if those views still lie within the general goal of social justice. Those with Network-Making Power perpetuated the Network Power of narrative, particularly one in which marginalized people—in this case, racially marginalized people—are cast as a collective

Networked Subject, the protagonist of a redemption narrative against White supremacy. To be clear, my views were not against anti-racism, but the particular brand of anti-racism that seemed to be favored among anti-racists in the field. However, my standpoint constituted a role that did not exist in the available *dramatis personae* of this narrative, so I was assigned one of the remaining, though inaccurate, roles.

The role of "Black man who sees anti-racist initiatives as misguided and wants to do something about it to better ensure the empowerment of marginalized students" is not a possibility within this network, so I was erased and replaced with one of the available roles: Uncle Tom, Coon, Sambo, etc. Because these were the available roles, anything I said would be interpreted negatively. Any opinion that went against the apparent infallibility of scholars of color were taken as the words of someone "dismissive of, inhospitable to, and aggressive towards" antiracism and its proponents (Baniya et al., 2019, p. 205). Standing one's ground after research, experience, and time has led one to a conclusion that prompts a revision—not a dismissal—of a favored ideology considered "toxic" and "harmful" (Baniya et al., 2019, p. 206). Asking colleagues to elaborate and engage in a conversation about all of the above is considered a kind of violence. Judith B. Lee, a social worker who utilizes empowerment theory akin to that put forth by Zimmerman,[4] cited the empowerment approach to social work as the building of a "Beloved Community" as "both the process and the hoped for outcome" of empowerment (Lee, 2001, p. 1). What Lee adds to empowerment theory is the necessity for what she calls the multifocal vision of empowerment, a vision that works well with social justice initiatives.

The multifocal vision of empowerment, along with the aforementioned components of the intrapersonal, the interactive, and the behavioral (what Lee calls the political), consists of seven "views":

1. Historical view
2. Ecological View
3. Ethclass perspective
4. Cultural/Multicultural perspective
5. Feminist perspective
6. Global perspective
7. Critical perspective (2001, pp. 49–50)

---

[4] Lee (2001) renders the components of empowerment "Personal," "Interpersonal," and "Political," which align with Zimmerman's "Intrapersonal," "Interactive," and "Behavioral," respectively. Because Zimmerman's take seems to be the most common, I use his renderings throughout my work.

Length of oppression—the Historical view—is utilized when considering the very real systemic aspects of oppression. As I wrote in my book, *A Critique of Anti-racism in Rhetoric and Composition: The Semblance of Empowerment*, (2019),

> Length of oppression is considered when considering the very real systemic aspects of oppression. The ecological view takes into consideration the material influences of the world on behavior and outlook. 'Ethclass' is synonymous with intersectionality and takes into consideration the various demographics one person can embody. The feminist component focuses on the political aspect of seemingly personal tribulations, that is, the personal is political. The critical denotes a challenge to hegemonic forces. The cultural and global recognizes how certain forces affect both our local considerations and those of other cultures and countries. (p. 33)

Lee's "Beloved Community" utilized a multifocal approach to progress, while engaging the three components of empowerment, and create a wider and more inclusive secure base. In essence, Lee's seven views should be considered, seen, simultaneously. Regarding her specific role as a social worker, but also relevant to our purposes as scholars and activists, Lee wrote,

> The social worker should maintain holistic vision in situations of oppression. The development of multifocal vision is needed to maintain a holistic view. We should be able to see both the forest and the trees, the wider scene and the individual picture—and attend to both with our clients. (2001, p. 60)

In theory, this would necessitate a look beyond any kind of network to get a better idea of the world and its players and, perhaps, a different narrative with a more dynamic *dramatis personae.*

In *Theory U: Leading from the Future As It Emerges*, Scharmer calls this holistic look beyond the confines of a network "presencing": "to sense, tune in, and act from one's highest future potential," insisting that "the future depends on us to bring it into being" (2016, pp. 7–8). What Zimmerman and Lee would call empowerment theory, Scharmer would call the "Primacy of Praxis": "[a]ll real learning is grounded in real-world praxis. There are three kinds of praxis: *professional praxis*—striving for performance excellence; *personal praxis*—striving for self-leadership; and *relational praxis*—striving to improve the quality of thinking, conversing, and acting together" (2016, pp. 225–226). This aligns with the empowerment components of the behavioral, the intrapersonal, and the interactional, respectively. Scharmer's claim that learning is situated in real-world performance, similar to Lee's argument that "The sharing of experience must always be understood within a social praxis" (2001, p. 57), speaks to Scharmer's point that looking beyond the boundaries of our respective networks is the key to innovation and generative change. Presencing is going beyond the status quo, beyond the emphasis on difference, and even beyond productive and innovative dialogue. Presencing and its inherent primacy of praxis, is stepping even beyond oneself and seeing the world, including oneself, as a vast and living organism. Here, there is no us against them; there is only "we." From this "we," we can "learn from the future as it emerges." That is, when we let go of familiar and preferred narratives and see from a bird's eye view, or from Lee's seven views, a more inclusive and more elaborately networked narrative emerges. This narrative is always evolving and always inclusive.

So, when applying a synthesis of these theories of empowerment to current antiracist initiatives by rhetoric and composition administrators or by the field, more broadly, another story emerges. More accurate roles are available for me and others in the emerging narrative. Dialogue toward a generative future brings forth a world in which different ideologies can merge into new and contextually sound ideas. With a broader network, broader meanings can come into play. Terministic screens widen, distinctions between protagonist and antagonist dissolve, diversity of viewpoint is not an inherently negative term, and no one is essentialized. This is easier said than done, but it can be done.

Rhetoric and composition administrators might want to examine, personally or professionally, the types of dialogue they are participating in and the types of dialogue they want to encourage in their programs and elsewhere. Here are some reflection questions readers might want to explore within their roles as administrators:

- How might systems and networks in your program, your department, and/or your institution encourage or push-back against the secure base?
- How might you encourage a multifocal vision of empowerment in your administrative work, the courses you teach, the committees you are on, and the conversations you have?
- How might you encourage more polyvocality rather than a monolithic perspective? How might you encourage dissenting views in your programs and elsewhere, even if those views go against popular social justice perspectives but still lie within the general goal of social justice?
- What social actors do you see in your home institutions that cast people in particular roles? How might you use your administrative

- work—archiving, document (re)design, curriculum development, assessment, etc.—to recast people in more accurate, inclusive roles?
- How might you incorporate Lee's seven views and/or Castells four major concepts in your administrative, teaching, and/or scholarly work to encourage a more inclusive networked narrative?

I believe that empowerment theory combined with understandings of network dynamics can assist us in overcoming the contention currently engulfing social justice in the field of rhetoric and composition, especially as it pertains to anti-racism. I believe it can help us develop a secure base, or what Lee would call a "Beloved Community," in which all can feel safe and heard. We all must take the courageous steps to opening up to all involved in the endeavor: perceived friends, perceived protagonists, perceived antagonists, and several different roles a more holistic viewpoint can allow. Although I have been critical of Baniya et al.'s essay, I couldn't agree more with its final sentiment: "We rise together" (2019, p. 210). I just want to see a broader and more inclusive "we."

REFERENCES

Baniya, S., Doan, S., Johnson, G. P., Kumari, A., Larson, K., Schwarz, V. M., Diab, K., Grayson, M. L., Grijalva, R. M., Hassel, H., Hendrickson, B., Hubrig, A., Messina, C. M. & Ruiz, I. (2019). Where we are: Dialogue and disciplinary space. A brief dialogue with members of the WPA-L working group and nextGEN listserv. *Composition Studies, 47*(2), 203–210.

Beavers, M., Brunk-Chavez, B. L., Green, N.-A., Inoue, A. B., Ruiz, I., Saenkhum, T. & Young, V. A. (2021). Abbreviated statement toward first-year composition goals. *Institute of Race, Rhetoric, and Literacy*. https://tinyurl.com/IRRL-FYCGoals.

Booth, W. (2004). *The rhetoric of rhetoric: The quest for effective communication*. Wiley-Blackwell.

Carter, G. M. (2021). Exploring the diversity of everyday experiences through the humans of the University of Wisconsin-Stout Facebook assignment. *Writers: Craft & Context, 2*(2), 17–29. https://journals.shareok.org/writersccjournal/article/view/39/21.

Castells, M. (2011). A network theory of power. *International Journal of Communication, 5*, 773–787.

Conference on College Composition and Communication. (2022a). The committee on accessing Whiteness for equity, understanding, and change within CCCC/NCTE. Conference on College Composition and Communication. https://cccc.ncte.org/cccc/committee-assessing-whiteness.

Conference on College Composition and Communication. (2022b). Committee for change. *Conference on College Composition and Communication*. https://cccc.ncte.org/cccc/committees/change.

Conference on College Composition and Communication. (2022c). CCCC officers & executive committee members. *Conference on College Composition and Communication.* https://cccc.ncte.org/cccc/about/leaders.

Conference on College Composition and Communication. (2022d). Social justice at the convention committee. *Conference on College Composition and Communication.* https://cccc.ncte.org/cccc/committees/socialjustice?utm_source=pocket_mylist.

Corrigan, P. T. (2019). White people are a problem: A conversation with Asao Inoue. *Teaching and Learning in Higher Ed.* https://teachingandlearninginhighered.org/2019/07/30/White-teachers-are-a-problem-a-conversation-with-asao-inoue/?fbclid=IwAR2RjUSCt6QTTyq-a95dLLnH_rWjBTeSUH31uE1ATxyhm6cA_ofauan1yr0.

Fisch, W. B. (2002). Hate speech in the constitutional law of the United States. *American Journal of Comparative Law, 50*(463), 463–492.

Grand Scholar Wizard. (2019, March 22). *The Cs chairs address.* Writing Program Administrators Listserv Archive. https://lists.asu.edu/cgi-bin/wa?A2=WPA-L;d7ba67ea.1903&S=.

Inoue, A. (2019a). 2019 chair's address: How do we language so people stop killing each other, or what do we do about White language supremacy? *College Composition and Communication, 71*(2), 352–369.

Inoue, A. (2019b). CCC chair's letter. *College Composition and Communication, 71*(2), 370–379.

Kohlrieser, G. (2012). *Care to dare: Unleashing astonishing potential through secure base leadership.* Jossey-Bass.

Kohlrieser, G. (2017a). Coach and mentor: The core of leadership. In D. Goleman, R. Boyatzis, G. Kohlrieser, M. Nevarez & M. Taylor (Eds.), *Coach and mentor: A primer* (pp. 194–234). More Than Sound.

Kohlrieser, G. (2017b). Staying calm in a crisis. In D. Goleman, R. Boyatzis, R. J. Davidson, V. Druskat & G. Kohlrieser (Eds.), *Emotional self-control: A primer* (pp. 50–52). More Than Sound.

Kohlrieser, G. (2017c). How secure base leaders maintain differences without breaking bonds. In D. Goleman, R. Boyatzis, A. Gallo, G. Kohlrieser, M. Lippincott & G. Pitagorsky (Eds.), *Conflict management: A primer* (pp. 220–250). More than Sound.

Lee, J. A. B. (2001). *The empowerment approach to social work: Building the beloved community* (2nd ed.). Columbia University Press.

Martin, B. & Saint Martin, F. P. (2014). Public mobbing: A phenomenon and its features (B. Martin, Trans.). In N. González González (Ed.), *Organización social del trabajo en la posmodernidad: salud mental, ambientes laborales y vida cotidiana* (para. 1–12). Prometeo Editores. https://www.bmartin.cc/pubs/14Gonzalez.html.

Matzke, A., Rankins-Robertson, S. & Garrett, B. (2019). Nevertheless, she persisted: Strategies to counteract the time, place, and culture for academic bullying of WPAs. In C. Elder & B. Davila (Eds.), *Defining, locating, and addressing bullying in the WPA workplace* (pp. 49–68). University of Utah Press.

Murray, D. (2019). *The madness of crowds.* Bloomsbury Continuum.

Patel, E. (2019, April 2). Whom do activists of color speak for? *Inside Higher Ed.* https://www.insidehighered.com/blogs/conversations-diversity/whom-do-activists-color-speak.

Scharmer, C. O. (2016). *Theory U: Leading from the future as it emerges.* Berrett-Koehler.

Smith, E. (2019). *A Critique of Anti-racism in Rhetoric and Composition: The Semblance of Empowerment.* Lexington Books.

Smith, E. & Abraham, M. (2022). *The lure of disempowerment: Reclaiming agency in the age of CRT.* Kendall Hunt.

Ward, K. D. (1998). Free speech and the development of liberal virtues: An examination of the controversies involving flag-burning and hate speech. *University of Miami Law Review, 52*(733), 733–766.

Writing Program Administrators Listserv. (2019). Listserv archive. https://lists.asu.edu/cgi-bin/wa?A1=ind1903&L=wpa-l#157.

WPA-L Reimagining Work Group and Moderation Board. (2021). WPA-L Participation Guidelines. https://sites.google.com/view/wpa-l-change-work/first-appointed-moderation-board?authuser=0.

Young, V. (n.d.). *Call for program proposals 2019: Performance-Rhetoric, Performance-Composition* [Pre-conference communication]. 2019 Conference on College Composition & Communication Annual Convention, Pittsburgh, PA, United States. Retrieved April 4, 2023, from https://cccc.ncte.org/cccc/conv/call-2019.

Zimmerman, M. A. (1995). Psychological empowerment: Issues and illustrations. *American Journal of Community Psychology, 23*(5), 581–599.

SECTION 2.
INTRA-CAMPUS AND INSTITUTIONAL NETWORKS: EXISTING AS A PROGRAM

Basic Writing

Chapter 5. "Basic Writing's Interoffice, Intercampus Actor-Network: Assembling Our History through Dolmagean Analysis" by John Paul Tassoni

Chapter 6. "Outsiders Looking In: Discursive Constructions of Remediation beyond the Academy" by Lynn Reid

First-Year Writing

Chapter 7. "Working Within the Rhetorical Constraints: Renovation and Resistance in a First-Year Writing Program" by Mara Lee Grayson

Chapter 8. "Negotiating Dominance in Writing Program Administration: A Case Study" by Emily R. Johnston

Writing Across the Curriculum

Chapter 9. "Networking Across the Curriculum: Challenges, Contradictions, and Changes" by Kelly Bradbury, Sue Doe, and Mike Palmquist

Writing Center

Chapter 10. "The Writing Center as Border Processing Station" by Eric C. Camarillo

Chapter 11. "Voice, Silence, and Invocation: The Perilous and Playful Possibilities of Negotiating Identity in Writing Centers" by Lucien Darjeun Meadows

The second section of the collection narrows in its application to how specific designations and educational delivery systems influence the affordances and structures of academic pathways that rest alongside conceptions of "traditional" undergraduate students and the administrators who work in these arenas. The subsections locate the chapters by area: basic writing, first-year composition, writing across curriculum, and writing center.

Beginning with basic writing, John Tassoni's chapter provides a critique of the "academic ableism" most often used as a heuristic to assign and ascribe narratives of "basic" at institutions. As he traverses the histories, practices, and beliefs of various institutional agencies, Tassoni makes the case for people, programs, and offices across campuses to recognize their stake in basic writing programs as being influenced by larger systems and networks.

Next, we turn our attention to Lynn Reid, who outlines historical naming and funding opportunities linked to "basic" writing. Reid conducts a situational analysis of the conception of "remediation" to provide a method for data visualization that "makes the perspectives of human and non-human actors visible." In her chapter, Reid argues the visualization of human and non-human actors provides readers with a more holistic picture regarding the rise and fall of "basic writing" as it is structured, unstructured, and re-structured in alignment with external mandates that supersede on-the-ground knowledges.

In Chapters 7 and 8, authors address systemic concerns in first-year writing. Drawing upon anecdotal and empirical data, Mara Lee Grayson examines how intersecting networks on the campus served, simultaneously and paradoxically, as barriers to and opportunities for equitable program redesign, and offers a conceptual framework through which WPAs in other institutions can honor disciplinary expertise and remain student-responsive in the face of administrative mandates. In Chapter 8, Emily Rónay Johnston questions how first-year writing programs function within the converging systems of institutional bureaucracies, academic elitism, and the capitalist structure of higher education, and capitulate to creating a hegemonic middle class.

Next, within the area of writing across the curriculum, Kelly Bradbury, Sue Doe, and Mike Palmquist discuss the gtPathways Writing Integration Program at Colorado State University within the framework of activity theory to provide insights into the many system and network forces at play in working to establish a writing across the curriculum program. The authors use activity theory to explicate how the larger networks of the institution inform, shape, and challenge the implementation and continuation of a WAC program.

Finally, in Chapters 10 and 11, we consider the writing center, which often functions interstitially. Writing centers in rhetoric and composition administrative work often function as spaces between places, where human and non-human actors converge to work alongside larger narratives of written production in university settings. In Chapter 10, Eric C. Camarillo examines the efficacy of understanding the writing center as "border processing station" through the lens of activity theory, arguing that in order to understand abilities and affordances within the systems in which writing centers are placed, we must spend time focusing on what *actually* happens, not necessarily what *should* be happening. In Chapter 11, Lucien Darjeun Meadows discusses identity disclosure in the writing center and the complexity of personal narrative when placed in larger academic systems, positing that greater attention to how the self exists within the system creates opportunity for change.

The aim of this section is to allow readers to select the campus entity within which they rest, and after selecting the area, to follow the authors, as you might a root system, noting how systems theory/analysis aided their growth in both insight and ability to maneuver existing problematic networks in their pursuit of change making and DEIBSJ. As we close this interchapter, we offer you a few reflection and discussion questions should you want to journal about your reading or use the book for a faculty book club or professional development. In particular, we encourage you to think about what you might take away or try from this section:

- Where do the rhetorics of basic, ableism, and remediation show up in documents, in meetings, in curriculum, in values, and in resources? Is there a reframing of language, ideology, and value that needs to happen?
- Where might the values of equitable program redesign ripple out to positively shape anti-racist program assessment and curriculum design, equitable hiring and promotion processes, mutuality within the rhetoric and composition classroom, and other DEIBSJ work?
- How might activity theory help you unpack the spheres of influence that shape program design, course design, hiring practices, community outreach, etc.?
- Who are the human actors and non-human actors that create positive and problematic processes? How might you examine human actors and non-human actors to examine what actually happens and not necessarily what should be happening?

CHAPTER 5.

BASIC WRITING'S INTEROFFICE, INTERCAMPUS ACTOR-NETWORK: ASSEMBLING OUR HISTORY THROUGH DOLMAGEAN ANALYSIS

John Paul Tassoni
Miami University

"TRYING TO FIND" BASIC WRITING

I tried to find basic writing (BW) at my university but found instead what BW tells. This being the case, it occurs to me that if you don't find this story that BW tells about its place, you might only learn what that place tells you about BW. Not that this is an unrelated or insignificant story: that place (depending on the place) might tell you something about equal opportunity or student needs, or about a drain on resources, or about errors and standards, or even about civilization in decline. And if you get the story of BW from those of us who actually teach and administer BW, you'll learn something about students with dyslexia and depression, students with unreliable cars and full-time jobs; you'll learn something about class and ethnicity, about teachers working for substandard pay, and even about some private concerns as to whether we, in the end, open doors to institutional and cultural transformation or unwittingly affirm an oppressive status quo. You'll also find us recounting stories about students who defy their "at-risk" designation to earn degrees and drastically improve their life chances, and you'll encounter tales about students whose struggles throw our teaching into crisis and propel us toward new methods and theories. Come to think of it, though, just about anyone in higher education can tell you something (actual or mythic, but something always telling) about BW; but while these things they tell you (or don't tell you) indeed intertwine, inform, and trammel the story of BW, they are not necessarily the story that BW tells. To get that story, you almost have to be trying to find BW.

Positioned in this way—"trying to find"—I draw on actor-network theory and Jay Dolmage's (2017) critique of academic ableism to describe BW's presence(s) among a system's aligned and competing interests and concerns. Theorists such as Bruno Latour (1999) and John Law (1999), as well as Ehren Pflugfelder (2015), Yrjö Engeström (1987), and Kate Crawford and Helen Hasan (2006) help me discern BW as not just a story of teachers, learning assistance staff, and "at-risk" students, but as what Pflugfelder (2015) would call a "strange entanglement" of institutional dynamics (p. 115), of humans, programs, and offices, many of which would fail to chart BW as a principal concern. While I am in total agreement with Lynn Reid (in this collection) whose chapter articulates the value of extending our focus beyond issues of localization to "the larger discursive network that influences basic writing today," my focus falls on the internal people, programs, and offices that reinforce a network in which BW persists (see Porter et al., 2000), as nebulous as that persistence sometimes is.

Any search for a BW program will convey volumes about its school's commitment to democratic access and student learning, what scholastic and cultural markers it uses to designate students worthy or unworthy of a higher education, what efforts it makes to open gates or shore-up walls, what kinds of professional labor it values, and what discourses it relies upon to describe itself amidst all these varied attitudes and practices. Toward this end, Dolmage's (2017) consideration of "steep steps," "retrofits," and "universal design" help me construct a story that intersects the histories, practices, and beliefs of entangled institutional agencies. This story/assemblage is designed to help agents/agencies recognize their involvement in BW's interoffice, intercampus actor-network. At the very least, knowing the story that BW tells at their particular schools, writing program administrators (WPAs) are in a better position to "find allies," as Ira Shor (1997) recommends (p. 102), in order to create new stories/trajectories where those allies find cause. Far from eschewing the broader, external forces that impact post-secondary education, the theories and stories I deploy in this chapter can help people, programs, and offices across campuses recognize their stake in BW and the political exigencies of their acknowledgment. When you try to find the assemblage that is BW, in short, you find that school's mettle: this is the story that BW tells.

STEEP STEPS, RETROFITS, AND UNIVERSAL DESIGN

One of the reasons you have to go searching for BW at my school is that BW, to some degree, has been hidden (intentionally forgotten) and to other degrees, people have just kind of lost track of it (accidentally forgotten it) or never really thought about it at all (very telling). My school is Miami University, a public ivy comprising a selective, central campus in Oxford, Ohio, and two open-admissions regional campuses. I principally work at the regional campus in Middletown, a town 25 miles east of the Oxford location. When I arrived at the school in 1994, BW offerings were taught through Middletown's Office of Learning Assistance (OLA), virtually without any oversight on the part of the English Department at either the central or regional campus. Students, referred to the course through an examination that tested their knowledge of grammar and punctuation, signed up for two concurrent writing workshops (English 001 and 002), and these sections operated as a two-credit, current-traditional, BW class. A free-standing BW course, English 007, staffed as well through the OLA, was not developed by that office until 1998. This course does not count toward graduation and does not appear in Miami's course catalog—its omission from this publication a prerequisite for its existence (DeGenaro, 2006). While English 001/002, on the other hand, did appear in the catalog when I joined Miami's faculty in 1994 and has so, I now know, since 1974, my colleagues on the College Composition Committee at Oxford expressed no knowledge of the courses' existence, let alone a stake in their operation.

As you might have guessed, no files labeled "Basic Writing" exist in our university archives or even in the English Department's WPA office; however, I learned that multiple institutional sites intersected with, foreshadowed, and named-without-naming the demographic, economic, pedagogical, and architectural matters shaping trajectories of BW at the school. Having encountered the work of Dolmage while he was still a doctoral student in our rhetoric and composition program, I found that a legend he had developed to image institutional approaches to disability could help me identify ways our department systematically managed its elitist and democratic impulses. With notes of thanks to Jay included, I published a series of articles that employed his legend to explain how BW had "left" the English Department and come to reside at the regionals' OLA. While my earlier works frame BW programming within cultural and pedagogical debates that shaped writing instruction during the time BW emerged at our main campus in the form of an Equal Opportunity Program (EOP) workshop, my approach focused almost exclusively on debates that informed English department actors and their eventual encounter with the OLA. Such a focus on one particular department, program, or course divorces local actants from other entities operating within the university structure and, thus, limits possibilities for positive and sustainable changes that might benefit not only BW students and teachers but strengthen, as well, institutions' (professed) commitments to social justice. Actor-network-theory helps me take that description of these impulses/trajectories and situate them as part of a broader system that circulates BW's interests and concerns.

I draw from Dolmage (2017) to extend descriptions of his legend and provide a more comprehensive and complicated view of the actor-network through which BW persists, pushes, and perishes at a variety of institutional sites—not just English departments and/or offices of learning assistance. I use the components of the legend, in other words, to describe the manner in which the network assembles in heterogeneous ways that block and/or facilitate the institution's responsiveness to BW (see Law, 1999). Dolmage's legend comprises the key terms—"steep steps," "retrofits," and "universal design"—I use to assemble "the internal tensions and contradictions" within the school's actor-network (Crawford & Hasan, 2006, p. 51). This assemblage includes, as Crawford and Hasan (2006) wrote, echoing the work of Engeström (1987), "both historical continuity and locally situated contingency that are the motive for change and development" (p. 51). Dolmage's legend helps me articulate the dynamic among various actors, including sites and events that have shaped our school's approach to diverse constituencies and, particularly, what room and direction these actants provide for BW. In conjunction with Dolmage's (2017) legend, actor-network theory's "ruthless applications of semiotics," as Law (1999) has characterized it, helps me to "take . . . the semiotic insight, that of the relationship of entities, the notion that they are produced in relations, and [apply] this [insight] ruthlessly to all materials—and not simply to those that are linguistic" (Law 1999, pp. 3, 4). Dolmage's (2017) legend, in short, helps me to describe the network trajectories of the assemblage that is BW at Miami University.

Simply, "steep steps" represent those systemic features/practices that restrict access: they work to mark certain demographics as mainstream business while keeping other constituencies at bay. In academia, such features might take the form of aptitude tests, or fluency in a prestige dialect (and BW curricula that privilege it exclusively), legacy admissions, tuition rates, cultural events on campus that consistently showcase a singular demographic, or even, as Dolmage (2017) points out, literal stairways. Meanwhile, "retrofits" are those features of a system that signal attempts, after the fact, to include previously marginalized groups. An actual ramp, for instance, indicates an attempt to include individuals with certain physical disabilities among a structure's activities. The retrofitted ramp, however, does not ensure that the individuals, once inside, will find other facilities accessible or the people anti-ableist. In this sense, the retrofit can come to represent institutional efforts, like the EOP, or Diversity Week, or a single "Learn Chinese" workshop that invites (although not necessarily through the front door) "non-traditional" constituencies or highlights, in effect, non-mainstream concerns (and reaffirms what is mainstream or essential in the process). A key concept toward determining the intent and effectiveness of systemic change/stasis, a retrofit can serve as an escape valve ("We've done our part; we need no further alterations") or instigate additional changes ("Are other features of our structure accessible too? What more do we need to do?").

The "more" that could be done prior to or even following a retrofit is reflected in "universal design" (UD). Unlike retrofits, which are by definition afterthoughts geared to provide special accommodations to certain segments of the population, UD asks from the beginning of the design process how all of its features might be aesthetically pleasing and functional for the greatest diversity of users (Alexander, 1995). In a previously published article that traces my department's approach to BW, I describe the significance of UD to BW in this way:

> Related to basic writing, universal design, then, would look for ways of integrating the issues and concerns of "at-risk" students into the mainstream business of the department and the institution more generally, rather than merely retrofitting onto its structure a single course [like the ENG 001/002 workshops] that is perpetually [not supposed to exist at a public ivy]. (Tassoni, 2006, pp. 102–103)

The passage goes on to describe UD as a challenge to what Mike Rose (1989) has called "the myth of transience" (p. 5), which characterizes BW as always a provisional (retrofitted) response to writing crises and new constituencies rather than part of the real work of postsecondary education. My 2006 work also calls on UD consultant Elaine Ostroff (2001), who indicates that such views of postsecondary education limit diversity in favor of "a mythical average norm" toward which activities tend to direct themselves (p. 1.12).

In *Academic Ableism*, Dolmage (2017) describes the ableist implications of such a "norm" and the ways in which UD represents an ongoing process that can destabilize this status quo in favor of more equitable designs. While Dolmage (2017) principally focuses on disability, an analysis of BW as actor-network could also lean on this notion of UD as process. This notion provides a sense of ways BW has emerged at various points at various sites in the university's history and how its actor-network might continue to create spaces to invite and support the multiple literacies, interests, and concerns BW represents. In the same light, however, steep steps and retrofits also represent processes that persist in this actor-network. They set and reset along the way but are always coming into being as effects of the institution's ambient rhetorics and related activities, as network trajectories shaping what Miami has become and what it still aspires to be.

Dolmage's (2017) legend helps assemble ambient rhetorics and institutional entities in such a way as to mark the circulation (and sometimes lack thereof) of BW concerns; or better yet, Dolmage's (2017) legend helps (actant/assemblage) BW tell the story of ways its concerns circulate throughout a network of competing and aligned interests. Understanding this movement of BW generated in relation to university entities leads me to, as Latour (1999) would say, "the summing up of interactions" among various offices, individuals, and ideologies "into a very local, very practical, very tiny locus" that is our BW program (p. 17). In this manner, one can explore the structures of the institution without being led away from these local sites "but closer to them" (Latour, 1999, p. 18). I might speak in terms of mainstream and periphery, current programming, and historical trends, but these elements all define the other; they are all elements of the system and are all part of the story that BW tells.

"THE INSTITUTION MORE GENERALLY"

In that 2006 work referred to above, I mention "the institution more generally," but in retrospect, I must not have meant it, and even if I did, I would have needed to understand BW as actor-network to avoid losing the local in favor of "the more generally" I sought to characterize. As it turns out, my earlier analyses drew upon Dolmage's legend to frame and discuss English department debates during the early years of the workshops that a member of its faculty had helped develop for EOP students: BW's broader actor-network receives scant attention in that earlier work. I traced the ways in which efforts to distinguish mainstream students from those students whom English faculty saw as needing remediation helped fuel the network trajectory that eventually led (after the death of the one English department member who had founded and oversaw the EOP workshops) toward ENG 001/002's being relocated to the regional campuses (alone), outside the house of English (and inside the OLA). Given efforts devoted then to distinguish mainstream students from those in need of remediation, it was easy to see that the English department was not prone to view the EOP students or other students considered to be in need of "remediation" as the department's business.

Within the English department, the EOP workshop, which comprised predominantly working-class and African American students, was never perceived as anything but a retrofit (the escape-valve kind) to a core institutional identity, which was marked by singular-plural standards (Fox, 1999), not to mention a White, affluent demographic. Under such circumstances, the retrofit could not hold. Anything resembling UD failed to enter the department's deliberations on writing instruction, deliberations which would not come to call for a truly plural view of standards (a view which might have situated the EOP workshops as a push toward broader change) but as a means to deprive non-traditional students of their "right to learn and use a dialect other than their own" (Freshman, 1975). In various notes addressed to the Director of Freshman Composition, English faculty affirmed the value of their traditions and standards (steep steps), one department member analogizing the school as an elitist playground in which one needed to learn the existing rules in order to join. My earlier article (Tassoni, 2006), in short, focused a good deal on individual, human actants and the ways in which they had come to (re)constitute the public ivy at a single site, the English department. The report did not expand its scope in ways that considered the assemblance of discourses that had driven these discussions, the ways, in other words, the broader institution itself served as actant in BW's actor-network.

Similarly, another previously published work on BW doings at Miami, one I co-authored with my colleague Cynthia Lewiecki-Wilson (Tassoni & Lewiecki-Wilson, 2005), reports on our attempts to revitalize the ENG 001/002 courses (previously the EOP workshops) as studio workshops. In a sense, we labored in the wake of debates that had resulted in the siphoning of BW concerns to not only the regionals, but out of the house of English itself. New to the school and ignorant of BW's actor-network, I was able to convince our department's College Composition Committee to form a subcommittee devoted to BW concerns, my argument being that the courses that constituted BW programming were, after all, English courses. Because BW programming was situated in the OLA, however, Lewiecki-Wilson's and my attempts to support, inform, and alter the BW landscape involved negotiations with that office, negotiations that rarely, we felt, led anywhere. Our 2005 *Journal of Basic Writing* article depicted our interactions with OLA staff as

> a series of scripts and counterscripts: pitting current-traditional pedagogies against process and (post)process pedagogies; the Office of Learning Assistance against the Department of English; adjuncts (hired through the Office of Learning Assistance to teach basic writing) against full-time faculty (who traditionally had steered clear of basic writing). (p. 79)

We describe the goals we did agree upon as "daunting, often involving the development of new courses and expanding the power and scope of writing centers university-wide"; we "lament our failure to generate third-space discussions in these meetings, meetings that in retrospect appear to us as but manifestations of rigid polarizations"; and we conjecture as to whether "we just needed more time in this [sub]committee to engage our differences [and move] toward understanding and improving conditions for students labeled basic writers" (Tassoni & Lewiecki-Wilson, 2005, p. 79). My colleague and I could label forces at work, but little did we consider that we were, in effect, merging with broader institutional arrangements. Pflugfelder (2015), drawing on the work of architect Lars Spuybroek (2009), describes the ways driving a car becomes a "strange entanglement of human-vehicle interaction" (Pflugfelder, 2015, p. 115). In the scenario above, the OLA and Lewiecki-Wilson and I struggle (from somewhere in the backseat) for control of the wheel in a car (Miami University), a vehicle (itself composed of multiple moving parts) we name as context earlier in the essay but never really acknowledge as actant itself.

I wonder now where those discussions with the OLA would have taken us had we considered the car we drove (the one that drove us?) in regard to the competing and overlapping principles represented in Dolmage's legend, all of which, I argue below, inform access initiatives at Miami. We (the OLA staff, Lewiecki-Wilson, and I) all wanted improved conditions, but were the human actors at these meetings sitting in car seats destined for step steps, retrofits, or UD? In other words, the passage I quote from above indicates that my colleague and I could identify segments of the actor-network at odds in our meeting with OLA staff and that we knew the rhetorical space of those meetings was too narrow. We did not, however, consider the extent to which these meetings coursed in a machinery we needed to better understand; our work existed in relation to these other parts of the system, not just in relation to the OLA. Our better understanding of the ways in which the institution itself served as an actor would have helped us locate and merge with the equipment (discourses, programs, administrators) in ways that best suited BW's needs. Just as Dolmage's legend facilitated my analyses of attitudes and beliefs shaping the English department's earlier considerations of BW, the legend proves equally helpful in naming mechanisms that drive "the institution more generally."

A Dolmagean analysis provides an especially useful vocabulary for identifying BW concerns and assembling those institutional agents that generate BW, react to it, and act upon it. Such an analysis involves converting Dolmage's legend into a series of overlays. In this manner, it is easier to understand the elements as not a sequence of (hoped-for) stages/improvements but a system of attitudes, beliefs, practices, as well as material and bureaucratic structures that persist, push, and perish simultaneously and continuously. Its network trajectories move horizontally across the current institutional structure and vertically in terms of the school's history: an allatonce, if you will. As an allatonce, the legend's features defy dichotomization. A Dolmagean reading of our institutional arrangements marks not an instance of the bad elitist selective campus (steep steps) pitted against a good, democratized (universally designed) regional campus but an ongoing interplay of inclusions and exclusions (enacted at all sites and defining each), retrofitted programs and entities (the regional campuses themselves being one of these retrofits) and ongoing efforts at deep, democratic change.

MORE "MORE TIME"

Reflecting on our early meetings with the OLA, Lewiecki-Wilson and I (2005) contextualized our differences through static fields (the OLA vs. Department of English; full-time faculty vs. part-time staff; etc.) that eschewed debates within each field. We failed to consider, as well, historical factors that had constructed and continued to inform this actor-network. Assembling the actor-network in which we worked, a Domalgean analysis could have helped us locate better the competing and aligned goals that transected our meetings and complicated our discourse, rather than perceive ourselves (as we did) settled into hypostatized local camps.

The OLA itself has evolved from an earlier entity, the Developmental Education Office (DEO). Of particular significance to BW's story, Miami's then-president Phillip Shriver (1973) projected the inaugural director of the DEO in these terms:

> [H]e [sic] should be aware of the educational problems of not only those students from underprivileged backgrounds but of those whose low standardized test scores or erratic high school records demonstrate a distinct academic deficiency. Included among such students at Miami would be those in the Educational Opportunity Program [EOP], a significant portion of the commuter group, veterans whose recent experience or time away from formal schooling results in academic handicaps, and some of the students from various special admission groups [i.e., including students selected based on physical handicap or English as a second language].

Shriver's proposed job description is significant for multiple reasons: (1) it emerges at approximately the same time the English 001/002 EOP workshops appear in Miami's course catalog; (2) it describes an administrative position for an office that would eventually come to house the university's BW programming; (3) it decidedly views that office's mission in terms of a deficit model, one that views "non-traditional" constituencies in terms of lack rather than in terms of diversity; (4) it names the multiple constituencies the president characterizes as "underprivileged" and likely to "demonstrate . . . academic deficiency"; (5) each of these constituencies represents a complicated and conflicted institutional history in terms of ways they have been invited into and excluded from the school's mainstream business (in order to affirm its mainstream); and (6) the office (now the OLA) and BW programming would eventually find themselves on the regional campuses alone, a development (siphoning) that speaks volumes to the ways in which the system manages diversity. Lewiecki-Wilson and I (2005) believed that "more time" might have helped us generate more productive dialogues with OLA stuff, but we already had more time and more institutional space in front of us and behind us (in the past) than we were prepared to even recognize, let alone sort out and herd toward anything resembling direction.

I do not have the space here to provide comprehensive histories of agencies relevant to all of the groups mentioned above in Shriver's proposed job description. What I will do, however, is use Dolmage's legend to quickly assemble a few of these constituencies and their histories. "Trying to find" these constituencies/histories, I spoke to various individuals across the campuses and interviewed retired faculty and staff. I reviewed documents I located (and ones people helped me to locate) in our WPA office, the university archives, the Equal Employment Opportunity Commission Office, and Personnel Office.

"SHOULD BE AWARE OF THE EDUCATIONAL PROBLEMS"

In the sections below, I rely on Dolmage's *Academic Ableism* (2017) to extend descriptions of steep steps, retrofits, and UD, particularly as features of his legend depict historical trajectories relevant to groups named in Shriver's proposed job description for DEO director—military veterans, EOP students, and students with disabilities. In the section following this one, I briefly reference implications for ESL students and the commuter group, demographics also named in Shriver's proposed job description, but I still need to research their histories at the time of this writing. Their histories, I do not doubt, are as significant as the others traced here. The commuter group eventually was absorbed into the regional campus student body—another instance of siphoning. The increase in international students currently generates much discussion regarding language standards across the curriculum. Reflective of its earlier discussions regarding BW students, the English department here in the last decade or so has even debated as to whether it was its responsibility to teach English to the growing number of international students and not the role of some other campus entity. So it goes . . .

STEEP STEPS AS NETWORK TRAJECTORY

As Dolmage (2017) points out, "[S]teep steps, physically and figuratively, lead to the ivory tower. The tower is built upon ideals and standards—historically, this is an identity that the university has embraced" (p. 44). Faced with new constituencies or other possible "threats" to this identity's ideals and standards, steep steps can become even more apparent. In the aftermath of the G.I. Bill, for instance, Miami, like other schools, performed its patriotic duty through attempts to accommodate returning WWII veterans; nevertheless, its administration at the same time worried about space needs. As a result, one program, which had been designed to provide vocational training to "salvage" students who might not have been successful in college curricula, was dropped, and in its wake the university president asked the Miami community to now critically consider "Who should be educated?" (Hanhe, 1947, p 10).

In response to this question, the university instituted a "pre-entrance test" that would gauge students' possible college success. The director of Student Counseling Services at this time called the test an "outstanding addition to the program" in its ability "to aid prospective students of very low academic ability to redirect their vocational planning" (Crosby, 1948, p. 84). This director saw it as a mark of success that, in the wake of this exam, a good number of prospective Miami students "changed from college plans to vocational training programs . . . while a still larger number made no further contact with the University . . ." (Crosby, 1948, p. 84). In short, faced with a class of students whose numbers and backgrounds exceeded those to which the institution was accustomed, a new hurdle was constructed to affirm just who would be college educated and who would be encouraged to go elsewhere. As these affirmations (and exclusions) were taking place, administrators such as Robert Miner (1948), Director of Student Affairs, reported that the veterans who remained "intermixed well with the student body and have renounced their identity as veterans in favor of being students first and foremost" (p. 74). As steep steps saw themselves reinforced in the form of canceled programs and pre-entrance tests, those populations who negotiated the steps would be lauded for their ability to assimilate and "renounce their identity" rather than generate any change to the school's identity.

For those who habitually find entry to the institution, steep steps might appear as neutral ground, rather than as a system of inclusions and exclusions. In a memo following passage of the Rehabilitation Act of 1973, for example, Shriver (1975) considers prospects for students with disabilities at Miami, only to affirm its literal steep steps. In the memo, he suggests that the school "list positively in our Catalog the accommodations [for students with disabilities] that we do have, rather than stressing what we do not have," but the memorandum does not seem to acknowledge ways that the university functioned as a system structurally designed to accommodate able-bodied norms and to invite people with disabilities as an afterthought. This rhetoric situates the institution in such a way as to allow for retrofits to an already integrated whole but not in a way that willingly gears itself to a revision of this integrated whole in anticipation of the greatest diversity of users. "I do not see that we are in any position to consider handling bed cases and wheelchair cases," wrote Shriver (1975), affirming an able-bodied "we" that excludes certain people with disabilities. He "believe[s] that there are some things we can do to help ambulatory students, including the deaf and the blind, the rheumatoid arthritics, etc." However, he did "not see Miami in any position to begin to prepare for wheelchair cases in light of the age of our buildings and extent of our campus." In the end, Shriver's 1975 memorandum expressed a desire for a situation in which "handicapped students . . . will self-select" their colleges "according to the nature of [the students'] handicaps," but does not articulate ways his university already pre-selects, through environmental and attitudinal dispositions, an able-bodied clientele.

Tellingly, he wrote in another memorandum on the subject: "I do not see the potential for non-ambulatory handicapped students in any significant numbers here. However, I see no reason why the Hamilton and Middletown Campuses could not provide these, with their provisions for ramps and elevators" (Shriver, 1976). As with BW, the regional campuses, as a glorious retrofit (the escape-valve sort), were seen as a principal site for difference management, as a way to capture constituencies, concerns, and interests the actor-network defined as peripheral. While various forms of steep steps helped establish a stable, normative clientele, the university could look ahead to the formation of a DEO, whose director would consider the interests and concerns of groups named above in Shriver's memo (EOP students, veterans, students with disabilities, international students, commuters) and consider how the university's steep steps might be retrofitted in ways that (at least) gestured toward expanded access.

RETROFITS AS NETWORK TRAJECTORY

By choice and sometimes by mandate (e.g., the Rehabilitation Act of 1973; Ohio Laws and Legislative Rules), the university will at times retrofit its steep steps in ways that invite constituencies it identifies as special (not mainstream) populations. Against the background of steep steps, of traditions focused on able-bodied, affluent, White norms, these retrofits are marked by what Dolmage (2017) calls "a chronicity—a timing and a time logic—that that renders them highly temporary yet also relatively unimportant" (p. 70). Like the "myth of transience" that so often guides BW funding and programming, this chronicity leads to "what might be called abeyance structures—perhaps allowing for access, but disallowing the possibility of action for change" (Dolmage, 2017, p. 77). As I say above, retrofits in this sense serve as escape valves. They gesture at inclusion but expect constituencies, once inside, to overcome differences or assimilate rather than challenge or alter what the institution might consider its core identity.

The institution will rhetorically position itself, when it comes to questions of access, as a stable, whole entity willing (kindly or under mandate) to flex toward constituencies it denotes as special; however, as Pegeen Reichert Powell (2013) argued, such an emphasis on students' abilities to adjust "treat[s] failure as the problem of the individual rather than that of the institution" (p. 98). This kind of steep-step stability is underscored as the university retrofits various programs and offices to its core identity, often with the stated goal of assimilating "non-traditional" groups. The EOP itself was drawn up, at least from the perspective of the school's upper administration, to "provide the necessary remedial education that will enable disadvantaged students to overcome their handicaps and complete their college degrees." It was expected that "students coming with different backgrounds [would] overcome the difference" rather than contribute difference (Shriver, 1969).

The implications of this dynamic were not lost on student Carter Richards, a Black Student Action Association (BSAA) member who in a 1971 newspaper interview voiced his concern that it is "always the blacks that must adjust to a community like this. We have been brought up in black homes in black neighborhoods. [But it] is the black who must adjust to the white student" (quoted in Nichols, 1971). Richards had an ally in EOP administrator Lawrence Young, who tended to see retrofits as opportunities to throw into relief the status quo and expose it to serious questions. "An unfortunate and distasteful fact of life in the West," he wrote in a column in 1978, "is that all integration starts with a token.... However, a token can agitate for further change. Remove that and you have a comfortable, anxiety-free, complacent, self-righteous, lily white, morally bankrupt status quo" (Young, 1978). Further change, movement toward UD, is necessary in these cases, or else, as Dolmage (2017) explained,

> [W]hite students know that the fakeness and ineffectiveness of diversity initiatives on campus maintain their white privilege sometimes just as powerfully as overt forms of discrimination do. If white students play along with the pantomime of tokenized diversity, they won't have to challenge their own privilege or lose their own positioning. (p. 45)

To take retrofits beyond pantomime, the actor-network must continue to ask what additional changes need to be made. While the influx of veterans to campus after WWII generated increased attention to spatial needs and a series of exclusionary practices to address those needs in a timely fashion, Miami's

Oxford campus nevertheless engineered a series of retrofits that pushed Miami toward more lasting changes. In *Miami University: A personal history* (1998), released the same year that Miami Middletown launched its studio program, the school's former president Shriver, renders a brief account of the post-war period, 1946–1952, focusing on the number of G.I.s returning to the Oxford campus. As there had been no construction at Miami during the United States' involvement with the war and little construction during the decade of the Great Depression that had preceded it, the campus, at least architecturally, was ill-prepared to accommodate so many returning students. Some "quick conversions," as Shriver (1998) describes them, had to be made. A physical education facility, for example, was converted into a men's residence hall. The university lined the basketball court with four-hundred double-decker, wall-to-wall bunks, creating what Shriver (1998) calls a "Spartan accommodation" (pp. 200–201).

Shriver's constructed memory of the post-war years, along with other such recollections, like Walter Havighurst's *Miami Years* (1984) and Robert White, Jr.'s *Oxford and Miami University during World War II: A remembrance* (1994), operate in conjunction with archival evidence to reveal discourses that continue to inform the school's considerations of democratic access. I've come to view the school's accounts of this post-war constituency as early signals of tensions that persist between its democratic aims and selective functions. Aided by the G.I. Bill, which provided tuition, fees, books, and sustenance funds for any person under twenty-six who had had his or her education interrupted by military service, students now flocked to Miami in increased numbers, many of whom were years older than those who had traditionally attended the school and many of whom brought with them literacies, concerns, and experiences far different than the university had previously entertained. While newly instituted pre-entrance exams did throw up steep steps for some of these new students, the "quick conversions" engineered to meet the immediate needs of those who persisted would point to deeper changes that the university would eventually make.

UNIVERSAL DESIGN AS NETWORK TRAJECTORY

Dolmage (2017) describes UD as "a way to move." He also describes it as "a world view." "Universal Design," he wrote, "is not a tailoring of the environment to marginal groups; it is a form of hope, a manner of trying. The push toward the universal is a push toward seeing space as open to multiple possibilities, as being in process" (Dolmage, 2017, p. 145). While groups like the EOP students and veterans might signal forms of "academic handicaps" and find themselves classified as the purview of a DEO director, the groups nevertheless have a history of challenging the status quo.

As retrofits, they resisted the status of "quick conversion" and spurred instead questions of the broader design. The presence of WWII veterans, for instance, helped administrators recognize that much more than difficulties with curricula could hamper students' persistence rates and led to the formation of the Office of Student Affairs, which provided, among other resources, psychological counseling (Crosby, 1948; Hahne, 1947; Minor, 1948). Other broader changes included the addition of more lights in more classrooms and the scheduling of night classes and summer classes to facilitate the schedules of the older adult students (Hahne, 1947). New academic buildings and residential buildings followed (Hahne, 1947), including residences for married students to provide more access for the non-traditional clientele. And despite the Director of Student Affairs' characterization of returning GI's having relinquished their identity as veterans, there are reports of global themes being incorporated into classes in order to invite returning veterans to draw on their recent experiences and reports as well of returning veterans winning writing contests by virtue of essays based on their war experiences abroad (Havighurst, 1984).

Thinking of tokenism (retrofitting) as an opportunity to agitate for broader changes, EOP administrators also actively sought means of redesigning the university structure in ways that diversified its actor-network. The program's inaugural director, Heanon Wilkins (1969), stressed from the EOP's very beginning that it "must be more than a mere show of tokenism by Miami University." The Office of Black Student Affairs, which housed the EOP, introduced practices that included: delays of suspension for students whose grade point averages were below passing in order to give the students more time to adjust; credit reductions, so that the students could spend more time on fewer courses; formation of a cultural center and additional cultural events reflective of the EOP students' own backgrounds; recruitment practices that looked beyond GPA in order to locate talented and committed students; the development of Black studies programming; an increase in Black faculty and staff; and office space for the BSAA in the student center. The BSAA is particularly worth mentioning here in that they were one of the student groups who supported students who occupied Oxford's ROTC building as part of a 1970 Vietnam War protest. As part of this protest, the BSAA's principal demands included extension of the EOP, particularly in the form of supportive services, like the ENG 001/002 writing workshops.

Just as Shriver's (1973) vision for the DEO's director intersected diverse constituencies likely to demonstrate "academic deficiencies," I look for BW in those intersections. What I find there are network trajectories indicating—to various degrees at various times—steep steps, retrofits, and/or UD. The sum of these histories and the movements (or lack thereof), culminating in BW's eventual situation on the regional campuses, is the story that BW tells.

CONCLUSION: "THE SUMMING UP OF INTERACTIONS"

BW tells me that: (1) more people, programs, and offices than would admit so have a stake in BW; (2) the attitudes and beliefs that these people, programs, and offices share (or fail to share) about BW still very much course through and intersect within the campuses and these coursings and intersections have not yet been documented in any sustained narrative, making it difficult for human actors to recognize their involvement/position in these chains of influence; and (3) critical histories such as the one I undertake here provide ways for actors to recognize their stake in BW by recognizing just how deep, how multiple, and how politically volatile these stakes can be. In short, BW's story persists, perishes, and pushes in its relation to institutional entities (demographics, offices, campuses) and those various network trajectories (steep steps, retrofits, UD) that assemble them, and it can serve rhetoric and composition program administrators (hereafter WPAs) well to know this story.

Listening to the story BW tells of its interoffice, intercampus actor-network, rhetoric and composition program administrators can position themselves better to "story change," as Steve Lamos (2012), borrowing from Linda Adler-Kassner (2008), might say. "Specifically," wrote Lamos (2012), "we should imagine new ways to identify and publicize BW as an institutional space explicitly dedicated to success for the increasingly diverse populations that are entering [predominantly White institutions] in greater numbers" (p. 18). Story changing, in this regard, involves intersecting campus units and histories relative to diverse populations and assembling them through the lenses of steep steps, retrofits, and UD to mark their trajectories. Dolmage (2017) warns of making the "interest convergence" argument that UD necessarily benefits all students, that such an argument might lead us to ignore specific pathways that bring students to our schools, as well as the ones that block their access (pp. 146–150). Lamos (2012), however, argues that critical and careful approaches to interest convergence dynamics can help remind those in power that BW persists and that diversity-conscious approaches to programming and curricula can benefit the contemporary neoliberal, predominantly White institutions as well, especially where their goals and interests include cultivation of a diverse student body and global engagement.

The story that BW tells encourages institutions toward UD while still recognizing the specific pathways that facilitate or curtail students' access. Dolmage's legend can help WPAs identify network trajectories circulating among institutional entities, those trajectories that align with as well as those that thwart educational access. At the same time, those entities (e.g., veteran affairs, disability offices, diversity councils, international education, etc.) can attend to the pathways that bring students to their offices. Not all ethnic-minority students or students with disabilities, military veterans, not to mention international students or regional campus (commuter) students, will seek or be referred to BW courses. Nevertheless, the programs and policies produced by agencies devoted to their concerns (e.g., at my school—the Diversity Council, OLA, the Disability Office, campus writing centers, Veteran Affairs, Global Initiatives, Department of Global and Intercultural Studies, Department of English, the Center for Teaching and Learning, Physical Facilities, etc.) all to various degrees map current and future areas of support for BW students. Doing so, they collectively mark movement toward UD in ways that can radically alter the brand of public ivies such as ours.

Identifying these entities as BW's actor-network, WPAs can better gauge university-wide policies and practices that determine the success of their BW students and identify human actors, beyond English departments, who might contribute to BW's transformative potentials. WPAs might also take it upon themselves to examine the histories of these various agencies at their schools, seeking the matter in which Dolmage's legend might unfold in their various files. You might not need to pursue as long a history as I trace in this chapter; however, the process itself, which can take you into various offices and archives, provides kairotic moments in which you can articulate to others the objectives of your search, your search for BW and the story that it tells. In bringing these other entities to the table (whether in the form of committees that discuss BW curricula, or communiques that inform other network actors of BW's doings, or even merely requests for documents via emails that help other actors in other offices connect with BW practices), WPAs help agents in the actor-network identify their stake in the ongoing (rather than transient) effort to make their school as accessible and as beneficial as it can be, not only for student writers whose skills challenge traditional standards, but also for the greatest diversity of users, those whose interests and concerns can retell tradition. At the same time, these efforts could very well help universities present a more effective message as they address the sorts of policy changes and initiatives proposed by the state legislatures, popular media, and non-profit organizations that Lynn Reid described in this collection, those policies and initiatives set to shape "the future of basic writing in the United States."

Given the extent to which "the tiny locus" of our BW programs represent "the summing up of interactions" among an institution's various offices, individuals, and ideologies (Latour, 1999, p. 17), WPAs can most immediately move their schools and their states toward UD through attention to relevant policies and practices within their programs. WPAs can make sure their instructors attend to the multicultural, anti-racist, and anti-ableist imperatives of BW programming;

and WPAs can ensure, as well, that their faculty are versed in vocabularies, such as those in Dolmage's legend, to help them trace the trajectories of this work. Likewise, WPAs can help design curricula that encourage BW students themselves to examine institutional entities that might curtail or facilitate their persistence rates, and these curricula can encourage students to compose accounts of their home and institutional lives in ways that thicken their own sense of agency in the story that BW tells. WPAs should use their interactions with other network actors to ensure that BW students' stories circulate through the broader network, that their challenges to the "mythical average norm" pulse through each of its trajectories (Ostroff, 2001, p. 1.12), story changing at each center of their schools' mainstream business.

REFERENCES

Adler-Kassner, L. (2008). *The activist WPA: Changing stories about writing and writers.* Utah State University Press.

Alexander, J. (1995). Introduction. In P. Welch (Ed.), *Strategies for teaching universal design* (pp. iii). Adaptive Environments.

Crawford, K. & Hasan, H. M. (2006). Demonstrations of the activity theory framework for research in IS. *Australian Journal of Information Systems, 13(2),* 49–68.

Crosby, R. C. (1948). *The report of the student counseling service. Annual report of the president, the vice president in charge of finance, the deans, and other administrative offices of Miami University.* Miami University.

DeGenaro, W. (2006). Why basic writing professionals on regional campuses need to know their histories. *Open Words: Access and English Studies, 1(1),* 54–68. https://doi.org/10.37514/OPW-J.2006.1.1.05.

Dolmage, J. (2017). *Academic ableism: Disability and higher education.* University of Michigan Press.

Engeström, Y. (1987). *Learning by expanding: An activity-theoretical approach in developmental research.* Orienta-Konsultit.

Fox, T. (1999). *Defending access: A critique of standards in higher education.* Boynton/Cook.

Freshman English Text and Program Committee (1975, February 11). *Response to the CCCC resolution on students' right to their own language.* Miami University.

Hahne, E. H. (1947). *The report of the president. Annual report of the president, the vice president in charge of finance, the deans, and other administrative offices of Miami University.* Miami University.

Havighurst, W. (1984). *The Miami years: 1809–1984.* New York, NY: Putnam.

Lamos, S. (2012). Minority-serving institutions, race-conscious "dwelling," and possible futures for basic writing at predominantly White institutions. *Journal of Basic Writing, 31(1),* 4–36. https://doi.org/10.37514/jbw-j.2012.31.1.02.

Law, J. (1999). After ANT: Complexity, naming, and topology. In J. Law & J. Hassard (Eds.), *Actor network theory and after* (pp. 1–14). Blackwell.

Latour, B. (1999). On recalling ANT. In J. Law & J. Hassard (Eds.), *Actor network theory and after* (pp. 15–25). Blackwell.

Miner, R. J. (1948). *Report of the director of student affairs. Annual report of the president, the vice president in charge of finance, the deans, and other administrative offices of Miami University.* Miami University.

Nichols, J. (1971, February 14). "Betrayal" to Miami Blacks just integration to Shriver. *Dayton Daily News.*

Ohio Laws and Legislative Rules. (2015, September 28). Section 3345.06: Ohio Revised Code. "Entrance Requirements of High School Graduates—Core Curriculum." Legislative Service Commission. https://codes.ohio.gov/ohio-revised-code/section-3345.06.

Ostroff, E. (2001). Universal design—The new paradigm. In W. Preiser & E. Ostroff (Eds.), *Universal design handbook* (pp. 1.3–1.12). McGraw-Hill.

Pflugfelder, E. H. (2015). Is no one at the wheel? Nonhuman agency and agentive movement. In P. Lynch & N. Rivers (Eds.), *Thinking with Bruno Latour in rhetoric and composition* (pp. 115–131). Southern Illinois University Press.

Porter, J. E., Sullivan, P., Blythe, S., Grabill, J. T. & Miles, L. (2000). Institutional critique: A rhetorical methodology for change. *College Composition and Communication, 51*(4), 610–642.

Rehabilitation Act of 1973. (1973). U.S. Equal Employment Opportunity Commission. https://www.eeoc.gov/statutes/rehabilitation-act-1973.

Reichert Powell, P. (2013). *Retention and resistance: Writing instruction and students who leave.* Utah State University Press.

Rose, M. (1989). *Lives on the boundary.* Penguin.

Shor, I. (1997). Our apartheid: Writing instruction and inequality. *Journal of Basic Writing, 16*(1), 91–104. https://doi.org/10.37514/jbw-j.1997.16.1.08.

Shriver, P. R. (1969, July 19). *Letter to alumni regarding creation of the Equal Opportunity Program* [Memorandum]. Miami University.

Shriver, P. R. (1973). *Memo regarding realignment of the EOO and the inaugural director of the Developmental Education Office.* [Memorandum]. Miami University.

Shriver, P. R. (1975, April 29). *Memo Regarding formation of a task force in response to the Rehabilitation Act.* [Memorandum]. Miami University.

Shriver, P. R. (1976, May 17). *Coming out of the report on the Rehabilitation Act.* [Memorandum]. Miami University.

Shriver, P. R. (1998). *Miami University: A personal history.* Miami University Press.

Spuybroek, L. (2009). *The architecture of continuity: Essays and conversations.* Nai010 Publishers.

Tassoni, J. P. (2005). Retelling basic writing at a regional campus: Iconic discourse and selective function meet social class. *Teaching English in the Two-Year Campus, 33*(2), 171–184.

Tassoni, J. P. (2006). (Re)membering basic writing at a public ivy: History for institutional redesign. *Journal of Basic Writing*, *25*(1), 96–124. https://doi.org/10.37514/jbw-j.2006.25.1.06.

Tassoni, J. P. & Lewiecki-Wilson, C. (2005). Not just anywhere, anywhen: Mapping change through studio work. *Journal of Basic Writing*, *24*(1), 68–92. https://doi.org/10.37514/jbw-j.2005.24.1.05.

White, Jr., R. (1994). *Oxford and Miami University during World War II: A remembrance*. The Smith Library of Regional History.

Wilkins, H. W. (1969, September 27). *Draft of a brochure for the Office of Black Student Affairs*. Miami University.

Young, L. (1978, February 24). Give me tokenism or give me less. *The Miami Student*.

CHAPTER 6.

OUTSIDERS LOOKING IN: DISCURSIVE CONSTRUCTIONS OF REMEDIATION BEYOND THE ACADEMY

Lynn Reid

Fairleigh Dickinson University

> Every 5 to 10 years, we experience cycles of remediation bashing . . . Usually at the end of a cycle or remediation bashing, there is regulation or policy created that is sometimes helpful and sometimes not.
>
> – Boylan qtd. in Levine-Brown and Weiss, An interview with Hunter R. Boylan

Since its institutionalization as a formal area of study in the 1970s, rhetoric and composition/ writing studies and its various subdisciplines have been shaped by actor-networks that are external to the discipline and even higher education itself. In his chapter in this collection, John Paul Tassoni seeks to map the networked knots and nodes that have a stake in basic writing (BW) on his campus at Miami University.[1] Tassoni's observation is that, "[M]ore people, programs, and offices than would admit so have a stake in BW" and that discourses of access comprising their conceptions of BW's history and function help sustain its place (precarious as it sometimes seems) at the university. Tassoni's work using networked theories to map the discursive influence that these various stakeholders have on BW in his local context serves as a useful model for a WPA interested in identifying similar patterns and opportunities on their own campuses. This chapter extends that discussion to include a conceptualization of the discursive networks within which BW operates on a more global scale, moving beyond the local institutional context to the broader professional and public discourses that shape BW across the US.

According to Bruno Latour (1988), "[T]he word network indicates that resources are concentrated in a few places—the knots and nodes—which are

---

1   My larger argument in this chapter draws on documents that use terms such as "remedial" and "developmental" to refer to what compositionists would consider basic writing courses, so I will use those terms interchangeably here.

connected with one another—the links and the mesh: these connections transform scattered resources into a net that may seem to scatter everywhere" (p. 180). In the fields of basic writing and developmental education, the actors who represent "the knots and nodes" where resources are most concentrated are increasingly distanced from both the actual work of teaching such courses and the scholarly communities that have studied them for the past fifty years. This chapter examines the relationships between just a few of the nodes in the larger discursive network that influences basic writing today: non-profit organizations, the popular press, and state legislators. My analysis suggests that given the enormous influence of these extra-institutional actors, writing program administrators who are responsible for basic writing programs must be aware of how both local campus actors (see also Tassoni in this collection) and stakeholders beyond the institution can exert rhetorical influence that can—and often does— dramatically alter the scope of a basic writing program (Reid, 2018).

It is no secret that remediation has historically been disparaged in both public and academic discourses (and as Mara Lee Grayson notes in her chapter in this volume, the weaponization of curricula to serve an exclusionary function in basic writing and other first-year composition (FYC) courses ought to give any WPA pause). Too often, however, conversations about the efficacy of basic writing are influenced by institutional needs, as remedial enrollments wax and wane depending on the exigence of the moment: students who place into remedial courses are admitted in higher numbers only when enrollment needs take precedence over an institution's "standards" (Soliday, 2002). Because the status of basic writing is perpetually in flux, remedial courses and programs have, unsurprisingly, rarely enjoyed institutional stability. In recent years, however, there has been a dramatic shift to curtail or even outright eliminate remediation in higher education (Mangan, 2013; Parker et al., 2014). This veritable "war on remediation" (Fain, 2012; Flannery, 2014; Landesman, 1999) has evolved as pressure increases to push students through college toward degree completion as quickly as possible.

Innovative models such as stretch (Melzer, 2005), studio (Grego & Thompson, 2007), and, most notably corequisite models such as the Accelerated Learning Program developed by Peter Adams and his colleagues at the Community College of Baltimore County (Adams et al., 2009) provide students with additional support as they progress through their coursework, while also making remediation less visible to administrators and other stakeholders. Tassoni's contribution to this volume offers another example of the ways in which BW is rendered invisible at the institutional level, although, as he noted, "multiple institutional sites intersected with, foreshadowed, and named-without-naming the demographic, economic, pedagogical, and architectural matters shaping trajectories of BW at the school." The efforts that make BW less visible, coupled with the pressure that BW instructors often face to reform developmental education with the goal of moving students through their degree programs more quickly (Two-Year College English Association, 2014), speak to a need for developmental educators to be included in the broader (often beyond the institution) conversations about developmental education (Two-Year College English Association, 2014).

When it comes to the administration of a basic writing program, it is important for WPAs to consider ideologies that are shaped by discourses beyond the university, as the influence of the popular media, legislative efforts, and nonprofit organizations can quite literally make or break a program. Despite this reality—one that is all too familiar to those of us who specialize in basic writing—there is little scholarship in WPA studies that looks closely at how a WPA responsible for a basic writing program might negotiate these external forces. The challenge lies in identifying where such conversations are taking place and, importantly, where power is concentrated in these extra-institutional discursive networks. The aim of this chapter is to examine one small portion of the discursive network centered on developmental education reform through an analysis of the following series of documents: the report titled *Remediation: Higher Education's Bridge to Nowhere* published by Complete College America (CCA) in 2012, *The New York Times* coverage of remediation from 2012–2019, and official documents from the state of Connecticut's highly-publicized shift away from traditional remediation, PA-1240. As Latour (2005) argued, a close reading of documents offers a useful method for analyzing an actor-network. Examining the processes through which a network forms requires, according to Latour, an analysis of the documents produced by different actors in a network to reveal the ways in which the network has been codified. My analysis reveals that nonprofit organizations such as CCA have heavily influenced the development of a crisis discourse surrounding developmental education, one that is strengthened through its circulation through intermediaries including the popular press and state legislators. The strength of this network has ensured that the notion that developmental education does not work and must be reduced or eliminated has become what Latour might refer to as a "black box," or a settled matter that represents an established fact. The problem with "black box" theories, Latour (1988) argued, is that they often hide the complexity of a topic behind the guise of an established truth (in this case, that developmental education is problematic and demands reform). What actor-network theory offers here is an analysis of *how* the "truth" that developmental education needs reform has been constructed through an assemblage of actors, mediators, and intermediaries, as well as through the creation of anti-groups that help to affirm boundaries within the network while also delegitimizing other perspectives (Braga & Suarez, 2018).

COMPLETE COLLEGE AMERICA AND DEVELOPMENTAL EDUCATION REFORM

In *Writing and School Reform*, Joanne Addison and Sharon James McGee (2016) analyzed the networks of influence on higher education policy that stem from high-stakes testing and, perhaps even more importantly, the agendas of private foundations. Their analysis centers primarily on the expansion and support of the Common Core Standards, with particular emphasis on the influence of the Bill and Melinda Gates Foundation, an organization that has provided a great deal of funding support to the Common Core Initiative. Importantly, Addison and McGee note the financial support from the Gates Foundation extends beyond "just the research, design, and implementation of the Standards" to include "how they are funding supporting networks," such as the National Writing Project where they have had opportunity to influence Common Core pedagogy as well (2016, p. 46). Through the development of the support network, nonprofits such as the Gates Foundation are able to exercise influence over multiple nodes in the network, strengthening their links and reinforcing a consistent message that is ultimately accepted as a black-boxed "truth."

The influence of the Gates Foundation on Common Core is but one example of the impact that a private non-profit organization can have on education policy and practice. One of the most powerful actors behind developmental education reform—influencing both the popular media and legislators—is CCA, a non-profit organization that has been heavily funded by the Bill and Melinda Gates Foundation. In materials related to college completion initiatives, CCA is regularly (and often uncritically) cited as a source of significant evidence in favor of eliminating traditional remedial sequences to move students toward graduation more quickly. The influence of the Gates Foundation in particular has been noted by Katherine Mangan (2013) as "unprecedented," largely due to his work through his own foundation and "intermediaries like Complete College America" (para. 2). Mangan furthers, "The influence of a major foundation and its grantees in state policy discussions makes some experts uncomfortable, since as a private entity Gates is not accountable to voters. They contend that the strategy bypasses colleges themselves and imposes top-down solutions, seeking quick fixes for complicated problems" (para. 5). As Nicholas Tampio (2019) has noted, the Gates Foundation offered strong support for the eventual implementation of Common Core Standards and, in the spring of 2019, announced a focused effort to engage in educational lobbying to define the value of a college degree, a move that Tampio argued will "disrupt higher education." Moreover, Philip Kovacs and Hazel Christie (2008) suggest Gates' funding supports "organizations [that] perpetuate discourses and narratives that stand in opposition to democratic school alternatives, ultimately reducing the likelihood that democratic school reform will ever take place" (p. 12).

In terms of basic writing, the work of CCA has been foundational to the construction of what has come to be known as the "completion agenda" (Lester, 2014; Two-Year College English Association, 2014). The completion agenda, promoted by "aims to collect more and better data about students' educational progress toward degrees, to enact new policies that incentivize increased graduation rates and improve the efficiency of degree production, and to tie funding to increased completion rates" (Humphreys, 2012), was spurred forward by President Obama's 2020 College Completion Initiative, which challenged colleges and universities to create clearer pathways for students to progress toward degree attainment (Pierce, 2015). While on the surface these appear to be laudable goals, little attention is paid to the complex circumstances that impact students' ability to complete coursework, leading to policy decisions that have far-reaching impacts on basic writing (Two-Year College English Association, 2014).

CCA: DEVELOPMENTAL EDUCATION REFORM AND "REMEDIATION: HIGHER EDUCATION'S BRIDGE TO NOWHERE"

The homepage of the CCA website immediately frames remediation as an educational crisis, emphasizing with red shading that "barriers to student success are clear: low credit enrollment, poorly designed and delivered remedial education, overwhelming and unclear choices, and a system out of touch with the needs of students who must often balance work and family with their coursework" ("Homepage"). To address this "crisis," CCA advocates a number of initiatives, including rethinking remedial education to include co-requisite courses that provide "just in time support," in favor of stand-alone remediation. The presence of crisis rhetoric is unsurprising here; Addison and McGee's (2016) analysis reveals that calls for accountability in response to crisis discourse and the exertion of influence from philanthropic organizations have a long history of interconnectedness, as crisis discourse fuels the perceived need for structured interventions, for example, standardized tests or privately-sponsored initiatives.

To highlight a perceived crisis in developmental education, CCA published a scathing and widely-cited 2012 report titled *Remediation: Higher Education's Bridge to Nowhere*. In this report, CCA reinforces the persistent message that remedial coursework is unquestionably a barrier to success. The "bridge to nowhere" is illustrated on the document's cover, with a graphic of a partially constructed bridge that repeats throughout the document to illustrate that remedial courses allow students to fall rather than cross safely to the next stage of their academic careers.

The negative association between remediation and college completion (the primary agenda of CCA) is made evident with a juxtaposition with drop-out rates. According to the report:

> Remediation is a classic case of system failure:
>
> Dropout exit ramp #1: Too many students start in remediation. More than 50 percent of students entering two-year colleges and nearly 20 percent of those entering four-year universities are placed in remedial classes. Frustrated about their placement into remediation, thousands who were accepted into college never show up for classes. With so many twists and turns, the road ahead doesn't seem to lead to graduation. Can an "open access" college be truly open access if it denies so many access to its college-level courses?
>
> Dropout exit ramp #2: Remediation doesn't work. Nearly 4 in 10 remedial students in community colleges never complete their remedial courses. Research shows that students who skip their remedial assignments do just as well in gateway courses as those who took remediation first. Never wanting to be in a remedial class in the first place and often feeling that they'll never get to full-credit courses, too many remedial students quit before ever starting a college class.
>
> Dropout exit ramp #3: Too few complete gateway courses. Having survived the remediation gauntlet, not even a quarter of remedial community college students ultimately complete college-level English and math courses — and little more than a third of remedial students at four-year schools do the same.
>
> Dropout exit ramp #4: Too few students graduate. Fewer than 1 in 10 graduate from community colleges within three years and little more than a third complete bachelor's degrees in six years (2012, pp. 2–3).

The emphasis here on "dropout exit ramps" is noteworthy, as it serves to align developmental courses with not simply slower progress toward a degree, but rather students' giving up altogether. In this report, CCA also emphasizes a racial disparity, pointing out that remediation can be a "dead end," symbolized by dead end yellow road sign throughout the report, accompanied by extensive lists of percentages that reflect student success in remediation based on racial demographics, a rhetorical move that implies that remedial courses inhibit the success of students from historically marginalized communities (2012, p. 6).[2] Additionally, the beginning of the report asks "Can an 'open access' college be truly open access if it denies so many access to its college-level courses?" (2012, p. 2). This language suggests that appeals to equity and accessible education from developmental educators and faculty at open-admissions institutions who support developmental education are divorced from the reality that students who enroll in those courses face and, in fact, ultimately do more harm than good to students who are academically at-risk. This powerful rhetorical move on the part of the authors of the CCA document shifts agency from professionals in the field and instead redirects it to CCA and its related initiatives.

To further establish its own expertise, for each of the above "dropout exit ramps," CCA proposes a solution: to prevent students from needing remediation, implement Common Core Standards in high schools, a move that directly reflects the values of the Gates Foundation (Addison & McGee, 2016). If current remedial models don't work, the report suggests, replace them with a co-requisite model and/or embedded tutoring. To help students progress through gateway courses, CCA suggests that extra support time is built into the credit-bearing class, such as in the co-requisite model, rather than offered in a separate, non-credited course.

THE POPULAR MEDIA AS ACTOR

In Latour's construction of ANT, documents exert agency as non-human actors that comprise a network. He wrote: "Instead of simply transporting effects without transforming them, each of the points in the text may become a bifurcation, an event, or the origin of a new translation. As soon as actors are treated not as intermediaries but as mediators, they render the movement of the social visible to the reader" (Latour, 2005, p. 128). Jenna Morton-Aiken's chapter in this volume further argues that textual evidence (archival records in her case) can allow WPAs to identify structures that might otherwise be invisible, allowing for a deeper critical reflection on existing knowledge. Below, I apply a similar logic to an analysis of *The New York Times* coverage of remediation to make visible the extent to which *The New York Times* has served as an intermediary for CCA's argument about reform in developmental education.

---

2   This assessment is true in some instances, particularly when placement into and advancement from BW courses is based primarily on the goal of assimilating students into a standard academic discourse (see Grayson in this collection). At the same time, however, BW courses can also provide needed time for students who, for a variety of reasons, may benefit from a slower pace and additional instructional support. While reform in some areas of developmental education is needed, I would argue that eliminating it entirely or dramatically reducing its availability can also introduce new barriers for some students.

BASIC WRITING IN THE POPULAR PRESS

The popular press functions as a non-human actor in the broader network of discourse about remediation and, as has been well-documented in the field's scholarship, often reifies the notion that remediation is ineffective and damaging to an institution's status. In "How We Failed the Basic Writing Enterprise," published as an open letter to the editors of *Journal of Basic Writing*, Lynn Quitman Troyka (2000) highlighted the many opportunities she perceives that basic writing as a field has missed to stabilize its image beyond the academy. Specifically, Troyka wrote, "Didn't we realize that most consumers of media, white- and blue-collar workers, professionals, homemakers, community leaders, legislators, educational administrators, and even faculty and students would be frankly repelled by what aspiring college students clearly did not know?" She continues, "Why did we not anticipate that the 114 newspapers, eager to sensationalize, would jump on the chance to print examples of college basic writers' writing before they took catch-up courses?" (pp. 114–115). Troyka's reference here is to an example of crisis rhetoric (Addison & McGee, 2016) that surrounded *The New York Times* review of Mina Shaughnessy's Errors and Expectations in 1979, a review that included the publication of some unedited writing produced by students in basic writing courses (Dember, 1975).

Published just a few short years after the now-infamous "Why Johnny Can't Write" *Newsweek* (Sheils, 1975) article that, according to Trimbur (1991), sparked the notion that the United States was facing a literacy crisis, *The New York Times*' publication of unedited writing from students placed into remedial courses did little to bolster public opinion about the writing abilities of that generation's newly admitted college students. Decades later, the discourse of literacy crisis reappears with *The New York Times* reviews of James Traub's (1994) controversial book, *City on a Hill: Testing the American Dream at City College*. In what was later honored as a New York Times Notable Book (Otte & Mlynarczyk, 2010), Traub offered an inside look at basic writing courses at City College, to evaluate the success of the Open Admissions experiment at CUNY. In an overwhelmingly positive review of *City on a Hill*, A. M. Rosenthall (1994) wrote of City College: "The admission requirement, Mr. Traub explained, was reduced drastically . . . Given the quality of education in so many New York City high schools by then, that was simply surrendering to mediocrity, and everybody knew it" (p. 7). The implication here is not subtle, as Rosenthall suggests that Traub's work reveals that Open Admissions—and its byproduct, remedial course offerings across CUNY—served to do little more than lower the standards of a once-great institution. The positive attention that Traub's work received was echoed in the coming years as *The New York Times* reported on the phase-out of remediation at CUNY's senior colleges in the late 1990s, much of which emphasized the watering-down of curriculum that was the natural byproduct of a senior college offering developmental courses (see Arenson, 1998; Gleason, 2000).

Given that *The New York Times* has long been recognized as an influential actor in the construction of the public image of remediation, it is important to consider how the paper has continued to cover remediation and developmental education in the current era of reform. In the section below, I offer a brief analysis of the relationships between actors and the discursive construction of remediation as a crisis in a small corpus of *The New York Times* coverage of remediation from 2012–2019.

REMEDIATION IS A ROADBLOCK TO STUDENT SUCCESS

Overwhelmingly, the articles I examined emphasized the notion that placement into remedial courses is a hindrance to student success and completion. This position was expressed by acknowledging two studies that "have found that community colleges unnecessarily place tens of thousands of entering students into remedial classes" (Lewin, 2012, para. 1). Alina Tugend (2016) extends this claim to add that colleges should "require fewer remedial classes to improve students' basic math and English skills." In another article, Lewin (2014) points out that "1.7 million students begin college in remediation . . . but only one in 10 remedial students ever graduate" (para. 7). Elizabeth Harris (2017) similarly wrote of remedial courses that "many students, frustrated that they are sitting in class without progressing toward a degree, drop out" (para. 2). Though *The New York Times* coverage has been consistent in suggesting that remedial courses are detrimental to student success, it is worth noting that much of this discourse has been constructed within the context of community college reform. In other words, dramatic changes to remediation are contextualized as one of several needed changes at the community college level, including better placement measures, more advising, and lower costs, all of which is closely aligned with the work of CCA and other proponents of the Completion Agenda. Despite these other concerns, though, the push to eliminate or radically reduce remediation is prominent in this coverage, thus providing a significant contribution to national conversations about these topics.

NAMED ACTORS/ACTANTS IN *THE NEW YORK TIMES* COVERAGE OF REMEDIATION

In the case of *The New York Times* coverage of remediation from 2012–2019, there was a great deal of consistency in terms of the actors who were most often named in the articles that I analyzed. Surprisingly, non-profit organizations were among the most frequently referenced sources of data about remediation and/or college completion rates across the corpus I analyzed. These nonprofits are listed below, along with indications of their relationships with CCA that were evident after a quick Google search of each one.

President of Education Trust

The president of Education Trust served as keynote speaker at the "2019 CCA Annual Convening" (Complete College America, 2019).

Jobs for the Future

Co-author with Complete College America on a report titled "Core Principles for Transforming Remedial Education" and recipient of $17 million in funding from the Gates Foundation. (Mangan, 2013).

National Center for Education Statistics

Their report "Remedial Coursetaking at U.S. Public 2- and 4-Year Institutions: Scope, Experience, and Outcomes" cites the CCA's *Remediation: Higher education's bridge to nowhere* report (Chen & Simone, 2016).

Gates Foundation

Complete College America was established with funding from the Gates Foundation (Mangan, 2013). The Gates Foundation provided almost 1.5 million in funding to Complete College America in 2020 (Complete College America, 2020).

Brookings Institute

Their article "Addressing Academic Barriers to Higher Education" cites data from Complete College America (Long, 2014).

American Association of Community Colleges

Their report "The State of College Completion Initiatives at U.S. Community Colleges" noted that data from Complete College America is controversial (Kilgore & Wilson, 2017).

The Writing Revolution

No obvious mention of Complete College America.

National Association on Teacher Quality

No obvious mention of Complete College America.

It is important to note that non-profit organizations (and their spokespeople) were referenced more frequently in these articles than were research centers associated with universities. In other words, the work of these non-profits (many of which translate the work of CCA) is forwarded through *The New York Times* coverage more than is scholarly work from research centers associated with universities. The research centers named included the Center on Education Policy at George Washington University, Pennsylvania's Alliance for Higher Education and Democracy at University of Pennsylvania, and Columbia Teachers College.

While these actors all provide perspectives that are useful in understanding current trends in remedial education, it is noteworthy that no specialists in rhetoric and composition were explicitly named (though several specific instructors at CUNY campuses were identified); the majority of the information that circulates in *The New York Times* coverage about remediation is based on perspectives from non-profits, research centers at institutions that do not offer remedial coursework, and, at times, college administrators. Individuals who specialize in teaching developmental courses are rarely referenced in these articles, further reinforcing the point that the prominent discourses about remediation are influenced by external actors. One article goes so far as to declare that "there is a notable shortage of high-quality research on the teaching of writing" (Goldstein, 2017, para. 35). Although basic writing has been heralded by some scholars as the starting point for the professionalization of the modern field of composition studies (Horner, 2000), that such a field of study even exists is hardly visible in these articles. While Goldstein's article does reflect some knowledge of composition studies' emphasis on the writing process, there is virtually nothing in any of the articles included in this study that points to expertise in rhetoric and composition to contextualize some of the concerns raised in the studies sponsored by non-profit organizations and university research centers. Given the already-marginalized status that basic writing typically enjoys in most institutions (Otte & Mlynarczyk, 2010), this erasure of disciplinary expertise in the public discourse about remediation is troubling. Add to that the emphasis on perspectives of non-profit organizations (many of which are associated with CCA), and it becomes clear that CCA exercises a great deal of influence over how the discourse about remediation and college completion is constructed for public audiences.

LEGISLATIVE INFLUENCE ON BASIC WRITING

The popular media is far from the only source of influential discourse about developmental education and remediation. At the state-level, developmental writing courses are increasingly influenced by legislative agendas. According to the Center for the Analysis of Postsecondary Readiness, 56 pieces of legislation that addressed developmental education were introduced across the country in 2017 and 15 were enacted, signifying that legislation does, in fact, play a critical role in the ways that developmental courses are structured and funded, along with how students are placed into such courses (Whinnery, 2017).

The influence of this so-called "legislative activism" has largely been the reduction, elimination, or complete reform of developmental reading and writing programs across entire states (Otte & Mlynarczyk, 2010; Schrynemakers et al., 2019). The Education Commission of the States identifies 33 states that have legislated placement and/or assessment policies for developmental courses (Education Commission of the States, 2022). The same source also highlights 26 states that have legislated the delivery and/or curriculum of developmental courses in formats such as corequisite course offerings, stretch models, studio or mandatory tutoring, and/or summer bridge programs—notably absent here are stand-alone developmental courses, which are becoming increasingly unpopular (Education Commission of the States, 2022). Miller et al. (2017) point to such examples in Florida, Wisconsin, and Idaho in anticipation of the potential for legislative interference into developmental courses in the Pennsylvania State system where they teach, noting concern that they might lose the credit-bearing developmental course at their institution in favor of a "reformed" alternative (p. 1).

PUBLIC ACT 12-40 IN CONNECTICUT

One example of how this larger network connects to a specific local context is the enactment of a statewide policy shift for developmental education, Connecticut State Colleges and Universities (2012) Public Act 12-40 subtitled "An act concerning college readiness and completion." This legislation focused explicitly to direct "public community colleges and state universities to reconfigure how remedial/developmental education is delivered," with three available options: college-level courses, college-level with embedded support, or an intensive college readiness program OR one semester of remediation (Connecticut, 2012, p. 1). In the case of the latter, students should progress to college-level coursework within a semester (Connecticut, 2012, p. 1). The legislation was initially proposed after a state legislator "attended a 'remediation institute' hosted by Complete College America" (Mangan, 2013).

Fain's (2012) report on PA 12-40 for *Inside Higher Ed* framed this move as a legislative effort to eliminate remediation across the state (though the official documents for PA 12-40 suggest otherwise). In the *NEA Today* article, Flannery (2014) referred to the legislation in Connecticut, Florida, Tennessee, and Georgia, "the war on remediation" (p. 4). This "war on remediation" could, as many have noted, result in some significant educational cost to students. Patrick Sullivan (2015) offers an insider's perspective on the implementation of PA 12-40 initiatives on his own campus at Manchester Community College. He noted one of the most controversial elements of the new legislation was that it pushed students who had placed below a standardized test cut-off out of college classrooms, as they were initially to be "remediated" at adult literacy centers before beginning college coursework. After some debate, the Connecticut community colleges and regional universities were permitted to develop transitional programming for these weakest students, ensuring that they wouldn't be denied access to higher education, but, as Sullivan noted, the original goal of dramatically reducing remedial offerings was eyed as a potential model for other statewide reforms across the United States.

The official documents generated for PA 12-40 include the senate bill itself, a two-page document that highlights the goals of the bill, and a 45-page report of results after the first year of implementation (State of Connecticut, 2012; Connecticut State Colleges and Universities, 2012; Brakoniecki et al., 2013). An analysis of this discourse identifies a discursive emphasis on three areas also visible in *The New York Times* coverage of remediation: the problem of high-stakes placement testing, the problem of low completion rates for students who begin in remedial courses, and the lack of alignment between high school and college curricula. Of particular concern for developmental educators was the move to dramatically shift the delivery of remedial coursework. According to the bill:

> Not later than the start of the fall semester of 2014 and for each semester thereafter, no public institution of higher education shall offer any remedial support, including remedial courses, that is not embedded with the corresponding entry level course, as required pursuant to subsection (b) of this section, or offered as part of an intensive college readiness program, except such institution may offer a student a maximum of one semester of remedial support that is not embedded, provided (1) such support is intended to advance such student toward earning a degree, and (2) the program of remedial support is approved by the Board of Regents for Higher Education. (State of Connecticut, 2012, p. 2)

The subtext here is that stand-alone remediation is not an effective approach for helping students to advance toward degree completion, an echo of the discourse of remediation reform that is also evident in *The New York Times* coverage. The supplemental document noted that "Common methods of remedial education are not successful for most students. Only 8% of community college students taking remedial courses earn a credential within three years" again invoking the discourse of reform (Connecticut State Colleges and Universities, 2012, p. 2).

The same document also includes a subtext which suggests that secondary education in Connecticut was not providing adequate instruction to prepare graduates for college-level work. This is visible in the bill's emphasis on implementing Common Core standards in Connecticut high schools and alignment of high school and college curricula, noting that because many students have not been engaged with Common Core curriculum, "Connecticut State Colleges and Universities, as well as other higher education institutions, have been partnering with priority school districts to redesign 12th grade math and English courses in order to minimize remediation needs" (Connecticut State Colleges and Universities, 2012, p. 2). In addition to its emphasis on the problematic nature of remediation, the above quote also suggests that a Common Core curriculum in high school has the potential to "solve" the remedial "problem" in the state, a position that fails to acknowledge the sociocultural and socioeconomic disparities that might influence a student's academic trajectory. The document *does* acknowledge that "African American, Hispanic and low-income students are disproportionately enrolled in remedial and developmental courses (72%, 70%, and 71% respectively, compared to 56% for White students and 29% for non-low-income students)" (Connecticut State Colleges and Universities, 2012, p. 1). But without context, those statistics do not offer a full picture of *why* students who represent these demographic groups often place into remediation and/or why such placement might impact completion.

More attention to the material and cultural concerns that often impact students' placement into remedial courses is evident in a section of the 2013 report by Brakoniecki et al. summarizing feedback from stakeholder surveys—after the bill was already passed into law. These survey results highlight some important challenges that students who place into remedial courses might face that simple skills assessments might not address. First, the socioeconomic needs of students are hinted at with the acknowledgment that access to technology is necessary and that online learning might be a barrier for some students. Perhaps most important, however, is the statement referring to "personal/life challenges" that impede student success (Brakoniecki et al., 2013, p. 23). As any basic writing instructor knows too well, students disappear from class for any number of reasons, few of which are generally academic in nature and instead are rooted in the socioeconomic and personal circumstances that too often impact student success (Whitfield, 2014). Additionally, the report acknowledged, "Students needed additional support through the registration process for their next semesters," which speaks to the difficulty that many students have with negotiating the bureaucracy and culture of college life, rather than their abilities to write grammatical sentences (Brakoniecki et al., 2013,

p. 23). As basic writing and developmental education scholarship suggests, students' personal challenges, socioeconomic backgrounds and access to funding and money, and abilities to navigate academic systems and networks are not *some of* the problems that students who place into remedial courses face; rather, these are *the* problems that hinder retention and persistence (see Adler-Kassner & Harrington, 2002; Soliday, 2002; Sullivan, 2015). Relegating these significant obstacles to a few lines results in a significant disconnect between disciplinary expertise and the legislative discourse regarding developmental education reform.

IMPLICATIONS FOR BASIC WRITING

The formation of an actor-network is dependent on the ability of a "key actor [to] successfully [align] a series of other elements [actants]" (Michael, 2017, p. 34) and to form associations with other actors (Latour, 2005). It is clear from the examples above that CCA has succeeded to form an actor-network by utilizing *The New York Times* and state legislatures to serve as intermediaries of its message regarding the need for reform in developmental education. To be sure, there is value in the initiatives that CCA promotes, and in certain institutional contexts, eliminating remedial courses in favor of another model works well. The work of teacher-scholars such as Peter Adams and his colleagues at the Community College of Baltimore County and Katie Hern of the California Acceleration Project has been invaluable in providing new pathways for supporting students who might otherwise fail to meet benchmarks for enrollment in credit-bearing composition courses. Additionally, Complete College America and the Gates Foundation have provided funding for countless important postsecondary initiatives across the country. Dismissing out of hand the positive impacts of these organizations and their missions would be a mistake.

At the same time, while it is crucial to avoid a situation wherein students are stuck in a remedial sequence for so long that it deters their progress, the corequisite model that is increasingly put forth as an alternative is not a panacea and nudging underprepared students forward more quickly does not necessarily meet every student's needs equally (Adams et al., 2009). Alexandros Goudas and Hunter Boylan (2012) argued that "to put the blame squarely on the shoulders of developmental education for its students' low completion rates, as most recent remedial research does, is an overgeneralization that does not account for other factors that contribute to high dropout rates" (p. 6). The CCA documents fail to acknowledge the complexity of college completion for students from diverse backgrounds, particularly for two-year college students who often must "stop-out" for personal reasons and therefore may not complete a degree in a designated time frame (Ernst et al., 2015, p. 4). In a presentation for the 2018

National Association of Developmental Education conference, D. Patrick Saxon et al. directly address the extent to which the relationship between placement in developmental courses and attrition is drawn from "seriously flawed research or [has] been misrepresented by advocacy groups to support their agenda," citing CCA as a specific example. Elsewhere, CCA has been critiqued for its work to target state governments and legislatures as sites for educational change by pushing performance-based funding models (Walters, 2012) and failing to acknowledge the complex socioeconomic, linguistic, and cultural concerns that might inhibit student progress toward a degree. As Tassoni notes in this volume, Basic Writing can easily function as a "retrofit" to a "core institutional identity," one that is not inclusive to the demographic of students that BW courses often support. His work illustrates the local impact of ignoring the socioeconomic and cultural forces that often shape BW.

The above is only a small representation of the evidence-based critiques that push back against the notion that developmental education is inherently damaging to students' chances of success. Rather than appearing in the pages of the popular press or in official documents or statements from state legislatures, these critiques are largely confined to the pages of scholarly journals with a much more limited readership. Richard Besel (2011) pointed to Latour's argument that in scientific discourse, "black box" theories are established "only after a particular theory has emerged victorious in this agnostic process against its competitors that it becomes reality and knowledge" (p. 124). By exerting influence across multiple nodes of the discursive network that surrounds basic writing and developmental education, including the popular press and state legislators, CCA has been able to establish a "truth" simply by engaging enough actors to repeat and reinforce the same message and pushing its critiques to the margins. As Jeanne Gunner (2002) noted, dramatic changes to a program that are supported exclusively by theory or scholarship from composition are "likely to have little effect on the larger ideological values that form the programs we administer and teach" (p. 8). In the current moment, only a fraction of the voices of experts in basic writing and developmental education are gaining traction in public discourse—namely those who are aligned with powerful non-profit organizations that are pushing an agenda of reform. While there is value in those perspectives, they are not the only perspectives on developmental education.

IMPLICATIONS FOR WRITING PROGRAM ADMINISTRATORS

Cultivating an awareness of the actor-networks that exert influence over writing programs is an essential skill for writing program administrators, one that is often framed through studies of institutional ecologies. Mary Jo Reiff et al. (2015) signaled a need for scholarship in writing program administration to read the complex and interconnected work of writing programs in ecological terms arguing that it's essential to "reveal the dynamic interrelationships as well as the complex rhetorical and material conditions that writing programs inhabit—conditions and relationships that are constantly in flux as WPAs negotiate constraint and innovation" (p. 16). Increasingly, teacher-scholars have incorporated critical analysis of the ways that WPA work functions within these complex networks into discussions of graduate training for future instructors and program administrators that focuses on scenario-based learning (Sura et al., 2009) and disciplinary reading (Reid, 2018). Overwhelmingly, though, existing work in this area focuses on locally-situated examples and fails to examine the larger social and discursive networks that exert pressure onto these local contexts.

In *Basic Writing as a Political Act*, Linda Adler-Kassner and Susanmarie Harrington (2002) recall a point made elsewhere by Joe Harris that "compositionists have a history of not communicating well why and how we do what we do to outside audiences" (p. 62). Rather than reacting to policy shifts (as many locally-focused profiles of BW illustrate), teacher-scholars in basic writing must make every effort to craft an effective public message about our field and the many different forms successful developmental support might take. These efforts are best begun in our local contexts, by encouraging administrators and trustees to consider the whole student with concrete examples of academic and personal successes and setbacks. Additionally, we must push back against the notion that developmental instruction is inherently a barrier for students from historically marginalized communities and instead take a more nuanced look at why some students benefit from basic writing courses while others do not. Much of the discourse that circulates about developmental education reform is situated in community college contexts, which are not universally the same across the country, nor are they the same as four-year institutions. Additionally, much of the discourse that pushes against the existence of basic writing courses and programs centers on the racism inherent in placing students based on evaluations that measure little more than linguistic diversity and socioeconomic status. I am in full agreement that such standards should be modified and, where appropriate, eliminated entirely. At the same time, however, basic writing courses have the potential to serve broader purposes and populations, including returning adult learners and adult basic skills students, students with disabilities who need a slower pace, students who are struggling with the cognitive impacts of trauma or mental health challenges, students who are just learning to speak English as an additional language, and students for whom the burdens of work and or home life make concentration difficult and an accelerated course pace nearly impossible.

Because basic writing programs are so deeply entwined with extra-disciplinary and extra-institutional networks and their discursive constructions of remediation, it is important that any WPA whose work includes the oversight of a basic writing program be attuned to these broader conversations to avoid repeating some of the failures that Troyka noted as endemic to the field. With that, a strict adherence to "Ed White's Law—assess thyself or assessment will be done unto thee" is also essential (Griffiths et al., 2017, para. 14). Strong assessment data can provide locally-focused counternarratives about remediation that can push back against the "war on remediation" that has eliminated or redefined developmental course offerings across the country. There is research that indicates that the elimination of remedial courses may actually disadvantage students from historically minoritized communities, if those students are also not close to the cutoff between remediation and mainstream courses (Boatman & Long, 2018).

The above were arguments that my writing program colleagues and I recently had to make in response to a suggestion from administrators that we eliminate one of our basic writing courses to allow students to move more quickly to graduation. While armed with scholarship and our own institutional data that illustrated a dramatic difference in need between students in all of our course levels, it was essential that we, as Tassoni describes in his chapter in this volume, "consider[ed] the extent to which these meetings coursed in a machinery we needed to better understand; our work existed in relation to these other parts of the system." Teacher-scholars in basic writing have long lamented the impact of stakeholders elsewhere in the institution and beyond on their programs (Reid, 2018). But to date, the field is lacking a comprehensive mapping of the actor-networks that are largely responsible for framing the national conversation about remediation. What are the black-boxed "truths" about remediation that are uncritically circulated? What individuals or organizations are driving these conversations and why? How many courses and programs have been altered or eliminated based on data that can be traced back to a single source? Morton-Aiken argues in her chapter in this volume that the curation of archives has the potential to reveal networks and illuminate connections that might otherwise be invisible to researchers. I argue that by applying this logic to a study of discourses that surround developmental education, we can see not only what those discourses are, but also how they circulate and what their tangible impacts might be.

To be clear, I agree with the notion that many approaches to developmental education in the US are in need of reform (including on my own home campus). But as Mary Soliday (2002) pointed out in *The Politics of Remediation,* institutions will always rely on attracting less-prepared students in times of economic crisis, often without the resources to support those same students through their coursework. To ensure that appropriate support is available for all students across a range of institutional contexts, it is imperative that rhetoric and composition program administrators combat the notion that a widely-adopted practice, such as eliminating remediation, is necessarily always the best practice in all scenarios. In a future that is dominated by actor-networks that seek to eliminate remediation, the expertise of developmental educators and the needs of students from historically marginalized communities are too easily erased if courses dedicated to these interests are eliminated. Without the input of administrator-teacher-scholars with expertise in basic writing, the extra-disciplinary forces presented above—the popular media, state legislatures, and non-profit organizations—rather than disciplinary experts will shape the future of basic writing in the United States.

REFERENCES

Adams, P., Gearhart, S., Miller, R. & Roberts, A. (2009). The accelerated learning program: Throwing open the gates. *Journal of Basic Writing, 28*(2), 50–69. https://doi.org/10.37514/jbw-j.2009.28.2.04.

Addison, J. & McGee, S. J. (2016). *Writing and school reform: Writing instruction in the age of common core and standardized testing*. The WAC Clearinghouse; University Press of Colorado. https://doi.org/10.37514/per-b.2016.0773.

Adler-Kassner, L. & Harrington, S. (2002). *Basic writing as a political act*. Hampton Press.

Arenson, K. (1998). Pataki-Giuliani plan would curb CUNY colleges' remedial work. *New York Times Online*. http://www.nytimes.com/1998/05/07/nyregion/pataki-giuliani-plan-would-curb-cuny-colleges-remedial-work.html.

Besel, R. (2011). Opening the "black box" of climate change science: Actor-network theory and rhetorical practice in scientific controversies. *Southern Communication Journal, 76*(2), 120–136.

Boatman, A. & Long, B. T. (2018). Does remediation work for all students? How the effects of postsecondary remedial and developmental courses vary by level of academic preparation. *Educational Evaluation and Policy Analysis, 40*(1), 29–58. https://doi.org/10.3102/0162373717715708.

Braga, C. & Suarez, M. (2018). Actor-network theory: new perspectives and contributions to consumption studies. *Cadernos EBAPE.BR, 16*(2), 218–231.

Brakoniecki, L., Fitzgerald, K. & Pritchard, A. (2013) An analysis of summer and fall 2013 developmental education pilots in Connecticut community colleges. *Connecticut Women's Education & Legal Fund*. http://www.ct.edu/files/pdfs/12-40-eval.pdf.

Chen, X. & Simone, S. (2016, September). Remedial coursetaking at U.S. public 2- and 4-year institutions: Scope, experiences, and outcomes. Statistical analysis report. *National Center for Education Statistics*. https://nces.ed.gov/pubs2016/2016405.pdf.

Complete College America. (2012). Remediation: Higher education's bridge to nowhere. https://completecollege.org/wp-content/uploads/2017/11/CCA-Remediation-final.pdf.

Complete College America. (2019). 2019 Annual Convening. *Complete College America.* https://completecollege.org/event/2019-annual-convening/.

Complete College America. (2020, January 9). *Complete college America receives nearly $1.5 million in grant funding.* Complete College America. https://completecollege.org/resource/complete-college-america-receives-nearly-1-5-million-in-grant-funding/.

Complete College America. (2022). Homepage. https://completecollege.org/

Connecticut State Colleges and Universities. (2012). Public Act 12-40, 1–2. https://www.ct.edu/files/pdfs/12-40-overview.pdf.

Dember, L. (1975, May 4). Capitalizing on poor writing. *The New York Times.* https://www.nytimes.com/1975/05/04/archives/capitalizing-on-poor-writing.html?searchResultPosition=2.

Education Commission of the States. (2022). *50-state comparison: Developmental education policies.* https://www.ecs.org/50-state-comparison-developmental-education-policies/.

Ernst, J., Guth, W., Hagen, C., Peterson, A. & Wolverton, T. (2015). Challenging the competition agenda. *At Issue, 5*(1), 1–8. https://www.ferris.edu/administration/academicaffairs/extendedinternational/ccleadership/publications/pdfs-docs/at-issue/AtIssue-2015_Challenging-the-Completion-Agenda.pdf.

Lester, J. (2014). The Completion Agenda: The unintended consequences for equity in community colleges. In M. B. Paulson (Ed.), *Higher education handbook of theory and practice* (Vol. 29, pp. 423–466). Springer.

Fain, P. (2012, June 19). Complete College America declares war on remediation. *Inside Higher Ed.* https://www.insidehighered.com/news/2012/06/19/complete-college-america-declares-war-remediation.

Flannery, M. E. (2014, November). The wrong answer on remediation. *NEA Higher Education Advocate, 31*(5), 3–5.

Gleason, B. (2000). Remediation phase-out at CUNY: The "equity versus excellence" controversy. *College Composition and Communication, 51*(3), 488–491.

Goldstein, D. (2017, August 2). Why kids can't write. *The New York Times.* https://www.nytimes.com/2017/08/02/education/edlife/writing-education-grammar-students-children.html.

Goudas, A. M. & Boylan, H. (2012). Addressing flawed research in developmental education. *Journal of Developmental Education, 36*(1), 2–6.

Grego, R. C. & Thompson, N. S. (2007). *Teaching/writing in thirdspaces: The studio approach.* National Council of Teachers of English.

Griffiths, B., Hickman, R. & Zöllner, S. (2017). Institutional assessment of a genre-analysis approach to writing center consultations. *Praxis: A Writing Center Journal, 15*(1), n.p. http://www.praxisuwc.com/griffiths-hickman-and-zoellner-151.

Gunner, J. (2002). Ideology, theory, and the genre of writing programs. In S. K. Rose & I. Weiser (Eds.), *The writing program administrator as theorist* (pp. 7–18). Boynton/Cook.

Harris, Elizabeth A. (2017, March 19). CUNY to revamp remedial programs, hoping to lift graduation rates. *The New York Times*. https://www.nytimes.com/2017/03/19/nyregion/cuny-remedial-programs.html.

Horner, B. (2000). Traditions and professionalization: Reconceiving work in composition. *College Composition and Communication, 51*(3), 366–398.

Humphreys, D. (2012). What's wrong with the completion agenda—and what we can do about it. *Liberal Education, 98*(1), n.p. https://eric.ed.gov/?id=EJ976714.

Kilgore, W. & Wilson, J. I. (2017). *The state of college completion initiatives at U.S. community colleges*. American Association of Collegiate Registrars and Admissions Officers. https://www.aacrao.org/docs/default-source/signature-initiative-docs/transfer/the-state-of-college-completion-initiatives-nbsp-at-u-s-community-colleges.pdf?sfvrsn=8589f844_4.

Kovacs, P. E. & Christie, H. K. (2008). The Gates' foundation and the future of U.S. public education: A call for scholars to counter misinformation campaigns. *Journal for Critical Education Policy Studies, 6*(2), 1–20.

Landesman, C. (1999). The remediation war at the City University of New York. *Academic Questions, 12*(4), 77–86.

Latour, B. (1988). *Science in action: How to follow scientists and engineers through society*. Harvard University Press.

Latour, B. (2005). *Reassembling the social: An introduction to actor-network theory*. Oxford University Press.

Lewin, T. (2012, February 29). Colleges misassign many to remedial classes, studies find. *The New York Times*. https://www.nytimes.com/2012/02/29/education/colleges-misassign-many-to-remedial-classes-studies-find.html.

Lewin, T. (2014, December 2). Most college students don't earn a degree in 4 years, study finds. *The New York Times*. https://www.nytimes.com/2014/12/02/education/most-college-students-dont-earn-degree-in-4-years-study-finds.html.

Levine-Brown, P. & Weiss, A. S. (2017). The current state of developmental education: An interview with Hunter R. Boylan. *Journal of Developmental Education, 4*(1), 18–22.

Long, B. T. (2014, June 19). Addressing the academic barriers to higher education. *Brookings Institute*. https://www.brookings.edu/research/addressing-the-academic-barriers-to-higher-education/.

Mangan, K. (2013, July 14). How Gates shapes state higher-education policy. *The Chronicle of Higher Education*. https://www.chronicle.com/article/how-gates-shapes-state-higher-education-policy/.

Melzer, D. (2005). Remedial, basic, advanced: Evolving frameworks for first-year composition at the California State University. *Journal of Basic Writing 34*(1), 81–106. https://doi.org/10.37514/jbw-j.2015.34.1.05.

Michael, M. (2017). *Actor-network theory: Trial, trails and translations*. Sage.

Miller, K., Wender, E. & Siegel-Finer, B. (2017). Legislating first-year writing placement: Implications for Pennsylvania and across the country. *The Journal of Writing Assessment 10*(1). http://journalofwritingassessment.org/article.php?article=119.

National Association on Teacher Quality. (2022). Homepage. *National Association on Teacher Quality.* https://www.nctq.org/.

Otte, G. & Mlynarczyk, R. (2010). The future of basic writing. *Journal of Basic Writing, 29*(1), 5–32. https://doi.org/10.37514/jbw-j.2010.29.1.02.

Parker, T. L., Barret, M. M. & Bustillos, L. T. (2014). *The State of developmental education: Higher education and public policy priorities.* Palgrave MacMillan.

Pierce, D. (2015). Building toward completion: Five years into President Obama's 2020 completion initiative, some community colleges find ways to move the needle on student success. *Community College Journal, 85*(4), 24–26.

Reid, L. (2018). Disciplinary reading in basic writing graduate education: The politics of remediation in JBW, 1995–2015. *Journal of Basic Writing, 37*(2), 6–34. ttps://doi.org/10.37514/jbw-j.2018.37.2.02.

Reiff, M. J., Bawarshi, A., Ballif, M. & Weisser, C. (2015). Writing program ecologies: An introduction. In M. J. Reiff, A. Bawarshi, M. Ballif & C. Weisser (Eds.), *Ecologies of writing programs: Program profiles in context* (pp. 3–18). Parlor Press.

Rosenthall, A. M. (1994). An American promise. *New York Times Book Review*, 7.

Saxon, D. P., Boylan, H. & Stahl, N. (2018, February 21–24). *The developmental education reform movement and the self-fulfilling prophecy.* National Association of Developmental Education Conference. [Conference presentation]. National Harbor, MD, United States.

Schrynemakers, I., Lane, C., Beckford, I. & K. Miseon. (2019). College readiness in post-remedial academia: Faculty observations from three urban community colleges. *Community College Enterprise, 25*(1), 10–31.

Sheils, M. (1975, December 8). Why Johnny can't write. *Newsweek*, 58. https://www.leetorda.com/uploads/2/3/2/5/23256940/why_johnny_cant_write__newsweek_1975___1_.pdf.

Soliday, M. (2002). T*he Politics of remediation: Student and institutional needs in higher education.* University of Pittsburgh Press.

State of Connecticut. (2012). Substitute Senate Bill No. 40, 1–3. https://www.cga.ct.gov/2012/act/pa/pdf/2012PA-00040-R00SB-00040-PA.pdf.

Sullivan, P. (2015). "Ideas about human possibilities": Connecticut's PA 12-40 and basic writing in the era of neoliberalism. *Journal of Basic Writing 34*(1), 44–80. https://doi.org/10.37514/jbw-j.2015.34.1.04.

Sura, T., Wells, J., Schoen, M., Elder, C. & Driscoll, D. (2009). Praxis and allies: The WPA board game. *WPA: Writing program administration, 32*(3), 75–88.

Tampio, N. (2019, May 16). New Gates-funded commission aims to put value on college education. *Associated Press* https://www.apnews.com/8fc174e4bb59213eb441f43e56584be2.

Traub, J. (1994). *City on a hill: Testing the American dream at city college.* Perseus Books.

Trimbur, J. (1991). Literacy and the discourse of crisis. In R. Schuster & J. Trimbur (Eds.), *The politics of writing instruction: Postsecondary* (pp. 277–295). Boynton/Cook.

Troyka, L. Q. (2000). How we failed the basic writing enterprise. *Journal of Basic Writing 19*(1), 113–123. https://doi.org/10.37514/jbw-j.2000.19.1.11.

Tugend, A. (2016, June 23). Revamping community colleges to improve graduation rates. *The New York Times.* https://www.nytimes.com/2016/06/23/education/revamping-community-colleges-to-improve-graduation-rates.html.

Two-Year College Association. (2014, March). TYCA White paper on developmental education reforms. *Teaching English in the Two-Year College,* 227–243. National Council of Teachers of English. https://cdn.ncte.org/nctefiles/groups/tyca/develop_educ_reforms.pdf.

Walters, G. (2012). It's not so easy: The completion agenda and the states. *Liberal Education* 98(1), 34–39.

Whinnery, E. (2017, Oct. 20). 2017 developmental state action update. *Center for the Analysis of Postsecondary Readiness.* https://postsecondaryreadiness.org/2017-developmental-education-state-legislative-action-update/.

Whitfield, P. (2014, May 9). Why teaching developmental English breaks my heart. *Inside Higher Ed.* https://www.insidehighered.com/views/2014/05/09/why-teaching-developmental-english-breaks-my-heart-essay.

The Writing Revolution. (2022). Homepage. *The Writing Revolution.* https://www.thewritingrevolution.org/.

CHAPTER 7.

WORKING WITHIN THE RHETORICAL CONSTRAINTS: RENOVATION AND RESISTANCE IN A FIRST-YEAR WRITING PROGRAM

Mara Lee Grayson
California State University, Dominguez Hills

First-Year Writing (FYW) occupies a marginalized position at the intersection of various ideological and administrative systems in the academy. That FYW is generally required for all students paradoxically undercuts its disciplinary significance (Crowley, 1998; Strickland, 2011), thereby contributing to the marginalized positioning of composition studies in English departments and in the university. Relatedly, the course is the epitomic representative of the adjunctification of the university, with most sections taught by contingent faculty, some with little training or experience in composition (Crowley, 1998; Hanson & de los Reyes, 2019; Kahn, 2013).

In light of these intersecting systems, as well as the inequitable origins of FYW (Crowley, 1998), it is all too common for writing curricula to work *against* what we know about composition instruction, often in ways that marginalize already-marginalized students (Inoue, 2014, 2016). Consider, for example, that, historically and nationally, students who are Black, Indigenous, or People of Color (BIPOC) and multilingual learners have been and still are disproportionately placed into developmental courses (Naynaha, 2016), largely because what is perceived as "writing failure [that] stems from irreconcilable differences between expectations of White, middle-class literacies in school and the raced, cultured, classed, and gendered home literacies that learners attempt to use in school" (Inoue, 2014, p. 331). As Siskanna Naynaha (2016) has noted: "Latinx students from a diverse range of backgrounds—from US-born and educated to longtime US residents to newly arrived immigrants; from first-generation to Gen 1.5 to 3rd- and 4th-generation Latinxs—are commonly placed in 'remedial' or 'developmental' writing courses despite the fact that . . . such courses may be unnecessary" (p. 199).

This chapter uses critical systems thinking (Melzer, 2013) to explore how writing program administrators (WPAs) at a Hispanic-serving campus within a

DOI: https://doi.org/10.37514/PER-B.2023.1848.2.07

large public university system used systemwide mandated revision as an opportunity to redesign its FYW program to align with contemporary composition theory. The chapter explores how, despite expectations that this revision would renew the campus's mission to provide access and equitable education, the new program was constrained by the same structures and ideologies that defined the old program. I examine, through anecdotal and empirical data, how intersecting networks of structures and stakeholders on the campus served, simultaneously and paradoxically, as barriers to and opportunities for equitable program redesign; describe how faculty worked within and across formal and informal networks to effect change; explore the limitations of programmatic change without institutional critique; and offer strategies for rhetoric and composition program administrators and teachers in other institutions to work through programmatic change while honoring the needs of our students and our disciplinary expertise.[1]

A NETWORK OF RHETORICAL CONSTRAINTS

Writing program administrators "answer to multiple groups, and those groups often have conflicting goals" (Miller-Cochran, 2018, p. 108). To examine the systems at play in writing program (re)design, I draw upon the metaphor of architecture, which Bryna Siegel Finer and Jamie White-Farnham (2017) have relied upon to highlight how various writing programs are built, and the conceptual framework of Critical Systems Thinking, which Dan Melzer (2013) has suggested is key to the creation of campus-wide writing programs.

The architecture metaphor, Finer and White-Farnham explained, "highlights the material, logistical, and rhetorical elements of a writing program" and "allows us to imagine these constituent parts of a writing program as its foundation, beams, posts, scaffolding—the institutional structures that, alongside its people, anchor a program to the ground and keep it standing" (2017, p. 4). Finer and White-Farnham identified the following parts: education, experience, and expertise of the WPA(s); conception of the program; population served; funding sources; staffing and day-to-day operations; assessment protocols; internal marketing and public relations; supportive technologies; related research and scholarship; unique pedagogical and/or administrative features; primary program documents; and soft skills like relationship-building, time management, and managing expectations (2017, pp. 9–17).

Though Finer and White-Farnham do not address systems thinking directly, their metaphor considers the system of the program and its relation to a broader

---

[1] This information is readily available through the university website and all names are pseudonyms.

educational bureaucracy. Systems thinking may be of use to WPAs seeking to redesign writing programs for it can "make the daunting task of changing an entire system more manageable because it emphasizes locating points of leverage where even small changes will affect the entire system" (Melzer, 2013, p. 76). In this view, the identification of architectural elements can be seen as a systems thinking process of sorts by which WPAs can explore "how structures and processes relate to each other within the system" and how the "conceptual model that defines their ideal of the system. . . . is compared with the structures, processes, and results of the actual system" (Melzer, 2013, p. 78).

Though the metaphor of architecture allows us to visualize the parts of the finished product, it, like a traditional systems framework, may not help us trace the processes of (re)design or the social, political, and historical contexts from which the program or the larger system of which it is a part emerged. The static nature of the metaphor may be limited, given that writing programs are "ideological entities" (Gunner, 2002, p. 7). Melzer (2013) has pointed out that, "historically in systems thinking the ideological is too often not acknowledged." In critical systems thinking (CST), however, "the interrogation of the system's ideologies is central and explicit" (p. 80). Thus, CST provides a useful framework for writing program (re)design, particularly when layered with a framework like writing program architecture, which exposes the concrete, material aspects of the program and the systems and networks of which it is a part. CST considers the social, political, and historical contexts of a given system, emphasizes "the exposure of inequalities and conflicts," and "works toward liberation rather than equilibrium" (Melzer, 2013, p. 80). This approach aligns with the rhetorical emphasis and critical pedagogies in writing studies.

Like writing program administration broadly, program (re)design is deeply rhetorical. Systems create constraints both practical and ideological, which "have the power to constrain decision and action" in our writing programs, even when they are less than clearly visible (Bitzer, 1968, p. 8). WPAs communicate with various audiences amid constraints that include program budgets (Fox, 2013; Miller-Cochran, 2018), hiring structures (Miller-Cochran, 2018), institutional history and campus culture (Finer & White-Farnham, 2017; Malenczyk, 2016; Melzer, 2013), sociopolitical influences on the academy (Welch, 2018), and our own identities and positionalities as WPAs (de Mueller & Ruiz, 2017; Finer & White-Farnham, 2017; Fox, 2013; Kynard, 2019; Perryman-Clark & Craig, 2019) and must often advocate simultaneously for the program, instructional faculty, and students. Fortunately, as Susan Miller-Cochran (2018) noted, "[o]ur rhetorical training prepares us well for the conflicted spaces in which we work—we know how to pay attention to context, audience, and to focus our purpose" (p. 111). That training may be especially valuable when WPAs "wish to play a role in transforming not just a course or a department, but their entire campus writing program, as well as the ideologies that inform the program" (Melzer, 2013, p. 76).

These ideological influences generally are more insidious than overt and, therefore, they can be difficult to interrogate. Writing programs are certainly not immune to—and in many ways are prime examples of—the labor imbalances that characterize the contemporary neoliberal academy (Welch, 2018; see also Carter in this collection), for example. Most insidious perhaps is Whiteness, an "ideology that works to normalize and promote white supremacy" (Nishi et al., 2016, p. 2) through conceptions of and attitudes toward identity, morality, knowledge, language, communication, behavior, and professionalism, all of which undergird the academic systems and educational institutions in which our work is situated (Grayson, 2020; Keisch & Scott, 2015; Nishi et al., 2016). While a direct interrogation of the ideological influences of Whiteness is outside the scope of this chapter, these foundational aspects of institutional inequity it maintains are necessary to acknowledge, for the system *of* Whiteness and the systems derived *from* Whiteness intersect with everything we do.

Fortunately, as the editors of this collection wrote in the introduction, "systems and network theories offer us a new lens for problem-solving because they allow us to zoom out and into complexities within our work." Understanding Whiteness and its relative, racism, as overarching, if often unseen, systems, enables us to conceptualize the macro dimensions of a problem and the various contexts surrounding our work when we face micro-level manifestations of inequity or make attempts at local change work in our programs. As Melzer (2013) explained of his own attempts at writing program revision, "WPAs had to make our ideologies explicit." This explicit identification is an important step to prevent "charging ahead without examining and critiquing the ideologies that informed the system" (p. 86). A critical systems approach can also help WPAs make sense of resistance they may encounter in their efforts toward change, and the competing, even contradictory systems and structures that bolster such resistance.

SYSTEMIC CHANGE, LOCAL IMPACT: CAMPUS CONTEXT

This IRB-approved research was conducted at South Lake State University (a pseudonym), a commuter campus in an economically and educationally underserved suburb of a metropolitan U.S. city. The campus's emphasis on access is a byproduct of the school's history and mission to enhance higher education opportunity for traditionally underrepresented students: originally founded in the mid-twentieth century to serve the local African American community, the school has historically graduated more Black students than any other college in the state. Now a designated Hispanic-serving Institution (HSI), the South Lake campus serves a student population that is 64% Latinx.[2]

In 2017, the public university system, via statewide mandates, eliminated developmental English courses and the use of placement testing for FYW and limited the FYW requirement to one semester of instruction. Though informed by research about developmental education (see Bailey, 2009), these changes disproportionately affected the students and faculty at South Lake. Approximately 80 percent of incoming South Lake students each year (double the state average) were placed in development writing, one or two courses for which students incurred fees but received no college credit. South Lake was tasked with revising placement structures and eliminating three of five required writing courses, a move that would have ripple effects across the university, from the general education program and the English major requirements to the job security of the many part-time faculty who relied financially on the five-course sequence. Through collaboration and with limited funding from the larger state university system, WPAs redesigned the FYW program to both better reflect contemporary composition theory and pedagogy and to establish a programmatic ethos that aligned with the university's mission of access and equity.

The composition program was revised using what Melzer (2015) called the Advanced Writing Framework (AWF): while many schools assume one semester of required writing instruction to be the norm, the AWF positions the stretch model, in which the FYW requirement is taught over two semesters, as the standard. The single semester option, in which the same curriculum as the stretch model is taught at a more rapid pace, is labeled "Accelerated." Melzer has argued that the AWF "acknowledges that *most* students . . . will need more than one semester of composition to succeed" and is more equitable, for it "disrupts the discourse of remediation while retaining support for underserved students" (2015, p. 83).

I joined South Lake immediately following the program revision, not long before two thousand incoming students would experience the curriculum for the first time. I found that, unlike more "heavily scripted" standardized curricula, there were no required assignments, "grading rubrics, semester schedules" or "assigned texts" (Cox, 2018, p. A6). In fact, the curriculum was standardized only in the sense that common program learning outcomes were designed and adopted. As well, faculty professional development (FPD) was mandated (though compensated) to acquaint FYW instructors with the new standards. My review of South Lake's new FYW program materials revealed a sound,

---

2 This information is readily available through the university website.

non-prescriptive curriculum and clear outcomes that emphasized genre awareness, rhetorical flexibility, and transfer (Wardle, 2007; Yancey et al., 2014).

The program, however, met considerable resistance. That first semester, I watched FPD workshops devolve into complaint sessions. Department and committee meetings alternated between outwardly contentious and silently saturated with passive aggression. Though some tried to put on a brave face for their new colleague, most faculty members I spoke to were, like the faculty members Genesea M. Carter has described in her chapter, "exhausted, resentful, and applying to other jobs." How had we gotten here?

I would later learn more through personal experience about the ways Whiteness, professionalism, and collegiality were weaponized in all departmental spaces (Grayson, 2022), including but not limited to the writing program. At the time, however, I was mostly struck by what I saw as two competing ideologies, each of which positioned a different vulnerable population as its priority: the program revisions were designed with student success and more ethical disciplinary practices in mind, systems of beliefs and ideas that positioned students and disciplinarity as central concerns. Some WPAs, however, along with the non-tenure-track faculty members (NTTF) who taught the bulk of FYW classes, were motivated by concerns about job security and classroom autonomy that positioned NTTF as a priority. I undertook this research in part to understand why these ideologies and concerns, which I saw as symbiotic and intersecting, seemed to stand in direct opposition at South Lake.

To understand how individuals experienced the program revision and its aftermath, I conducted structured, semi-structured, and open interviews with ten tenured, tenure-track, and NTTF faculty members, including both WPAs involved in the revision and teachers of FYW courses. The reticence and hostility of many instructors with regards to the programmatic changes and the faculty involved with them, however, made formal interviews less than ideal at times. Therefore, I also engaged in casual conversations with faculty members. I reviewed official program documents and anonymous assessment surveys completed by the NTTF who teach FYW courses at South Lake State University.

INTERSECTING NETWORKS OF RENOVATION AND RESISTANCE

Though perspectives on the new curriculum varied considerably, some patterns emerged. I found that, to comply with mandates and ensure the success of the program, faculty members worked within and across three intersecting networks: formal, informal, and invisible networks.

Many interviewees expressed that they had been relieved by the mandates. Daphne, a former department chair and literature scholar who had taught composition for eight years, long had wanted to revise the program. Prior to the revision, there had been little oversight of composition instruction; as a result, curricula and instructional practice varied dramatically from one classroom to the next. There was no assessment, and lecturer evaluation was a "a pro forma process" that was "dated and problematic."[3]

Other interviewees expressed similar sentiments. Mark, a professor of composition, rhetoric, and cultural studies, admitted that FYW instruction had been "haphazard and higgledy-piggledy. There was more freedom, but a freedom by default. Some people were doing terrible work and taking advantage of that, like trying to teach a literature class in a comp class." Suzanne, a British literature scholar, explained that "'composition program' was a misnomer. It was not a program at all, just a bunch of courses listed under the English department . . . It was a comp program in name only." Not formally trained in composition, Suzanne did not feel confident critiquing the program. Then untenured, she was also concerned about retaliation, having been warned early on that "people here hold grudges."

FORMAL NETWORKS OF RENOVATION

State universities had a year to comply with the mandates and a lump sum of funds to aid the transition. (None of the participants could provide an exact figure for that lump sum.) At South Lake, a task force, which Daphne chaired, was formed. Other members included Mark; Henry, a tenured professor of rhetoric and composition who became composition director following the revision; the writing across the curriculum (WAC) coordinator; a literature professor who previously had served as composition director; the department chair; the director of the university's embedded tutor program; and the college's associate dean. Daphne, who had "grown frustrated with the lack of meaningful conversation around writing, zero professional development, faculty doing the same things, many of which were detrimental to students," formed a network of support with the new WAC coordinator: "Finally, there was someone with the disciplinary knowledge to give names to what I saw. I personally wasn't equipped to take up that battle . . . My instincts were confirmed by somebody else."

Henry said he had lobbied against the adoption of a shared assignment across FYW classes, a move for which the WAC coordinator advocated. Otherwise, he found the collaboration to be "relatively seamless," though short notice and

---

3 All names are pseudonyms.

ambiguity in the mandates led the task force to spend time "trying to figure out exactly what we could and could not do to comply."

Mark thought the formal networks that established and supported the task force presented obstacles. He'd had concerns about the previous program, but he wasn't entirely comfortable with the new program either. Mark thought the rhetorical emphasis quickly became a "battering ram" that pushed aside other visions of composition. He added: "Ideally, there should be spaces in a rhetorical approach for creativity and disruption." He admitted that he didn't voice his frustration: "I saw the inevitability of it all and I didn't find it worth it in terms of stress. Was I ready to take on this lonely fight? Could I secure enough allies? The budget, the chancellor, the provost all supported it."

Mark's comments bring to mind the thought processes Carter has identified in her chapter as a "natural reaction for WPAs working within the scarcity and competitive mindset of the neoliberal university supersystem—a system that prizes self-denial, emotional exploitation, workaholism, people-pleasing, and codependency." Among these are thoughts such as "But I cannot say no," "There is nothing that can be done," "The Provost says I must," and "I don't want to make waves."

Systems-level change requires structures "composed of numerous actors in the system" who interact with "other high-leverage components of the system" to "gain better leverage within the bureaucratic system" (Melzer, 2013, p. 92). Those who have the most leverage in a writing program, however, are not necessarily those involved with its day-to-day operations. Most participants noted that the taskforce excluded more faculty members than it included, and all participants noted that there was no sense of working with people impacted as a whole. Notably excluded were the NTTF who taught FYW.

Adjunct faculty rarely are afforded such opportunities, the result of the academic labor system and how our field constructs labor identities. As Gina Hanson and Chloe de los Reyes (2019), both NTTF, have pointed out, adjunct faculty are rarely identified as compositionists, even when composition is their area of expertise. There is instead a hierarchy of labor identity in which

> one rank theorizes practices and training for the other rank, who is somehow supposed to enact those practices without the capacity to theorize themselves. In other words, this two-tier distinction constructs us as composition workers (in need of training and skill development) rather than composition thinkers (capable of contributing to the field and our individual composition programs). (p. A9)

As a result, NTTF often "feel removed from the discipline, despite their expertise in the classroom" (Fedukovich & Hall, 2016, p. A4). In this way, we see how labor systems intersect with systems of disciplinary knowledge production and ideologies that subsequently shape work within writing programs.

Despite—or perhaps because of—its reputation as a "teaching subject" (Harris, 1997), the field has sought to establish composition as an autonomous academic discipline with a body of knowledge and ways of knowing distinct from English and literature. Since "adjuncts are constructed as the workers and not the thinkers, they become something our field wants to distance itself from" (Hanson & de los Reyes, 2019, p. A9). Adjuncts are positioned as workers outside of the knowledge production of our discipline, a broader systemic dynamic that was reflected in the configuration of the South Lake task force. A critical systems approach enables one to speculate that including NTTF on the task force might have helped in "defining an alternative model of the system" rather than reinforcing the labor dynamic already in place (Melzer, 2013, p. 84). Instead, the task force replicated the same labor inequities to which NTTF had grown sadly accustomed. As one NTTF put it: "If you are not in the inner circle, you have no sway regarding anything." For some NTTF at South Lake, being excluded wasn't jarring because it wasn't unusual. Layla, a NTTF who graduated from the department's literature MA program, remarked: "I can't be bothered being angry about it. That's how it's always been. It doesn't even surprise me anymore."

In the WPA Henry's view, the state's timeline contributed to a less than equitable task force structure. He admitted: "We could, *should* have had more time for adjunct participation in the process, rather than having to work quickly and essentially present them with program changes as a fait accompli, with an implementation date of immediately."

Following the redesign, a NTTF representative was elected to serve on the composition committee that assisted the composition director with oversight of the program. In the year of implementation, the university also supported three FPD sessions per semester to familiarize those teaching FYW with foundational concepts of the curriculum. These sessions emphasized teaching genre (Devitt, 2009), providing feedback on writing (Haswell, 1983; Lindemann, 2001), assets-based practices for working with multilingual learners and Generation 1.5 students (Nielsen, 2014), and, at my urging, considerations of instructor positionality (Taylor et al., 2000).

Two-thirds of respondents to the NTTF survey distributed after the fall semester praised these formal networks of support, noting the following:

- "Marvelous support! Best we've had in decades."
- "The training sessions and ensuing conversations have been terrific."
- "Semester meetings were enlightening and imaginative."

- "[Henry] was consistently helpful when I reached out."
- "I feel completely comfortable asking questions and seeking advice."

Institutional problems, however, contributed to what multiple participants called the "low morale" of NTTF. All FYW instructors were supposed to receive stipends for attendance at FPD sessions, but stipends for fall weren't processed until halfway through spring. Though FYW courses were supposed to be capped at 17, a figure already larger than the CCCC recommendation of 15, an enrollment surge resulted in caps of 20 in both fall and spring. The curriculum included a stretch model, for which students should have had the same instructor during fall and spring, but, due to course assignment procedures outlined in the collective bargaining agreement (CBA), many instructors who taught in fall were not rehired in spring. Henry suggested that this "drop-off was *profoundly* greater than it would have been with a little more foresight."

In what can be dismissively conceptualized as oversights or a series of unfortunate events, we see how the various macro systems at and beyond South Lake contributed to the micro problem of instructor morale in the local context of the writing program. University enrollments, staffing procedures, and payroll processing problems are not discrete concerns but "components of the system" and evidence of the conceptual models that undergird it. As Melzer (2013) noted, "conceptual models dictate the way the system operates, but at the same time the way the system is structured reinforces the conceptual models" (p. 78). In this way, even the lack of foresight Henry noted is part of a system of thinking and doing that devalues foresight and, arguably, is, at best, ambivalent toward outcomes like high course caps and instructor drop off, which foresight might have prevented.

Participants attributed many challenges to the lack of support received from Mott Hall, the metonymic catchall assigned to upper administrators with offices in the so-named building at the north end of campus. Of Mott Hall, Daphne said, "In theory the support is there. But in practice, where is the support?" Pointing to a pattern of upper-level administrators leaving the campus after only a year or two, Suzanne noted, "there's no consistency or accountability . . . When we need help, we're left kind of on our own." At the time of implementation, South Lake's President, Provost, Vice Provost, Vice President of Faculty Affairs, and Dean of Undergraduate Studies had all been in their positions for less than a year.

Participants also felt that the occasional cross-campus conferences hosted by the state university system were largely ineffective because they weren't intended for WPAs but also for deans, admissions and retention specialists, and student support services staff, resulting in what Henry called a "rhetorical problem" of audience. He was also struck by the differences between the writing programs on other campuses and the one at South Lake: "Other campuses either a) previously had many less students deemed 'developmental' than we had here or b) were already well along in using models such as stretch." Most participants believed that South Lake should have received more funding to aid in the redesign.

In keeping with its mission to provide access to higher education, South Lake was, at the time of the program rollout, the only non-impacted campus, guaranteeing admission to those who were officially accepted by the state university but turned away from other campuses. Admission, however, does not guarantee access or equity, particularly when the campus is not "student-ready" (McNair et al., 2016), and participants noted that the campus lacked financial or spatial resources to support the growing student population. As Willa, a NTTF who graduated from the department's BA and MA programs, discovered, "students don't see this as a real college." Of course, when the bodies in the classroom aren't valued, the instructors who work with them aren't valued either.

INFORMAL NETWORKS OF RESISTANCE

Curricular revision comes with labor. For NTTF who teach multiple courses on numerous campuses, updating a syllabus or redesigning a curriculum may demand time they really don't have. For NTTF, programmatic change is also a reminder that decisions are out of their control and that they are viewed as "contingent," or, worse, "disposable" (Fox, 2013). Many NTTF do not voice their concerns, if they have them, for fear that, if they make waves, they will not be offered classes in the future or that their contracts, if they have them, will no longer be renewed (Cox, 2018).

A different dynamic was observed at South Lake, where NTTF were vocal and persistent. One fall FPD meeting was derailed by an instructor (trained outside the field of writing studies) who insisted that teaching rhetoric was a disservice to "these students," who needed "basic skills training." When WPAs pointed out how basic skills models perpetuate the marginalization of already marginalized students, the instructor walked out. Another instructor walked out in the middle of a discussion of multiple Englishes. "Those who were vocal tended to get attention," Daphne said, "and the friction and negative feelings they shared set the stage for a rough implementation."

In ideal conditions, "faculty do not operate as independent contractors but develop expertise and judgment in collaboration with others and apply those talents to common goals" (Penrose, 2012, p. 120). That NTTF had been excluded from early on made it difficult for NTTF to see themselves as part of the community later. As Anicca Cox (2018) found, "feelings of being undervalued or misplaced in the institution often correlated with a perceived lack of autonomy in teaching practices" (p. A7). In other words, even when the curriculum is not standardized and instructors *do* have autonomy over how they implement broad learning outcomes, as was the case at South Lake, NTTF may feel like they do not.

The diverse traditions and bodies of knowledge that make up the "continually expanding and evolving knowledge base" of composition studies attest to the richness of our discipline, but those whose primary engagement with the field is via a tenuous position in the labor system may not recognize this: "a contingent faculty member moving from one writing curriculum to another may instead see the goals, and thus the knowledge base, of the profession as haphazard and idiosyncratic. Faculty who see the profession's knowledge base as idiosyncratic are not likely to see their own knowledge validated" (Penrose, 2012, p. 114). If professional identity is intrinsically connected to autonomy and expertise, curricular revision may threaten not only the employment of NTTF but also their professional identities as writing teachers.

By spring, a deep fissure had formed between the tenured and tenure-track faculty involved in WPA work and the NTTF teaching in the program. Interviewees reported participating in or overhearing "private conversations" about the program that involved "denigration of individuals" and "implicit bias" against students. Communication in the South Lake writing program operated in accordance with what Pamela Grossman et al. (2001) called "pseudocommunity," a dynamic wherein a group of individuals pretend they are already a community without ever establishing shared norms or values. In pseudocommunity, which "pivots on the suppression of conflict," group interactions are governed by "the tacit understanding that it is against the rules to challenge others or press too hard for clarification" (Grossman et al., 2001, p. 962). In keeping with these norms, most conversations about the program revision were private, conducted between individuals rather than openly among the entire faculty affected by it. In the absence of open conversation or a critical consideration of how all faculty members operated within and as parts of the various systems at work at South Lake, both responsibility and blame fell on individuals. Daphne explained: "As a former chair, I had greater credibility with many people . . . but this divided us."

Some WPAs feel torn between their institutional roles and their ideological orientations. As Fox (2013) has asked: "[H]ow can someone . . . who wants to be in solidarity with labor and working class negotiate a simultaneous identity as a 'manager'" (p. A5)? Henry, for example, negotiated this conflict by working toward the continued employment of NTTF, regardless of their pedagogical effectiveness. How equitable is an emphasis on academic freedom and instructor autonomy if it supports faculty at the expense of students?

Program assessment in the year following the revisions demonstrated that, despite the emphasis on rhetorical awareness, FYW sections on the South Lake campus were still taught using a wide variety of outdated theoretical models and pedagogical approaches, including current-traditional rhetoric, literary criticism, and models that Mary Lea and Brian Street (1998) have called *study skills* (emphases on grammar, surface features, and discrete skills) and *academic socialization* (emphasis on a singular discourse of higher education). These approaches have been discredited in contemporary composition scholarship due to their ineffectiveness (Lea & Street, 1998) and their rootedness in White cultural hegemony (Inoue, 2016), which is especially problematic given that most students at South Lake are from historically underserved and underrepresented racial, ethnic, and socioeconomic backgrounds.

Alongside the curriculum, WPAs also revised and formalized NTTF evaluation processes. That year, three NTTF were not recommended for reappointment, including the instructor who pushed for so-called "basic skills." Though her teaching was out of alignment with program goals and contemporary best practices, that the most vocal opponent of the curriculum was recommended for nonrenewal highlights the dangers NTTF experience when trying to assert autonomy as instructors. Negative evaluations resulted in fear and resentment among already disgruntled instructors.

This particular instructor filed a successful grievance against the department and resumed teaching the following year. On paper, she had fulfilled her contractual obligation to teach the courses she had been assigned to teach. Nowhere in the CBA is it stated that NTTF must be teaching equitably or effectively, that their work must align with contemporary composition theory, or that they must not harbor deficit attitudes toward students. The FPD offered during the rollout at South Lake, which was meant to help NTTF engage with contemporary disciplinary perspectives, was deemed to be in violation of the CBA due to its mandatory nature. Though the defining characteristic of a NTTF position is contingency, many NTTF at South Lake had long histories with the program. The CBA ensures that NTTF who teach in six consecutive semesters receive contracts, which is a considerable labor victory in a neoliberal academic system. While these contracts help retain teachers who are effective, they also interfere with the removal of those who are not. To point, one NTTF who was nonrenewed following numerous consecutive warnings in previous reviews was retained for almost three years thereafter, finishing out his contract.

Until 2017, in the program's forty-year history, there had been little FPD and no program assessment. Though high failure and attrition rates hinted toward the FYW program's ineffectiveness, there had been no investment in ensuring that students were receiving equitable, up-to-date writing instruction. Despite the increased formality of the revised evaluation process, Daphne said that there was still "not any concerted effort to publicly confront those who insist upon ideas that have largely been discredited. Some of it is probably faculty burnout—or just not giving a shit." Of the continued resistance and resentment of NTTF, she lamented: "We are reaping what we sow."

This dynamic frustrated those NTTF who possessed disciplinary expertise and supported the new curriculum. Because of the diverse training and experiences of NTTF, adjunct faculty members who have disciplinary training and are active in the field often find themselves working alongside "last-minute hires with little to no vetting," including instructors who "know nothing about composition at all" (Hanson & de los Reyes, 2019, p. A6). By the end of the year, Michael, who had a doctorate in composition and rhetoric, had resigned as the lecturer representative due to "resistant posturing and toxic attitudes" among fellow NTTF. In his letter of resignation, he explained: "I refuse to represent to the committee ongoing challenges to the revised curriculum. I find the curriculum to be disciplinarily sound, thoughtful, and well-suited to our students' needs . . . I cannot in good faith represent pervasive positions and attitudes that I find intellectually vacant or morally abhorrent."

Michael's frustration may have been compounded by his committee position. As Casie Fedukovich and Megan Hall (2016) pointed out, "[T]here are potential relational challenges created when a non-tenure-track faculty member works closely with program administrators" (p. A8). Some NTTF thought Michael was getting "special treatment," but, due to policies preventing NTTF from participating in discussion and evaluation of other NTTF, Michael was often asked to leave the room during official meetings. Though the position ought to have encouraged "cross-tier collaboration" (Fedukovich & Hall, 2016), the existing system reinforced professional distinctions.

DISCUSSION: INVISIBLE NETWORKS

Most participants believe the program is on the right track. Henry said he was "proud of the progress that we've made in bringing the comp program here into the 21st century." For Daphne, working on the program revision taught her "to advocate for certain positions against the status quo, damning the consequences in some cases." Suzanne was cautious, noting that she was "still waiting to come out on the other end." Willa was resigned: "I'll just keep doing what I'm doing until they tell me to stop doing it and do something else," she said.

Resignation appears to be the result of department and campus culture, insidious and influential networks that lie beneath the formal and informal networks of renovation and resistance identified by participants. Stuart McDougal (2010) argued "[e]ven in times of great change, a department exists within three contexts: that of its own culture and history, that of the culture and history of the college or university, and that of the culture and history of the profession" (p. 360). The influence of these contexts was evident at South Lake. The department's laissez faire approach to hiring and evaluation resulted in a cadre of NTTF with little to no disciplinary expertise, yet the WPA demonstrated little interest in calling out unsound approaches to writing instruction. The university's history of serving a predominantly transfer population from the local two-year colleges resulted in limited resources for first-year students. There were limited resources for FPD. Perhaps most problematic were the ideological underpinnings that perpetuated deficit approaches to instruction and assessment.

Looking at the revision through a critical systems lens, we see that even with the new curriculum, the deficit approach, undergirded by ideology and long-standing practice, was particularly difficult to shake. Though Melzer (2015) claimed the advanced writing framework (AWF) "disrupts the discourse of remediation while retaining support for underserved students" (p. 83), I suggest, and as was clear during the transition at South Lake State University, this is not as simple a solution as we might wish it to be. In his analysis of discourse surrounding the Early Start program, a 2012 effort by the California State University to curb remediation, Melzer noted that the language used in policies, press releases, news reports, and statements from WPAs and instructors perpetuated the same discourse of remediation that has, for generations, defined basic writing initiatives. It is arguable that Melzer too replicates the same semantic structures he claims to disrupt. When making the argument that assigning the single semester course the "accelerated" label, thereby framing the stretch option as the norm, Melzer explained: "most students need more than a single semester of focused, integrated reading and writing instruction by a composition specialist to help prepare for the complexities of academic literacies" (2015, p. 95). True though this may be, Melzer's use of words and phrases like "need" and "help prepare" perpetuate the dominant deficit-model discourse that, as he admits, has "remained virtually unchanged" over time (2015, p. 90).

Paradoxically, then, Melzer's own use of this language is further evidence that his assertion is correct: despite good intentions—"and sometimes *because* of those good intentions—the discourse of remediation and basic skills remains dominant," and "we unintentionally replicate the dominant discourse of the Remedial Writing Framework even as we argue against it" (2015, p. 86, p. 101). The AWF changes the language but not the hierarchical structure of required college writing courses, and it doesn't change the racist assumptions (White) faculty and administrators hold of BIPOC students. It merely replaces one set of hierarchical terms for another, somewhat less problematic yet hierarchical set. At least that's what happened at South Lake.

Failure and withdrawal rates in FYW remained high, despite the program revision. Because the new curriculum was not implemented more equitably *inside the classroom*, the deficit model prevailed. To point, here are a few comments from the NTTF survey:

- "I found students pretty unprepared for the rigor of the class. Their knowledge of English, and particularly basic grammar, was very dismal."
- "And as with the last ten years of students few knew citation or were open to learning it until they realized they would fail without its proper use."
- "The students that I am seeing this school year are woefully underprepared. Their level of competence is even lower than what I have seen in the past, and they appear to have no desire to perform even the most simple of tasks."
- "No, students aren't ready. At all. And that's for the already watered down standards."

Henry acknowledged that there were "voices of nostalgia for the good old days of wild irresponsibility" when instructors with limited disciplinary knowledge had autonomy over the curriculum, but the euphemistic nature of his statement minimizes the implications and outcomes of such irresponsibility. For many instructors, the new curriculum merely cemented their views of students as remedial. Thus, while South Lake is built around a model of access and opportunity, FYW instruction on the campus has functioned and continues to function as a gatekeeper to student success, echoing historical national trends, particularly for students of underrepresented racial formations (Crowley, 1998; Inoue, 2014, 2016; Naynaha, 2016).

Fewer than half of Black and Latinx students who enroll in four-year colleges graduate within a six-year period (Tate, 2017). While the non-credit-bearing developmental courses BIPOC are disproportionately placed into historically have contributed to low graduation rates, so too do the racist assumptions about language that undergird the teaching of academic discourse. As Asao Inoue (2016) reminded us, "no matter what antiracist motives a teacher or WPA may have . . . we all work within conditions and systems that have branded some language as less communicative, less articulate, subjective and in subjection to the dominant white discourse" (pp. 141–142). The commonplace argument (taken up by those at South Lake who argued for "basic skills education") that the role of FYW is to teach all students the language practices of the academy is flawed because access in a racist system is about more than discourse: "You can earn the keys to the kingdom, but if no one gives you access to the lock at the front gate, those keys are useless" (Inoue, 2016, p. 142).

That most instructors and WPAs, particularly on the tenure track, historically have been and still are White compounds this problem. BIPOC teachers and WPAs may be more cognizant of the racialized aspects of language and writing instruction but are often "ignored or aggressively silenced by white colleagues" (García de Mueller & Ruiz, 2017, p. 30). At South Lake, those NTTF who identified as BIPOC were generally more amenable to the new curriculum than those who identified as White. However, because they also tended to be newer to the profession, most lacked the contractual protections offered by the CBA, which privileges seniority.

One of Henry's goals following the program revision was "to stabilize the corps of adjuncts." Henry's allegiance to faculty is honorable but short-sighted, if it doesn't consider how staffing and scheduling procedures work within the larger systems of the university and the discipline. One of writing studies' most noted labor activist scholars, Seth Kahn (2013), has pointed out that "failing to hire and evaluate contingent faculty rigorously, carefully, and supportively" is actually one of the "ways that senior faculty contribute to contingent labor exploitation" (p. A13). Hiring and evaluation practices must be "ethical and meaningful": while WPAs must prioritize the hiring and support of qualified instructors, "if we make it a priority *not* to retain faculty who aren't doing the job well simply because they're convenient then we can go a long way toward addressing the darker, deeper underbelly" of the adjunctification of composition (Kahn, 2013, p. A15), one defined as much by assumptions about FYW and who is qualified to teach writing as it is by the institutional labor hierarchies that perpetuate our discipline's continued marginalization.

RENEWAL: WRITING PROGRAM ADMINISTRATION AS RHETORICAL INQUIRY

Since I conducted this research, we have made additional programmatic changes to better support both students and instructors, including updating an upper-division writing course that hadn't been reviewed in two decades and developing yearlong faculty learning communities toward antiracist writing instruction and writing across the disciplines. These initiatives are promising, but much work remains.

The department culture at South Lake was described as "toxic" by multiple participants, who cited "ad hominem attacks" against women WPAs; a drastic imbalance in service workload requirements between men and women on the tenure track; "microaggressions" toward BIPOC; "mansplaining" and other discursive methods of silencing women faculty members; "White savior" attitudes; and a general "anti-intellectual" devaluing of disciplinary expertise in composition and rhetoric. I have written elsewhere about my own experiences trying to do antiracist work within these contexts (Grayson, 2022). Until these deeper cultural and ideological problems in the program are addressed, WPAs' best efforts will be insufficient to challenge the deficit orientation that prevails in the FYW program. Attempts to effect change via WPA work are limited if they focus "on the classroom without adequately theorizing the institution," for such approaches perpetuate a "trickle-up theory of change that pins political hopes on the enlightened, active individual" (Porter et al., 2000, p. 617).

As we know, WPAs cannot go it alone. Yet change work is often relegated to the individual, a dynamic that both obscures and in fact illuminates the broader institutional systems in operation. That antiracist work, for example, is often relegated to individual efforts and subjected to neoliberal box-checking tendencies (Dugan, 2021) is indicative of an institutional system rooted in Whiteness (Tate & Page, 2018) and the broader social, political, and ideological supersystems of which all educational institutions are a part (Keisch & Scott, 2015; Shenhav-Goldberg & Kopstein, 2020). After all, as I have explained elsewhere in this collection, "institutions exist in order to, well, exist. That's the only way they have power. Thus, initiatives that focus on individuals rather than systems generally are implemented in lieu of broader structural changes."

We are not immune to these dynamics as WPAs. Too often, as the editors of this collection have noted in the introduction, "rhetoric and composition administrators do not approach higher educational supersystems as a series of internetworked systems and networks." I would add that, if WPAs are not looking beyond the walls of the siloes in which they operate, it is because those walls have been erected to keep the silo operating in isolation. In other words, our isolation is itself evidence of the workings of the ideological and institutional networks and systems at play beyond the more immediate levels of our writing program's architecture. Critical systems thinking better enables us to examine these systems, the multiple, even competing, roles we play within them, and how we can use our positionality to effect change.

Many WPAs resist rather than embrace the managerial aspects of their work (Fox, 2013). As Donna Strickland (2011) has said, "If we are to truly work for the material benefit of administrators, teachers, and students alike," we must acknowledge and take advantage of the administrative roles we play in the systems of our institutions, especially during times of change (p. 122). Partly because many see administrative structures as emblematic of academia's increasing neoliberalization, programmatic change is likely to be viewed with skepticism, irritation, and resistance, especially when mandated (Melzer, 2013; Welch,

2018). Often, we equate resistance with activism—yet resistance that doesn't account for how our own resistance perpetuates inequity cannot be considered activism. Though justified in resentment of a system that devalues our contributions, resisting contemporary theory and pedagogy as an act of resistance against the institution misses the mark. Activism ideally moves us toward change, but a reactionary resistance to pedagogical change on the sole grounds that it *is* change hurts foremost the students we teach.

Instead, if we acknowledge that institutions are rhetorically and systematically constructed and, therefore, "can be rewritten . . . through rhetorical action," we can employ institutional critique as a "rhetorical methodology that will lead to change and restructuring" (Porter et al., 2000, pp. 610, 613). Our institutional critique must be informed by our understanding of the various systems and networks in which our labor is situated on both macro and micro levels, from the local architecture of the program, the funding structures of the university, and the formal and informal networks of communication among program faculty to the historical conception of our discipline and our writing programs and the ideological systems that undergird all of contemporary education.

To better account for these various, intersecting systems, we might examine how our institutions are configured spatially and push for office layouts, access to shared department areas, and webpage design and navigation that reflect the systems we wish to create in our writing programs. We might consider how information about the writing program is disseminated to participants within the system. If there are differences between the narratives provided to administrators, presented in department meetings, and conveyed in outward-facing materials like webpages or student brochures, we might explore why those stories differ and how they function rhetorically. For example, we might consider what beliefs about audience inform the telling of those stories and what messages those various stories—and the very existence of variation—tell the actors within the system. To effect change, we must know how the institution operates, what it values, which parts of the system function as constraints, and which parts are vulnerable to influence.

Carter noted in her chapter "one of the best ways to resist assimilation by the neoliberalism university system is to change our mindset about what we 'can' and 'cannot' do" and suggests that WPAs "focus their attention on their own agency." With this call in mind, and in keeping with the approach of institutional critique, I suggest we recognize the limitations and affordances of our work in context and cultivate an agentive relationship to our environment. This is especially important for those whose positions are precarious: only by examining the situation and the multiple forces working within and upon it can we identify opportunities for transformation through discursive action. When facing programmatic challenges, we must draw upon our rhetorical training and do the following.

Recognize contexts. What traditions, beliefs, and ideologies sustain the program? How do those traditions and ideologies sustain inequity? These questions require we approach institutional critique as ethnographers. We should take advantage of our emic positions as actors within the system and our experience as researchers by recording what we know about the program, seeking out answers to what we don't know, observing our daily interactions with other actors in the system, and reflecting upon what we learn. This interrogation of context is integral to understanding the rhetorical situations we face.

Identify audiences. Who has a stake here? Who are the various actors involved? A high-level university administrator who began her career as a compositionist or teacher educator may be more open to disciplinary perspectives than an administrator whose background is in finance. When working with the finance-oriented administrator, it may be beneficial to emphasize (and justify) the funding required.

Acknowledge constraints. What don't we have access to? What don't we know? In a college without the resources necessary for a programmatic overhaul, it may be especially important to identify the scope of a project early on. Large public universities tend to have more moving parts than can be easily accounted for, so figuring out what information and resources are needed and who has access to them may be significant.

Locate available means of persuasion. What do stakeholders want? What resources do we have? Where are the "fissures and the points of leverage" (Porter et al., 2000)? A vague statement in a university policy, for example, may be a space where we can offer an interpretation that works to the benefit of our program. An administrator tasked with ensuring the campus complies with a statewide order may be eager to ensure change happens and may have some leverage in the supersystem of the university than we do, thereby becoming an important point of contact.

Seize kairotic opportunities, like mandated revisions, to convey significant messages. When change is required, we are forced to consider the work we are doing and, ideally, imagine how we might do it better. While some stakeholders will resist critical reflection and become more resolute in their current practices, others will be more open. Our work, then, is to initiate change not by pushing back against the resolute but by developing the attitudes and belief systems of those who are listening, those who can, as members of the same system, ultimately help to disseminate that message. Institutional change, when it happens, is a long process. If we want change to be deeper than surface-level fixes, if we want to move beyond mere reform toward an institutional revolution of sorts, we must begin with the foundations: the culture and ideology that sustain the system. By laying the first stones of a new foundation, we can begin to build a new system in which change is inevitable.

Perhaps by using rhetorical tools we already have, we will feel less powerless in the face of programmatic change and administrative mandates that seem out of our control. This approach does make us complicit in the neoliberalization of higher education. Instead, by exploring the real-world situations and in which we are, variously and sometimes simultaneously, rhetors, actors, audiences, and change-makers, we afford ourselves kairotic opportunities to practice what we preach in the FYW classroom. Put simply, looking at challenges as rhetorical situations brings us closer to the frameworks that define our discipline.

REFERENCES

Bailey, T. (2009). Challenge and opportunity: Rethinking the role and function of developmental education in community college. *New Directions for Community Colleges, 145*(24), 11–30.

Bitzer, L. F. (1968). The rhetorical situation. *Philosophy & Rhetoric, 1*(1), 1–14.

Cox, A. (2018). Collaboration and resistance: Academic freedom and non-tenured labor. *Forum: Issues about Part-Time and Contingent Faculty, 22*(1), A4-A13.

Crowley, S. (1998). *Composition in the university: Historical and polemical essays*. University of Pittsburgh Press.

Devitt, A. (2009). Teaching critical genre awareness. In C. Bazerman (Ed.), *Genre in a changing world* (pp. 337–351). The WAC Clearinghouse; Parlor Press. https://doi.org/10.37514/PER-B.2009.2324.

Dugan, J. (2021). Beware of equity traps and tropes. *Educational Leadership, 78*(6), 35–40.

Fedukovich, C. & Hall, M. (2016). Using cross-tier collaboration to support professional identity. *Forum: Issues about Part-Time and Contingent Faculty, 19*(2), A3-A10.

Fox, S. (2013). Looking in the WPA mirror: Balancing roles and taking actions. *Forum: Issues about Part-Time and Contingent Faculty, 16*(2), A1-A16.

García de Mueller, G. & Ruiz, I. (2017). Race, silence, and writing program administration: A qualitative study of U.S. college writing programs. *WPA: Writing Program Administration, 40*(2), 19–39.

Grayson, M. L. (2020). *Race talk in the age of the trigger warning: Recognizing and challenging classroom cultures of silence*. Rowman and Littlefield.

Grayson, M. L. (2022). Antiracism is not an action item: Boutique activism and academic (anti)racism. *Writers: Craft and Context, 2*(2), 58–67.

Grossman, P., Wineburg, S. & Woolworth, S. (2001). Toward a theory of teacher community. *The Teachers College Record, 103*(6), 942–1012.

Gunner, J. (2002). Ideology, theory, and the genre of writing programs. In S. K. Rose & I. Weiser (Eds.), *The writing program administrator as theorist* (pp. 7–18). Boynton/Cook.

Hanson, G. & de los Reyes, C. (2019). Identity crisis: Daring to identify as more than "just" adjunct composition instructors. *Forum: Issues about Part-Time and Contingent Faculty, 22*(2), A4-A15.

Harris, J. (1997). *A teaching subject: Composition since 1966*. Prentice Hall.

Haswell, R. H. (1983). Minimal marking. *College English, 45*(6), 600–604.

Inoue, A. B. (2014). Theorizing failure in US writing assessments. *Research in the Teaching of English, 48*(3), 330–352.

Inoue, A. B. (2016). Friday plenary address: Racism in writing programs and the CWPA. *WPA: Writing Program Administration, 40*(1), 134–154. http://association database.co/archives/40n1/40n1inoue.pdf.

Kahn, S. (2013). "Never take more than you need": Tenure-track/tenured faculty and contingent labor exploitation. *Forum: Issues about Part-Time and Contingent Faculty, 16*(2), A12-A16.

Keisch, D. M. & Scott, T. (2015). U.S. education reform and the maintenance of White supremacy through structural violence. *Landscapes of Violence, 3*(3), 1–44.

Kynard, C. (2019). Administering while Black: Black women's labor in the academy and the "position of the unthought." In S. M. Perryman-Clark & C. L. Craig (Eds.), *Black perspectives in writing program administration: From the margins to the center* (pp. 28–50). Conference on College Composition and Communication; National Council of Teachers of English.

Lea, M. R. & Street, B. V. (1998). The "academic literacies" model: Theory and applications. *Theory into Practice, 45*(4), 368–377. https://doi.org/10.1207/s15430421tip4504_11.

Lindemann, E. (2001). *A rhetoric for writing teachers* (4th ed.). Oxford University Press.

Malenczyk, R. (2016). Opening plenary address: Locations of administration; or, WPAs in space. *WPA: Writing Program Administration, 40*(1), 114–133.

McDougal, S. Y. (2010). The remaking of a small college English department. *Pedagogy, 10*(2), 345–362.

McNair, T. B., Bensimon, E., Cooper, M. A., McDonald, N. & Major, Jr. T. (2016). *Becoming a student-ready college: A new culture of leadership for student success.* Jossey-Bass.

Melzer, D. (2013). Using systems thinking to transform writing programs. *WPA: Writing Program Administration, 36*(2), 75–94.

Melzer, D. (2015). Remedial, basic, advanced: Evolving frameworks for first-year composition at the California State University. *Journal of Basic Writing, 34*(1), 81–106. https://doi.org/10.37514/jbw-j.2015.34.1.05.

Miller-Cochran, S. (2018). Innovation through intentional administration: Or, how to lead a writing program without losing your soul. *WPA: Writing Program Administration, 42*(1), 107–122.

Naynaha, S. (2016). Assessment, social justice, and Latinxs in the US community college. *College English 79*(2), 196–201.

Nielsen, K. (2014). On class, race, and dynamics of privilege: Supporting generation 1.5 writers across the curriculum. In T. M. Zawacki & M. Cox (Eds.), *WAC and second language writers: Research toward linguistically and culturally inclusive programs and practices* (pp. 129–150). The WAC Clearinghouse; Parlor Press. https://doi.org/10.37514/per-b.2014.0551.

Nishi, N. W., Matias, C. E., Montoya, R. & Sarcedo, G. L. (2016). Whiteness FAQ: Responses and tools for confronting college classroom questions. *Journal of Critical Thought and Praxis, 5*(1), 1–34. https://doi.org/10.31274/jctp-180810-55.

Penrose, A. M. (2012). Professional identity in a contingent-labor profession: Expertise, autonomy, community in composition teaching. *WPA: Writing Program Administration, 35*(2), 108–126.

Perryman-Clark, S. M. & Craig, C. L. (2019). Introduction: Black matters: Writing program administration in twenty-first-century higher education. In S. M. Perryman-Clark & C. L. Craig (Eds.), *Black Perspectives in writing program administration: From the margins to the center* (pp. 1–27). Conference on College Composition and Communication; National Council of Teachers of English.

Porter, J. E., Sullivan, P., Blythe, S., Grabill, J. T. & Miles, L. (2000). Institutional critique: A rhetorical methodology for change. *College Composition and Communication, 51*(4), 610–642.

Shenhav-Goldberg, R. & Kopstein, J. S. (2020). Antisemitism on a California campus: Perceptions and views among students. *Contemporary Jewry, 40*, 237–258.

Strickland, D. (2011). *The managerial unconscious in the history of composition studies.* Southern Illinois University Press.

Taylor, E., Tisdell, E. J. & Hanley, M. S. (2000, June 2–4). *The role of positionality in teaching for critical consciousness: Implications for adult education* [Paper presentation]. Adult Education Research Conference, Vancouver, Canada.

Tate, E. (2017, April 26). Graduation rates and race. *Inside Higher Ed.* https://www.insidehighered.com/news/2017/04/26/college-completion-rates-vary-race-and-ethnicity-report-finds.

Tate, S. A. & Page, D. (2018). Whiteliness and institutional racism: Hiding behind unconscious bias. *Ethics and Education, 13*(1), 141–155.

Wardle, E. (2007). Understanding "transfer" from FYC: Preliminary results of a longitudinal study. *WPA: Writing Program Administration, 31*(1/2), 65–85.

Welch, N. (2018). "Everyone should have a plan": A neoliberal primer for writing program directors. *WPA: Writing Program Administration, 41*(2), 104–112.

White-Farnham, J. & Finer, B. S. (2017). Writing program architecture: An introduction with alternative tables of contents. In B. S. Finer & J. White-Farnham (Eds.), *Writing Program Architecture: Thirty Cases for Reference and Research* (pp. 3–24). Utah State University Press.

Yancey, K., Robertson, L. & Taczak, K. (2014). *Writing across contexts: Transfer, composition, and sites of writing.* Utah State University Press.

CHAPTER 8.

NEGOTIATING DOMINANCE IN WRITING PROGRAM ADMINISTRATION: A CASE STUDY

Emily R. Johnston
University of California, Merced

> **Kumeyaay Land Acknowledgment:** *The University of California, San Diego campus where the Dimensions of Culture Program lives sits on unceded Kumeyaay territory. The Kumeyaay have been in San Diego for over 10,000 years and today, Kumeyaay tribal members are living within twelve distinct sovereign bands across the United States (Viejas Enterprises, 2015). Every program that the university houses is embroiled in a paradox of claiming a public service mission while enacting that mission on unceded land. Higher education institutions across the United States live on unceded indigenous lands. This shared reality represents one way in which first-year writing programs intersect across the United States.*

Administering first-year composition (FYC) is a project of advocacy. In FYC, we guide first-year students in transitioning to college and developing their communicative agency. We support graduate teaching assistants (GTAs) as they navigate the institution and prepare for careers in higher education. We employ adjuncts and contingent faculty seeking more secure employment in a highly unstable job market. Yet, FYC administrators are complicit in maintaining the status quo of promoting a college degree as a ticket to opportunity, freedom, and success. As fellow contributor Iris Ruiz (2016) asserted in her monograph, *Reclaiming Composition for Chicano/as and Other Ethnic Minorities: A Critical History and Pedagogy*, the implicit goal of FYC is not to challenge power hierarchies, but "to create and maintain a hegemonic middle class [by] encourag[ing] students to think and write in ways that will make them good citizens of the academic (and larger) community and viable candidates for good jobs" (p. 43). Indeed, as the Conference on College Composition and Communication (CCCC) (2021) describes in the *CCCC Statement on White Language Supremacy*, the emphasis on Standard Academic English in FYC and educational institutions more broadly

DOI: https://doi.org/10.37514/PER-B.2023.1848.2.08

coerces student-writers to assimilate into "a worldview that is simultaneously pro-white, cisgender, male, heteronormative, patriarchal, ableist, racist, and capitalist" (para. 4). How can we come to terms with the fact that our field exists to bolster a White supremacist, cisheteronormative, patriarchal, ableist, meritocratic elite? How do we reckon with administering FYC programs, if it means that we're reinforcing the very systems of dominance that create the conditions of struggle facing our students, faculty, and staff—including ourselves?

This chapter attempts to answer these questions through a case study of an FYC program whose explicit aim is teaching writing as a tool for speaking truth to power: the Dimensions of Culture Program (DOC) at the University of California, San Diego (UCSD). This case study reveals that DOC, like any FYC program, capitulates to, while also resisting, power imbalances shaping our field and institutions. Only from reckoning with *how* our programs both reinforce and transform systems of dominance, I contend, can we fulfill the democratizing potential of higher education. Indeed, when we identify the systems that make our programs function, the conditions in which complicity occurs, and where we can impact change, we create conditions for agency within and against the converging systems of institutional bureaucracies, academic elitism, the capitalist structure of higher education in the United States, and White supremacy.

METHODOLOGY

This chapter uses the methodology of a case study to analyze DOC's struggle to hold onto its legacy as a counterhegemonic FYC program at an elite university. Intersectionality grounds my analysis. First articulated by Kimberlé Williams Crenshaw (1989), intersectionality is a framework for making simultaneously visible *both* efforts to undermine *and* capitulations to power hierarchies within single-axis social systems that eschew contradiction and treat differences as mutually exclusive categories. As Vivian M. May (2015) put it, intersectionality "underscores how we can participate in forms of dominance, harm, and subordination even as we also fight hegemonic relations and pursue justice" (p. 5). This case study centers intersectionality to examine how DOC, in our struggle to advocate for students, faculty, and staff, *both* exercises agency within *and* experiences subordination to the hegemonic systems of UCSD, FYC, and higher education.

To situate DOC in its particular historical and institutional context as an FYC program that resulted from minoritized student demands for culturally-relevant education at UCSD, I also draw on cultural-historical activity theory (CHAT). Emerging from activity theory (Engeström, 1996; Engeström et al., 1999), a framework for understanding human activity as complex, socially-situated phenomena, CHAT (Prior et. al, 2007) is a tool for understanding how the work of writing program administration (WPA), like the activity of writing itself, "is situated in concrete interactions that are simultaneously improvised locally and mediated by historically-provided tools and practices" (p. 17). CHAT reminds us that FYC programs are not the sum-total of their activities, but rather, parts of larger systems with particular histories, cultures, values, and interests.

CHAT, approached intersectionality, allows me to conduct an *intersectional cultural-historical activity-based case study* of DOC as an FYC program *in process*—as it *both* teaches writing through the theory and practice of social revolution *and* belongs to a large research university focused on capitalistic growth and research prestige. Taken together, CHAT and intersectionality help me ask several interconnected questions: what are the systems, both local and global, in which DOC participates? How do those systems intersect? How does DOC's positionality within those intersecting systems both facilitate and detract from the counterhegemonic change the program promotes? I draw on institutional research about UCSD as well as my own knowledge and experience as the Associate Director of DOC. To address these questions, I use the seven elements of CHAT used to analyze texts and contexts (Prior et al., 2007) to examine the following, in no particular order:

- How DOC came to be (production);
- How people feel and think about DOC (representation);
- How DOC circulates its work on/beyond campus (distribution);
- How the campus community takes up DOC (reception);
- How people interact in DOC (socialization);
- What activities happen in DOC (activity);
- The historical, institutional, cultural contexts in which DOC operates (ecology).

This case study by no means attempts to be comprehensive in its analysis of these elements in DOC, but rather, to highlight some areas where tensions, contradictions, and the need for ongoing power negotiations lie. It is my hope that writing program administrators can apply pieces of this case study and my analysis to their home institutions to facilitate and foster meaningful systemic change within their programs.

AN INSTITUTIONAL PROFILE OF THE UNIVERSITY OF CALIFORNIA, SAN DIEGO

UCSD, where DOC lives, is widely known as a preeminent research institution, within the University of California (UC) system and the global ecology of higher education. Opening its doors in 1960 to advance climate change research and the growing field of engineering, the university has become particularly prestigious in the fields of science, technology, engineering, and math (STEM) (Regents, 2023). The Scripps Institute of Oceanography is among the largest marine biology laboratories in the world. UC San Diego Health, the academic health system, is a national leader in pulmonology, neurology, and cardiology, among other medical specialties (Brubaker, 2020). It is worth noting the number of students graduating with STEM degrees from UCSD is three times the national average (Clark, 2016). At STEM-oriented UCSD, writing programs are relatively underfunded and obscured. We must fight for institutional resources and recognition, which contributes to the culture of faculty competition that runs rampant in higher education.

The material wealth surrounding UCSD exacerbates competition. UCSD is located in La Jolla, one of the wealthiest neighborhoods in San Diego County. The campus is expanding with new student housing, a living and learning neighborhood, research centers, a light-rail transit line (Regents, 2022b), and even a Target in the student center. And the undergraduate student body is rapidly increasing. In Fall 2016, the university enrolled 8,630 new students (Regents, 2017). By Fall 2021, that number jumped to 11,148, the number of new students increasing by several hundred each year in between (Regents, 2022c). Additionally, the international student population at UCSD has become among the highest in the US, and while fewer international students have enrolled since the onset of the pandemic, in Fall 2019, they constituted 25 percent of the student body (Robbins, 2020). As the campus infrastructure and student population grow, resources for the writing programs do not. The current distribution of university resources disproportionately impacts multilingual international student-writers as well as faculty and staff supporting larger numbers of incoming students in their transition to the university. Coupled with the extant marginalization of writing amidst the STEM culture of UCSD, institutional growth exacerbates a sense of powerlessness in the writing programs, fueling imposter syndrome, demoralization, and burnout, and fortifying institutional hierarchy.

FIRST-YEAR COMPOSITION AT UCSD

To understand how the writing programs operate within the institutional ecology of UCSD, one has to understand the unique position of FYC at the university. Undergraduate education at UCSD functions on the college system, adapted from Oxford and Cambridge universities, in an effort to create a small liberal arts experience for students within a large research institution. Each of the university's seven (soon to be eight) undergraduate colleges houses its own FYC program, which teaches composition in alignment with the college's intellectual theme. In addition to these seven (soon to be eight) writing programs, the university is also home to the Analytical Writing Program (AWP). Independent from the colleges, AWP offers writing courses to students across colleges who have not yet satisfied the UC's Entry Level Writing Requirement, which they must successfully complete before enrolling in their college's writing program (Regents, 2022a).

While the college system generates diverse, innovative approaches to writing at UCSD, it also creates a culture of isolation for the writing programs. Each FYC program varies radically—from its curriculum and the structure of writing instruction to its degree of collaboration with the other writing programs. Some programs offer composition as small studio classes taught by graduate teaching assistants (GTAs), faculty, and adjuncts, while other programs offer composition as large lectures taught by faculty, with breakout discussion sections facilitated by GTAs and adjuncts. GTAs, adjuncts, and faculty teaching in the writing programs come from myriad departments and disciplines, such as literature, sociology, ethnic studies, visual arts, history, Latin American studies, and education studies. Their breadth of disciplinary backgrounds enriches students' learning experiences, but it also means that many instructors come into the writing programs with little to no background in composition pedagogy; and, unless their program has a compositionist on the administration, instructors may get little explicit mentorship and instruction in the teaching of writing. Some of the writing programs provide comprehensive training in writing pedagogy, while others prioritize training in the teaching of content specific to their college's mission. What's more, some programs collaborate extensively with one another, deliberating on pedagogical approaches and curriculum, while others prefer to operate independently. UCSD is just now, for the first time, convening a Council of Writing Directors following a review of writing instruction at the university. While the formation of the council is promising for advocating for writing on campus, the college-based structure of FYC can make it difficult to generate the collective power we need to be frontliners of first-year students' experiences.

This culture of isolation exacerbates, and is exacerbated by, the devaluation of WPA work in higher education. As the editors wrote in the introduction, WPA work "plugs directly into campus-wide conversations in ways not easily felt or understood by all faculty or administrators." Moreover, across many colleges and universities, writing is perceived as *a skill* that can be performed with minimal training and research (Kahn, 2017), not as *a legitimate field of scholarly inquiry*. As the thinking goes, students learn how to write, and teachers learn how to teach writing, through osmosis. At UCSD, this assumption obscures the contributions the writing programs make to the university's prestige and undermines our values as an institution.

In FYC, and possibly only here, students engage explicitly with questions of what it means to be a knowledge-maker. Current research showed FYC is among the strongest predictors of student success and student retention, and that when students succeed in their FYC courses, that success shapes their overall satisfaction with their education and contributes directly to high graduation rates (Garrett et al., 2017). Given UCSD's recent progression to the third best public college in the nation, according to the Forbes America's Top Colleges List and based on factors such as maintaining high retention and graduation rates (Rubalcava, 2022), this finding suggests that the writing programs at UCSD contribute significantly to the institution's success. Yet, to date, the writing programs are not acknowledged in the university's coverage of its rankings, despite the chancellor's acknowledgment of the importance of writing to overall student experience (University of California San Diego, 2014). The devaluation of writing at UCSD not only undermines the goals of the institution, but it also maintains writing studies' marginalized status in higher education. Ultimately, this coerces writing programs at UCSD and elsewhere into fighting to justify our existence.

Like many FYC programs, the writing programs at UCSD are staffed primarily by contingent faculty and staff. In this way, DOC is part of a systemic ecology of unprotected, low-wage WPA work. While program directors at UCSD are tenured teaching faculty, those of us who are associate or assistant directors hold hybrid contracts as both non-tenured faculty (union represented) and staff. The hybridity of our positions can compound the isolation and devaluation of writing at UCSD. We are often the primary administrators in our programs with expertise in composition studies, yet we do not sit on the Academic Senate and cannot participate in faculty voting around or on faculty committees that make decisions about such matters as curriculum, campus planning, campus budget, and more. At the same time, as associate/assistant directors, we are often responsible for high-impact administrative functions. We provide pedagogical leadership, supervising, training, and mentoring to GTAs as well as, in some programs, to guest tenured faculty from different disciplines who teach FYC courses in the college writing programs. We develop curriculum, designing program-wide learning outcomes and building assessment structures for FYC courses. We adjudicate high-impact procedures, such as academic integrity cases and harassment and discrimination cases. The responsibilities we hold do not match the precarity of our positions, another intersection linking DOC and other writing programs across the nation (WPA Executive Committee, 2019). Scarce resources and minimal job security shortchanges GTA training, faculty development, and, ultimately, student learning. This ecology often leads to high turnover in the college writing programs and perpetuates the devaluation of writing studies in higher education.

In some ways, the college-based structure of FYC at UCSD is a source of strength. It allows students to experience the capaciousness of writing, and faculty and instructors to fuse writing instruction with their disciplinary expertise. Yet for these potentials to be fully realized and to offset the existing constraints around community-building and knowledge-sharing at UCSD, university administration must invest in writing. In the absence of that investment, FYC programs at UCSD capitulate to a capitalist, meritocratic culture of competition in our fight for much-needed resources. This fight detracts our attention away from pedagogical innovation and maintains the grind culture of academia.

THE DIMENSIONS OF CULTURE PROGRAM

The very creation of DOC stems from radical student resistance to an ecology of exclusion at UCSD and in higher education more broadly. Housed in Thurgood Marshall College, named after the first Black justice on the U.S. Supreme Court, DOC teaches composition through the theory and practice of social revolution. In the 1960s, as the student movement for civil rights gathered momentum across the United States, the Black Student Council (BSC) and the Mexican American Youth Association (MAYA) at UCSD came together to demand an undergraduate college dedicated to the histories, cultures, and lived experiences of working-class Black, Brown, and White students (Ferguson, 2015). Originally named Third College when it formed in 1970, this college eventually became Thurgood Marshall College, and DOC, originally Third College Writing, was established as the academic program for incoming Marshall students new to the university (Regents, 2022c). DOC's roots in anticapitalistic, antiracist student activism make FYC somewhat of an anomaly at UCSD.

Given this history, from the vantage point of DOC, UCSD's prestige has been shaped as much by student activism as by cutting-edge research. For example, within DOC, the Chicano Legacy Mural is one of the university's most significant achievements. This 17 x 54-foot mosaic portraying the Chicanx Movement takes up one full side of a lecture hall on campus and results from the vision of UCSD's Movimiento Estudiantil Chicano de Aztlán (MEChA), a student-run organization supporting Chicanx and Latinx students, and persistent collaboration from faculty and staff, including Jorge Mariscal, the former director of DOC (Clark, 2011). Along with subsequent public art installations on campus, including the Black Legacy Mural in the university's student center in 2015, the Chicano Legacy Mural provides a permanent reminder of both minoritized students' demands for institutional representation and the university's promise to invest in them. We teach this history in DOC. We assign the original student demands authored by BSC-MAYA that formed the college, the Lumumba/Zapata Demands (Black Student Council and the Mexican American Youth Association, 1969), at the beginning of the DOC sequence, and we teach the Chicano Legacy Mural as part of a unit on UCSD student activism as students produce their own arguments for campus change in the capstone course of the DOC sequence.

At the same time as DOC upholds a legacy of student demands for counterhegemonic education, as an FYC program, DOC is also bound up in the university's requirement that students become proficient academic writers. DOC makes transparent this both/and positionality through curriculum, which "outline[s] the contradictions of U.S. history and culture and ask[s] students to consider the extent to which the nation's founding principles of life, liberty, and the pursuit of happiness have been realized for all" (Mariscal, 2013), while it also helps students "develop the critical reading, drafting and revision, and metacognitive processes necessary to succeed at UCSD and beyond" (Dimensions of Culture Program, 2022). Like all FYC programs at UCSD, but *un*like FYC programs at other institutions, DOC teaches writing through specific content so that we can simultaneously uphold the legacy of our college home and orient students its intellectual theme and prepare them for success as writers in and beyond the academy.

In DOC, we mediate our contradictory position at the university by emphasizing academic writing not as something to master, but as something to facilitate student agency—a tool used to speak truth to power with material impact. We manifest this principle through the sequencing of curriculum and the learning outcomes that ground them. In the introductory course of the year-long sequence, students *practice* critical reading through coming to terms with U.S. history from the perspectives of disenfranchised groups. In the argumentation course that follows, students *practice* persuasive writing through a rhetorical analysis of arguments for justice in the Civil Rights Movement and contemporary struggles for justice. In the capstone course, students *practice* research by proposing student-led interventions into campus culture issues. We purposefully emphasize *practice* in the curriculum to acknowledge students as agents of their own learning and to challenge ideologies of *mastery* and *assimilation* that Standard Academic English espouses. The sequencing of the curriculum emphasizes grounding action in critical consciousness. In critically examining the conditions that have enabled injustice to thrive in the United States early on in the sequence, DOC students are better positioned to imagine different futures at the culmination of the sequence.

The challenge facing us daily is aligning our teaching practices with DOC's focus on naming and resisting oppressive power structures. A primary way we confront this challenge is through antiracist writing pedagogy education for DOC GTAs. In DOC, the term antiracist writing pedagogy refers to a teaching philosophy and toolbox of practical methods for centering issues of race, racism, and racial justice in FYC, alongside constant pedagogical self-reflection. As antiracist educators, we work with each other and our students to uncover how Standard Academic English is a form of White language supremacy (Inoue, 2019a) and White rhetorical and communication supremacy (Young, 2021). Antiracist writing pedagogy education in DOC supports instructors and students in engaging at their own levels of experiences while taking ownership of their pedagogical and writerly development.

This education of unlearning has compelled DOC to replace traditional grading with contract grading across the lower-division DOC sequence, so that we can better support students' development of their own writing process and their agency as writers. Utilizing contract grading means that we assess student writing based on completion, revision, and documentation of learning rather than on the subjective quality of the writing. In DOC, we've developed our own brand of contract grading by blending elements of specifications grading (Nilson, 2015) and elements of labor-based contract grading (Inoue, 2019b). We draw from Linda Nilson's framework to establish clear, detailed criteria (specifications) for each assignment, grade student work on a pass/fail basis, and allow students to revise any assignment that does not pass. So that the final course grades students earn more accurately reflect their learning, all assignments map onto explicit learning outcomes we have designed for the DOC sequence:

1. Defining, describing, and explaining promises and paradoxes in U.S. history, society, and culture.
2. Examining, giving examples of, and imagining interventions into the contradiction between the American promise of equality and reality of structural inequities.
3. Relating, synthesizing, and integrating the social and historical contexts of struggles for justice in the US, from the precolonial period through to the present day.
4. Reflecting on, communicating about, and asking questions about positionality in relation to U.S. history, society, and culture.
5. Recognizing, sharing, and committing to new interests, attitudes, and/or values about social justice.
6. Identifying and assessing learning style, learning needs, and learning resources in relation to critical reading, writing, and thinking.

At the core of our approach to grading is radical compassion: an endeavor to build trust and community between instructors and students by reimagining the FYC classroom as a space for shifting entrenched power structures that force students "to adopt a normative White voice that devalues the specific practices of language and lived experiences of minoritized communities" (Johnston et al., 2022, p. 17). We use contract grading to subvert the notion that the teacher is the sole arbiter of good writing and, instead, we center the diverse literacies and knowledges that our students bring into the classroom.

Given our curriculum, DOC has developed a reputation as the social justice writing program among UCSD's FYC programs. Some students even refer to DOC as the "Social Justice Warriors" writing program that "inDOCtrinates" students into a liberal agenda. What's more, DOC exists on a UC campus nicknamed **U**niversity of **C**alifornia for the **S**ocially **D**ead (UCSD), located as it is in wealthy La Jolla and lacking a college town feel. DOC's reputation as a social justice program on a "socially dead" campus, as it intersects with the current moment of politicized polarization and an invigorated Alt-right, poses compounded risks to fulfilling the revolutionary aims of the students and faculty who founded DOC's Marshall College home. We don't want to water-down curriculum, at the same time as we must prioritize the safety of students, TAs, staff, and faculty, and attempt to engage students and help them succeed as writers regardless of their political orientations. With few program faculty and staff with job security and structurally supported academic freedom, risk-taking is risky.

Despite our best intentions to be revolutionary educators, DOC capitulates to dominance in myriad ways. Analyzing DOC's position within its UCSD home and in the field more broadly allows us to name these capitulations. Indeed, they are all systemic, based on existing networks and supersystems, and cannot be resolved through individual actors. Rather, they require vigilance so that we can attend to their harmful impacts.

- In helping students satisfy the University of California Writing Requirement, which stipulates that they "develop the command of argumentative strategies and the control of voice that will enable them to present their ideas cogently and persuasively" (UC Student Affairs, 2017), we reproduce colonialist ways of knowing, which reinforce individualism, rationality, self-control, and persuasion (Inoue, 2015, p. 48–49).
- In requiring students to follow academic citation conventions (APA, MLA), we valorize the individual over the collective. These citation styles shore up a Western understanding of source use, giving credit

to individual authors and obscuring how knowledge emerges through varying degrees of collaborative authorship.
- While we utilize contract grading, in assigning letter grades at the end of the course, we condone a grading scale set by the university and subscribe to meritocracy.
- In assigning a rigorous workload of reading and writing assignments and expecting students to attend tri-weekly lectures in a lecture hall with limited accessibility, we privilege able-bodied, affluent students with few to no barriers in caring for their mental and physical health.
- In employing the least expensive laborers (GTAs and adjuncts) to take on the affective and intellectual labor of grading and responding to student writing, we participate in capitalism. While we have found ways to offset the burden on GTAs and adjuncts through comprehensive pedagogical training and subsidizing their professional development, many must go into debt and take on additional employment to survive.

A CONCLUSION WITH A FEW PLACES TO START

An intersectional cultural-historical activity theory can make visible the misfit of the institutional structures that contain our daily practices as writing instructors and administrators. This case study has revealed both alignments and disconnects between DOC's stated intentions and the program's impact. We teach FYC through the theory and practice of social revolution. At the same time, students experience our curriculum as, at once, emancipatory and coercive; administrators and faculty take significant pedagogical risks in teaching DOC curriculum, while also participating in an academic culture of competition that fuels isolation and demoralization; we resent and also consent to the dominance of STEM as the gold standard of academic prestige by participating in a system that devalues writing.

In naming contradictions in DOC, I intend to call attention to the larger power dynamics that we all face in our daily work as FYC administrators. I hope this builds solidarity across FYC administrators. I hope this invites reflection on how our programs' positional differences uniquely shape our negotiations with dominance—and by extension, on how our work as writing program administrators *is* a project of negotiating dominance at the same time as it is one of advocacy. I hope this chapter sparks ideas for how we might make more intentional choices about how to engage power in our programs, at our institutions, and in our fields.

While each institution has its own unique sets of structural constraints and affordances, the channels our programs must go through to approve curriculum and learning outcomes, which inevitably shape how we assess student writing, to approve or deny student access to credit-bearing writing courses, among other routine practices in WPA work, are overwhelmingly determined by units of leadership that seldom set foot in an FYC classroom. Perhaps the university will never change. Perhaps our negotiations with dominance will persist. Perhaps FYC will continue to be treated as a service, not a legitimate field. I propose that we resist the urge to settle these uncertainties once and for all and instead, move toward our contradictions to learn what they might teach us. Here are a few places to start:

- How can we leverage the particular histories of our programs and the broader successes of the institutions in which they live to secure more resources?
- How can writing pedagogy education in our programs influence future writing studies teacher-scholar-administrators to become more cognizant of the larger ecosystems in which FYC operates?
- How can we refuse to feel defeated by the systems in which we participate and instead, develop more intentional terms of that participation?

REFERENCES

Black Student Council and the Mexican American Youth Association. (1969). *Lumumba-Zapata College: B.S.C.-M.A.Y.A. demands for the third college, U.C.S.D.* https://library.ucsd.edu/speccoll/DigitalArchives/ld781_s2-l86-1969/.

Brubaker, M. (2020, July 27). UC San Diego ranked #1 by U.S. news & world report. *UC San Diego Health Newsroom.* https://health.ucsd.edu/news/releases/Pages/2020-07-27-uc-san-diego-ranked-number-one-by-us-news-and-world-report.aspx.

Clark, C. (2011, May 16). Groundbreaking Chicano Legacy 40 años mosaic to be unveiled. *This Week @ UCSD.* https://library.ucsd.edu/dc/object/bb74124759.

Clark, C. (2016, June 29). UC San Diego tops list for highest number of women graduates in STEM. *UC San Diego News Center.* https://ucsdnews.ucsd.edu/pressrelease/uc_san_diego_tops_list_for_highest_number_of_women_graduates_in_stem.

Conference on College Composition and Communication. (2021). *CCCC statement on White language supremacy.* Conference on College Composition and Communication. https://cccc.ncte.org/cccc/white-language-supremacy.

Crenshaw, K. W. (1989). Demarginalizing the intersection of race and sex: A Black feminist critique of antidiscrimination doctrine, feminist theory and antiracist politics. *University of Chicago Legal Forum, 1*(8), 139–167.

Dimensions of Culture Program. (2022). Syllabus for dimensions of culture 1: Reading diversity. University of California San Diego. https://marshall.ucsd.edu/doc/doc1/index.html.

Engeström, Y. (1996). Developmental studies work as a testbench of activity theory: The case of primary care medical practice. In S. Chaiklin & J. Lave (Eds.), *Understanding practice: perspectives on activity and context* (pp. 64–103). Cambridge University Press.

Engeström, Y., Miettinen, R. & Punamäki-Gitai, R. L. (Eds.). (1999). *Perspectives on activity theory.* Cambridge University Press.

Ferguson, S. (2015). *Philosophy of African American studies: Nothing left of Blackness.* Palgrave Macmillan.

Garrett, N., Bridgewater, M. & Feinstein, B. (2017). How student performance in first-year composition predicts retention and overall student success. In T. Ruecker, D. Shepherd, H. Estrem & B. Brunk-Chavez (Eds.), *Retention, persistence, and writing programs* (pp. 93–113). Utah State University Press.

Inoue, A. B. (2015). *Antiracist writing assessment ecologies: Teaching and assessing writing for a socially just future.* The WAC Clearinghouse; Parlor Press. https://doi.org/10.37514/per-b.2015.0698.

Inoue, A. B. (2019a). How do we language so people stop killing each other, or what do we do about White language supremacy? *College Composition and Communication, 71*(2), 352–369.

Inoue, A. B. (2019b). *Labor-based grading contracts: Building equity and inclusion in the compassionate writing classroom.* The WAC Clearinghouse; University Press of Colorado. https://doi.org/10.37514/PER-B.2022.1824.

Johnston, E., Solomon, A. S. & Kim, J. (2022). Sharing lessons learned: Intersectional collaboration, collective accountability, and radical care in antiracist programming. *Writers: Craft & Context, 3*(1), 13–23.

Kahn, S. (2017, August 7). Bad idea about writing: Anybody can teach it. *Inside Higher Education.* https://www.insidehighered.com/views/2017/08/07/colleges-should-hire-writing-instructors-right-experience-and-expertise-and-give

Mariscal, J. (2013). Ties to the origin of "Third College." *Dimensions of culture program history.* Thurgood Marshall College, UC San Diego. https://marshall.ucsd.edu/doc/history-of-doc.html#Ties-to-the-Origin-of-Third-Co.

May, V. M. (2015). *Pursuing intersectionality, Unsettling dominant imaginaries.* Routledge.

National Council of Teachers of English. (2021, June). *CCCC statement on White language supremacy.* Conference on College Composition and Communication. https://cccc.ncte.org/cccc/white-language-supremacy.

Nilson, L. B. (2015). *Specifications grading: Restoring rigor, motivating students, and saving faculty time.* Stylus Publishing.

Prior, P., Solberg, J., Berry, P., Bellowar, H., Chewning, B., Lunsford, K., Rohan, L., Roozen, K., Sheridan-Rabideau, M. P., Shipka, J., Ittersum, D. V. & Walker, J. R. (2007). Resituating and remediating the canons: A cultural-historical remapping of rhetorical activity. *Kairos, 11*(3). http://kairos.technorhetoric.net/11.3/topoi/prior-et-al/core/core.pdf.

Regents of the University of California. (2017). Student profile 2016–2017. *UC San Diego Office of Institutional Research.* https://ir.ucsd.edu/_files/stats-data/profile/profile-2016-2017.pdf.

Regents of the University of California. (2022a). Analytical writing program. https://awp.ucsd.edu/.
Regents of the University of California (2022b). Campus transformation. https://plan.ucsd.edu/campus-transformation.
Regents of the University of California. (2022c). Dimensions of Culture Program. https://marshall.ucsd.edu/doc/index.html.
Regents of the University of California. (2022d). Student Profile 2021–2022. *UC San Diego Office of Institutional Research*. https://ir.ucsd.edu/undergrad/publications/21_22_StudentProfiles.pdf.
Regents of the University of California. (2023). UC San Diego turns 60. UC San Diego. https://today.ucsd.edu/story/uc-san-diego-turns-60.
Robbins, G. (2020, November 16). UC San Diego's foreign enrollment hits record. The pandemic may stop it from going higher. *The San Diego Tribune*. https://www.sandiegouniontribune.com/news/education/story/2020-11-16/uc-san-diego-foreign-student-enrollment.
Rubalcava, A. (2022, September 9). UC San Diego ranked no. 3 best public college by Forbes. *UC San Diego Today*. https://today.ucsd.edu/story/uc-san-diego-ranked-no-3-best-public-college-by-forbes.
Ruiz, I. D. (2016). *Reclaiming composition for Chicano/as and other ethnic minorities: A critical history and pedagogy*. Palgrave Macmillan.
University of California San Diego. (2014). Strategic plan report: Defining the future of the public research university. *UC San Diego Strategic Plan*. https://plan.ucsd.edu/report.
Viejas Enterprises. (2015). Viejas band of Kumeyaay Indians. *Viejas band of Kumeyaay Indians*. http://viejasbandofkumeyaay.org/viejas-community/kumeyaay-history/.
WPA Executive Committee. (2019, 17 July). Evaluating the intellectual work of writing program administration. *Council of Writing Program Administrators*. http://wpacouncil.org/aws/CWPA/page_template/show_detail/242849?model_name=news_article.
Young, V. A. (2021). 2020 CCCC chair's address. *College Composition and Communication, 72*(4), 623–639.

CHAPTER 9.
NETWORKING ACROSS THE CURRICULUM: CHALLENGES, CONTRADICTIONS, AND CHANGES

Kelly Bradbury, Sue Doe, and Mike Palmquist[1]
Colorado State University

In this chapter, we share the story of Colorado State University's gtPathways Writing Integration Project through a lens of activity theory, highlighting the ways in which each of us, over the course of fifteen years, has met with institutional networks that have and continue to inform, shape, and challenge the goals and the work of the project. Readers can glean from our story insights about the complexities involved in undertaking, developing, and maintaining a socially just writing across the curriculum program amidst an array of changing institutional players and forces. While it is in many ways a story of missed opportunities, it is also a story of localized triumphs, perseverance, and long-term dedication to supporting meaningful work happening from the bottom up.

> I think this is a great solution to the problem.
> – Vice Provost for Undergraduate Affairs, Late September, 2005

> In its current form, unfortunately, it's likely to fail.
> – Mike Palmquist, Early October, 2005

In 2005, facing a mandate from the Colorado legislature that writing instruction be integrated into core courses in the arts, humanities, and social sciences, the vice provost for undergraduate affairs at Colorado State University (CSU) came up with a promising idea. With support from the provost as well as the vice provost for graduate affairs, he secured 75 new graduate teaching assistant lines, all of which would be held by the graduate school and allocated as needed to departments teaching the core courses.[2] Drawing on his experience years earlier

---
1 Authorship is alphabetical.
2 With the exception of Psychology 100, these courses are housed in the College of Liberal Arts. The psychology department is located in the College of Natural Sciences.

as a faculty member at an elite liberal arts college, he envisioned the graduate students in these new lines working with faculty members to provide meaningful feedback to students on their writing.[3]

When word of the new initiative filtered down to the writing studies faculty in the English department, through the dean and then through the department chair, in the way this sort of information typically flows, we found ourselves intrigued by the idea, pleased by the commitment of resources (more than a million dollars on an annual basis), and concerned that it had been planned without input from faculty members with expertise in writing instruction. In a meeting to discuss the initiative, Mike was asked to reach out to the vice provost and report back to the group. As one of twelve university distinguished teaching scholars, he had already worked closely with the provost and vice provost and, in addition, was an emerging leader in the WAC community. He had also been involved, at the vice provost's request, in state-wide discussions of how to implement the legislation that had created the state-wide Guaranteed Transfer Pathways (gtPathways) program.[4]

In his meeting with Mike, the vice provost expressed both great optimism in his vision for integrating writing into gtPathways courses and fond memories of the writing his students had done at his previous institution. His vision was straightforward and elegant: faculty members teaching the core courses would help the GTAs develop the skills they would need to respond to the meaningful and substantial writing assignments the faculty members would design for their courses. When Mike, who since 1991 had been working with his colleagues to redesign a WAC program that took into account the resistance typical of faculty at research-intensive universities (Palmquist, 2000), suggested that more than three decades of WAC research pointed to a dismal outcome for the plan, the vice provost began to pivot, and the conversation turned toward modifications that might lead to greater success.[5] By the end of the meeting, the vice provost had agreed to support professional development for both GTAs and faculty led by a team of writing studies faculty.

With support from the vice provost in place, the writing studies faculty began exploring options for developing a robust training program that would work in concert with the existing WAC program. Early agreements among the group included the need for program leadership from a senior faculty member, significant release time for the program leader, review of course assignments, and

---

3   CSU was (and remains) the only institution in the state to take this comprehensive (and expensive) approach to addressing the state-mandated writing requirement.
4   gtPathways refers to a set of general education courses (totaling roughly 30 credit hours at various institutions) that the Colorado Commission on Higher Education guarantees to transfer across all public colleges and universities in the state.
5   To be fair, it would not be inaccurate to report that this pivot was far from instantaneous.

a robust professional development program for the GTAs and faculty members involved with gtPathways courses. A plan was developed, and a meeting was scheduled with the dean.

Unfortunately, convinced that faculty in the college would view the gtPathways writing requirements as not only an infringement of their right to teach their courses in the manner they deemed best but also as an unfunded mandate that would consume time they might prefer to devote to other areas of their academic lives, the dean refused to sign off on the plan. While the dean approved of placing a senior faculty member in charge of what had by then become known as the gtPathways Writing Integration Project (gtPathways Project), the dean opposed any form of faculty professional development, pointing out that it implied a level of control that writing studies faculty should not—and would not—have over the design of assignments in gtPathways courses. The argument that professional development workshops and faculty consultation would be voluntary, compensated, and likely to lead to improved learning outcomes was rejected as overreach.

With these limits in place, the dean asked the department chair and the writing studies faculty to develop a "better" plan and tasked one of the associate deans with managing further discussion of the project. Planning continued throughout the spring and summer of 2006, with an expectation that Mike would lead the project.

That changed in the fall of 2006, when Mike became director of The Institute for Learning and Teaching (TILT), a new unit put in place by the provost to enhance learning and teaching across the university. When no other members of the writing studies faculty were able to take the lead on the gtPathways Project, Mike enlisted the aid of two vice provosts (one who had originated the project and a second to whom he was reporting as director of TILT) in convincing the provost to allocate an additional tenure line to lead the project (additional in the sense that the provost had already given the department a new line to replace Mike as a computers-and-writing specialist). With an agreement for a new tenure line in place, Mike approached the department chair with what he thought was good news.

Surprisingly, the department chair did not welcome the offer of a new tenure line. Faced with anger from what he viewed as the core of the English department—the literature faculty, a group to which he belonged—who had seen their numbers decline over the previous year (complicated largely by the 2003 recession), he initially refused to accept the new line, pointing out that the literature faculty would be angry with him if he did so. After further discussion, which included the observation that refusing the tenure line would result in adding the writing studies faculty to the groups that were upset with him, the chair agreed to accept the new line under the condition that it would not take the place of other (literature) lines he had already requested, and, in consultation with the writing studies faculty, Mike developed a plan to fund the project (see Appendix A). The dean subsequently agreed to the plan, and Mike drafted a memorandum of understanding (MOU) that defined the duties of the new hire and specified that the new line would not replace any other requested lines (see Appendix B). Sue was subsequently hired into the new tenure line, and she took on leadership of the project.

In what follows, we share the story of the evolution of the gtPathways Project in hopes that it can provide writing program administrators insights into the many forces at play in working to establish a writing program and, more specifically, a writing across the curriculum program. We draw on activity theory to help us consider the larger set of networks that have—and continue to—inform, shape, and challenge the gtPathways Project. Activity theory and, in particular, Yrjö Engeström's (1987, 1990, 2014) elaboration of Lev Vygotsky's (1978) subject-object-tool model, provides a useful lens through which we can interrogate and draw conclusions about the institutional forces that have shaped the project over the past 15 years, among them the conflicting goals, perceived pressures, and confining systems and networks felt by key players involved with the project. We hope that sharing our story and analyzing it through activity theory will provide insights into practices that can be used to establish complex undertakings in writing studies and, more specifically, writing across the curriculum.

APPROACHING THE PROJECT THROUGH ACTIVITY THEORY

> I have found that Engeström's systems version of activity theory offers insight into the central problematic of my research: how university students learn to write specialized discourse and write to learn specialized knowledge.
> – David Russell, 2009, p. 42

In the introduction to their influential edited collection, *Writing Selves/Writing Societies: Research from Activity Perspectives*, Charles Bazerman and David Russel characterized activity theory as "a set of related approaches that view human phenomena as dynamic, in action" (2003, p. 1). It focuses, they observed, on how "human-produced artifacts" (an umbrella term under which they included activities as wide-ranging as "utterances or text, or shovels or symphonies") that can be understood best not as distinct "objects in themselves" but rather as objects and, more to the point, activities that achieve meaning within the larger context of the systems in which they are situated (p. 1).

Also referred to as cultural-historical activity theory (CHAT) and sociocultural activity theory, activity theory provides a robust theoretical framework that can help writing program administrators understand the rise, function, operation and, in some cases, the demise of intra-campus initiatives such as the gtPathways Project.[6] As an intellectual movement, activity theory emerged from work carried out by Soviet psychologists in the 1920s and 1930s to develop psychological theories that better addressed the work of groups, and in particular theories that could provide alternatives to Western theories that focused on the individual. Key voices in that effort included Alexei Leontiev, Aleksandr Luria, Sergei Rubinstein, and Lev Vygotsky. Jeanne Pau Yen Ho and her colleagues (2016) characterize activity theory as moving through three phases.[7] The initial phase is characterized by Vygotsky's three-part model of subject, object, and mediating artifact (see Figure 9.1).[8]

Following the translation of their work, activity theory became a powerful framework for understanding the work of groups. Yrjö Engeström would play a central role in that emergence, drawing on Leontiev's work to expand Vygotsky's triadic activity model of *subject*, *object*, and *mediator* into a more complex model that is distinguished by its stronger focus on cultural and historical factors that shape the work of an activity system. His model, and more importantly his extensive efforts to explore the use of activity theory to understand complex, socially mediated actions and decision-making, marked a second phase in the development of activity theory (see Figure 9.2).

The most recent elaboration of activity theory focuses on the ways in which activity systems interact with each other or are embedded in larger systems of activity (see Figure 9.3). In this way, we might explore how the activity systems associated with a college or university might interact with or otherwise influence each other, perhaps through shared membership, shared goals (objects), similar rules (sometimes referred to as *norms*) or reliance on the same or similar tools. This third-stage approach might also be used to explore how a given university program (or, again, an activity) is embedded within other (and perhaps overlapping) activity systems, such as departments, colleges, schools, and divisions as well as how they are shaped by activity systems such as local communities, professional organizations, and, in the case of public institutions, governmental entities and regulatory agencies.

---

6   For more about activity theory, see Cole (1996), Engeström (1987, 1990, 1993, 1999a, 1999b, 2014), Engeström and Miettinen (1999), Kaptelinin (2005), Leontiev (1978, 2005), Rubinštejn (1987), and Vygotsky (1978, 1986, 1989). For more about its application to writing studies, see Bazerman and Russell (2003a, 2003b) and Russell (2009).

7   Some scholars (e.g., Behrend, 2014; Ho et al., 2019) view Leontiev's elaboration of Vygotsky's model as a second phase in the development of activity theory. Since Vygotsky and Leontiev were not only contemporaries but collaborators, their work might reasonably be viewed as falling within the first stage.

8   This description of activity theory is drawn in large part from Mike's exploration of the origins and operation of the WAC Clearinghouse in a collection, also published by the WAC Clearinghouse, honoring the work of Charles Bazerman (Palmquist, 2023). The re-use of text and figures is intentional and done so with permission.

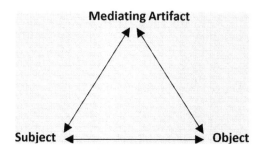

Figure 9.1. A model of the first phase of activity theory.

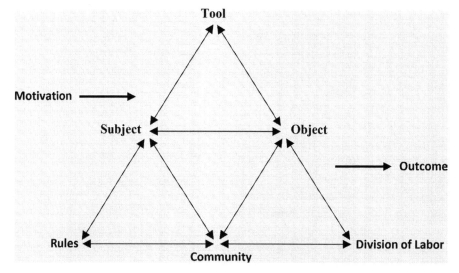

Figure 9.2. Engeström's model of activity theory.

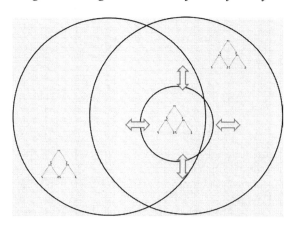

Figure 9.3. Interactions among embedded and overlapping activity systems.

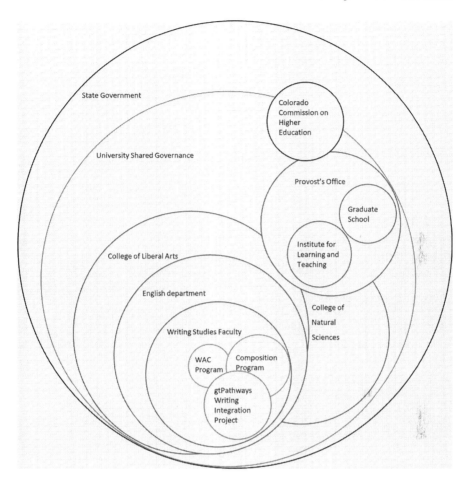

Figure 9.4. Overlapping and embedded activities shaping the gtPathways Writing Integration Project.

Over the past three decades, activity theory has been used to explore a wide range of complex systems. Scholars have focused on writing studies (Bazerman & Russell, 2003a; Russell, 1995, 2009), instructional technology (Behrend, 2014; Chung, 2019), distributed leadership (Ho et al., 2015; Takoeva, 2017), design thinking (Winstanley, 2019; Zahedi & Tessier, 2018), education (Abdullah, 2014; Al-Huneini et al., 2020; Carvalho, 2015; Pearson, 2009), human computer interaction (Draper, 1993; Kaptelinin & Nardie, 2012; Nardi, 1995), and software development (Dennehy & Conboy, 2017; Hoffmann et al., 2020), to name only a few areas.

In the case of the gtPathways Project, we find activity theory in general, and Engeström's model in particular, to be a useful framework within which to understand the influence on the development and operation of the project of activity systems within the larger state and university structures that pursue goals that are often aligned but sometimes in conflict. The primary motivating factor in the origin of the project—an act passed by the Colorado state legislature and its subsequent implementation by the Colorado Commission on Higher Education—was subsequently filtered through the Office of the Provost, the Graduate School, the Colleges of Liberal Arts (CLA) and Natural Sciences (CNS), the English department, and the writing studies faculty. In turn, the eight departments that offered the courses, seven from the CLA, and one from CNS, their faculty groups, and the courses themselves shaped the intra-campus operation of the project. Finally, and not inconsequentially, the entire project was approved at the curricular level (through modification of the grading requirements for individual courses) by the Faculty Council, a key part of the university's three-part shared governance system. In some ways, the multiple activity systems shaping the creation and operation of the project resemble a set of Russian matryoshka dolls placed inside a basket that is set on a table and available to family and friends who might want to pick it up and play with it. The potential for arranging, rearranging, breaking, and even disposing of it seems quite high. In Figure 9.4, we've tried to convey the activity systems (with the exception of professional and local communities) that influence and shape the project as a set of overlapping and embedded spheres.

REVISITING THE EARLY AND MIDDLE YEARS (2007–2020)

You only need one advocate.

– Marty Townsend

From the outset, the gtPathways initiative was fraught with difficulty. Some of the challenges came from the departments that were newly required to integrate writing and some came from the CLA dean's office, which oversaw all but one of the departments involved in the project (Psychology). As might be expected when viewed through the lens of activity theory, the departments and faculty faced with the required and seemingly major curricular changes cried foul, arguing that their academic freedom was being challenged. Many argued that they could not be expected, as disciplinary faculty, to "teach writing" and especially grammar. In response, Sue, who had been hired as the first Director of the gtPathways Project, pointed out that they were being asked to *assign* writing—and that professionally trained GTAs would assist with assignment design, the development and explanation of writing expectations, and grading. Still, the faculty were not convinced. To their credit, they pointed out that most of the faculty teaching the affected courses were not in tenure lines and hence could be viewed as an unstable workforce that would offer little continuity and low availability for either professional development of their own or oversight of the GTAs who would be under their watch. Additionally, many senior faculty members in these departments argued that their GTAs would be so overwhelmed with the work of grading student papers that they wouldn't be able to get their own graduate work done.

The CLA dean and associate dean, which received the majority of this pushback, found themselves on the defensive (as the dean had foreseen). The dean arranged a meeting in which the chairs of departments leveled their anger about the new requirement against Sue and the acting Director of Composition who accompanied Sue to the meeting. Insults were thrown and anger vented, while Sue and her colleague listened carefully and acknowledged that departments were being asked to undertake a major curricular shift. Following the meeting, the dean and associate dean, as a response to pressure, modified the initial requirements for the GTA professional development course. The course was reduced from three credit hours to one credit hour; it would be taught in the first half of the semester; and it would focus strictly on grading and responding. It would be taught by the gtPathways director alone, and the director would be permitted no interaction with faculty members unless they sought it out. In addition, the planned preservice orientation for the GTAs was limited to nine hours the week prior to the start of the fall term.

We realized, of course, that placing restrictions on the director's interaction with faculty and limiting what could be accomplished in the GTA professional development course runs counter to best practices in WAC and writing program work, including (as Jenna Morton-Aiken argued in this collection) the need for meaningful conversations and active listening between the director and the faculty. Nonetheless, Sue settled into acceptance of the constraints and focused on what she could accomplish, focusing on GTA professional development and adjusting her priority to this new professoriate while directing the rest of her energy toward other parts of her workload distribution, which included 40 percent research and 20 percent service. In the summer before she began directing the gtPathways Project, Sue went to the International Writing Across the Curriculum Conference and the Writing Program Administrator Conference, where she brought her concerns to many fora and gained confidence that she had whole professional associations behind her. One person at the WAC Conference expressed actual envy of Sue's position, saying "Oh, for an initiative with low expectations!" and WAC pioneer Marty Townsend told Sue that she needed only one advocate. Mike was that advocate, as he was now directing TILT and serving as associate vice provost for learning and teaching.

Prior to the start of the semester, positive news arrived. The CLA dean's office developed an MOU, with help from Sue, that established expectations for writing assignments in the gtPathways Project (see Appendix C). The MOU established that both low-stakes and high-stakes writing could be assigned throughout the semester and that, at a minimum, one formal high-stakes assignment would be required. While the MOU was intended to reduce anxiety about the amount of writing that would need to be assigned, Sue viewed the MOU as the foundation for discussing writing as not only a form of assessment but more importantly as a tool for enhancing teaching and learning. The pedagogy course for the GTAs could now focus on not only how to grade and respond to final products of writing but also on intervention drafts, on writing-to-learn activities, and on writing-to-engage assignments in gtPathways courses.

In the first year, the pre-service orientation was well attended, but many of the graduate students—some of whom had been in the field doing research—were angry about being asked to come to campus early. Participating departments had been slow to send information to them, and some of the GTAs had picked up on the negative reactions of their faculty mentors. Many arrived at the pedagogy class with skepticism. Sue set her sights on gaining their trust and instilling a belief that they would learn something of value. Sue also pointed out that their appointments were a pretty good deal—a paid position with a full tuition stipend. She also told them, without any initial evidence to support the claim, that their involvement would positively affect their own writing and their career aspirations, particularly if they thought they might want to teach at the college level. As it turns out, those GTAs, many of whom were destined to become part of the new professoriate, emerged as key people to focus on. Many were happy to have graduate support, and most began to see the value of their work with students as a CV builder. Further, because they did not arrive with a set of expectations regarding the courses in which they would serve as assistants, they quickly saw ways in which writing activities and assignments could advance the teaching and learning goals in their courses. Indeed, in time it became clear that they would be the ones to take writing for engaged learning seriously.

Sue initially made grading and responding to writing the focus of the one-credit pedagogy class, surprising the GTAs by showing them a robust literature in these areas and, more generally, conveying that the best practices around writing instruction are not folklore but grounded in theory and research. The GTAs began to show interest in the pedagogical opportunities presented by writing, and some began to imagine action research that they might undertake in their classrooms. One GTA created a bridge between their supervising faculty member and Sue, which led to a research project that became an article through which the disciplinary faculty and Sue gained an important publication.

In the second semester of her first year as director, in an effort to sustain the GTAs' professional development, Sue encouraged them to think of themselves as writing ambassadors to their departments, drawing on the work of Paula Gillespie at Marquette University. The GTAs began to develop writing workshops for their departments, eventually delivering workshops that, in some cases, were also offered as part of TILT's Master Teacher Initiative program, which was operating in all of the colleges. With the GTAs developing pedagogical expertise and visibility around writing, Sue and the graduate students began producing a gtPathways newsletter and developed language that they could use for their CVs to explain what they knew about writing assignments, including how to grade and respond effectively, efficiently, and ethically. Eventually, some of the GTAs told Sue that the capacities around writing integration had helped them obtain teaching positions after completing their degrees.

Moreover, many of the GTAs were themselves transformed not only as teachers but as writers, and when their graduate committee members saw this, the faculty began to understand the potential impact of writing integration not only on undergraduates but also on the graduate students who were responding to undergraduate writing. The success with the GTAs was redemptive, and Sue found that she cared less and less about the recalcitrant faculty members and departments within her own college. At the same time, she began to propose WAC research projects which became important to the initiative and to the broader WAC community (Cavdar & Doe, 2012; Doe et al., 2013; Doe et al., 2016; Gingerich et al., 2014).

While Sue became increasingly confident that the intra-campus gtPathways initiative was making a difference, especially given the systematic obstacles that were overcome, she was also increasingly impressed that Mike was able to spearhead a WAC initiative in the first place, especially given the significant pushback of faculty and the low support of leadership. After Sue left the directorship of the gtPathways Project in 2013, it went consecutively to three senior tenured faculty members in the department, each of whom stayed the course, deepening institutional commitments wherever they could as they worked on the project.

FLASHING FORWARD

> DEPARTMENT OF ENGLISH ANNOUNCEMENT for gtPATHWAYS WRITING INTEGRATION DIRECTOR: Seeking a non-tenure-track faculty member to assume additional duties with gtPathways writing integration, GTA professional development, and program administration.
>
> – Spring 2020 job posting

> With apologies for the long delay, I am writing to see if you remain interested in the gtPathways [director] position. Due to the current COVID-induced budgetary challenges, the position has been changed somewhat.
>
> – Spring 2020 email correspondence

In 2020, Kelly became director of the gtPathways Project. Like Sue before her, Kelly's directorship centers on training the gtPathways GTAs through the pre-semester orientation and one-credit course. During these trainings, GTAs engage critically with scholarship that examines how writing can foster learning, engagement, and critical thinking. They learn about and work to implement best practices in responding to student writing, designing effective writing assignments, and developing appropriate grading criteria. Kelly and her students discuss strategies for dealing with assessment challenges, such as the writing challenges faced by many non-native English speakers, common difficulties with grammar, and poor uses of sources that can lead to unintentional plagiarism. They also consider inclusive teaching practices through awareness of issues of linguistic supremacy, linguistic justice, and cross-cultural writing differences.

Ideally, Kelly's job also involves engaging faculty in similar conversations. We say *ideally* because, through her third year as the director, she has had no faculty members express interest in discussing—or even sharing—the ways in which they integrate writing in their courses. Just as Sue realized during her tenure as director, Kelly quickly learned that her energies are best spent making a difference from the bottom up, so to speak—working to engage and inspire the GTAs who may share their knowledge with faculty members in their home departments and who are working, in some cases, to become future faculty. Centering the GTAs as the foci for the work of the project seems to fall in line with faculty perceptions of the project as well, as the only two faculty members to reach out to Kelly in the past three years have invited her to visit with graduate students in their department about how they as GTAs can integrate writing into their classes and implement best practices in writing assignment design.

As the email correspondence that serves as an epigraph to this section indicates, the position of gtPathways Project director changed substantively in 2020. Those changes included the faculty status of the director. While all previous directors had been tenured or in tenure-track positions, none of the tenure-line faculty were able at the time to serve as director. The selection of Kelly, who was in a non-tenure-line position, marked a significant change in the position. Additionally, the directorship was reduced from a two-semester position to a one-semester (fall) position, with the director returning to a full teaching load during the spring semester. This change reduced the opportunities Kelly would otherwise have had to reach beyond the primarily GTA-focused professional development work conducted in the first half of the fall semester. In addition, the length of the pre-semester GTA orientation was reduced from nine to six hours, further limiting opportunities to move beyond nuts-and-bolts training during the orientation.

Noteworthy, as well, was the discovery that through administrative and department leadership turnover, awareness of the responsibilities of the departments, the faculty, and the GTAs funded by the project had been muddied and, in some departments, had disappeared. For example, when Kelly reached out to department chairs to inquire about low (or no) GTA registration for the required course, she learned that the newly appointed graduate advisor in one department was unaware that the GTAs in their department funded through the gtPathways Project were required to register for the course. It follows, then, that the advisor was unaware which and how many GTAs were tasked with helping to integrate and respond to writing in gtPathways courses. When Kelly reached out to upper administration in the CLA to clarify the number of GTAs assigned to the department, she learned that no upper administrator was overseeing the project or holding departments accountable.

When a senior associate dean was assigned to work with the gtPathways Project, Kelly knew she had the support to repair the broken networks between the gtPathways Project and participating departments. With the support of the associate dean, Kelly has been able to raise awareness and re-extend the work of the project. In the fall of her second year as director, department funding was secured to provide Kelly a spring-semester course release so she could work with the WAC program, now housed in the writing center (which Mike directs) on institutional initiatives related to and extending beyond the gtPathways project. And in fall 2022, a revised MOU was developed that spelled out more clearly the responsibilities of the gtPathways Project, the English department, the CLA, and the departments participating in the project (see Appendix D). These shifts in awareness and engagement at the department and college level, provide us with optimism about securing additional support for the project in the future.

FLASHING BACK: EXPLORING A COMPLEX NETWORK OF ACTIVITY SYSTEMS

> The University will require departments who receive GTA lines funded through the AUCC/gtPathways Writing Initiative to decide whether they will participate in the professional development program supported by TILT and the University Composition Program or provide their own training for the GTAs at department expense. Departments can choose to provide their own training only with approval of the College.
>
> – Draft MOU, January 3, 2007

The planning of the gtPathways Project was influenced by the goals (objects, in activity theory terminology) of several groups at and beyond CSU. Its origins in the Provost's Office reflected mandates issued by the Colorado Commission on Higher Education, which in turn was working to implement a law passed by the state legislature and signed into law by the governor. The deans of CLA and CNS, in an effort to ensure that the departments involved in the initiative would be in agreement with its requirements, worked with more than a dozen department chairs, who in turn worked with their faculty to assess and provide feedback on the initiative. Key issues addressed in discussions included the impact on curriculum of the new requirement that 25 percent of the final grade would be based on writing assignments in gtPathways courses, the implications for faculty academic freedom of the new requirement, the labor required to manage the GTAs who would provide feedback to students, the implications of increasing the number of funded graduate students in affected departments, the funding required to implement the project, the responsibilities and authority of the faculty members directing the project, and the role of existing governance structures in overseeing the project.

These issues played out in ways that illustrate the complex manner in which the nested and overlapping systems within higher education operate. In particular, they highlight several key aspects of activity theory, both within a given activity system and across systems. Below, we discuss efforts to understand and address contradictions revealed through the recognition of competing goals and priorities, the rules that influenced how the project was developed and operated, the manner in which labor was carried out, and the outcomes of the project. We hope these aspects can provide insights into how initiatives such as the gtPathways Project are influenced by the systems and networks within which they operate.

Contradictions, Rules, and Rule Changes

> I could only contact faculty by going through an associate dean who would carefully decide what messages to allow through. As a result, I had to be fairly covert in my efforts to contact faculty. In time, I learned that if the faculty saw how they could benefit from the work (their grad students became better writers as they GTA'd and the faculty themselves got involved in pedagogical research and publication), I could reach them and connections led to conversations about best practices with regard to assignment and rubric design, among other things.
>
> – Sue Doe

When the tenure line into which Sue was hired in spring 2007 was approved, general agreement existed about her role and the shape of the gtPathways Project. A MOU had been circulated among key players in the Provost's Office, the College of Liberal Arts, the English department, and the writing studies faculty, and it was used to guide the design of the project (see Appendix B). Unfortunately, not long after her hire, Sue found little support from college leadership for her work as project director. In her first semester, she was told by the dean that there was to be no direct communication between the project director and faculty members, chairs, or graduate coordinators in the departments that offered the gtPathways courses. All communication was to be run through the dean's office. This differed from the approach taken by the College of Natural Sciences, which authorized the project director to work directly with the faculty member who was in charge of the introductory psychology course. Importantly, it seems to reflect a recognition by the CLA dean of the potential conflicts—referred to as contradictions in Engeström's model of activity systems—across activity systems embedded within the larger college activity system as well as in the activity systems in which the college itself was embedded, conflicts that centered largely on questions of control over curricula. Concerns about who controlled the curriculum were, at that time (though this has diminished over the years), particularly salient, given what were then perceived as demands for oversight of course curricula by the Colorado Commission on Higher Education and, on a larger level, by the state legislature. These concerns also reflect a natural and continuing conflict over control of the curriculum among the departments, the colleges, and the Provost's Office. These conflicts shaped (again, using a term drawn from Engeström's model of activity systems) the rules that shaped activity within the gtPathways Project activity system.

Significantly, the rule against direct contact distanced the project director from the departments and course instructors, creating a situation that would lead to a lack of understanding of the goals of the project, its benefits to students and faculty members, and the responsibilities of the GTAs funded through the project. The decision—again, a rule that shaped activity within the gtPathways Project—to require that 25 percent of the course grade be based on writing was complicated by the large enrollments in the core courses involved in the project. The allocation of new GTA lines to these courses was based on the recognition that faculty members could not be expected to grade and respond to 100–200 students from any one class. The original ratio had been set at 1:90 (GTA to undergrad), a ratio that was judged to be sufficient to allow GTAs to respond to student writing in no more than 20 hours in any given week. Over time, departments began to recognize that they could ask the GTAs to carry out other duties during weeks in which writing was not assigned, which led to changes in GTA activity during the semester. Essentially, and largely as members of the writing studies faculty had warned against during the planning phase of the project, mission creep set in. Over time, as noted earlier in this chapter, changes in department leadership and staffing of the gtPathways courses combined with limited interaction between the departments and the gtPathways Project director led to the rationale for the GTA assignments being "lost" (in some departments) or at least becoming less clear than had initially been the case.

Eventually, the rule against direct outreach by the gtPathways Project director revealed a contradiction in the activity system that led to additional changes in how the project operated. After the project was launched and many faculty members expressed uncertainty about how to develop effective and appropriate writing assignments, the CLA dean's office sought information from the project director that it could share with faculty. Based on information provided by Sue, the CLA dean's office drafted a MOU between the college and the departments stipulating that faculty members teaching gtPathways courses would meet the objectives of the initiative if both informal and formal writing were assigned (see Appendix C). Departments were informed that they could not ignore or avoid the mandate, and the MOU stipulated that there had to be at least one formal writing assignment in each course. The MOU, as a result, provided the director of the project a basis for talking with faculty members who asked about how they might integrate writing-to-learn and writing-to-communicate assignments as the ends of a spectrum of authorized writing tasks.

An additional change in the rules governing how the gtPathways Project operates would also occur as its first semester of operation approached. What had been proposed as a three-credit full-semester graduate course in pedagogy as the main mechanism for preparing the disciplinary GTAs was recast (and diminished) by the CLA dean's office into a one-credit, five-week course with a singular focus on grading and responding. This was a departure from its original vision as a course focused on broader issues related to writing integration, such as how to connect assignment design and assessment to project goals. Departments were also given the option to create their own course rather than require their GTAs to take the course created by the writing studies faculty. Two CLA departments took the option of creating their own courses. One used this model for a few years before acknowledging that the labor resources involved in offering the course were too burdensome and redirected GTAs to the gtPathways Project training. The second department maintains their separate course to this day. Interestingly, a third department decided to withdraw its gtPathways course from the university's core curriculum rather than be forced to adhere to the rules imposed by the CLA dean's office.

A final initial change in the rules has also had a lasting impact on the operation and sustainability of the gtPathways Project. The director of the University Composition Program and Sue, as project director at the time, had argued strongly for annual assessments of student writing and GTA response to writing in the gtPathways courses. They explained that starting the project off with a well-designed assessment could provide useful data that could aid departments in course redesign, and, down the road, help justify retention of the newly funded GTA lines. Unfortunately, all suggestions of assessment were rejected. Approximately eight years into the project, when the idea of assessment was brought up again, the idea was again jettisoned. This stood in contrast to a demonstrated need for assessment. Only a few years into the project, when the Great Recession hit campus and budget cuts were implemented, the vice provost who had initiated the project informed Mike that the project (and its more than million-dollar annual cost) were on the chopping block. Working together, Mike and Sue created a memo that argued successfully for continued funding of the project. The basis for that memo was a series of studies by Sue and Karla Gingerich, the faculty member who coordinated the Introduction to Psychology course, which demonstrated improved writing skills among students in the psychology major, improved writing skills among the GTAs assigned to the course, and improved learning outcomes in areas about which students had written in the course. Due to its excellent assessment practices, the only course outside of CLA essentially saved not only the project but the more than 70 GTA lines associated with it.

Division of Labor

The gtPathways Writing Integration Project runs in parallel with the university's traditional writing requirement, which stipulates that undergraduate students meet both an intermediate and an advanced composition course prior to graduation. These core requirements address the written competency of the gtPathways transfer expectations as well, and in 2016 were re-instantiated in revisions to the competency expectations adopted by the Colorado Commission on Higher Education. The University Composition Program's offerings exist alongside other core requirements in the All-University Core Curriculum (AUCC) for foundational math, science and diversity, equity, and inclusion literacies. Importantly, the intermediate and advanced writing courses are taught primarily by a combination of instructors in contingent positions and roughly three dozen English department GTAs. These GTAs receive substantially more professional development than the gtPathways GTAs, yet all GTAs are compensated equally.

The faculty members in the departments in which gtPathways GTAs reside typically believe that the time required for responding to student writing is far more substantial than that required in most other GTA assignments at the university. Accordingly, recognizing this disparity, some departments have resisted efforts to provide additional professional development to gtPathways GTAs. This contradiction between the goals of the departments and the project director has proven intractable. While departments have clearly conveyed that they are not inclined to take advice on how to assign writing, much less how to grade it, they have also expressed skepticism about their own ability to integrate writing into their courses in meaningful ways. When this skepticism has manifested itself as concern about being asked to become grammar experts, the project director has had ready answers and has been able to direct attention toward the use of writing-to-learn and writing-to-engage activities.

Yet a more fundamental contradiction informs some of the resistance directed toward the project, resulting in clear opposition to any form of professional development, including opportunities to explore best practices in the teaching of writing and the ways in which writing activities and assignments can contribute to department efforts to meet disciplinary and course objectives. This resistance seems to be rooted in the belief that CLA faculty are already outstanding teachers. As such, they are convinced they already possess the knowledge and experience to assign writing successfully and to prepare their GTAs to respond effectively and efficiently to student writing. With this in mind, they have contended that the "excess" funded hours of GTA work can be better directed toward other work, including the GTAs' own graduate schooling. The result, beyond the initial reduction in the GTA pedagogy course to five weeks and one credit hour, has been a significantly narrower professional development program for gtPathways GTAs.

One additional factor associated with the labor required to teach gtPathways courses is that most instructors in these courses are in contingent positions. The single exception is in the introductory psychology course where the GTAs, all of whom are advanced doctoral students, are instructors-of-record and are led by a course director whose sole job is to make the course and the GTAs successful. The course director has understood from the start of the project that GTAs can benefit as writers themselves from designing, integrating into their courses, and responding to writing assignments. With clear opposition to professional development at the department and college level, it took far longer than expected to build awareness among the faculty members teaching the gtPathways courses of the benefits available to them and their GTAs that could come from working with the project director. But perseverance proved effective and some of the instructors teaching the gtPathways courses have become aware of these benefits and have taken advantage of them. Through a persistent effort to build relationships one by one, the project directors have been able over the past 15 years to convince some instructors of the value of the resources and relationships available through the project. The most effective strategy for building relationships has been the creation of informal partnerships and networks that tap into the faculty reward system. When faculty in contingent positions saw that their work in writing integration could make their teaching more effective and more satisfying, and when course directors and other tenure-line faculty associated with these courses saw that research and publication opportunities abounded in the realm of writing integration, relationships were strengthened, and opportunities began to expand.

Competing Goals

A challenge that evolved over time is the level of commitment to the original mission of the project on the part of the faculty and administration. Fundamentally, and from the start, the departments offering gtPathways courses have pursued goals that are, at least to some extent, at odds with the goals of the gtPathways Project. For example, the economics department is currently assigned 10 GTA lines, but it doesn't require its GTAs to take the gtPathways professional development course. Consequently, GTAs in economics do not receive training in WAC and writing scholarship, and they are likely to receive only minimal training on how to grade the specific assignments their professors assign. From the start of her work as project director, Kelly has found it challenging to connect with administrators and faculty in the department. There does not seem to be a willingness to work with the project director to create, revise, and implement writing assignments.

One of the central problems that comes into clearer focus when viewed through an activity theory lens is the disconnect between the central actors (or community members) in this system. In the project's current iteration, Kelly trains the GTAs but has had very little communication with the disciplinary faculty mentoring the GTAs. Kelly recalls a few graduate students last year saying that they wish their faculty advisors would read the same writing scholarship they were reading, as they felt they were receiving mixed messages and felt that while they were learning about best practices in designing, integrating, and responding to writing assignments, they were not seeing those best practices enacted—or supported—by their mentors. For example, while GTAs are learning that providing positive feedback is important for writers' engagement and learning, their faculty mentors may be telling them to just assign a grade or fill out a numerical rubric. Additionally, as GTAs are taught to consider best practices for designing effective writing assignments, they may see the assignments they are assessing as not meeting those criteria.

As Mara Lee Grayson noted in her chapter in this collection, it is important to recognize how the networks at work within our institution—or, as we view it, the institutional and state activity systems that nest within or overlap each other—can be seen as being in opposition. Over the years, the GTAs in the gtPathways Project have almost certainly recognized this, particularly if they have noted differences in the narratives presented by the faculty members they have assisted in the classroom and the narratives shared by Sue, Kelly, and the other project directors.

REFLECTIONS AND CONCLUSIONS

> This course's intensive, five-week exploration through various pedagogies and theories regarding the evaluation of student writing has proven to be an exceptional asset to my role as a GTA and adjunct instructor. Despite my three years of experience as the latter, I discovered after our first gtPathways orientation the extent to which I had been teaching with a deficit of knowledge of research-based best practices. . . . I now feel comfortably equipped with strategies for creating classroom exercises that serve student growth holistically by actively involving students in the process of their own learning.
>
>   – Department of Journalism and Media Communication GTA

As we look back on the evolution of this initiative from its conception to its current iteration, one conclusion stands out. As the epigraph above shows, our work has helped GTAs gain a deeper understanding of the role writing can play in their teaching and in their own learning. They've recognized that even as GTAs tasked (in some cases solely) with responding to undergraduate student writing, they can "teach through their feedback." They've learned that focusing on the content in others' writing, working to see the strengths in others' writing, and offering specific praise and critique can foster others' learning. They've considered—and, we think, have continued to contemplate—the roles linguistic justice, linguistic diversity, and cross-cultural writing differences can (and should) play in our teaching of and responding to writing. And they've taken this knowledge with them as they have moved forward professionally, in some cases becoming the future professoriate, in other cases becoming non-academic social workers, journalists, political scientists, psychologists, historians, musicians, and philosophers. Thus, despite the challenges we faced, the opportunities that were not embraced, and the conflicting goals, shifts in our division of labor, and contradictions that complicate the story of the gtPathways Writing Integration Project, we remain cognizant of the important work being done with the graduate students. Importantly, we see that work having long-term influence on not only the GTAs but also on those they work with now and in the future.

For rhetoric and composition administrators who have experienced similar competing goals and missed opportunities, we suggest stepping back, taking stock of the situation, and, as appropriate, regrouping your efforts or shifting your focus. We've found it useful to use the analytic framework offered by activity theory as we examine the challenges we encounter. The contradictions within a given activity system provide a good starting point for that examination. Asking about their underlying causes can help us determine whether they arise from inadequate or inappropriate tools, from questionable use of those tools, from conflicting rules or norms, from potentially problematic distribution of labor, or from conflicting motivations and goals. Equally important, asking about whether the challenges we face come from conflicting goals and motivations associated with embedded or overlapping activity systems, as we saw in our analysis of the gtPathways Writing Integration Project, can provide insights that can lead to the development of useful strategies for addressing conflicts. We encourage you to work with colleagues and mentors to consider how best to move forward—or to step away (temporarily or permanently). If you have not yet experienced a similar situation, it may be useful to lay a foundation for responding to challenges down the road by developing a support system across campus. If challenges arise in the future, you'll have a network of colleagues you can work with to find a path forward—perhaps one that involves pivoting to a different initiative or pulling back on your efforts until the time is right to re-engage.

Looking back, we see what happened with the gtPathways Writing Integration Project as a reflection of Miller's (1993) textual carnivals and, in particular, local manifestations of disciplinary politics that led to missed opportunities that continue to plague the project. The meaningfulness of these missed opportunities is only now beginning to be realized as we see English departments, specifically, and the liberal arts, more generally, struggling to identify themselves as relevant to students and to higher education as a whole, particularly in institutions that are grappling with mid-pandemic strategic planning. This moment may present opportunities for writing program and WAC administrators, but much hinges on how the initiative is engaged in coming years. Today, the university is in a different moment institutionally than it was in 2005, when we had not yet experienced the Great Recession, much less the COVID-19 pandemic. Certainly, opportunities remain, and new opportunities continue to present themselves. For our institution, it lies in department, college, and university leadership that has recognized the role of disciplinary writing activities and assignments as a high impact practice. Nevertheless, the saga of missed opportunity was there from the start of this WAC initiative and continues today with new variations. We press on to make this right.

REFERENCES

Abdullah, Z. (2014). Activity theory as analytical tool: A case study of developing student teachers' creativity in design. *Procedia—Social and Behavioral Sciences, 131*, 70–84. https://doi.org/10.1016/j.sbspro.2014.04.082.

Al-Huneini, H., Walker, A. S. & Badger, R. (2020). Introducing tablet computers to a rural primary school: An activity theory case study. *Computers & Education, 143*, 1–10. https://doi.org/10.1016/j.compedu.2019.103648.

Bazerman, C. & Russell, D. R. (Eds.). (2003a). *Writing selves/writing societies: Research from activity perspectives*. The WAC Clearinghouse; Mind, Culture, and Activity. https://doi.org/10.37514/PER-B.2003.2317.

Bazerman, C. & Russell, D. R. (2003b). Introduction. In C. Bazerman & D. R. Russell (Eds.), *Writing selves/writing societies: Research from activity perspectives*. The WAC Clearinghouse; Mind, Culture, and Activity. https://doi.org/10.37514/PER-B.2003.2317.1.3.

Behrend, M. B. (2014). Engeström's activity theory as a tool to analyse online resources embedding academic literacies. *Journal of Academic Language & Learning, 8*(1), A109-A120.

Carvalho, M. B., Bellotti, F., Berta R., Alessandro, D., Sedano, C. I., Hauge, J. B., Hu, J. & Rauterberg, M. (2015). An activity theory-based model for serious games analysis and conceptual design. *Computers & Education, 87*, 166–181. https://doi.org/10.1016/j.compedu.2015.03.023.

Cavdar, G. & Doe, S. (2012). Learning through writing: Teaching critical thinking skills in writing assignments. *PS: Political Science and Politics, 45*(2), 1–9.

Chung, C.-J., Hwang, G.-J. & Lai, C.-L. (2019). A review of experimental mobile learning research in 2010–2016 based on the activity theory framework. *Computers & Education, 129*, 1–13. https://doi.org/10.1016/j.compedu.2018.10.010.

Cole, M. (1996). *Cultural psychology: A once and future discipline*. Cambridge University Press.

Dennehy, D. & Conboy, K. (2017). Going with the flow: An activity theory analysis of flow techniques in software development. *Journal of Systems and Software, 133*, 16–173. https://doi.org/10.1016/j.jss.2016.10.003.

Doe, S. R., Gingerich, K. J. & Richards, T. L. (2013). An evaluation of grading and instructional feedback skills of graduate teaching assistants in introductory psychology. *Teaching of Psychology, 40*(4), 274–280.

Doe, S. R., Pilgrim, M. E. & Gehrtz, J. (2016). Stories and explanations in the introductory calculus classroom: A study of WTL as a teaching and learning intervention. *The WAC Journal, 27*(1), 94–118. https://doi.org/10.37514/WAC-J.2016.27.1.06.

Draper, S. (1993). Critical notice: Activity theory: The new direction for HCI? *International Journal of Man-Machine Studies, 37*(6), 812–821.

Engeström, Y. (1987). *Learning by expanding*. Orienta-Konsultit.

Engeström, Y. (1990). *Learning, working and imagining: Twelve studies in activity theory*. Orienta-Konsultit.

Engeström, Y. (1993). Developmental studies of work as a testbench of activity theory: The case of primary care medical practice. In S. Chaiklin & J. Lave (Eds.), *Understanding practice: Perspectives on activity and context* (pp. 64–103). Cambridge University Press.

Engeström, Y. (1999a). Activity theory and individual and social transformation. In Y. Engeström, R. Miettinen & R.-L. Punamäki (Eds.), *Perspectives on activity theory* (pp. 19–38). Cambridge University Press.

Engeström, Y. (1999b). Innovative learning in work teams: Analyzing cycles of knowledge creation in practice. In Y. Engeström, R. Miettinen & R.-L. Punamäki (Eds.), *Perspectives on activity theory* (pp. 375–404). Cambridge University Press.

Engeström, Y. (2014). *Learning by expanding* (2nd ed.). Cambridge University Press.

Engeström, Y. & Miettinen, Reijo. (1999). Introduction. In Y. Engeström, R. Miettinen & R.-L. Punamäki (Eds.), *Perspectives on activity theory* (pp. 1–18). Cambridge University Press.

Gingerich, K. J., Bugg, J. M., Doe, S. R., Rowland, C. A., Richards, T. L., Tompkins, S. A. & McDaniel, M. A. (2014). Active processing via write-to-learn assignments: Learning and retention benefits in introductory psychology. *Teaching of Psychology, 41*(4), 303–308. https://doi.org/10.1177/0098628314549701.

Ho, J. P. Y., Chen, D.-T. V. & Ng, D. (2016). Distributed leadership through the lens of activity theory. *Educational Management Administration & Leadership, 44*(5) 814–836. https://doi.org/10.1177/1741143215570302.

Hoffmann, D., Ahlemann, F. & Reining, S. (2020). Reconciling alignment, efficiency, and agility in IT project portfolio management: Recommendations based on a revelatory case study. *International Journal of Project Management, 38*(2), 124–136. https://doi.org/10.1016/j.ijproman.2020.01.004.

Kaptelinin, V. (2005). The object of activity: Making sense of the sense-maker. *Mind, Culture, and Activity, 12*(1), 4–18.

Kaptelinin, V. & Nardie, B. (2012). *Activity theory in HCI: Fundamentals and reflections*. Morgan and Claypool.

Leontiev, A. N. (1978). *Activity, consciousness, and personality*. M. J. Hall (Trans.). Prentice-Hall.

Leontiev, A. N. (2005). The genesis of activity. *Journal of Russian and East European Psychology, 43*(4), 58–71.

Luria, A. (1979). *The making of mind: A personal account of Soviet psychology*. M. Cole (Trans.). Harvard University Press.

Miller, S. (1993). *Textual carnivals: The politics of composition*. Southern Illinois University Press.

Nardi, B. A. (1995). *Context and consciousness: Activity theory and human-computer interaction*. MIT Press.

Nardi, B., Whittaker, S. & Schwarz, H. (2002). NetWORKers and their activity in intensional networks. *Computer Supported Cooperative Work, 11*, 205–242. https://doi.org/10.1023/A:1015241914483.

Palmquist, M. (2000). Notes on the evolution of network support for WAC. In M. D. Goggin (Ed.), *Inventing a discipline: Essays in honor of Richard E. Young* (pp. 373–402). National Council of Teachers of English.

Palmquist, M. (2023). Opening up: Writing studies' turn toward open-access publishing. In P. Rogers, D. Russell, P. Carlino & J. Mariner (Eds.), *Writing as a human activity: Implications and applications of the work of Charles Bazerman* (pp. 195–226). The WAC Clearinghouse; University Press of Colorado. https://doi.org /10.37514/PER-B.2023.1800.2.08.

Palmquist, M., Mullin, J. & Blalock, G. (2012). The role of activity analysis in writing research: Case studies of emerging scholarly communities. In L. Nicholson & M. P. Sheridan (Eds.), *Writing studies research in practice: Methods and methodologies* (pp. 231–244). Southern Illinois University Press.

Pearson, S. (2009). Using activity theory to understand prospective teachers' attitudes to and construction of special educational needs and/or disabilities. *Teaching and Teacher Education, 25*(4), 559–568. https://doi.org/10.1016/j.tate.2009.02.011.

Rubinštejn, S. L. (1987). Problems of psychology in the works of Karl Marx. *Studies in Soviet Thought, 33,* 111–130. https://doi.org/10.1007/BF01151778 (Original work published 1934).

Russell, D. R. (1995). Activity theory and its implications for writing instruction. In J. Petraglia (Ed.), *Reconceiving writing, rethinking writing instruction* (pp. 51–78). Erlbaum.

Russell, D. R. (2009). Uses of activity theory in written communication research. In A. Sannino, H. Daniels & K. D. Gutierrez (Eds.), *Learning and expanding with activity theory* (pp. 40–52). Cambridge University Press. https://doi.org/10.1017/CBO9 780511809989.

Takoeva, V. (2017). *The re-appearing act of leadership: An exploration of leadership practice through the lens of cultural-historical activity theory* [Unpublished doctoral dissertation]. University of Birmingham.

Vygotsky, L. S. (1978). *Mind in society: The development of higher psychological processes.* M. Cole, V. John-Steiner, S. Scribner & E. Souberman (Eds.), Harvard University Press.

Vygotsky, L. S. (1986). *Thought and language.* A. Kozulin (Ed. & Trans.). MIT Press. (Original work published 1934).

Vygotsky, L. S. (1989). Concrete human psychology. *Soviet Psychology, 27*(2), 53–77.

Winstanley, L. (2019, September 2–5). *Mapping activity theory to a design thinking model (ATDT): A framework to propagate a culture of creative trust* [Paper presentation]. International Association of Societies of Design Research Conference, Manchester, United Kingdom. https://iasdr2019.org/uploads/files/Proceedings/vo-f -1180-Win-L.pdf.

Zahedi, M. & Tessier, V. (2018, June 25–28). *Designerly activity theory: Toward a new ontology for design research* [Paper presentation]. Design Research Society Conference, Limerick, Ireland.

APPENDIX A: PLAN PRESENTED TO THE ENGLISH DEPARTMENT EXECUTIVE COMMITTEE

November 27, 2006
To: English Executive Committee
From: Mike Palmquist
Re: Supporting gtPathways GTA Professional Development and WAC

For more than a year, the rhetoric and composition faculty in English have worked to develop a plan to support the use of writing in gtPathways courses at the University. Our plans were developed to support President Penley's decision to require that all gtPathways courses in the social sciences (many with enrollments of over 200 students per section) would base at least 25 percent of the course grade on written work. The new AUCC core now codifies this requirement for the social science courses in the core. To support this initiative, the President provided funding for 74 new GTA lines in the social sciences in CLA and psychology in CNS.

This summer, the Provost's office approved the rhetoric and composition faculty's plan to support the professional development of GTAs involved in the gtPathways writing initiative. That plan involved providing me with release time and staff support to work with social science faculty and GTAs. My appointment as TILT director resulted in the development of a new plan, in which I proposed to provide this support through per-section hiring of instructors who had previously served as composition lecturers. For a variety of reasons, this plan was rejected by the rhetoric and composition faculty. A new plan, outlined below, reflects discussions with the rhetoric and composition faculty, [Vice Provost] Tom Gorell, and [Vice Provost] Alan Lamborn.

This plan will provide gtPathways GTAs with an intensive semester of professional development designed to enhance their ability to respond fairly and effectively to student writing. The key elements of the plan involve:

- Notifying GTAs of the conditions of their employment as gtPathways GTAs in their appointment letters and contracts.
- Assigning GTAs to a class for 15 hours per week in the first semester of their GTA assignment and for 20 hours per week thereafter.
- Requiring GTAs to sign up for E607 Teaching Writing in the first semester of their GTA assignment.
- Requiring GTAs to participate in workshops throughout their assignment.
- Providing opportunities for one-on-one consultation and grading review conferences to GTAs.

To support this plan, I propose reconfiguring base funding for the gtPathways writing initiative to support the hire of a new assistant professor of rhetoric and composition. If approved, I would also offer funding from TILT to help bridge the cost of this position over the next two years. In the third year, funding would be provided through the funds assigned to the Provost's office to expand the tenure-track faculty at CSU.

The department is currently conducting a search for an assistant professor in rhetoric and composition. I propose hiring a second assistant professor from this pool. This hire would teach a normal load and undertake the full range of scholarly activity typical for a new assistant professor. It is possible that this person would also serve as the director of writing across the curriculum.

This plan provides an effective means of continuing our efforts to support writing-across-the-curriculum. Through agreements with the Dean and Provost, it should also provide a means of expanding our tenure-track faculty without reducing replacement or new hires in coming years.

APPENDIX B: DRAFT MEMORANDUM OF UNDERSTANDING FOR THE AUCC/ GTPATHWAYS WRITING INITIATIVE

January 3, 2007
Parties:
Provost's Office
College of Liberal Arts
Department of English
Institute for Learning and Teaching
Graduate School

1. A new tenure line will be created to support the AUCC/gtPathways Writing Initiative.
2. Bridge funding for the line will be provided in FY 08 from . . .
3. The creation of this line will not take the place of lines that would otherwise have been allocated to the College of Liberal Arts or the Department of English.
4. The faculty member in this line will:
   - serve as AUCC/gtPathways Writing Initiative coordinator
   - teach at least two and as many as three sections of E607 Teaching Writing during each academic year[9]

---

[9] The course referred to in this MOU as E607 Teaching Writing became the 1-credit, 5-week course we refer to in our discussion and is now titled E608: Integrating Writing in the Academic Core.

- supervise the adjunct faculty who will teach other sections of E607
- develop workshops for and consult with GTAs

- support faculty teaching AUCC/gtPathways courses in their efforts to incorporate writing into their courses
- serve as director of the University's Writing-Across-the-Curriculum program

5. Over time, these responsibilities are likely to be shifted to other faculty members of the composition and rhetoric faculty, as part of their regular rotation of administrative responsibilities.
6. The Institute for Learning and Teaching will provide support for the AUCC/gtPathways Writing Initiative through funding for up to two sections of E607 Teaching Writing taught by experienced lecturers and supervised by the AUCC/gtPathways Writing Initiative coordinator.
7. The University will require departments who receive GTA lines funded through the AUCC/gtPathways Writing Initiative to decide whether they will participate in the professional development program supported by TILT and the University Composition Program or provide their own training for the GTAs at department expense. Departments can choose to provide their own training only with approval of the College.
8. Departments who choose to participate in the TILT/Composition Program professional development program will assign GTAs to 15 hours of classroom support and 5 hours of professional development in their first semester as a GTA and 20 hours of classroom support in subsequent semesters. Departments will also require GTAs to:

- enroll in E607 Teaching Writing in the first semester of their GTA assignment
- participate in writing workshops and other professional development opportunities throughout their assignment

9. This agreement is subject to revision by agreement of all parties. The English Department can withdraw from the agreement only by relinquishing the tenure line, or through mutual agreement of the other parties.

APPENDIX C: MEMORANDUM OF UNDERSTANDING—COLLEGE OF LIBERAL ARTS

WRITING IN AUCC COURSES IN LIBERAL ARTS
Effective Fall 2007

All AUCC courses in Categories 3B, C, D and E of the core must satisfy the following requirements regarding writing. These must be clearly stated on the syllabus for the course.

Goals for writing in AUCC courses:

There are two goals for writing assignments in AUCC courses:[1]

(1) to improve students' comprehension of course content and,

(2) to improve students' proficiency in writing.

Note 1: Both of these goals are best achieved when students receive feedback on their writing assignments and have an opportunity to make use of that feedback.

1. Writing requirements:

(1) At least 25 percent of the course grade must be based on written work that satisfies the following :

    a. At least one writing assignment must be an out-of-class piece of written work.[2]

    b. In-class written work, such as on exams, must be in the form of essays.

Note 2: While this represents a minimum standard, to maximize the benefits to students of more writing multiple opportunities to write and respond to feedback are recommended, such as:

1. Several out-of-class writing assignments.

OR

2. One or more rewrites of an out-of-class writing assignment.

(2) Expectations of written work must be clearly stated on the syllabus. Among other things the instructor considers appropriate, those expectations should include students demonstrating:[3]

1. The ability to convey a theme or argument clearly and coherently.
2. The ability to analyze critically and to synthesize the work of others.
3. The ability to acquire and apply information from appropriate sources, and reference sources appropriately.
4. Competence in standard written English.

Note 3: Instructors should use their own discretion in communicating to students the relative importance of the various expectations in their own writing assignments in terms of how they will be graded.

2. Plagiarism Statement:

More writing in AUCC courses also brings the risk of increased incidents of plagiarism. It is strongly recommended that instructors have a statement in their syllabus that clearly states that plagiarism is not acceptable and is a form of academic dishonesty. An example is:

Plagiarism is a form of academic dishonesty. As per university policy "Any student found responsible for having engaged in academic dishonesty will be subject to an academic penalty and/or University disciplinary action."

On page 38 of the *2006–2007 General Catalog,* plagiarism is defined:

"Plagiarism includes the copying of language, structure, ideas, or thoughts of another, and representing them as one's own without proper acknowledgement. Examples include a submission of purchased research papers as one's own work; paraphrasing and/or quoting material without properly documenting the source."

APPENDIX D: 2022 MEMORANDUM OF UNDERSTANDING—COLLEGE OF LIBERAL ARTS

GUARANTEED TRANSFER PATHWAYS WRITING INTEGRATION PROJECT DISTRIBUTION OF RESPONSIBILITIES

Effective Fall 2022

The purpose of this MOU is to lay out the responsibilities of the English Department and the College of Liberal Arts (CLA) in their shared commitment to ensuring the effectiveness and longevity of the Guaranteed Transfer (gt) Pathways Writing Integration Project. Implemented in Fall 2007, the gtPathways Writing Integration Project supports the meaningful integration of writing into the majority of CLA's All University College Curriculum (AUCC) courses with the goals of improving undergraduate writing proficiency and enhancing comprehension of course content. As the 2007 MOU between the Provost's Office and the College of Liberal Arts (titled "Writing In AUCC Courses In Liberal Arts") notes, with this initiative, the College of Liberal Arts is committed to supporting the Faculty Council approved minimum of 25% of the final course grade in designated AUCC courses for writing assignments, designed to foster students' learning and communication skills. To meet these goals, faculty teaching many of these courses are assigned GTAs funded by the graduate school whose job it is to assist faculty in commenting on, responding to, and grading undergraduate student writing and who receive professional development training to do this work effectively.

RESPONSIBILITIES OF THE ENGLISH DEPARTMENT AND THE COLLEGE OF LIBERAL ARTS

The English Department will:
- Provide a pre-semester general orientation for GTAs in August.
- Offer 3 sections of E608: Integrating Writing in the Academic Core (1 credit) each fall.
- Determine and hire the instructor of record for E608 and the pre-semester orientation. This person shall carry the title of Director of the gtPathways Writing Integration Project. The appointment of the director shall be approved by the Rhetoric and Composition Faculty Committee.
- Maintain the gtPathways Writing Integration Project website.
- When compensation is possible, support the Director in conducting annual or biennial assessments of student writing performance and learning fostered by the work of the gtPathways Writing Integration Project.

The College of Liberal Arts will:
- Ensure that departments understand and implement practices consistent with the gtPathways Writing Integration Project expectations laid out below.
- Designate the CLA Associate Dean for Academic Programs as the point of contact in the Dean's Office for the gtPathways Writing Integration Project.
- Distribute to faculty teaching gtPathways courses the 2007 MOU titled "Writing In AUCC Courses in Liberal Arts," which lays out the goals and requirements for writing integration in gtPathways courses. (See below.)
- Distribute to departments communications from the Director of the gtPathways Writing Integration Project such as an annual report or newsletter.
- By June 1 each year, secure from departments the names of faculty and courses that will have gtPathways GTAs. Knowing this information makes connections with faculty and associated GTAs more feasible.
- Secure from each department one syllabus, a few sample writing assignments, grading criteria, and papers to aid the Director of the gtPathways Writing Integration Project in ensuring the GTA training reflects current practices across departments. Samples should be updated every two years.

- Facilitate communication between the Director and participating faculty to aid the Director in formally assessing student writing performance and learning, consistent with Higher Learning Commission accreditation requirements and University expectations.

EXPECTATIONS OF DEPARTMENTS WHO RECEIVE FUNDED GTA POSITIONS TO SUPPORT THE GTPATHWAYS WRITING INTEGRATION PROJECT

Participating departments should:
- Select graduate students to serve as GTAs for faculty teaching designated gtPathways courses with the writing requirement. These GTAs must support faculty in commenting on, responding to, and grading undergraduate student writing.
- Ensure that gtPathways GTAs attend the pre-semester orientation and complete E608 so they have the training they need to effectively comment on, respond to, and grade undergraduate students' writing.
  - <u>If participating departments choose not to have their gtPathways GTAs attend the pre-semester orientation and complete E608</u>, they must provide their own GTA training specific to ensuring GTAs can meaningfully comment on, respond to, and grade undergraduate writing in designated gtPathways courses.
  - If departments choose to provide their own professional development training for GTAs, they must submit their detailed training plan to the CLA Associate Dean for Academic Programs.

CHAPTER 10.

THE WRITING CENTER AS BORDER PROCESSING STATION

Eric C. Camarillo
Tarrant County College, Northwest

Writing centers align closely, and often overlap, with other areas of writing studies and research. This is especially the case with composition and writing program administration work. In some institutional contexts, writing centers exist within composition programs or are a part of larger writing programs. Certainly, writing centers are as equally affected by institutional systems and contexts. The editors' noted in the introduction,

> As writing program administration, writing center administration, and writing across curriculum/communities scholarship shows, it is downright challenging—and sometimes impossible—to do meaningful work, sometimes *because of* the existing systems and networks that define the parameters of our jobs, our spheres of influence, our resources, and our agency.

Systems and networks also often delimit the work of writing centers as much as they form the borders of that work. If writing center administrators aim to change the nature of writing center work, then they must find ways to engage with those systems and institutional networks. Activity theory is one such method of theoretical engagement. As Yrjö Engeström (2015) explained,

> Third-generation activity theory expands the analysis both up and down, outward and inward. Moving up and outward, it tackles multiple interconnected activity systems with their partially shared and often fragmented objects. Moving down and inward, it tackles issues of subjectivity, experiencing, personal sense, emotion, embodiment, identity, and moral commitment. (p. xv)

In activity theory, objects can be purposes or goals, but they can also be motivating factors and "generators and foci of attention, volition, effort, and meaning" (Engeström, 2015, p. xvi). What activity theory offers writing centers, then, is a better way of understanding the work we *really* do rather than the work

DOI: https://doi.org/10.37514/PER-B.2023.1848.2.10

we aspire to do. Activity theory can help writing center directors and staff better understand and account for the systems in which we're placed, the stakeholders to whom we answer, and the borders of our work. That is, activity theory allows researchers to examine the tensions that exist within an activity system (see also Bradbury et al. in this collection). Samuel Van Horne wrote in his dissertation *An Activity-Theory Analysis of how college Students Revise after Writing Center Conferences*, "Activity systems can be situated in networks of other activity systems, so this framework is helpful for analyzing how different contexts of activity interact and influence each other" (2011, p. 26). Through this lens, we can examine how a student's behavior (their writing habits) necessarily changes when visiting or after visiting a writing center. Like any border place, the writing center functions as an activity system within a larger institutional network.

In the introduction to this collection, the editors wrote of the importance of systems theories in creating environments where social justice can emerge in sustainable ways, especially for administrators. In particular, through these critical action-analyses that highlight social, epistemic, eco-critical, and network theories as practices, as means of professional/corporate interaction, we can open working spaces that can serve differing communities in useful ways. Activity theory allows writing center administrators to take a wider view of the kind of impact writing centers have on students and to find better, more useful ways of serving their locally diverse student populations.

Yet, the writing center isn't just a border. It is itself bordered. And like all border areas, there are limitations to how flexible the boundaries are and to what extent border crossing will be tolerated. Writing centers (and other sites of hegemonic privilege) tend to protect their borders, their boundaries, in order to prevent what might be viewed as chaos. A "center" necessarily centers bodies and discourses, normalizing them and flattening difference. The very name and nature of writing centers, then, may be regulatory and immutable. This may especially be the case when writing centers try to help students meet professor expectations. In Nancy Grimm's (1996) work on "the regulatory role of the writing center," she recounted a story of working with an African American writer in an advanced composition class. While the assistant director "appreciated the unique rhythms and metaphors of the paper . . . a week later the young man returned with his paper, which had been marked by his professor for problems of diction and questions of appropriate word choice" (p. 12). In helping the student change the paper to meet the professor's needs, "the normalized writing practices of the institution remained unchallenged, and the writing center had again functioned to keep things in place" (Grimm, 1996, p. 12). The extent to which liberation is possible in writing centers, then, may be limited by both a writing center's history, the expectations of faculty, and other sorts of institutional networks.

As my title implies, this chapter draws comparisons between writing centers and border processing stations, a "real-world" place that secures and maintains the integrity of country borders. To be clear, though, the comparisons here are purely metaphorical. Border processing stations are imbued with actual imperial power. They control and regulate the physical movement of bodies and can even determine the life or death of those who enter their spaces. Writing centers don't, even as they work to maintain (deliberately or otherwise) hegemonic power structures within their larger institutions. The comparison between these two types of centers, then, relies mostly on their similar power to filter, exclude or change, particularly when relying upon and deploying a set of standardized practices.

To this end, I'm drawing on the border processing station as a metaphor for the student experience with writing centers. In *Postcomposition*, Sidney Dobrin (2011) complicates the use of space-based metaphors, arguing that "to employ metaphors of space to simply describe the conditions of subjectivity in relation to writing or writing pedagogy is to reduce the potential for what we can ultimately come to know about the phenomena and function of writing" (p. 40). Metaphors can be used to describe this relationship, but description alone is not enough to develop a theory. However, Dobrin eventually noted, "when talking about space, we must acknowledge that we cannot escape space as a metaphor, escape all representation as metaphor" (2011, p. 40). He asserted that descriptive metaphors are a necessary transition for the development of any theory.

To approach a comparison between writing centers and border processing stations, the chapter begins with an account of writing center spaces or writing centers as places. From there, the chapter discusses how the work of writing centers is often described in writing center scholarship before moving into an application of activity theory to writing centers, examining the various moving pieces that can potentially make up a writing center's activity system and how this system may brush up against institutional networks. Finally, the chapter will close with a discussion of how best to account for potentially exclusionary and border-protecting actions in which writing centers engage in order to craft a fundamentally more equitable center.

THE SPACE OF WRITING CENTERS

As a field (another spatial metaphor), writing centers often theorize and write about their physical spaces. Jackie Grutsch McKinney (2013) asserted, "[T]he idea that a writing center is—and should be—a cozy, homey, comfortable, family-like place is perhaps most firmly entrenched" (p. 20). Spaces also often figure into the lore of writing centers. According to Randall Monty (2016) in *The*

Writing Center as Cultural and Disciplinary Contact Zone, writing center studies "has been historically and inextricably linked to physical space" (p. 10). The most common bit of lore is that writing centers began in basements of academic buildings or libraries before finally emerging from their subterranean origins. One important note here is that "space" and "place" are being used interchangeably in this chapter, but scholars and other theorists treat these terms separately. For instance, Dobrin (2011), in his discussion of geographic principles, noted, "Space is marked and defended; places have 'felt value': they have been given identity. Places are divisions of space to which meaning and organization have been attached" (p. 40). Places offer security; space is less limiting.

Dobrin's (2011) discussion of space and occupation is especially relevant for this chapter. He argued, "What occupies space, then, are bodies: specific bodies that mark and identify segments of the space they occupy" (p. 51). The bodies, the people, in spaces then turn these spaces into places. In this way, the places people occupy become a synecdoche for the people themselves. Asao Inoue (2015) takes Dobrin's ideas further, casting place as an element in a larger writing (assessment) ecology. For Inoue, a "place" need not be in a physical space. He wrote, "I use the term place to identify both the rhetorical context and material conditions of the production of assessment (judgment) of writing in the classroom, which includes places like writing groups, the remedial location, an evaluation rubric . . ." (p. 159). Inoue draws on Dobrin to highlight the conflict that arises as spaces are defined into places.

The idea of conflict directly contradicts the grand narrative that writing centers assert for themselves, particularly the idea of the writing center as cozy home (McKinney, 2013). McKinney wrote when writing center administrators fill "writing centers with touches of home, [they] may be marking it as familiar and comfortable for directors and tutors, who are often . . . of a certain class (upper or middle class) and cultural background (white American)" (2013, p. 25). Her argument ties into Dobrin's notion of struggle over spaces. Dobrin (2011) explained,

> Space is defined by the boundaries imposed by its occupiers. To make the partitions/borders/boundaries appear natural—nonexistent, if possible—and nonpolitical is the ultimate goal of use: to identify occupations as appropriate, as natural, as correct. This is my space; it always has been. This is the manufacture of consent; this is hegemony. This is how space is used; this is how it has always been used. (p. 55)

Dobrin's conception of space allows a stronger connection between the idea of a writing center and the border processing station metaphor. The occupiers of a space define what the space is and, through this defining, create a place that appears to be natural and, therefore, correct. Those who do not occupy the space, but merely visit, are targets for correction. Dobrin noted, "[P]laces may be safe, but they are safe only for those who make them" (2011, p. 55). Writing centers, as outgrowths of composition and, more largely, the hegemonic academic values of institutional networks, are only safe for those who occupy them—much like border stations.

Finally, it's important to remember that writing centers don't just exist in physical spaces. The coronavirus pandemic spurred many writing centers, many of which may have only offered face-to-face services, into virtual spaces. As I note elsewhere, "The difference in mode creates new possibilities for bias and prejudice, unconscious or otherwise, that need to be considered, navigated, and mitigated" (2022, p. 19). Online spaces are no less bound by systems and networks than physical spaces, and we should take a social justice lens to online work as well.

WHAT HAPPENS IN WRITING CENTERS

Writing center scholars talk frequently about the work that goes on in the writing center. In his foundational article, Stephen North (1984) asked, "What is the Idea of a Writing Center?" (p. 437). There are many approaches to answering this question. Many scholars and administrators attempt to answer North's other call to describe our work, most often a kind of talk, that goes on in the writing center space (p. 444). Anis Bawarshi and Stephanie Pelkowski (1999) discussed how traditional writing centers reinforce histories of colonialism; Grimm (1996) highlighted the regulating function of writing centers; Laura Greenfield (2011/2019) presented the function of racism and linguistic discrimination in writing center practice; Romeo García (2017) argued writing centers should develop decolonial frameworks in order to best serve their locally diverse student populations; and there are others. The writing center is a highly discursive space where "talk is everything" (North, 1984, p. 444), so focusing on the activities that occur within the writing center space, and how they reinforce or breakdown the borders of institutional networks, offers valuable insights into how writing centers currently work and how they can be transformed.

There are best practices in the field of writing centers, particularly regarding the traditional face-to-face writing consultation (or session or conference). From North (1984), writing centers adopt a constructivist point of view for observing student writing; rather than worry about specific texts, writing centers focus on the writing process of students. More directly, writing centers take the writing process itself as their purview. This practice enables writing centers to work with a wide variety of documents from an increasingly diverse student body. Jeff Brooks (1991), in his "Minimalist Tutoring: Making the Student Do All the Work," introduced the notions of authority and power in the writing center, ensuring students retain agency over their documents. These ideas also solidify into specific practices like making sure the paper is physically closer to the student or that the consultant never wrote on the document. Building on North's social constructivist stance, Andrea Lunsford (1991) weaved collaboration as an integral part of writing center work; and in "Collaboration, Control, and the Idea of a Writing Center," she frames collaboration itself as the work of the writing center.

However, these best practices and, perhaps, traditional writing center work focus more on individuals and their individual actions. Lucien Darjeun Meadows, in this collection, noted how social systems theory can help writing center administrators better understand writing center work by looking at the system of a writing center interaction rather than the individual parts. Meadows' particular focus is on disclosure and concealment and the ways in which writers and writing tutors may, or may not, "come out" to each other. Even without necessarily revealing part of their identities, Meadows wrote,

> [T]here is so much coming out on the part of a writer in any session. Writers must admit they feel their writing needs another set of eyes, must admit the elements of their writing that concern them, and must admit their writing voice and style to consultant-writers with the text under discussion.

Yet, despite these pressures to come out or disclose, social systems theory and the holistic view of a student can allow writing center administrators to resist traditional hegemonic systems and, as Meadows encouraged "to find liminal borderland—room to create, experiment, and play." Meadows argued being able to queer the writing center consultation in this way, to bend it away from hegemony, turns the writing consultation itself into a kind of third space, a border or in-between space.

While many writing center scholars and administrators write about the work that *should* be going on in writing centers, few of them write about what actually happens in writing centers. Van Horne (2011) utilized activity theory as a framework for analyzing the revision process for students. While he's mostly examining the behavior of students, Van Horne also makes observations of the writing tutors. He found

> [T]he writing consultants did not try to promote situation redefinition by moving the discussion away from the text

toward a conversation about the strategies the student used to produce the draft. They conducted the conference at the level of the student in order to fulfill the student's agenda. This contradicted the main philosophy of the writing center, which was that a conference should be a productive conversation about the ideas in a piece of writing. (2011, pp. 1–2)

In activity theory, a situation definition is generally a set of expectations one has for a particular kind of space or activity. When students had a plan for their writing, they also generally shared a situation definition of the writing center with the tutors. That is, this type of prepared student expected from the writing tutor what the writing tutor expected to give. In contrast, students without a plan for their writing had mismatched situation definitions for the writing center; their expectations did not match the expectations of the writing consultants. However, despite being trained in process-oriented, minimalist, and collaborative tutoring, these consultants did not attempt to shift the students' perspectives. While Van Horne's study is admittedly small (he only observed eleven students), his methods are detailed.

ACTIVITY SYSTEMS AND WRITING CENTERS

Van Horne's conceptual framework offers writing center practitioners ways of re-thinking how their work is done and how their spaces are created, particularly regarding the various end goals of writing center work and engagement with institutional networks. When viewed as an activity system, we can see writing centers functioning as microcosms of larger cultural values. Engeström (2015) claimed, "[H]uman learning is pervasively shaped according to normative cultural expectations. Such expectations are extremely diverse, and they change historically. Thus, human learning processes are also very diverse and continuously change" (pg. xviii). Larger cultural views and values, then, influence what "good" learning looks like or change perspectives on how people "should" learn, which necessarily changes the processes and procedures for sites like writing centers. Yet, students are not just entering into the writing center's activity system—they also become part of that system and can influence it as well. Engeström asserted that a prescribed process from an instructor may not always be followed by the learner, that the learner may deploy their own process for learning. How can our systems allow students to develop and deploy their own processes without attempting to process the students themselves?

Before going further, we should first examine the components of a writing center's activity system and some of the various other systems with which it interacts. Aside from discussing what actually occurs in a particular writing center (rather than on what *should* occur), Van Horne (2011) also discusses the boundaries of writing center work and how other academic sites, specifically classrooms, relate to the writing center. He asserted, "But for all of the writing about how faculty should or should not use the writing center, there is little research on the actual ways that instructors integrate a writing center's services into their pedagogy" (2011, p. 223). However, better understanding the relationship between faculty and the writing center is critical to understanding how students themselves interact with the writing center. Van Horne recognizes that the writing center's activity system exists within "a network of other activity systems in which students are completing many kinds of writing assignments" (2011, p. 223). What are the components, then, of a writing center's activity system? While Van Horne is also examining how social structures mediate activity, the scope of this chapter is much narrower. However, we can still draw on the adaptation of Engeström's (2015) model of activity systems that Van Horne applies to writing centers.

In Van Horne's diagram, we can see the various activities that occur (or should occur) in the typical writing consultation. He has provided pertinent labeling of this activity system in at least two stages: an initial visit to the writing center with a rough draft and what happens after that session. Van Horne locates the student as the subject in this activity system and "Ideas about the topic" or "Current draft" as the object of the activity, depending on which stage the writer is in. The outcomes in each lead, eventually, to a new draft of the paper. However, the tools used to mediate the activity vary, it's likely that these tools change relative to the subject-student.

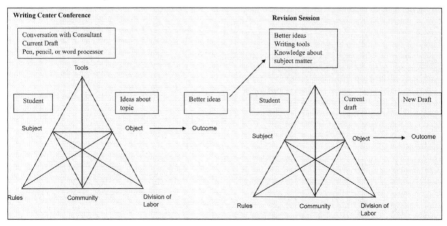

Figure 10.1. Van Horn's depiction of Activity Systems of the Writing Conference and Revision Session.

Viewing the writing center and the classroom as activity systems allows us to see the motivations some students have when entering our spaces and how institutional networks may pressure them into engaging with us. Do students choose to come to the writing center? If so, why? Or are students compelled to come to the writing center? Does the professor require writing center visits of all students? Does the professor require visits only for certain students? When a student enters our spaces, we need to consider what brought them there. Students do not always visit because "more often than not, they are genuinely, deeply engaged with their material, anxious to wrestle it into the best form they can" or because "they are motivated to write" as North (1984) contends (p. 443). Sometimes they come just to fulfill the requirements of the course or to get the necessary points. We must question at what point a student experiences a border or a harbor, and by whom that systematic understanding is enforced.

The writing center visit can just as easily become another barrier rather than a truly integrated part of a writer's process. As Engeström (2015) noted, "[T]he concept of activity is necessarily connected with the concept of motive" (p. 54). However, Engeström also discussed the all-controlling nature of activities and activity systems. He asserted, "Under the conditions of division of labor, the individual participates in activities mostly without being fully conscious of their objects and motives" (p. 54). In terms of writing centers and writing classrooms, students may be required or recommended to visit the writing center without fully understanding what the purpose is, which could especially be the case when the professor requires all students to visit the writing center.

However, these compelled visits may disproportionately affect students whose writing is viewed as somehow "aberrant" or "basic." These students may be ostensibly identified by their language use, but Greenfield (2011) noted the role race and racism play in such identifications. She argued that students of color are asked less to learn a particular dialect (in this case, dominant academic discourse or what might be called Standard English) and more to rid "themselves of all linguistic features that may identify them with communities of color" (p. 46). When students are referred to or coerced (through grades) into the writing center to have their writing "fixed," what's being changed is more than just surface-level linguistic features. Writing centers are also playing a role in changing parts of the student's very identity. In this way, we see how the activity system, and the larger institutional network, may control individual behavior, may contribute to border processing, rather than the individual being a truly empowered agent.

When discussing what work goes on in the writing center and what writing centers should be producing, one should also examine why and how certain policies or rules are adopted over others, who controls these policies, and who benefits from them. There are common practices that seem to span writing centers: reading a paper aloud, not writing on the paper, asking questions over providing answers, and so on. Within the framework that Van Horne (2011) provides us, these policies become part of the "tools" section of the triangle because they mediate the writing consultation activity, determining what can be done and what cannot. For example, the main rule of the writing center that Van Horne observed is "consultants did not write on student papers" (2011, p. 60). This type of policy was popularized in Brooks' (1991) idea of minimalist tutoring, resisting the imagery of writing consultants as editors. Yet, this focus on what *not* to do did not necessarily control the editing impulse. As Van Horne observed, "If the rule was supposed to prevent consultants from . . . making too directive suggestions to students, the rule was not effective. I observed consultants tell students exactly which word to use or which punctuation mark to use" (2011, p. 61). This policy helped mediate writing consultations that might be considered more directive than a consultant modeling a sentence for a student or even physically adding the punctuation marks themselves.

This aspect of writing center work, of enacting best practices without thinking of their various negative effects, is particularly deleterious for students who come from places of difference or who use nonstandard discourses. As García (2017) wrote, "The power of whiteness continues to shape contemporary forms of management and control of practices and writing center scholarship" (p. 32). Writing centers (and their administrators), even as they seek inclusion, diversity, or student empowerment, as they seek to produce better writers, are always working from places of hegemony, their implicit practices serving to reinforce traditional power structures. Grimm's (1996) story of an African American student writing in Black Vernacular English (BVE) results in the student changing the paper in order to meet the expectations of the dominant academic discourse. In Grimm's telling, the consultant did not feel comfortable, or empowered, to confront this standardizing force. Indeed, both the writing center and the student became objects in the activity system of the institutional network, with the professor's policies demarcating the border both for the student and the writing center.

Within the realm of activity theory, these invisible, unquestioned practices or values help produce the object of an activity system. In most cases, what is produced by the writing consultation activity is a real draft or new draft of an assignment. Van Horne (2011) makes space for the product to be "better ideas" in his model of activity systems, but these ideas are then used to produce or enhance some form of writing. What this model of activity system does not make space for, though, is better writers as its object. Ultimately, this may be because student-writers and the consultants who work with them have different aims and end goals. As Engeström (2015) explained, the actions of instructors and students are

> dialectically intertwined. This means that the prescribed and planned process the instructor is trying to implement must be compared and contrasted with the actual process performed by the learners. The two will never fully coincide. The gap, struggle, negotiation, and occasional merger between the two need to be taken as key resources for understanding the processes of learning as processes of formation of agency. (p. xix)

If writing centers are working to produce better writers, as North (1984) urges, ultimately, we are also producing more independent and empowered writers, who may be less willing to make the changes we recommend or to respond to the questions we ask.

There are contradictions inherent in activity systems, such as the one above. Students who have thought less about their projects or feel less ownership over their writing may be likelier to cede authority to writing consultants (Van Horne, 2011). They are, thus, likelier to be more responsive to direct suggestions and recommendations but less responsive to the Socratic style of questioning that may characterize writing center work. Students who have a stronger sense of agency over their writing projects may demonstrate the inverse: more responsive to the conversational model of the consultation and more resistant to directive methods. Yet, the contradiction lies in the use of the writing center—how boundaries and borders of agency are realized and by whom.

Although North (1984) posited, "Nearly everyone who writes likes—and needs—to talk about his or her writing," it can be argued that writing centers typically serve writers who are identified as struggling or basic (pp. 439–440). In the eyes of many faculty, serving this student population is the *raison d'etre* of writing centers. Engeström (2015) explained, "The essential contradiction is the mutual exclusion and simultaneous mutual dependency of use value and exchange value in each commodity" (p. 68). That is, even as writing centers work to produce independent writers, the existence of writing centers relies on the presence of "dependent" writers. Or rather, writing centers rely on identifying certain writers as basic, an act that disproportionately affects students of color, students from nonstandard discourses, and students from low socioeconomic backgrounds.

While not discussing activity systems specifically, Greenfield (2019) analyzes the conservative and liberal impulses that influence the policies of writing centers and how these policies don't necessarily translate into actions. In critiquing the liberal practices of writing centers, Greenfield asserted, "Seeing it as futile to change their environments, many liberals work from a defeatist perspective in a way that serves to perpetuate the disparities in power they would otherwise critique" (2019, p. 52). This results in a lack of meaningful action to change environments or to change the activity system. Instead, what results is a kind of cognitive dissonance. Specifically, Greenfield points to the "Students' Right to Their Own Language" resolution from the Conference on College Composition and Communication. She argued, "These educators cite the resolution to pay lip service to valuing difference without drawing a tangible roadmap to change" (2019, p. 53). That is, what writing center administrators say they do is not necessarily reflective of what actually occurs in their spaces. This lack of a map from intentions to actions may be the result of the writing center's activity system which, because it so closely overlaps with the writing classroom, prevents this kind of change from becoming the object of the system. The use of one spatial metaphor as an attempt to escape another spatial metaphor is potentially troubling but working at the level of description is arguably necessary for identifying how a writing center's structural elements impact and affect the student experience. As others in the collection also note, by being transparent about our programs' positionalities within their larger systems of operation, we make it more possible to transform those systems. Transforming complex, invisible systems begins by working with what we can define.

CONCLUSION

This chapter offered a brief activity theory analysis of writing centers, examining the tensions that arise between the student and the writing center and the institutional network. This chapter highlighted how what writing centers say they do does not always, or even often, match up with what actually occurs in the writing center. Like any activity system, the writing center gives rise to contradictions between stated and enacted goals or objectives and these contradictions then inform the ways in which actors understand and interact with perceived borders or boundaries on their own agencies. However, without the language of activity theory, writing center administrators (and rhetoric and composition administrators more generally) may be less prepared to grapple with these contradictions and change the objects, or what is produced, from their systems. The writing center has products. Its existence as an activity system necessitates them. However, we lose the ability to determine these products if we lack the awareness of the tools that mediate our activities. We may find ourselves producing something antithetical to our mission statements or enacting policies that unwittingly oppress the students who come into our spaces. This risk is intensified if the students who come into the writing center are compelled to be there, moved by the activity system of the classroom or the larger institution. What activity theory offers writing centers, then, is a way to be more intentional and deliberate in how they work with students, writing instructors, and their institutions.

To better understand their activity systems, writing center administrators, and rhetoric and composition administrators more broadly, might expand upon Van Horne's model of the writing consultation's activity system. What Van Horne examined in his study was a slice of the work that goes on in the writing center. There are other branches of the system that are worth examining, especially along the Community and Rules points of the triangle. There are activities and decisions occurring well before the student enters into the writing center's physical or virtual space. When thinking about the rules of the writing center, administrators might interrogate where those rules came from and whom they benefit. These rules don't only need to concern the writing consultation itself; the rules around appointment-making, paper formatting, or other more procedural tasks are also worth investigating. When it comes to community, administrators might examine who they're hiring onto their staff and what backgrounds tutors or other professionals are bringing into the writing center. We know that the people in a place shape the definition and nature of that place; how do writing center staff affect the writing center as a place? How do they influence the writing center's activities? If writing tutors and other professional staff are all from similar backgrounds, there may be a greater danger of hegemony being reinforced in writing sessions, in document creation, in workshop presentations, and other manifestations of writing center work. However, diversity is one way to counter hegemony. Of course, diversity may extend beyond race/ethnicity, gender, and socioeconomic status. We might also think of diversity in terms of majors or areas of study, nontraditional student status, or other types of non-academic experience a tutor brings with them. While administrators need not fully diagram the larger view of their writing centers, it may be worthwhile to perform a sort of audit of the rules that govern behavior in the center and the sorts of people who inhabit it.

Woven into this discussion are metaphors of vision and space. To invoke the writing center as a border processing station is to invoke the hegemonic power writing centers, and spaces like it, wield in order to maintain their activity systems. This chapter relies on these spatial metaphors in order to make apparently neutral functions more visible. The danger of hegemonic power is not just that it oppresses, excludes, or forcibly transforms those who are considered aberrant, but that the processes by which it performs these functions often go unchallenged because the underlying motivations for these functions are unseen. While students have their own motivations for visiting or not visiting a writing center (and sometimes this motivation has a coercive cause), writing centers also have their own motivations when creating policies and procedures that dictate how they work with students. The work to recognize, name, and potentially change these motivations remains ongoing.

REFERENCES

Bawarshi, A. & Pelkowski, S. (1999). Postcolonialism and the idea of a writing center. *The Writing Center Journal, 19*(2), 41–58.

Brooks, J. (1991). Minimalist tutoring: Making the student do all the work. *Writing Lab Newsletter, 15*(6), 1–4.

Camarillo, E. (2022). An idea of a writing center: Moving toward antiracism in asynchronous sessions. *WLN: A Journal of Writing Center Scholarship, 46*(7–8), 19–26.

Dobrin, S. (2011). *Postcomposition.* Southern Illinois University Press.

Engeström, Y. (2015). *Learning by Expanding: An activity-theoretical approach to developmental research.* Cambridge University Press.

García, R. (2017). Unmaking gringo-centers. *The Writing Center Journal, 36*(1), 29–60.

Greenfield, L. (2011). The "standard English" fairy tale: A rhetorical analysis of racist pedagogies and commonplace assumptions about language diversity. In L. Greenfield & K. Rowan (Eds.), *Writing centers and the new racism: A call for sustainable change and dialogue* (pp. 33–60). Utah State University Press.

Greenfield, L. (2019). *Radical writing center praxis: A paradigm for ethical political engagement.* Utah State University Press.

Grimm, N. (1996). The regulatory role of the writing center: Coming to terms with a loss of innocence. *The Writing Center Journal, 17*(1), 5–25.

Inoue, A. (2015). *Antiracist writing assessment ecologies: Teaching and assessing writing for a socially just future.* The WAC Clearinghouse; Parlor Press. https://doi.org/10.37514/per-b.2015.0698.

Lunsford, A. (1991). Collaboration, control, and the idea of a writing center. *Writing Lab Newsletter, 16*(4–5), 1–5.

McKinney, J. G. (2013). *Peripheral visions for writing centers.* Utah State University Press.

Monty, R. (2016). *The writing center as cultural and interdisciplinary contact zone.* Palgrave.

North, S. (1984). The idea of a writing center. *College English, 46*(5), 433–446.

Van Horne, S. A. (2011). *An activity-theory analysis of how college students revise after writing center conferences* [Doctoral dissertation, University of Iowa]. Iowa Research Online. https://ir.uiowa.edu/etd/1187.

CHAPTER 11.

VOICE, SILENCE, AND INVOCATION: THE PERILOUS AND PLAYFUL POSSIBILITIES OF NEGOTIATING IDENTITY IN WRITING CENTERS

Lucien Darjeun Meadows
University of Denver

Every day in writing centers, consultants and writers negotiate, voice, silence, and invoke complex systems of identity. Consultants and writers come out, pass, or seek alternative options as they navigate rhetorical situations of context, text, and audience. As a doctoral candidate and writing center consultant of intersecting and often invisible identities—I am a gay man of mixed Cherokee and Euroamerican descent—I must often consider if, when, how, and why to come out about my identities in some way during a consultation. I regularly encounter writers who also are navigating such situations. We are all passing, in differing extents, identities, and levels of risk. We try to pass as fascinated in every writing consultation, administrative meeting, and classroom, to promote community. We try to pass as more-heterosexual or more-White in certain spaces, to remain safe. We try to pass as a peer in our writing center consultation, a friend to our colleague, an authority in a publication. Identity is nuanced and generates different experiences, but we all navigate disclosure across various, changing rhetorical contexts.

In this chapter, I discuss the disclosure of identities in writing centers from a social systems theory standpoint; here, writers, consultants, and writing centers act not in isolation but in systems where, as Werner Schirmer and Dimitris Michailakis (2019) stated, "Systems are complex entities that consist of a number of elements and their relations" (p. 2). Discussions of disclosure and concealment often focus on the individual as the active agent, where one must simply choose to come out, and is always free to do so. Or, the community is the active agent, where one is forced into concealment or disclosure according to the pressures and expectations of their social/cultural milieu. Social systems theory helps researchers move away from, and queer, this more binary approach.

Because social systems theory centers on understanding systems and contexts, we gain knowledge of a phenomenon like disclosure in writing centers through knowing the systems in which it exists and functions, and we also gain awareness of writing center work as a rhizome in dialogue with writing program administration work.

Social systems theory recognizes what Hans Van Ewijk (2018) termed the "complexity" of communication and social reality. Writers come into our centers with networks of histories, present concerns, and futures voiced and unvoiced just in relation to the writing project at hand, as well as further networks as relevant to them as writers, students, scholars, and community members. Through social systems theory, consultants and writing center professionals recognize the numerous social systems and networks each individual must constantly navigate, including the subsystems of the different communities present in the writing center for each writer on each visit. We recognize that these systems are always more multifaceted and multivalent than we can ever fully know. As writing center administrators and consultants approaching this work through social systems theory, even though we necessarily focus our attention onto the writing project and the writer's discrete goals for this work at hand, we seek to recognize and honor the knowable and unknowable complexities of the writer's full person.

Thus, social systems theory is relational and holistic work, as scholars including Stephan Fuchs (2001) and Haim Shaked and Chen Schechter (2016) wrote, a stance echoed by Schirmer and Michailakis' description of this theoretical approach and practice as "creative, autonomous, and empathic thinking" (2019, p. 5), characteristics also quite applicable to the daily tasks of many writing center administrators and consultants. Approaching disclosure through social systems theory enables us to honor this complexity, even as we seek to understand and support these writers' processes. In the following pages, I will discuss current conversations on navigating identity in writing centers, offer lived scenarios and reflections on coming out and remaining silent for consultants and for writers, introduce the alternative concept of invocation, and extend scholarship on social systems theory and queer theory to offer targeted and tangible takeaways for writing center administrators and for consultants to use in training and tutoring sessions. It is also my hope rhetoric and composition program administrators will read this chapter with an openness for how they might apply my analyses and recommendations to their programs.

NAVIGATING IDENTITY IN THE WRITING CENTER

As a collaborative, conversation-based space within academia, writing centers provide opportunities and challenges for navigating identity in consultations for consultants and writers. Writing centers are themselves often marginalized in the larger academic community. As Eric C. Camarillo wrote in this collection, "The writing center isn't just a border. It is itself bordered." Similar to other spaces discussed in third-space research, writing centers offer a space not-classroom but not-unacademic, where writers work alongside consultants who are not-professors but also not-classmates. Writers discuss their writing in a space that is outside of grades while still rigorous; and administrators, Harry Denny (2010b) stated, "must engage in a sort of perpetual disclosure" to the larger university (p. 119). In this empathic, intellectual space between academia and community, writers and consultants construct and position texts. These texts include the identities of the consultant and the writer. How do we generate our identities, and writers' identities, in sessions? Who are we, as consultants? Who do we imagine each writer to be? How do we, as Andrea Lunsford (1991) wrote, mediate and construct knowledge and identity via collaborative dialogue in a tutoring session? How are these issues complicated by the invisible identities held by consultants and writers?

Most identities exist along a multidimensional spectrum of visibility. While some identity categories tend to be more visible than others (race and sex, according to Denny), in our increasingly intersectional world, these categories—alongside gender, ability, sexual orientation, socioeconomic class, and many other categories—can be strikingly invisible. For several years, I worked in a space where the (White) members of senior leadership would frequently comment, when issues of diversity were brought forward, "We're all White people here," or some variation thereof, despite over 25% of total staff openly identifying as Black peoples, Indigenous peoples, or other peoples of color (BIPOC). Such comments would also be made even in smaller groups, where openly BIPOC individuals comprised 50%—or more—of staff "here" in the room. What are the identities we think we see, and what are the identities we misinterpret or occlude?

More students, staff, and faculty on college campuses nationwide hold diverse identities, according to organizations including the Modern Language Association and the Human Rights Campaign. Writing centers, also, witness this increasing diversity. Thus, the disclosure and negotiation of identity is relevant regardless of whether a particular consultant or writer holds a marginalized and/or invisible identity. Discussions of identity, as Jonathan Alexander and David Wallace (2009) argued, "are critical because they provide opportunities for all students to deconstruct one important aspect of our collective narration of culture" (p. 305). Who we are and who we imagine ourselves to be, who our peers and colleagues and writers are and are imagined, and who our texts' audiences are and are imagined generates particular ways of seeing and being in the world. These aspects connect to often-hegemonic systems of sociocultural and political narratives, and it is possible, Camarillo asserted in this collection, "writing centers . . . are always working from places of hegemony, their implicit practices serving to reinforce traditional power structures." If we, as writing center administrators and consultants, remain unaware of these connections, we may reproduce hegemonic systems for ourselves and the writers we serve, as Anis Bawarshi and Stephanie Pelkowski (1999) cautioned. And what would it mean to reinforce a hegemonic system on writers or on ourselves, especially during more vulnerable discussions of coming out, passing, and issues of identity?

Despite increasing awareness of and need for increased scholarship on marginalized identities in writing centers, the current state of the scholarly conversation remains sparse. In 2013, Andrew Rihn and Jay Sloan reviewed over 30 years of writing center scholarship and found only 14 articles with substantive analysis of queer topics. On my university's databases, my September 2022 search for peer-reviewed articles with "writing center" as the key subject yielded thousands of results. A similar search for "writing center" and "queer"—or terms for specific queer identities, as well as "LGBT" and acronym variations thereof—yielded fewer than 100 total unique results. Further, searching for "writing center" and "Native American"—or specific names of Indigenous Nations, Tribes, and communities, as well as "Indigenous," "First Nations," and "Métis"—yielded fewer than 50 unique results. In both cases, few results held extended discussion of these key terms in relation. Also, few results engaged social systems theory, despite how this approach engages systems of being, identity, communication, and meaning-making—elements seen in writing centers daily—in new and consequential ways.

Meanwhile, certain cornerstone texts of writing center scholarship, like Stephen North's 1984 article "The Idea of a Writing Center," remain, according to Elizabeth Boquet and Neal Lerner (2008), extreme singular influences that dominate the conversation and limit space for others to join. When we privilege certain systems of communication and identity, we exclude other systems. Exclusion always exists; most individuals are excluded from most systems and organizations due to formal requirements (e.g., age or health) or ascriptive requirements (e.g., interest level). Still, individuals and communities also find meaningful inclusion through what Niklas Luhmann (2005) termed "function systems" (p. 226). Here, we relate to each other through shared functions, such as "consultant" or "writer" in a writing center, or as "scholars" in academic discourse. We need diversified citations that bring more voices into our community. We need our scholarship to better represent the diversifying function system of our field.

Despite challenges in meaningful and substantive engagement of diverse topics and voices in scholarship, writing centers remain pivotal sites for authenticity and empowerment. Marilyn Cooper (1994) believed "the goal of empowering students can best be achieved in a writing center" (p. 103), even as Kathryn Valentine and Mónica Torres (2011) admitted "identity confounds any easy assumption of equity and equality in the tutoring session" (p. 195). What happens when identities are confounded by the decision of the consultant or the writer to come out about their marginalized and potentially invisible identity? What about when the consultant or the writer chooses to remain silent, particularly when we recognize and witness this silence?

WHEN THE CONSULTANT SPEAKS

Human communication is a fraught system and process of interpretation dependent on mutuality and openness. What we say (and, further, what we think we say or what we mean to say) is generally never unequivocal, Hans-Georg Gadamer (1960) described. As consultants, by deciding whether to come out or to pass in a session, and by reflecting on choices made and their effects, we learn alongside Rihn and Sloan (2013) how "the writing center can become a key site for investigating what it means to negotiate identity on the fly, in unpremeditated moments of intimacy" (p. 9). So, what happens when we—the consultant—come out in a session?

I'm meeting with a transfer undergraduate writer about her critical essay, where she is asked to take a controversial word, describe controversies surrounding this word, and generate a solution through research and reflection. This writer chose "pioneer." She mentions, "Native American readers might not like my views. I planned on asking my consultant if they were a Native American, but then I saw I was working with you, so I didn't." I look surprised, then say, "Funny you should say that! I'm of Native and Euroamerican descent." Now she looks surprised, and says, "Is that right? I never would have guessed! You don't look Native American. I'm fascinated by Native Americans. I love their culture. I love their skin and how they look." The writer repeatedly expresses her surprise and fascination that I am Native and her fascination with "their culture," before sharing her experiences as a Caribbean immigrant and first-generation United States citizen, through which we return to her essay.

In this scenario, I disclosed my Native identity to this writer as a response to her concern about her essay's impact on Native audiences, and to disrupt and question her assumptions of visible and invisible markers of Native identity. Yet, Denny (2010b) explained, consultants' disclosures of invisible identities are "precarious," because doing so makes consultants subject to rejection (p. 119), as well as, like Alexander and Wallace (2009) noted, fetishizing and tokenizing. Within the hegemonic systems of academia, present even in writing centers, questions of agency are complicated for consultants and writers alike. Yet, as Elise Dixon (2017) explained, "opening up spaces of discomfort is a key part of the meaning-making process" (para. 4). Empowering growth often occurs when one, perhaps due to discomfort, pushes beyond unquestioned beliefs into a space for more authentic dialogue, allowing writers to synthesize new perspectives and a diverse range of texts. It is not the responsibility of the consultant to come out in a session, and this chapter will consider, later, how alternatives to direct disclosure might be more impactful and useful for administrators and consultants. However, by coming out and serving as a teacher-learner in the alongside space with the writer in this way, the consultant occupies a contingent space where their identity might be engaged and where their identity might become the text of a lesson, even if the consultant does not wish to be a lesson or text. As a result, the writer and consultant can then begin to navigate the resulting communication system.

Communication becomes complicated when disclosing—or discussing—identity, as such conversations usually focus more on feelings and experiences rather than on observable data. "When we think about how we communicate feelings and experiences," Schirmer and Michailakis asserted, "the latter cannot be transmitted, and in contrast to knowledge and news, they cannot even be sent or received" (2019, p. 12). Because of these gaps, communication, especially in subjective or internal matters like identity disclosure, exists not as a pure transmission of knowledge between individuals within a system, but as the systemic concept of "an emergent reality" in itself (Schirmer and Michailakis, 2019, p. 15). As scholars of writing centers and programs, we recognize that we never fully know what a writer means or intends to say. Still, we can study systems of communication, analyzing their patterns of expectations, normative behaviors, and sanctions. Similar to the "social facts" named by sociologist Émile Durkheim (1895), these systems of communication manifest in writing centers. Through this systematic study, we move from this gap of knowledge toward emergent understanding, standing with writers as their consultants.

For example, in Canada in 2002, professor Tracey Swan found students in her social work course reacted positively to her disclosure of her lesbian identity. Such professor (or consultant) disclosure—"using one's life as a text," she wrote (2002, p. 7)—augmented students' navigation of heterosexism, homophobia, and client diversity in their professional and personal development. Her decision to come out made oppression tangible and generated room to question discrimination and stereotypes, enhance critical awareness of how language intersects with oppression across contexts, and generate authentic dialogue. At the same time, though, Swan found such disclosure to blur personal/professional boundaries in inappropriate ways, demand "a reciprocal gesture that the student might not be ready to offer" (2002, p. 9), and silence students if they then worry about offending the discloser. However, the impact of disclosure may depend as much on *who* discloses and *how* they disclose than on *what* is disclosed, making the timing of disclosure a key consideration—especially in a writing center, where we often have only a single session with a given writer. Further, Swan, as a professor, occupies a different situation than that of a peer consultant, who often holds no grade-based power, meets with writers for only one session, serves only one writer at a time, and works in a shared professional space. The writing center is a much more contingent space than a term-long class. Consultants must draw upon their multiple identities in this emergent space within a single session and without professorial authority, raising the stakes of this system.

How does a consultant navigate the spaces between coming out, subsequent discussions, and the return to the writer's text and goals for that session? How can a consultant come out in a way that honors, as Denny (2010a) encouraged, their own "obligation to complicate and make possible a whole range of understanding" (p. 106)? And how does our coming out to the writer complicate the rhetorical orientation of the writer's text? If a text is problematic, for example, in presenting all Native American peoples as inhabiting one culture or mindset, what happens when the writer learns this text is being read by a Native person who might not fit into the writer's notions of what Native identity looks like and means? At the same time, how can a consultant's coming out open a mutual consideration of what Joe Salvatore and Judith McVarish (2014) called "risk-taking, questioning, critical thinking, and most importantly, self-reflection," without taking the focus of the session away from the writer and their goals (p. 49)?

WHEN THE CONSULTANT IS SILENT

But what about when we, as consultants, choose not to come out in a session, even when faced with questionable interpretations of our own identities in a writer's text?

I'm meeting with a first-year undergraduate writer about her editorial, where she is responding to the destruction of a park to build a commercial development. I ask, "Why should this park be preserved?" She says, "It's historically significant." I encourage her by asking, "How so?" She responds, "The Native Americans used to use it. It was important to them and Native American culture. I know that's all in the past now, but it's still relevant." When we look at her essay, I observe aloud that the paragraph on the Native influence is uniquely in past tense, and the language moves between discussing one tribe and broad cultures without distinction. She confirms her past tense as intentional, as "they don't live there anymore," and the conflation as also intentional, because "tribes saw the natural world in similar ways." We move on, returning here only when relevant to larger themes (e.g., making a thesis map).

I wondered, throughout this consulting session and in the weeks and months to come, whether I made the "right" choice in remaining silent about my Native identity with this writer. What would have happened if the writer learned that her text, which presented Native peoples as extinct, was being read by a Native person? How would that complicate the text's obligation to its perceived readership, its potential readership, and to our larger world? But also, what did it mean for me—or for any consultant of a marginalized identity being invoked in a potentially problematic way by a text—to remain silent about and during this invocation?

In this session, while my agency as a consultant—as a reader, mentor, and guide for this writer's navigation of her professor's prompt—is retained, my agency as an individual—and as a collaborative partner in meaning-making—is diminished. Accordingly, Alexander and Wallace (2009) argued, "When we cannot speak our truths, our sense of agency is restricted" (p. 304). How is not speaking a kind of speaking? Refraining from explicit questioning of material can be implicit endorsement of such material. By letting "dominant assumptions," as Richard Miller (1994) wrote, "pass through the classroom unread and unaffected" (p. 391). I would add, unchallenged, we replicate and condone hegemonic, colonialist attitudes and structures.

Across writing centers and writing programs, we help writers build transferable skills in rhetoric, voice, and agency that transcend academic boundaries. I wonder how a consultant's coming out can open routes to building these skills. I wonder how silence and passing can close such routes, or whether silence and passing can ever open such routes. In an interview with Travis Webster (2021), the writing center director "Cara," a self-described "'feminist queer woman,'" shared, "'I am advocating for speaking up. It's not about, "Well did you say, have you considered all of your audiences," no, saying, "This is offensive" and "This is wrong" and just really speaking up and being an ally'" (p. 63). Must one always speak up in some way, whether through coming out or through other questioning, to be an ally? I continue to feel conflicted about how I handled this situation with this editorial writer.

Yet, entertaining the binary notion of full silence or full passing, especially for identities that impact our verbal, interpersonal, and physical ways of being in the world, feels disingenuous and unlikely. In this scenario, due to my physical appearance, the writer (to my knowledge) did not suspect that her text was being read and discussed by a Native person. In other scenarios, however, if our identities are apparent or partially intuited by writers, what does it mean for them to know we are choosing to pass instead of coming out?

WHEN THE WRITER SPEAKS

Because communication is an emergent social system, every dialogue between writer and consultant is a network of utterances, such as verbal and nonverbal communicative acts, generated via what Schirmer and Michailakis (2019) called "selections"—that is, conscious and unconscious choices between communicative possibilities. Sometimes, consultants select verbal silence, as I did in the scenario above. Sometimes, consultants select verbal and/or nonverbal voice, as in the first scenario. Throughout our consultations, we can ask: what is said? How is it said? What nonverbal acts accompany this saying? These questions help reveal the selections behind every utterance and show that every utterance, even every moment of every dialogue, is contingent. What is said—here? What is said—to whom? What is said—in this moment? But the consultant is only one actor in this network of utterances. What about when we consider the complexity of coming out or remaining silent for the other person at the table, the other half of this consulting relationship: the writer?

I'm meeting through an online video-and-text session with a first-year graduate writer about his summer internship application, where he is asked to discuss his personal, academic, and professional reasons for applying. He is in the brainstorming stage, so we dialogue, using the platform's synchronous text-based messaging system about what brought him to his field and this internship. After I ask, "Tell me about what you enjoy researching in your program?" he is silent for over two minutes, thoughtful, reflective. In the small video picture of the writer in one corner of the platform's screen, I can see his brow furrowing as he works to formulate his response. Watching the messaging system, I see him start several sentences—"Because," "I," "There is," and "I am"—before backspacing. Then, he types in one continuous span, "I am a Yemeni Muslim. My faith and my family are very important to me, and I've seen many challenges. I want to help those who don't have voice because I know what that feels like." I thank him for sharing his story and affirm the importance of who we are to how we shape our lives, before we return to discussing his knowledges, skills, and career paths—as influenced by his identity—and how they connect to this internship. His responses come quickly for the remainder of the session, and he generates a full essay outline.

Regardless of a writer's explicit or implicit coming out or passing, there is so much coming out on the part of a writer in any session. Writers must admit they feel their writing needs another set of eyes, must admit the elements of their writing that concern them, and must admit their writing voice and style to consultant-writers with the text under discussion. Also, as part of rapport-building initial conversation, they must admit background information about themselves (e.g., their major and some feelings about themselves, their college trajectory, and their writing), often all before the first five minutes of a session have passed. Harriet Malinowitz (1995) described how queer students, "dealing in myriad situations with issues of secrecy, concealment, and disclosure" in most departments across campus, must generate and sustain a "rhetorical self-consciousness" to navigate their daily lives (p. 254). While she wrote about queer students, such rhetorical complexities occur daily in many students' lives, to varying degrees, and particularly in the lives of students with marginalized or invisible identities.

One could say it this way, or one could not; one could opt to disclose their identity in one moment, or not. Differences abound when thinking of how, in representing dialogue, whether through face-to-face verbal encounters or through text-based platforms, we also represent the social system of communication with the inclusion or exclusion of the psychological systems of thought, feeling, and experience. How might this scenario have moved differently if we were face-to-face, or if we were online without video? Communication is contingent, unpredictable, and always shaded in multivalence and situational particularities.

With this in mind, I wonder about the consultant's responsibility when a writer comes out in the consulting session. Writing center administrators and consultants often describe their work as somewhere along the spectrum of teacher and counselor, facilitator and mentor, voice and sounding board. Opting to disclose, or not, can be a useful move for consultants to help writers gain insight and broaden metacognition. In situations when the writer discloses, as in this scenario, consultants become teacher, counselor, and learner all at once within a system of multidimensional possibility, as consultant and writer teach each other about each other in the work of developing rhetorical awareness and incorporating multiple perspectives into our claims and ways of operating within academia.

A writer's coming out might not be a shift away from the text at hand but the addition of another valuable text. If so, consultants can foster an atmosphere of mutual respect, trust, and valuing by avoiding assumptions about what meanings a writer's identity may hold, and instead, as Valentine and Torres urged, work toward "the more complicated stories of racial and ethnic identities merging in our institutions" (2011, p. 206). But what would it mean to complicate a moment of disclosure with invocation of rhetoric, text, audience? In this intricate interpretive system of selections and utterances, the spectrum of visibility and invisibility in identity must complicate our notions of what coming out might look like.

WHEN THE WRITER IS (VISIBLY) SILENT

Some writers choose to come out in the consultation. Some writers remain silent, and as consultants and administrators, we might never know—nor need to know—what silences may be in play. But sometimes, due to a not-quite-invisible identity, we notice this silence.

I'm meeting with a senior undergraduate writer about her business proposal, where she outlines her team's research and development plan for an eco-friendly beauty product. This writer presents as a woman in clothing, hair, makeup, and name on her appointment; yet, her deep voice and name on her student email presents masculine characteristics. When asked to read her essay aloud, she looks startled and nervous. I discuss why we read aloud and share that it is also perfectly fine to have the writer and consultant take turns reading, or to have the consultant read, but that we love to hear the work in the writer's voice, when possible, if they are comfortable. She agrees to read and begins very quietly, reaching a volume more like our initial conversation level by the end. Though she fidgets and avoids eye contact when our discussion approaches passages describing her "woman-owned company" and a company "made for women, by women," she returns to her calm, engaged demeanor when we discuss these passages in the same non-judgmental tone as all others—focusing on her intended audience of executives, and honoring her authority as the scholar and business owner.

Sometimes, writers of visible and/or invisible identities will come out directly in a consulting session, explicitly making space to bring meaning and voice into the conversation. Other times, consultants may be aware the writer likely holds a marginalized identity but is choosing not to come out, as in the scenario above. Speech and silence, action and inaction, and all choices are communicative behavior. So, as theorists Paul Watzlawick et al. (2011) described, one cannot *not* communicate in the presence of another person. For this writer, answering my invitation for her to read her work aloud by breaking eye contact and shifting in her seat is an act of communication. And while I am aware of this writer's initial reluctance to read aloud, and I could imagine a possible identity-based reason for this hesitance, I feel it would be harmful to voice my thoughts on these concerns or to treat her any differently than any other writer. My own silence on her silence is also an act of communication, just as much as my discussion of alternatives to the writing center's reading-aloud policy.

By treating this writer just as I would any other writer, I tried to avoid what Alexander and Wallace (2009) called "forms of othering that are often used to acknowledge the existence of the marginalized while keeping them in the margins" (p. 303). This writer's anxiety may have been related to a fear of outing or of her gender identity becoming an additional party in this conversation she wished to keep focused on her writing. Or not. Regardless, equitable and consistent practices across consultations are useful, even if such practices themselves require constant flexibility to move, realize, and grow to meet each writer's individual needs—to "*listen more*," as Anne DiPardo (1992) recommended for a Black consultant with a Native writer—especially in the vulnerable topic of identity (p. 140). In this session, I realized a potential complication to writing centers' policies of having work read aloud, often by the writer. Even alongside its goals of helping writers gain empowerment, voice, and authority, this standard procedure of reading aloud could out a writer against their will to their consultant or others in the room.

To verbally disclose identity is an act of communication, arguably just as much as to choose to not verbally disclose (and/or to non-verbally disclose) is an act of communication. With Watzlawick et al.'s (2011) theory of the omnipresence of communication in mind, I wonder how consultants can avoid assumptions that coming out (visibly, audibly) is preferable to passing, or that passing is preferable to coming out. Though consultations can occur without need for personal pronouns, should consultants always share their pronouns and ask writers for their own? With many professional introductions expanding beyond offering name and role (or major) to offering name, role, and pronouns, the absence of pronoun inclusion is a communicative act, and this act may be noticed and felt by our colleagues and those we serve. How, then, can we hold spaces of both voice and silence as emergent systems of communicative acts? Is it ever useful or acceptable to invoke a perceived non-disclosed identity, as one housed in the writer or consultant, or as one housed in potential readers?

WHEN WE TALK AROUND AND THROUGH, WITHOUT EXPLICIT DISCLOSURE

I wonder about these situations—the consultant coming out, the consultant remaining silent, the writer coming out, the writer remaining silent. I wonder if these scenarios generate a binary, where our options are either full disclosure (by consultant or writer) or full silence. I want us to queer this binary to imagine other possibilities. Queer theory enables us, as Jan Cooper (2004) wrote, to "attend to the complex experiences of individuals interacting with each other within and across cultures" (p. 36), where binaries and static positions are just one way of being in the world. Other ways of being—many other ways of being—involve triangulations, septangulations, and fluid positions in systems and sequences that we all, in some way, inhabit.

I'm meeting with a junior undergraduate writer on her prospectus, where she proposes traveling to major United States military archives to research silences of queer veterans. After she reads the abstract, we dialogue. I say, "This sounds like new research." She responds, "Yes—and important to do for folks both in and outside the queer community." I mention, "I attended a conference featuring a keynote by Matthew Shepard's father. So powerful. These stories inspire empathy and voice." The writer agrees. Time is limited, so we skip some sections of her choice, including "Personal Relevance," which includes a sentence where she comes out as lesbian. But she pauses in moving from the section before to the section after, and I cannot help but scan the page and see her sentence. When we move on, there is a different feel to the session—she is more relaxed, more direct in discussing her work.

Beyond the two binary options of coming out or remaining silent, we have options for self-conscious, critical existence and use of multiple discourses—of passing, of coming out; of acculturation, of subversion; and more. Communication systems are emergent systems, and they are, Schirmer and Michailakis (2019) described, changeable, unpredictable, and difficult to plan. Most writing center administrators and consultants would agree that the writing center echoes this dynamic space. Each consultation brings new challenges, questions, and rewards one may never have been able to predict. Accordingly, Boquet (2002) wrote, "To function as an apparatus of educational transformation" as writing centers and consultants, "we must imagine a liminal zone where chaos and order coexist" (p. 84). As in the last scenario, disclosure and silence are both communicative acts. We can further multiply communicative possibilities by acknowledging, like Watzlawick et al. (2011), that every communicative behavior has a content aspect (i.e., what is communicated) and a relational aspect (i.e., how it is communicated). It is an act of communication that this writer chooses not to read her "Personal Relevance" section aloud, another act that she pauses in silence as our eyes move over this section, another act that she glances at me and sees my reading during her brief pause, and another act that her demeanor changes after this shared, and charged, silence.

Honoring and invoking this metacommunicative relational aspect, we work toward invoking Gloria Anzaldúa's work of the "border residency/consciousness" (1987, p. 79). In this border space, we negotiate these emergent communicative systems as multiple contradictory contexts, identities, audiences, and rhetorical strategies, even while we continue to exist in the dominant discourses. In border residency/consciousness, we exist not as fixed points or static identities but as strategic and contextualized systems of potentiality. Jicarilla Apache scholar Loyola K. Bird concurs, stating consultants should prioritize discussions of context, situation-dependent linguistics, student needs, and "what it means to move 'between worlds'" (Gray-Rosendale et al., 2003, p. 88). There is much to be gained when existing not as either-or, but as in-between.

One productive possibility of border consciousness is how it lets us see consultations as what Nancy Welch (1999) called "potential spaces" (p. 54). These potential spaces, Welch argued, do not necessarily arise out of full-adherence-to or full-resistance-to academic expectations and conventions, but, rather, out of queering hegemonic systems of space to find liminal borderland—room to create, experiment, and play. This space energizes writers and consultants to decide when and how they, Denny wrote, "choose to resist or further challenge and question" (2010a, p. 110). Such rhetorical decisions generate transferable skills beyond the consultation and across academia, professional trajectories, and community engagements. By opening potential spaces, we re-envision with Welch how "an estranging gap becomes now a space of potential and play" (1999, p. 57). This potential and play generated "both a view of and a space apart from the surrounding world" (Welch, 1999, p. 59), and new possibilities for negotiating passing and coming out and liminal/border consciousness emerge. We recognize the writer's text as another audience, another system of being, and another being at the table—a being with communicative needs with whom the writer and consultant, in this potential space, can consider and engage.

WHEN WE "COME OUT" TO—AND WITH—AND FOR—THE TEXT

In social systems theory, psychological and social systems of communication are often defined as "closed" systems in that they cannot exceed their predefined boundaries. It is impossible for one individual to read another's mind or feel their emotions or sense their pain as their own. One's thoughts, perceptions, and sensations cannot be downloaded to another. They must be shaped through shared social systems of communication to relay our individual psychological systems. According to Luhmann (1992), because communication can only express these social utterances, one could say that communication cannot think or feel, and psychological systems cannot communicate. What is one to do? We can turn to play, potentiality, and emergence.

When "the tutorial [consultation] becomes a potential space," as Welch wrote, the consultant and writer come together to consider the needs of a third party: the writer's text (1999, p. 60). Writer and consultant consider the text, its contexts, and importantly, its audiences. And by considering these potential audiences, sessions become emergent spaces where writers and consultants work together in "trying out, not closing out, different constructions of reality" (Welch, 1999, p. 64). Attention to the playful, transformative possibilities of considering these social systems of text and audience as other communicative parties at the table help us consider and express the implications of coming out to, with, and for the text and its audiences.

Lisa Ede and Andrea Lunsford (1984) discussed two rhetorical positions on negotiating audience: the "Audience Addressed," or concrete, living individuals who will read a particular text; and the "Audience Invoked," or constructed, imagined individuals who will likely never hold the text in question but are still present in its consideration (p. 156). Both audiences, Audience Addressed and Audience Invoked, fit into the potential categories of self, friend, colleague, critic, mass audience, and future audience. Audience Invoked, though, also exists as past audience, such as a historical figure, and as anomalous audience, such as a fictional figure. When writing consultations become potential spaces of play that question and refigure communicative systems, writers and consultants can consider potential audiences and the psychological impact of the text on these audiences, whether they will literally be at the table at some point (Audience Addressed) or may never be, though they still exist however imaginatively in the same social system as the text (Audience Invoked).

Audience Invoked, then, becomes a way for consultants and writers to acknowledge diverse voices and perspectives and to consider the writer's text as it might impact the Invoked. If a text portrays Native American cultures as singular and extinct, as in the earlier scenario, one solution is for the consultant, if applicable, to share their Native identity to bring a new Audience Addressed to the table and enable the writer to consider the impact of their text on one example of such an audience. Another way, accessible to all consultants and another option for consultants who choose not to invoke their personal identity, would be to bring a new Audience Invoked to the table—an imagined Native American reader, presenced as a unique psychological system and not as an abstract representation or generalization—to achieve the same results: helping the writer consider the impact of their text on a new audience.

Swan (2002) found her self-disclosure to her students as a lesbian person had effects including making tangible experiences of marginalization and oppression, encouraging growth away from unconscious assumptions, provoking critical awareness and consideration of diverse perspectives, and creating space of mutual trust and confidence in disclosure. However, all of these effects but the last can be achieved with the consultant's introduction of a relevant Audience Invoked. Perhaps the final effect can be achieved also, and more effectively.

Introducing a new reader through Audience Invoked sidesteps the consultant-writer power imbalance, giving both writer and consultant a third-person, less risky, and more accessible way to voice concerns and questions without the fear of offending someone physically at the table with them. Watzlawick et al.

(2011) discuss how communicative relationships tend to exist as symmetric (i.e., based on equal power, such as learner-learner) or complementary (i.e., based on unequal power, such as manager-employee), and communicative systems tend to maintain the existing relationship, whether symmetric or complementary. If a consultant discloses their own marginalized identity to generate an Audience Addressed for a writer, the resulting communication, however productive, will tend to maintain the complementary communicative relationship of consultant-writer. However, if a consultant generates an Audience Invoked with a writer, the communication that results, particularly between writer and Audience Invoked, will dwell in a symmetric communicative system more accessible and engaging for writer and text.

Thus, if disclosure for Swan means "using one's life as a text" (2002, p. 7), it would work well to use the life of an Invoked one as a text, to place consultants and writers in a more mutual space of interpretation. This is not to encourage passing where coming out is desired and felt relevant. After all, the adage that personal stories are a highly effective way to touch hearts and change minds continues to be true. Voicing marginalized perspectives through Audience Invoked does provide another option for folks wishing not to come out, for whatever reason, and importantly offers all consultants, regardless of their identity categories, a means to work toward inclusion.

NEXT STEPS

We work in an emergent field, where communicative acts reverberate outward in ways we could never predict with each new consulting session and staff meeting. I seek to open the doors (and windows) into this discussion and invite dialogue. Ours is a collaborative field, where we generate knowledge "by negotiating collaboratively toward new paradigms of perception, thought, feeling, and expression" (Bruffee, 1984, p. 646). In writing centers, we inspire border consciousness and create potential spaces, according to Bawarshi and Pelkowski, through helping ourselves and our writers, "look prior to and outside of these discourses" (1999, p. 54). My chapter itself is a text and discourse, with room to grow, evolve, and expand through our collaboration, our questions and future research possibilities.

In 2008, Boquet and Lerner declared, "Writing center scholarship must manage, more often than it does now, 'both-and' rather than 'either-or'" (p. 186). This statement remains true today, as writers and consultants nationwide are increasingly diverse, often in increasingly intersectional ways. Powerful work is being generated by diverse writing center scholars, often before they leave their graduate programs. For example, consider: Elizabeth Witherite's thesis on writing center tutors' perceptions of social justice issues (2014, Indiana University of Pennsylvania), Hillery Glasby's dissertation on queer doing and being in the writing classroom (2016, Ohio University), Abbie Levesque's thesis on queer writing and queer writing center practices (2017, Northeastern University), Talisha Haltiwanger Morrison's dissertation on racism and antiracism from Black writing tutors at predominantly White institutions (2018, Purdue University), and Hillary Weiss's dissertation on the complexities of coming out in community-based writing groups (2020, Wayne State University).

However, there are still many gaps and silences. What might a qualitative study reveal in surveying the effect on writers of consultant-disclosure in the consulting session? What would we learn if we studied one identity category and its disclosures, silences, and invocations in writing center sessions? How has disclosure changed in and since 2020, with our widespread shift to online learning, heightened attention to systems of racial and cultural oppression, and changing relational expectations amid the COVID-19 pandemic and its various continuances? We have much room to expand this ongoing conversation.

At the same time, writing center administrators and consultants have access to tangible and scalable practices to promote identity-based invocation while remaining present and emergent in our positionality. For administrators, we can re-align our writing center's strategy, leadership, and hiring practices with campus-wide diversity, equity, and inclusion (DEI) policies and goals. We can leverage relationships with existing campus offices to support enhanced training for our staff and deepen existing work in our centers. We can partner with campus and community DEI offices, and/or national writing center organizations and resources, to pursue impactful hiring processes in materials (e.g., incorporating diversity statements), qualifications (e.g., evaluating what is truly required), and language (e.g., showing transparency in decision-making timelines, pay levels and benefits, and day-to-day duties). For consultants, we can support continued education in the campus or community through paid training time or schedule flexibility. We can support continued education in the writing center by implementing staff meetings or a space within existing meetings to discuss DEI books or films, dialogue about identity-based moments from tutoring sessions, role-play scenarios, and invite consultants to share relevant knowledges and experiences as holders of complex systems of identity.

Today, and at no cost, writing center administrators and consultants can work together to generate sentence frames for center-wide use in tutoring sessions when marginalized and/or silenced identities are invoked by the writer or their text, to help provide structure and build confidence in what can be a challenging and complicated topic. These sentence frames could include: "What audiences are we not thinking about here?" "What readers can you imagine feeling positive about this section/paragraph/sentence?" and "Who might feel not-so-positive here?" "What exceptions to this claim might a different reader ask?"—and starting each session's discussion of the text's rhetoric or audience with, "What audiences are at the table?"

Throughout these practices and across the writing center staff, we help each other by acknowledging our own individual sense of self, being, and boundaries. We are not alone in negotiating systems of identity within ourselves, among our centers, or with the students and texts we serve. The choice to come out, remain silent, or use Audience Addressed/Audience Invoked in a given session will not make—or break—the larger educational system. Rather than a burden, systems of identity and possibilities for their navigation in a consultation are spaces of sacred play. The liminal space of the writing center within academia becomes a generative space of possibility for all of us to learn and play alongside writers and texts.

Writing centers and programs present a transformative environment in which to consider identity. How consultants, writers, and administrators navigate coming out, remaining silent, and alternative possibilities in regard to marginalized is a line of study with room for many voices to join. While every consultant, writer, and administrator might not navigate decisions of identity disclosure on a daily basis, we all live in an intersectional world and participate in complicated systems of communication. We—as makers and advocates of texts—have a responsibility to consider all the voices at the table, our Audiences Addressed, and all the voices who might not be present nor welcomed, our Audiences Invoked. Together, we can leverage communicative systems to move with writers toward consideration of how their texts, and even our consulting sessions, navigate, revel in, and honor these complexities.

ACKNOWLEDGMENTS

I am deeply grateful for the insight of scholars who reviewed drafts of this chapter and provided instrumental feedback, including Megan Kelly, Elijah Null, Juli Parrish, Sara Sheiner, and Alison Turner. I warmly thank editors Genesea M. Carter and Aurora Matzke for the opportunity to contribute to this project, their incisive guidance, and for modeling an inclusive, inspiring approach to editing and publication.

REFERENCES

Alexander, J. & Wallace, D. (2009). The queer turn in composition studies: Reviewing and assessing an emerging scholarship. *College Composition and Communication*, *61*(1), 300–320.

Anzaldúa, G. (1987). *Borderlands/La frontera: The new mestiza*. Spinsters/Aunt Lute Books.

Bawarshi, A. & Pelkowski, S. (1999). Postcolonialism and the idea of a writing center. *The Writing Center Journal, 19*(2), 41–58.

Boquet, E. H. (2002). *Noise from the writing center*. University Press of Colorado; Utah State University Press. https://doi.org/10.2307/j.ctt46nwjt.1.

Boquet, E. H. & Lerner, N. (2008). After "The idea of a writing center." *College English, 71*(2), 170–189.

Bruffee, K. A. (1984). Collaborative learning and the "conversation of mankind." *College English, 46*(7), 635–652.

Cooper, J. (2004). Queering the contact zone. *JAC, 24*(1), 23–45.

Cooper, M. M. (1994). Really useful knowledge: A cultural studies agenda for writing centers. *The Writing Center Journal, 14*(2), 97–111.

Denny, H. C. (2010a). Facing sex and gender in the writing center. In H. Denny (Ed.), *Facing the center: Toward an identity politics of one-to-one mentoring* (pp. 87–112). University Press of Colorado; Utah State University Press.

Denny, H. C. (2010b) Queering the writing center. *The Writing Center Journal, 30*(1), 95–124.

DiPardo, A. (1992). "Whispers of coming and going": Lessons from Fannie. *The Writing Center Journal, 12*(2), 125–144.

Dixon, E. (2017). Uncomfortably queer: Everyday moments in the writing center. *The Peer Review, 1*(2). thepeerreview-iwca.org/issues/braver-spaces/uncomfortably-queer-everyday-moments-in-the-writing-center/.

Durkheim, É. (1895). *The rules of sociological method: And selected texts on sociology and its method*. Free Press.

Ede, L. & Lunsford, A. (1984). Audience addressed/audience invoked: The role of audience in composition theory and pedagogy. *College Composition and Communication, 35*(2), 155–171.

Fuchs, S. (2001). *Against essentialism: A theory of culture and society*. Harvard University Press.

Gadamer, H.-G. (1960). *Truth and method*. Bloomsbury.

Glasby, H. (2016). *Politics and pedagogies of queer doing and being in the writing classroom: Rhetoric and composition's LGBTQ student-writers* [Doctoral dissertation, Ohio University]. OhioLINK Electronic Theses and Dissertations Center. http://rave.ohiolink.edu/etdc/view?acc_num=ohiou1470906834.

Gray-Rosendale, L., Bird, L. K. & Bullock, J. F. (2003). Rethinking the basic writing frontier: Native American students' challenge to our histories. *Journal of Basic Writing, 22*(1), 71–106. https://doi.org/10.37514/jbw-j.2003.22.1.08

Levesque, A. (2017). *Queer writing and queer writing center practices*. [Master's thesis, Northeastern University].

Luhmann, N. (1992). What is communication? *Communication Theory, 2*(3), 251–259

Luhmann, N. (2005). Inklusion und exklusion. In N. Luhmann (Ed.), *Soziologische aufklärung 6* (pp. 226–251). VS-Verlag Press.

Lunsford, A. (1991). Collaboration, control, and the idea of a writing center. *The Writing Center Journal, 12*(1), 3–10.

Malinowitz, H. (1995). *Textual orientations: Lesbian and gay students and the making of discourse communities.* Heinemann.

Miller, R. E. (1994). Fault lines in the contact zone. *College English, 56*(4), 389–408.

Morrison, T. H. (2018). *Nooses and balancing acts: Reflections and advice on racism and antiracism from Black writing tutors at predominantly White institutions* [Doctoral dissertation, Purdue University]. Purdue e-pubs. https://docs.lib.purdue.edu/dissertations/AAI10788542/.

North, S. (1984). The idea of a writing center. *College English, 46*(5), 433–446.

Rihn, A. J. & Sloan, J. D. (2013). "Rainbows in the past were gay": LGBTQIA in the WC. *Praxis: A Writing Center Journal, 10*(2), 1–13.

Said, E. (1983). *The world, the text, and the critic.* Harvard University Press.

Salvatore, J. & McVarish, J. (2014). Vulnerability: A metalogue. *Teacher educators rethink self-assessment in higher education: A guide for the perplexed* [Special issue]. *Counterpoints, 380,* 47–59.

Schirmer, W. & Michailakis, D. (2019). *Systems theory for social work and the helping professions.* Routledge.

Shaked, H. & C. Schechter. (2016). Systems thinking among middle school leaders. *Journal of Educational Management Administration & Leadership, 45*(4), 699–718.

Swan, T. A. (2002). Coming out and self-disclosure: Exploring the pedagogical significance in teaching social work students about homophobia and heterosexism. *Canadian Social Work Review/Revue Canadienne de service social, 19*(1), 5–23.

Valentine, K. & Torres, M. F. (2011). Diversity as topography: The benefits and challenges of cross racial interaction in the writing center. In L. Greenfield & K. Rowan (Eds.), *Writing centers and the new racism: A call for sustainable dialogue and change* (pp. 192–210). University Press of Colorado; Utah State University Press.

Van Ewijk, H. (2018). *Complexity and social work.* Routledge.

Watzlawick, P., Bavelas, J. B. & Jackson, D. D. (2011). *Pragmatics of human communication: A study of interactional patterns, pathologies, and paradoxes.* Norton.

Webster, T. (2021). *Queerly centered: LGBTQA writing center directors navigate the workplace.* University Press of Colorado; Utah State University Press.

Weiss, H. (2020). *Coming out as complex: Understanding LGBTQ+ community writing groups* [Doctoral dissertation, Wayne State University]. Wayne State University Dissertations. https://digitalcommons.wayne.edu/oa_dissertations/3414/.

Welch, N. (1999). Playing with reality: Writing centers after the mirror stage. *College Composition and Communication, 51*(1), 51–69.

Witherite, E. (2014). *Writing center tutors' perceptions of social justice issues: A multiple method qualitative study* [Master's dissertation, Indiana University of Pennsylvania].

SECTION 3.
PERSONAL AND RELATIONAL NETWORKS: EXISTING AS AN ADMINISTRATOR

Self-Care

Chapter 12. "Is Resistance Futile?: Struggling against Systematic Assimilation of Administrative Work" by Genesea M. Carter

Scheduling

Chapter 13. "'It's Complicated': Scheduling as an Intellectual, Networked Social Justice Issue for WPAs" by Julia Voss and Kathryn Bruchmann

Archiving

Chapter 14. "Flexible Framing, Open Spaces, and Adaptive Resources: A Networked Approach to Writing Program Administration" by Jenna Morton-Aiken

As we open the third section, Personal and Relational Networks: Existing as an Administrator, the work of the authors becomes further characterized by managerial tasks. Chapter 12 begins with the task of self-care, a task Genesea M. Carter says is necessary to managerial success but rarely supported by the neoliberal systems which guide higher education. Carter points readers to (1) attention toward the concept of a rhetoric and composition administrator as a constructed persona that is problematically perpetuated by larger systems of communication within the field, and (2) the ways in which the body functions as a supersystem in and of itself that must be actively monitored to sustain change-making efforts. Carter encourages administrators and the field at large to re-write the field's narratives about work, to be mindful of the language we use about the work we do, and to set work-life boundaries; these three recommendations can help administrators mindfully navigate academia writ large as a system, so as to not suffer burnout, when working toward more equitable educational settings for those within our care.

Next, in Chapter 13, Julia Voss and Kathryn Bruchmann delve into a discussion of course and classroom scheduling, examining the campus-wide networks of stakeholders involved in the delivery of writing instruction and its infrastructure. They make interesting comparisons between institutional characteristics of the student body, tuition, and selectivity and the types of classrooms used, encouraging administrators to critically consider the systems at work when they complete the routine task of scheduling and classroom assignment.

Finally, Chapter 14 closes the collection with a discussion of archiving. In this chapter, Jenna Morton-Aiken names the rhetorical power of organizational habits and archival principles for the compositionist as both individual instructor and program administrator. Taking the reader through her experience archiving information during her graduate studies, Morton-Aiken argues that we are all archivists, whether we're working in digital archives, Sharepoint or Google Drive, office file cabinets, or other digital or analog spaces. Morton-Aiken calls for program administrators to pay attention to and critically engage with archiving: the *how* and *why* administrators archive enables or constricts the ways in which they and others are able to facilitate changes in their programs and beyond.

The purpose of this section is to consider the routine work of the administrator, and its relationship to systems that affect it. Self-care, scheduling, and archiving are just a few of the common tasks that can easily be checked off of a list with little time for critical attention to the systems at play. Why is it so easy to skip self-care in systems of higher education? Why can scheduling be complicated by networks of power? And how can archiving contribute to DEIBSJ? This section challenges the manager to pause and consider various networks that shape the common and necessary tasks of the rhetoric and composition administrator. As we close this interchapter, we offer you a few reflection and discussion questions, should you want to journal about your reading or use the book for a faculty book club or professional development. In particular, we encourage you to think about what you might take away or try from this section:

- How might workplace boundaries improve the equity and health of your program and department? How might you encourage others in your program or department to set workplace boundaries as well?
- How might the infrastructure of course scheduling promote or impede change making? How might the rhetoric of space and place fit into conversations about course scheduling, particularly which courses or meetings get scheduled in which spaces?
- What does archival work, knowledge management, and content coding tell you about what information and knowledge is privileged and prioritized? Are there new systems you or others can put into place to enact DEIBSJ in your classroom, program, or department?
- What are some of the additional "day-to-day" tasks of the program administrator that may inhibit or promote equity work? What gaps still exist regarding these activities in the larger literature?

CHAPTER 12.

IS RESISTANCE FUTILE? STRUGGLING AGAINST SYSTEMATIC ASSIMILATION OF ADMINISTRATIVE WORK

Genesea M. Carter
Colorado State University

In the second season of Star Trek's *The Next Generation* (TNG) episode, Captain Picard and crew are introduced to the Borg, a cybernetic alien species. The Borg were not the typical enemy the U.S.S. Enterprise crew met during their exploration of the Milky Way galaxy. Unlike other alien species, the Borg's objective was to assimilate all biological life into "The Collective," a hivemind driven by their quest for total domination and complete perfection. The Borg's motto, "Resistance is Futile," often declared by thousands of Borg in unison, terrified Picard's crew and television viewers alike. As a humanoid species with a shared consciousness across millions of Borg drones, the Borg function as a systematic network: they physically plug into the Collective mainframe where they have their own docking stations and receive the Collective directives through network downloads.

I open my chapter with the Borg supersystem because it is a fitting—albeit dramatic—metaphor for the many working environments rhetoric and composition administrators experience within the neoliberal university supersystem. Much has been written about the professional, emotional, and invisible labor of administration work, such as Diana George's *Kitchen Cooks, Plate Twirlers, and Troubadours* (1999), Theresa Enos and Shane Borrowman's collection *The Promise and Perils of Writing Program Administration* (2008), and, more recently, Courtney Adams Wooten et al.'s *The Things We Carry: Strategies for Recognizing and Negotiating Emotional Labor in Writing Program Administration* (2020). Many hallway conversations, conference workshops, and Facebook feeds are filled with how the system of academia reduces humane working conditions and increases emotional and cognitive overload. A common theme in the scholarship and side conversations are rhetoric and composition administrators' worries about setting boundaries and saying no due to workplace (covert or overt)

DOI: https://doi.org/10.37514/PER-B.2023.1848.2.12   271

retaliation, feelings of powerlessness, and fears over letting students and colleagues down (McGee & Handa, 2005).

However, a (often) missing piece of the conversation and scholarship about rhetoric and composition administrators' work culture is how neoliberal ideals and values have shaped rhetoric and composition administrators' identities, motivations, and work mindset. While much has been written about the neoliberal university more generally, very little scholarship on rhetoric and composition administration explores how the neoliberal university functions as a system directly affecting rhetoric and composition administrators' (hereafter administrators) wellbeing. Systems theory is an important framework to consider in this conversation because, as we write in the Introduction, it provides "a tangible way to engage in identifying the gaps, the in-between, and the silences that result in broken systems and people." Therefore, my chapter is not a critique of the administrators who are caught-up in an all-consuming system, as many of us have been conditioned that this administrative life is normal or that nothing can be done about it. Rather, I want to draw attention to system processes that affect our personal and professional lives and impede the meaningful change we want to create for ourselves, our colleagues, and our students.

The neoliberal university supersystem, according to Evelyn Morales Vázquez and John S. Levin (2018), "relies on the idealization and needs of faculty members as entrepreneurial workers" (para. 3). In this model, administrators "operat[e] in the position of middle management, are often tasked with maintaining viable writing programs on skeletal budgets with overwhelmingly contingent faculties" (Scott, 2009, p. 184). Administrators in the United States and elsewhere are probably familiar with the neoliberal buzzwords of the ideal university employee: the employee exhibiting "flexibility," "competitiveness," "entrepreneurial spirit," "economic rationale," "adaptability to precarious environments" and "emotional detachment" (Vázquez & Levin, 2018, para. 3). In this system, workaholism, scarcity mindset, managerial processes, economic priorities, and emotional disembodiment are prized. Resistance, push-back, self-care, and boundaries are discouraged or even disciplined.

In this chapter, I focus on how the neoliberal university supersystem functions as a top-down collective defining and shaping administrators' work mindsets and identities. In this hybrid essay genre, which blends research, narrative, and reflective exercises, I first provide an overview of social science scholarship on neoliberalism to show how neoliberal university supersystems affect administrators' workloads, job satisfaction, and personal care. Social science scholarship can give administrators language and framing to better understand how the neoliberal system shapes our work and, often, hides from view how we might resist neoliberalism. Second, I use mindfulness theory, neuroscience, and psychology to encourage readers to adopt what I call a "mindful work mindset" (MWM) to counteract the demands of the neoliberal university supersystem. In this section, I offer mindfulness and boundary exercises for administrators to try for personal and professional self-care. Ultimately, my objective is to support your examination of your own (conscious or unconscious) roles in the neoliberal university supersystem, how you might resist neoliberal work expectations, how you might reclaim your personal and professional identities, and how you might (re)establish meaningful personal and relational networks.

As you read this chapter, I would like you to consider one or more of these questions, perhaps with a journal by your side, to guide your reflection and mindfulness:

- What do I value most about my administrative work and why?
- What do I value least about my administrative work and why?
- What is my biggest concern about how administrative work affects my personal life?
- What is my biggest concern about how administrative work affects my professional life?
- What parts of this chapter resonate with my experiences as an administrator and why?
- Do I feel like I can set boundaries and say no? And when/if I do set boundaries or say no, do I feel like I am letting students, faculty, or others down?
- How does the neoliberal supersystem function in my program, department, college, or university? In what ways am I required or encouraged to perpetuate the supersystem?

WHEN UNIVERSITY SYSTEMS RESEMBLE THE BORG: AUDITING CULTURE, WORKAHOLISM, FRAGMENTATION, AND COMPULSORY CITIZENSHIP BEHAVIOR

I draw from psychology, anthropology, business administration, and public administration research to highlight four negative outcomes of neoliberalism that impact administrators as human beings: auditing culture, fragmentation, compulsory citizenship behavior, and workaholism. Auditing culture, fragmentation, compulsory citizenship behavior, and workaholism are the byproduct of the neoliberal university supersystem. My purpose in this section is to introduce readers to social science research that could help them better understand the work culture they have been foisted into or unwittingly adopted. Until we can recognize the supersystem dynamics affecting our work culture and pressures, it is very difficult to resist, internally and externally. (Readers should also hop over to Bradbury et al.'s chapter on activity systems in this collection, as their observations about how activity systems "interact with or otherwise influence each other, perhaps through shared membership, shared goals (objects), similar rules (sometimes referred to as *norms*) or reliance on the same or similar tools" offers readers another perspective of how systems shape how we see ourselves and the work we do.)

I am personally invested in this conversation because I have experienced this supersystem, as perhaps all readers have, and have felt its emotional and professional toll. Coming out of my doctoral program in 2013, I took a 4-4 tenure-track job at the University of Wisconsin-Stout (UW-Stout), which I knew would be a difficult teaching load for me as an ambivert and empath. During faculty orientation, the provost announced faculty turnover was 47%, which was demoralizing to hear before the semester began. During my four years there as an assistant professor and also as the Director of First-Year Writing (with one course release each semester), I experienced the emotional and professional exhaustion working at a university with high teaching loads and low salary. (My salary for nine months was $51,000 gross, which barely covered student loans and the cost of living.) Because of the low salaries, especially among faculty in the humanities, many of us took overloads, taught courses during the three weeks of winter break, and taught in the summer. It felt like the campus was generally burned out. At least in my pockets of campus.

My own workload, with the internal pressure to publish enough to be considered competitive for a job with a lower teaching load, caused me to have adrenal fatigue and chronic exhaustion, which is still affecting me years later. Most everyone around me, it seemed, was exhausted, resentful, and applying to other jobs. And I was exhausted, resentful, and applying to other jobs. At that time, I thought taking a position with a lower teaching load might reduce the exhaustion, but it did not. In 2017, I accepted the position at Colorado State University (CSU), and the exhaustion of my CSU colleagues was the same at UW-Stout if not higher. Ten years post-graduation, rather than being resentful about the academic climate, I have poured myself into understanding *why things are the way they are*. In my research for this collection and chapter, I've learned a few things: the neoliberal university supersystem keeps us in the cycle of exhaustion; as well, being trained in a field where overwork seems to be the norm (and do I dare to say prized in some circles), sets-up graduates to accept neoliberal work environments as the norm. But my personality as a problem-solver and ever-questioner means I ask "why?" quite a bit. Why do we prize exhaustion?

Why are we taught exhaustion is normal? Why do we think we can't say no? Why do we think if we set workload boundaries, we're disappointing colleagues and students? These questions and more drive my research.

According to anthropologists Cris Shore and Susan Wright (2015), the neoliberal university model has fostered an "audit culture" with significant consequences (p. 430). In their study of how neoliberalism has shaped European university systems, Shore and Wright explained, "The introduction of audit and accounting changes the nature of the organizations so that their activities become increasingly focused on the measures by which their performance is judged" (2015, p. 430). The perceived "positive outcome" of auditing culture is it "delivers efficiency, commensurability, and accountability" in addition to "transposable templates for managerial control and make possible new forms of remote surveillance" (Shore and Wright, 2015, p. 430). Despite the perceived benefits, Shore and Wright identified seven consequences of academic audit culture as identified by international scholars:

1. "loss of organizational trust"
2. "elaborate and wasteful gaming strategies"
3. "a culture of compliance and large compliance costs, including the appointment of new specialists preoccupied with creating position (mis)representations of performance"
4. "defensive strategies and blamism that stifle innovation and focus on short-term objectives over long-term needs"
5. "deprofessionalization, a disconnect between motivation and incentives, lower employee morale, and increased stress and anxiety"
6. "'tunnel vision' and performing to the measure, with a focus solely on what is counted, to the exclusion of anything else"
7. "and the undermining of welfare and educational activities that cannot be easily measured" (p. 430).

I don't know if it reassures us to know our international colleagues are experiencing similar demands. Perhaps it's a bit reassuring. If anything, it reveals that higher education institutions, acting as supersystems, rely on compliance, quantified methods, auditing culture, loss of autonomy, and personal self-sacrifice to maintain their output: more students, more classes, more sports, more awards, and more money. As we can probably all guess, auditing culture does little to benefit staff, faculty, and students.

Working very hard, often defined as "workaholism" or "overwork" depending on the context, is a by-product of the neoliberal supersystem. Because context is important to defining whether one is a workaholic or an overworker, researchers studying workaholism often struggle to agree upon definitions (Peiperl & Jones,

2001; Schaufeli et al., 2009). According to Wayne Oates (1971), who coined the term "workaholism," it is "the compulsion or the uncontrollable need to work incessantly" and likened workaholism to a type of addiction (p. 11). More recently, Wilmar B. Schaufeli et al. (2009) defined workaholism "as the tendency to work excessively hard (the behavioral dimension) and being obsessed with work (the cognitive dimension), which manifests itself in working compulsively" (p. 322).

It is worth noting there is a difference between workaholics and overworkers: whether or not workers feel valued by the organization. According to Maury Peiperl and Brittany Jones (2001), workaholics are "those who work too much but feel that the rewards arising from their work are at least equitably distributed between themselves and the organizations that employ them (if not slightly more favorable to them)" and overworkers are "people who work too much (in their own terms) just as workaholics do but at the same time feel that the returns of their work are inequitably distributed in favor of the organization" (p. 374). Peiperl and Jones (2001) concluded, "Workaholics, then, have a clear reason to continue their extreme work behavior; overworkers, by contrast, may be trapped in a pattern of working that is neither sensible nor equitable" (p. 374). We administrators might lean into the workaholism category or lean into the overwork category, depending on the task or situation.

Based on the scholarship, it seems whether an administrator is a workaholic or overworker depends on context and personal feelings of choice: does the administrator want to work to the extreme? Or do they feel trapped in a system where they feel they must work to the extreme or the _____ (insert program, students, initiatives, etc.) will collapse? Sometimes administrators believe they must be workaholics or overworkers; sometimes they choose to be workaholics or overworkers; sometimes their tenure and promotion requirements require them to be workaholics or overworkers. Regardless, the consequences are the same. Workaholism and overwork results in loss of morale, increased mental and physical health issues, and non-existent collegiality (Berg & Seeber, 2016; van Dernoot Lipsky & Burk, 2009). The rhetoric and composition administration scholarship, social media posts, and listserv conversations bear the human consequences to be true: many administrators are burned out, disenchanted, resentful, and mistrustful.

Whether administrators choose or feel obligated to work excessively, workaholism and overwork often leads to compulsory citizenship behavior (CCB). CCB is also called the good soldier syndrome, where employees place the needs of the organization above their own needs for the "good" of the organization (Hayat et al., 2019; Soran et al., 2017; Vigoda-Gadot, 2006). For example, if an administrator is burned out but feels they must attend all meetings they are invited to for the good of students, faculty, their program, the department, etc., this is a sign of the good soldier syndrome. Or, if an administrator feels they must single-handedly continue an initiative without compensation for the good of the students, faculty, program, etc., this is a sign of the good soldier syndrome. According to Eran Vigoda-Gadot (2006), CCB "may be viewed as another means by which those with authority and power take advantage of other, less powerful individuals who simply cannot resist or say 'no'"; it is "anything but spontaneous behavior" (pp. 83, 85). Similarly, Fang Liu et al. (2019) defined CCB as "personal participation in extra-role activities that always go against one's will" (pp. 1–2). Most frequently, CCB occurs when employees are expected to complete tasks or adopt roles not defined in their job descriptions and when employees do not receive formal rewards for the additional work they do (Vigoda-Gadot, 2006, p. 85). For example, if the provost asks the administrator to develop a new course or participate in a new outreach program, the administrator may experience CCB if they feel they must participate and cannot say no due to being already over-extended or if the request is outside of their job description. And they may feel they must say yes to maintain the goodwill of the provost.

A result of workaholism, overwork, and CCB is professional and personal "fragmentation" (not to be confused with psychology's fragmentation of personality) which results in fractured professional and personal identities. According to Vázquez and Levin (2018), fragmentation "denies the roles that personal histories or professional goals play in how faculty members experience their work and their academic identities" (paras. 3, 6). For example, administrators may experience fragmentation when they are unable to enact goals or initiatives they are socially, politically, professionally, or ideologically committed to, such as having a budget for ongoing professional development, offering long-term contractual work to non-tenure-track-faculty, or adopting anti-racist assessment practices and curriculum. Fragmentation may materialize through burnout, disillusionment, anger, workaholism, people-pleasing, or codependency—or a myriad of other possibilities depending on administrators' coping mechanisms, trauma, and upbringing (Burke & Cooper, 2008).

It is important to note CCB is different from organizational citizenship behavior (OCB), as OCB is personally driven. With OCB, employees commit to extra-role activities that "serv[e] their private interest, including impressing the management" (Liu et al., 2019, p. 2). However, even if administrators choose to go above and beyond to serve their private interest, they are setting a norm for working beyond their job descriptions and signaling to those around them—graduate students, colleagues, the chair, the dean, etc.—they are willing to do more with the same compensation. This doesn't mean administrators shouldn't do extra work that serves their personal and professional interests. It simply means they should be aware of how their OCB may affect the program or department: it may cause others in the program or department to feel like they have to commit to extra roles or activities, or it may cause others in the department or college to expect the administrator to continue to take on extra activities and roles without compensation.

So why does overwork, workaholism, fragmentation, OCB, and CCB happen in academia? It may be because many academics all have a high level of public service motivation driving them to serve. According to Tse-Min Wang et al. (2020), there are "four types of motives" in public service motivation: "Compassion, Attraction to Public Service, Commitment to Public Values, and Self-Sacrifice" (p. 2). Organizations with high public service motivation, such as non-profits, government, and higher education, draw employees interested in interweaving their personal identities with the public's greater good (Ingrams, 2020). Tse-Min Wang et al. (2020) explained, "Individuals with high [public service motivation] can be seen as 'moral exemplars' who pursue their moral goals to achieve a life characterized by deep integration of self and public morality" (p. 3). I would argue many in rhetoric and composition choose to become program administrators because of a high public service motivation: to change students' lives for the better, to support students' rights to their own language, and to improve non-tenure-track faculty's working conditions, among other reasons. An administrator who has a high sense of public service motivation also has a high sense of moral obligation for the work they do—which may exacerbate CCB, fragmentation, overwork, and/or workaholism.

Perhaps most painful about working within the neoliberal university supersystem is little scholarship that neoliberalism makes our programs, departments, colleges, and universities better. Jodie-Lee Trembath (2018), anthropologist and expert on modern university life, wrote on her academic blog, "[T]here has been no evidence, statistical or otherwise, that increasing 'quality control measures' in universities has actually improved quality in universities by any objective criteria" (para. 16). Rather, research overwhelmingly suggests the human cost outweighs any financial benefit.

It is possible, at this point in the chapter, you are feeling frustrated, disenchanted, and, maybe, hopeless. Or, possibly, the light bulb has turned on and you are able to make connections between your work experiences, your university system, and your own values and expectations. Or maybe these thoughts are running through your mind:

- But I cannot say no.
- There is nothing that can be done.

- If I don't do it, no one will.
- The provost says I must.
- I don't want to make waves.
- I don't want to make people mad at me.
- I just need to keep my head down.
- I don't want to lose my job.

If you are thinking one or more of these statements, you are not alone. They are a natural reaction for administrators working within the neoliberal university supersystem—a supersystem that prizes self-denial, emotional exploitation, workaholism, people-pleasing, and codependency. However, resistance is not futile, even if it feels like it. And it's important to be aware of what we tell ourselves about our agency because if we hear "I can't" enough, our brains will believe it as true. As Lucien Darjeun Meadows wrote in his chapter in this collection,

> [C]ommunication is an emergent social system, every dialogue between writer and consultant is a network of utterances, such as verbal and nonverbal communicative acts, generated via what Schirmer and Michailakis (2019) called "selections"—that is, conscious and unconscious choices between communicative possibilities.

While Meadows' chapter focuses on communication between writer and writing center consultant, his analysis rings true for the communication selections of within ourselves and to ourselves. What we believe and say to ourselves becomes a brain pathway, like an over-skied slope, that becomes hard to undo. Mindfulness and self-reflection about what we say and believe about ourselves acts like fresh snow renewing the mountain.

In this next section, I introduce readers to a new way of thinking about work: a boundary- and mindfulness-based mindset I call "mindful work mindset" (MWM). MWM is based on scholarship on mindfulness theory, psychology, psychotherapy, and neuroscience. For MWM to occur, administrators must better understand their inner selves first. One of the challenges of working within a systems-based, fast-paced modern life is administrators are often so focused outward—on helping others—they forget to focus inward. As Jenna Morton-Aiken, in this collection, wrote, "WPAs are in the business of connecting people and resources, elevating voices, and putting people in touch with the right systems." And this is all true. However, we cannot continue "doing good stuff" without connecting with our own selves first. In our efforts to do good work, we cannot—we must not—places ourselves last.

WHAT CAN I DO ABOUT IT?: A MINDFUL WORK MINDSET TO RESET THINKING AND BEING

Not surprisingly, the neoliberal university supersystem conflicts with administrators' reasons for entering the profession in the first place. Quite simply: we (generally) love the work. For many of us, our administrative work "is the expression of our soul, our inner being" and "puts us in touch with others, not so much at the level of personal interaction, but at the level of service in the community" (Fox, 1995, p. 5; see also Gini, 1998). Writing Program Administrators (WPAs) such as Courtney Adams Wooten and colleagues (2020), Megan McIntyre (2019), Bruce Horner (2007), and Susan H. McLeod (2007) and others have written about the love many WPAs have for the work they do while also feeling burned out, frustrated, disillusioned, disappointed, and angry at many facets of that work. So how do we do the work we love and feel called to do within a broken system?

I believe one of the best ways to resist assimilation by the neoliberalism university system is to change our mindset about what we "can" and "cannot" do. Neoliberalism thrives as a supersystem because it takes away (or tries to take away) the agency of the employees. Additionally, neoliberalism thrives in academia because academia is a rewards-based system where the rewards are often couched in what Allison Laubach Wright (2017) called "the language of excellence" (p. 272). The neoliberal university supersystem uses rewards and the language of excellence to continue demanding, consuming, and growing. As long as the people in the supersystem acquiesce, the supersystem will continue. However, as much as it may not feel like it, we do have agency, and we do not have to resign ourselves to the expectations and demands of the neoliberal university model. We may not be able to convince upper administrators to abandon neoliberalism, but we can focus our attention on our own agency, and we can encourage our colleagues and graduate students to claim their own agency. But first, we need to be aware of our emotions and what our bodies are telling us about our work mindset.

For this next section, I include three steps towards a mindful work mindset, which I have developed with therapists and practitioners to help me practice self-care in the workplace. As a result, grappling with (and oftentimes resisting) a mindful work mindset helped me better understand my personal and professional needs and relationships as an administrator working within the neoliberal university supersystem. Each step below, which can be done in any order but is purposefully organized from big picture to small picture reflection, includes exercises you might want to try.

STEP 1. ADOPT MINDFULNESS TO BETTER UNDERSTAND HOW YOU RESPOND TO YOUR WORK STRESSORS

Recent scholarship shows academics around the world are in perpetual states of chronic stress (Brown & Leigh, 2018; Coetzee et al., 2019; Gill & Donaghue, 2016; Smith & Ulus, 2019). Part of this stress is working within the neoliberal supersystem. Other parts of the stress are rooted in a myriad of places, including public service motivation, internal pressures, fear of failure, and scarcity mindset.

As a result, the body goes into fight or flight mode to manage the stress. Because the brain does not know the difference between an actual threat (such as being chased by a bear) and a perceived threat (emotional stress), the body will respond to work-related emotional stress the same way it responds to you being chased by a bear: your hypothalamus sets off the alarm which causes the adrenal glands to release hormones, including adrenaline and cortisol (American Psychological Association, 2023; Mayo Clinic, 2019). Many academics reap the "benefits" of adrenaline and cortisol because it allows the body to push through exhaustion and long hours. However, when the body believes it is constantly under attack, for example, being in hours and days of stress due to course scheduling problems or working under a tight deadline, the body relies on adrenaline which causes the body to become chronically stressed and depleted of adrenal hormones (Kearns, 2020; van Praag et al., 2004). And while the chronic stress may result in tangible benefits—more publications, more initiatives, better professional development, etc.,—the results of chronic stress include anxiety, depression, digestive problems, headaches, sleep problems, and concentration and memory problems, among others (Gottlieb, 1997; Wilson, 2014).

Before we administrators can resist the neoliberal supersystem in meaningful ways, we need to heal a little bit (or a lot) from our chronic stress and reduce our body's adrenaline response. One way to do this is through mindfulness. Mindfulness, defined by Jon Kabat-Zinn (2003), is "the awareness that emerges through paying attention on purpose, in the present moment, and non-judgmentally to the unfolding of experience moment by moment" (p. 145). Research showed that mindfulness improves "emotional regulation," supports "decreased reactivity and increased response flexibility," and "promotes empathy" (Davis & Hayes, 2011, p. 199–202).

To get you started, here are some mindfulness-based reflection questions you might free write about (now or later) to help you process your chronic stress and adrenaline responses:

- What work situations cause me to feel anxiety or an adrenaline rush? Do I know why they do cause those reactions, or do I need to spend more time understanding my body's reaction?
- Where do I find work-related tension or anxiety in my body? In my solar plexus? In my neck? In my stomach? In my throat? Do certain work situations cause me to feel tension, anxiety, nausea, acid reflux, or some other discomfort or pain?
- Do I feel like my throat is closing up, or do I feel a ball of tension in my throat before, during, or after work tasks and situations?
- Do I feel like I can't take a work break on-campus to attend to my needs: going to the bathroom in a relaxed state, leisurely eating my meals, stretching or walking, etc.?
- Are there days I dread going to campus, addressing certain tasks, meeting with certain people, etc.?
- Are there times I cannot fall asleep because I do not want to go to work the following day?

Take note of your body's reaction to these questions and your mental, emotional, and physical responses. If you find yourself resistant to some or all these questions, you might want to ask yourself where the resistance is coming from. With such a heavy topic as this one, give yourself time to process and feel. It is okay to stop reading here if you need a break or if you feel emotions bubbling up to the surface.

To better understand the roots of my chronic stress and adrenaline responses, I had to slow down and listen to my body. I did not know how to do that, so I worked with therapists, medical doctors, acupuncturists, and other practitioners to learn how to listen to what my body was telling me. I learned my body was always in a heightened state of anxiety, particularly when it came to my academic work. The adrenaline rush was always there. But I needed to train my body to relax and to let it know I wasn't being "chased by a bear" all day, every day.

I want to share with you three exercises I developed with the help of therapists and practitioners to increase my mindful awareness around my body's chronic stress and automatic adrenaline responses. You will get the most out of these exercises if you practice them at least for a week—but even after one or two days you will see a benefit. While I list the practices below that have significantly helped me, I encourage you to develop your own MWM that help you reflect upon your body's automatic stress responses. The end goal of your MWM should be to help bring awareness to your body and thoughts, so you can make the best choices to support balance and self-care in your administrative work.

Exercise #1: Breathwork to Lower Your Stress Response and to Learn to Listen to What Your Body is Telling You

If you are experiencing a stressful day or if you are stressed out about your next task, such as responding to email, set your timer for three to five minutes, close your eyes, and breathe in through your nose and out through your mouth. Allow your body to relax and focus your thoughts on your breath. When you are feeling an adrenaline response, your body will get the most out of breathwork. If your brain is sending you messages that you cannot slow down and take a break, be aware that this messaging is your brain trying to protect you from the "bear" (e.g., emails, student complaints, the upcoming meeting, course preparation, etc.). Messages such as "If I stop now, I won't get it done" or "I don't have time to take a break" are your brain's protection response; they are not true. You *will* get it done. (More to come on the brain's resistance in the next section.)

After your breathwork, take one to five minutes and write down what thoughts, emotions, and feelings you experienced. Do you feel tired? Do you feel pain in your left shoulder? Are you hungry? Do not judge your thoughts, emotions, and feelings. Notice them and use your notes later to make decisions about how you can address what your body, brain, and heart are telling you about your workday and your emotions around your work tasks.

Exercise #2: Noticing and Retraining the Brain's Automatic Stress Response

If you are feeling stress around a particular task—for me, it's opening my email in the morning—do not open your email when you are in a heightened response state. We often experience adrenaline or anxiety responses around a particular work task because the brain is in fight or flight mode, and it is releasing enough adrenaline and cortisol to complete the task. Even if you believe, rationally, you should not be in a stress response, the body will act based on habit. The brain needs to be taught it can "stand down." To retrain your brain's response, either complete exercise #1, go for a short walk, watch a video clip that will make you laugh or smile, or do another task until the stress resides. You might find it helpful to have a conversation with your brain to remind it that you have "got this" and that it does not need to go into an automatic stress response. Before checking email, I often have a conversation with my brain such as "I know you are trying to protect me by creating a stress response. But I will be fine, and I have the tools to take care of the emails I might receive. Thanks for protecting me, but I have got this."

Keep a Post-It note by your desk or open your smart phone's note app and record what tasks or situations create a stress response in your body. Notice what stress responses feel automatic: that is, the reaction does not feel warranted, but your body is producing that response regardless. When you have a moment of calm, perhaps over the summer when you have more mental and emotional processing time, look at the list and decide what task(s) you want to retrain your body's response. Do not feel compelled or guilted into fixing the responses all at once; do not judge yourself for your list; do not allow negative self-talk such as "I should not be stressed out by this" or "I must be the only one with this problem" (you are not!). You are retraining your brain's habits, which takes time and practice.

Exercise #3: Carry a Notebook and Write Down Everything You Want to Say—Good, Bad, and Ugly

If you find yourself in meetings that leave you feeling frustrated, silenced, angry, hopeless, and/or bored, take notes in your notebook or on your laptop about what is said and what you would like to say back, unfiltered. Be honest in your notes about what you believe is right, what you disagree with, and what you wish you could say. After the meeting and when you have mental and emotional processing time, look back over your notes. Note trends you see, such as particular people you frequently disagree with or what you would really like to say but do not. To find a way forward for future meetings, reflect on the following questions and develop an action plan:

- Is it true I cannot say what I want to say? Or is the brain trying to keep me safe with its stress response?
- Am I keeping quiet because of perceived repercussions that may not actually happen, or am I keeping quiet because I know there will be actual repercussions?
- How might I revise my unfiltered notes into keywords or phrases that I can say in future meetings?
- Are there others in the program or department I can speak with honestly, so they can help me formulate my ideas or thoughts in ways that will be heard?
- Is there a legitimate reason why I cannot say what I want or need to say? Will I lose my position, will it affect my annual review, will I lose necessary cultural capital, etc.?

Exercises #1–#3 are data collection: the information you have gathered by completing one or more exercises tells you quite a bit about your work mindset and your body's reaction. Once you have data, you can make a plan about how to identify and set boundaries to redefine what you want from work and what your colleagues and administrators can expect from work. If you have the means, I highly recommend working with a therapist who is versed in systems and organizations to help you further change your mindset and set boundaries.

Step 2. Identify and Set Boundaries to (Re)Define What You Want from Work—and What Work can Expect from You

Just as teachers might reestablish classroom norms throughout the term if student-teacher boundaries get too porous, administrators may need to reestablish (or define for the first time) boundaries around their time and job descriptions. Academic social workers Janice M. Rasheed et al. (2010) defined boundaries as "the arrangement both between subsystems and within systems outside of the family.... The function of boundaries is to protect the integrity (differentiation) of the subsystem" as "every subsystem has different functions and makes specific demands on its members to prevent interference from other subsystems" (p. 218). Boundaries teach people how to treat our emotional, physical, and mental spaces. As children, we learn about boundaries from how we are raised and treated; we carry those boundaries into our teenage years and adulthood. Many of our workplace boundaries (or lack of boundaries) can be traced back to how we were raised and the boundaries that were modeled to us by the family members who raised us or had authority over us (Burn, 2016; Katherine, 1991; van der Kolk, 2014). When boundaries are crossed, even accidentally, we might feel like we have been taken advantage of, abused, neglected, and/or disrespected (Burn, 2016, p. 13).

For example, I repeatedly had an anxiety response whenever there was disagreement between faculty in a regular meeting I attended. If I anticipated disagreement before the meeting started, anxiety appeared before the meeting began. In all cases, my anxiety disappeared as soon as I walked out of the meeting room. I suffered for two years not understanding why I had such a targeted anxiety response. It was not until after reflecting on my family role—I am the eldest and was raised to be the peacekeeper and problem-solver—that I instantly understood my body's reaction: my body was sending me signals to solve and fix the workplace conflict like I had been trained to do in my family. Realizing how my family role carried over into my professional life allowed me to acknowledge the root of my body's anxiety response. Then I was able to develop strategies with my therapist for how to set emotional and mental boundaries, such as reminding myself that I do not need to problem-solve other faculty's conflicts. Mentally and emotionally setting boundaries before heading into meetings have helped lessen my body's anxiety response.

Setting boundaries may be challenging, especially if we have to retrain our body's automatic physiological response in addition to changing our ways of engaging, thinking, and responding (Kreiner, 2007; van der Kolk, 2014). Moreover, administrators may find it exceedingly difficult to set boundaries if having no boundaries creates cultural capital, gives us a seat at an important table, or gets us more program funding. However, if we do not set boundaries, no one will set them for us. We can only be responsible for ourselves—and our professional and personal satisfaction depends on how we choose to live in the world (Trefalt, 2013).

Drawing from the professional practice of Shawn Burn (2016), Anne Katherine (1991), Caroline Knowles (1997) and others, here is a partial list of workplace boundaries you might consider setting to support your MWM:

- Create a memorandum of understanding (MOU) with your department chair and/or dean that refines your job description during the academic year and/or the summer.
- Become less available for last-minute requests or tasks that cannot be completed quickly. Set boundaries with phrases such as "Other work obligations prevent me from completing this today" or "I will need X days to complete your request."
- If you have multiple long meetings in a day and do not have time for self-care, arrive late to a few of your meetings. Do not sacrifice eating, stretching, down time, etc., for meetings.
- Resist the urge to become the program or department's problem-solver unless it directly corresponds with your professional role. Refer students and faculty to the correct person who can address or solve their problem. Phrases such as "I only have five minutes to talk," "That sounds horrible, but I am not the right person to resolve it," or "I don't have time to talk right now; send me an email, so I can get you on my calendar," are ways to set boundaries on your time and emotions.
- Close your office door and tape a printed message to your door with the message "I am under a tight timeline and cannot be interrupted except for emergencies." Liberally use this boundary to protect your mental health.
- Block out enough "busy" time in your university calendar for rest time, mealtimes, breaks, writing time, etc. Resist feeling compelled or guilted into multiple meetings in a day that negatively affect your mental and physical health.
- Disable all email notifications on your laptop and smart phone to prevent distractions and anxiety responses.
- Set email away messages after hours, on the weekends, or during busy weeks explaining senders can expect a response within 48–72 hours.
- Avoid checking email on the weekends or after hours regardless of department norms.

- Practice not apologizing unless the situation warrants it. (If we were raised with the idea that setting boundaries is "being mean," you might find yourself inclined to apologize a lot. It takes some practice to realize setting boundaries is not "mean.")

Setting boundaries takes time. You will need to decide which boundaries you want to set, the amount of effort/time it will take to set them, any potential challenges, and your existing emotional and mental bandwidth. I recommend setting one or two boundaries a semester. Start with easier boundaries and work your way up to boundaries that feel more complicated and challenging. You might even consider talking with a therapist or psychologist familiar with organizational systems who will help you set boundaries and help you respond to colleagues who break your boundaries.

Step 3. Be Prepared for Your Brain to Resist—and that's Okay

Do not be alarmed if your brain and body resist your MWM. Resistance may feel like anxiety responses, feelings of fear, or brain messaging such as "You can't say no!" or "Don't set that boundary—everyone will be mad at you!" These examples of resistance may happen for different and overlapping reasons: people-pleasing tendencies, a lack of practice with boundaries, and the brain's wiring, among other reasons.

The reward system of academia further entrenches the brain's wiring to be resistant to boundaries. A reward system, Kerry Ann O'Meara (2011) explained, is "a set of interconnected and interacting elements that work together (and against each other at times) to regard, ignore, or disregard faculty and their contributions" (p. 162). In a reward system like academia, faculty and staff are "'disciplined' or socialized towards a certain set of behaviors" (O'Meara, 2011, p. 161). Reward systems are effective at shaping behavior because the brain is designed to seek out pleasure rewards and avoid negative experiences. When the brain receives a reward, which could be a thank you note, a salary raise, or a smile, it releases dopamine, known as the "feel good hormone," which reinforces behavior in alignment with the reward system (Psychology Today, 2021, para. 1). Neuroscientist Marc Dingman (2019) explained the brain's reward system is not simply focused on dopamine release; the reward system "also concerns learning and the development of motivation to try to achieve the experience again" (p. 157). For example, if a writing center administrator receives a dopamine release through workplace problem-solving and people-pleasing, the brain will be more inclined to problem-solve and people-please even if those actions are at odds with the administrator's boundaries. However, if the writing center administrator decides they want to set boundaries and stop people-pleasing at work, the brain will resist because this is not what it expected—and because no dopamine release comes with set boundaries. But this is key (and underline it one hundred times if you must): just because the brain resists doesn't mean the writing center administrator should stop setting boundaries. If our brains tell us we're "mean," "not good colleagues," and/or "letting people down" when we set boundaries, it doesn't mean it is true.

The brain will also resist MWM due to evolutionary biology. The brain is designed to keep us alive and safe and, as a result, prefers consistency and repetition, so it can be prepared for what might happen throughout the day (Jensen & McConchie, 2020). The brain does not like mental and emotional change because it fears change will put us in physical danger. Therefore, once we have established consistent actions over many months and years, such as staying late at work or answering emails after hours, the brain becomes accustomed to these actions. If we change those actions, the brain will send a "Stop! Don't do that!" signal, such as an anxiety response or negative thought, to convince us to continue doing what we have always done (Stanley, 2019). The brain will use personal experiences, fears, and the ego, among other persuasive strategies, to keep you from changing your behavior. This brain response is evolutionary designed to keep us alive (Stanley, 2019; Wickremasinghe, 2018). But we don't need to be afraid of our brain's alarm system. Just because the alarm has been set off doesn't mean we are doing anything wrong. In the moment, it is important to deeply breathe and tell the brain "Everything is okay. Thank you for protecting me. I am taking over control now. I've got this." Speaking to the brain reminds us that the evolutionary biological responses are not in charge—we are.

CONCLUSION

As many conference presentations, hallway conversations, and Facebook feeds attest, administrators often feel "resistance is futile" against the neoliberal university supersystem and their home institution system. Sometimes administrators' feelings of futility are conscious and other times they are unconscious. And sometimes they can find ways to resist the neoliberal university supersystem by developing their own personal and relational networks, boundaries, and self-care. And other times administrators let the system sweep them up, and they ignore their mental and physical health "for the good of the _____" (insert students, equitable working conditions, program needs, collegiality, etc., here).

For all the readers who are learning to reclaim their bodies and boundaries: good for you. You are a model for the rest of us. Please share your tips and strategies at conference panels, in scholarship, and on social media. For the readers who are not sure how to reclaim their selfhood or are afraid to set boundaries: I know it is hard to resist the system, but I believe in you. Talk to your fellow administrators about how you might develop a personal network of support and adopt a mindful work mindset to reclaim yourselves from the collective supersystem. In order to keep doing the good work you want to do, it is important for you to set healthy work expectations in your program and department and to develop clarity around how you show up for your personal and professional self. This administrative work is demanding, and you deserve to take care of yourself first. As the saying goes, "You cannot pour from an empty cup." And this is true for us administrators: to do the meaningful administrative work we want to do—the new curriculum we want to design; the new Celebrations of Student Writing we want to initiate; the new anti-racist program assessment we want to facilitate—we have to turn inward, first, and take care of ourselves. Then the rest can (and will!) follow.

REFERENCES

American Psychological Association. (2023, November). Stress effects on the body. *American Psychological Association.* https://www.apa.org/topics/stress/body

Berg, M. & Seeber, B. K. (2016). *The slow professor.* University of Toronto Press.

Brown, N. & Leigh, J. (2018). Ableism in academia: Where are the disabled and ill academics? *Disability & Society, 33*(6), 985–989.

Burke, R. J. & Cooper, C. L. (2008). *Long work hours culture: Causes, consequences and choices.* Emerald Publishing.

Burn, S. M. (2016). *Unhealthy helping: A psychological guide to overcoming codependence, enabling, and other dysfunctional giving.* CreateSpace Independent Publishing Platform.

Coetzee, N., Maree, D. J. F. & Smit, B. N. (2019). The relationship between chronic fatigue syndrome, burnout, job satisfaction, social support and age among academics at a tertiary institution. *International Journal of Occupational Medicine and Environmental Health, 32*(1), 75–85.

Davis, D. M. & Hayes, J. A. (2011). What are the benefits of mindfulness? A practice review of psychotherapy-related research. *Psychotherapy, 48*(2), 198–208.

Dingman, M. (2019). *Your brain explained: What neuroscience reveals about your brain and its quirks.* Nicholas Brealey Publishing.

Enos, T. & Borrowman, S. (Eds.). (2008). *The promise and perils of writing program administration.* Parlor Press.

Fox, M. (1995). *The reinvention of work: New vision of livelihood for our time.* HarperOne.

George, D. (1999). *Kitchen cooks, plate twirlers, and troubadours: Writing program administrators tell their stories.* Heinemann.

Gill, R. & Donaghue, N. (2016). Resilience, apps and reluctant individualism: Technologies of self in the neoliberal academy. *Women Studies International Forum, 54*, 91–99.

Gini, A. (1998). Work, identity and self: How we are formed by the work we do. *Journal of Business Ethics, 17*, 707–714.

Gottlieb, B. H. (Ed.). (1997). *Coping with chronic stress.* Springer.

Hayat, Z., Batool, I., Hayat, S. & Amin, U. (2019). Emotional instability, employee work outcomes among academia: Compulsory citizenship behavior and leadership style as moderators. *Review of Economics and Development Studies, 5*(3), 551–562.

Horner, B. (2007). Redefining work and value for writing program administration. *JAC, 27*(1/2), 163–184.

Ingrams, A. (2020). Organizational citizenship behavior in the public and private sectors: A multilevel test of public service motivation and traditional antecedents. *Review of Public Personnel Administration, 40*(2), 222–244.

Jensen, E. & McConchie, L. (2020). *Brain-based learning: Teaching the way students really learn.* Corwin.

Kabat-Zinn, J. (2003). Mindfulness-based interventions in context: Past, present, and future. *Clinical Psychology: Science and Practice, 10*, 144–156.

Katherine, A. (1991). *Boundaries: Where you end and I begin.* Hazelden publishing.

Kearns, A. (2020, April 16). Is there such a thing as adrenal fatigue? Adrenal fatigue: What causes it? *Mayo Clinic.* https://www.mayoclinic.org/diseases-conditions/addisons-disease/expert-answers/adrenal-fatigue/faq-20057906.

Knowles, C. (1997). *Family boundaries: The invention of normality and dangerousness.* University of Toronto Press.

Kreiner, G. E. (2007). The struggle of the self: Identity dysfunctions in the contemporary workplace. In J. Langan-Fox, C. L. Cooper, R. J. Klimoski & E. Elgar (Eds.), *Research companion to the dysfunctional workplace: Management challenges and symptoms* (pp. 75–89). Edward Elgar Publishing.

Liu, F., Chow, I. H. & Huang, M. (2019). Increasing compulsory citizenship behavior and workload: Does impression management matter? *Frontiers in Psychology, 10*, 1–10.

Mayo Clinic. (2019, March 19). Chronic stress puts your health at risk. Healthy lifestyle: Stress management. *Mayo Clinic.* https://www.mayoclinic.org/healthy-lifestyle/stress-management/in-depth/stress/art-20046037.

McGee, S. J. & Handa, C. (2005). *Discord and direction: The postmodern writing program administrator.* University Press of Colorado; Utah State University Press. https://doi.org/10.2307/j.ctt4cgqc0.

McIntyre, M. (2019). Snapshots of #WPALife: Invisible labor and writing program administration. *Academic Labor: Research and Artistry, 3*(1), 64–86.

McLeod, S. H. (2007). *Writing program administration.* Parlor Press; The WAC Clearinghouse. https://wac.colostate.edu/docs/books/mcleod_wpa/wpa.pdf.

Oates, W. (1971). *Confessions of a workaholic: The facts about work addiction.* World Publisher.

O'Meara, K. A. (2011). Inside the panopticon: Studying academic reward systems. In J. C. Smart & M. B. Paulsen (Eds.), *Higher education: Handbook of theory and research, volume 26* (pp. 161–220). Springer. https://doi.org/10.1007/978-94-007-0702-3.

Peiperl, M. & Jones, B. (2001). Workaholics and overworkers: Productivity or pathology? *Group & Organizational Management, 26*(3), 369–393.

Psychology Today. (2021). Dopamine. *Psychology Today.* https://www.psychologytoday.com/us/basics/dopamine.

Rasheed, J. M., Rasheed, M. N. & Marley, J. A. (2010). *Family therapy: Models and techniques.* Sage Publication.

Schaufeli, W. B., Shimazu, A. & Taris, T. W. (2009). Being driven to work excessively hard: The evaluation of a two-factor measure of workaholism in the Netherlands and Japan. *Cross-Cultural Research, 43*(4), 320–348.

Schirmer, W. & Michailakis, D. (2019). *Systems theory for social work and the helping professions.* Routledge.

Scott, T. (2009). *Dangerous writing: Understanding the political economy of composition.* Utah State University Press.

Shore, C. & Wright, S. (2015). Audit culture revisited: Rankings, ratings, and the reassembling of society. *Current Anthropology, 56*(3), 421–444.

Smith, C. & Ulus, E. (2019). Who cares for academics? We need to talk about emotional well-being including what we avoid and intellectualize through macro-discourses. *Organization, 27*(6), 840–857. https://doi.org/10.1177/1350508419867201.

Soran, S., Sesen, H. & Caymaz, E. (2017). The relationship between compulsory citizenship behavior and leadership: A research by accommodation businesses. *Research Journal of Business and Management, 4*(3), 303–309.

Stanley, E. A. (2019). *Widen the window: Training your brain and body to thrive during stress and recover from trauma.* Avery.

Trefalt, Š. (2013). Between you and me: Setting work-nonwork boundaries in the context of workplace relationships. *Academy of Management Journal, 56*(6), 1802–1829.

Trembath, J. (2018, June 14). The neoliberal university is making us sick: Who's to blame? *The Familiar Strange.* https://thefamiliarstrange.com/2018/06/14/neoliberal-universities-whos-to-blame/.

van der Kolk, B. A. (2014). *The body keeps score: Brain, mind, and body in the healing of trauma.* Penguin Publishing Group.

van Dernoot Lipsky, L., with Burk, C. (2009). *Trauma stewardship: An everyday guide to caring for self while caring for others.* Berrett-Koehler Publishers.

van Praag, H. M., de Kloet, R. & van Os, J. (2004). *Stress, the brain and depression.* Cambridge University Press.

Vázquez, E. M. & Levin, J. S. (2018, January–February). The tyranny of neoliberalism in the American academic profession. *AAUP: American Association of University Professors.* https://www.aaup.org/article/tyranny-neoliberalism-american-academic-profession#.X6mqrS9h3BI.

Vigoda-Gadot, E. (2006). Compulsory citizenship behavior: Theorizing some dark sides of the good soldier syndrome in organizations. *Journal for the Theory of Social Behavior, 36*(1), 77–93.

Wang, T.-M., van Witteloostuijn, A. & Heine, F. (2020). A moral theory of public service motivation. *Hypothesis and Theory, 11*, 1–15.

Wickremasinghe, N. (2018). *Beyond threat*. Triarchy Press.

Wilson, J. L. (2014). Clinical perspective on stress, cortisol and adrenal fatigue. *Advances in Integrative Medicine 1*(2), 93–96.

Wooten, C. A., Babb, J., Costello, K. M. & Navickas, K. (Eds.). (2020). *The things we carry: Strategies for recognizing and negotiating emotional labor in writing program administration*. University Press of Colorado; Utah State University Press.

Wright, A. L. (2017). The rhetoric of excellence and the erasure of graduate labor. In S. Kahn, W. B. Lalicker & A. Lynch-Biniek (Eds.), *Contingency, exploitation, and solidarity: Labor and action in English composition* (pp. 271–278). The WAC Clearinghouse; University Press of Colorado. https://doi.org/10.37514/PER-B.2017.0858.2.17.

CHAPTER 13.

"IT'S COMPLICATED": SCHEDULING AS AN INTELLECTUAL, NETWORKED SOCIAL JUSTICE ISSUE FOR WPAS

Julia Voss and Kathryn Bruchmann
Santa Clara University

Scheduling isn't a task most rhetoric and composition program administrators (hereafter WPAs) enjoy (Crowley, 2002; Holmstein, 2002). The Portland Resolution (Hult et al., 1992) buries scheduling toward the bottom of its list of WPA responsibilities, signaling its low status by grouping it with mundane bureaucratic work. Scheduling is the ultimate managerial task, connecting WPAs to local institutional networks populated with upper administrators, instructors, and students, linked together by policies and resources. The responsibilities and priorities of these stakeholders and the values built into the policies that guide their work—shaped by the financial, labor, and space resources available in the local institutional ecology—determine the conditions for writing instruction, helping dictate the extent to which writing programs can provide the just and effective teaching and learning conditions that define disciplinary best practices.

Despite the role scheduling plays in constituting institutional networks and enacting disciplinary knowledge about writing instruction, the process of course scheduling has not been systematically examined in the WPA literature (Voss, 2020). To begin filling this gap, this study reports on survey data on course scheduling from 120 North American colleges and universities, providing preliminary findings about the impacts of different network configurations on the course scheduling process and the types of classrooms in which writing courses are taught. We also consider how institutional and student body characteristics affect these outcomes. Our findings begin to outline current practices, suggesting avenues for intervention at the local, disciplinary, and professional levels.

DOI: https://doi.org/10.37514/PER-B.2023.1848.2.13

REAPPRAISING COURSE AND CLASSROOM SCHEDULING FROM A NETWORK PERSPECTIVE

Course Scheduling

Our field's lack of knowledge about course scheduling raises questions about how these managerial systems affect writing programs' ability to deliver instruction that meets disciplinary standards and ideals. Despite the research on the impact of class size and course load on outcomes (Farrell & Jensen, 2000; Haswell, 2004; Horning, 2007), WPA scholars have not yet researched how decisions about course scheduling and classroom placement are made or how these decisions affect instruction. Although WPAs are responsible for ensuring the working conditions the Wyoming Resolution (Robertson et al., 1987) and Indianapolis Resolution (Cox et al., 2016) articulate, their ability to do so has been hampered by the framing of managerial work as non-bureaucratic (Strickland, 2011). While labor-focused WPA scholarship has addressed managerial concerns like staffing, it has typically done so through case studies of individual programs and accounts from contingent faculty, attending to the qualitative but lacking a quantitative perspective. As a result, writing studies' tendency to dismiss the managerial aspects of WPA by reconceptualizing them theoretically or framing them locally/anecdotally fails to account for its structural, systematic nature and its effects on writing instruction. Scheduling is a task that is institutionally embedded and connected to other stakeholders through local networks, but guided by disciplinary knowledge and local data, making it a complex intellectual task.

Classroom Scheduling

In addition to developing the schedule of courses, scheduling also includes the placement of courses into classrooms, another neglected aspect of WPA work that draws writing programs into other networks of stakeholders. The Conference on College Composition and Communication (CCCC) Position Statement on the Principles for the Postsecondary Teaching of Writing (2015) asserted that reasonable working conditions are an integral part of writing pedagogy: "Instructors also require adequate resources—including (but not limited to) time, reasonable class sizes, and physical surroundings—to provide sound writing instruction" (Adler-Kassner et al., para. 28). Advocacy relating to physical working conditions has focused on faculty offices, computers, and copy machines (LaFrance & Cox, 2017). However, less attention has been paid to the working conditions found in teaching spaces. There has been little published on classrooms more broadly, especially the traditional classrooms in which most writing classes are taught, featuring stationary desks set in rows and a front "stage" area for the teacher containing the room's display technologies. As Bre Garrett and Matthew Dowell argue in their collection chapter on accessible conference design, the design of physical spaces like classrooms is an essential consideration for writing studies and writing programs.

Considering classroom design specifically, Todd Taylor (2006) links the design of the traditional classroom to a teacher-centered, lecture-based pedagogy, where passive students listen to an instructor occupying a position of focus and authority at the front of the room. As Garrett and Dowell remind us in their chapter, this design and respective pedagogies makes numerous able-bodied assumptions about how—and even whether—students will enter and navigate the classroom and how they will create and consume knowledge within it. On the other hand, process-oriented writing instruction, Taylor argued, is "student-focused" and engages students in small group work, group and solo composing, and large group discussion, with the instructor serving as a guide and mentor who works as much with individual students and small groups as with the class as a whole, aligning with "active learning" pedagogies advocated throughout higher education in the twenty-first century.[1] While process-oriented teaching and active learning have often failed to explicitly address accessibility, there are strong parallels between the problematic normative ability assumptions made by teacher-centered instruction and the traditional classrooms designed to facilitate it.

While the small body of work on classrooms in writing studies discusses the benefits of active learning for all students,[2] scholarship of teaching and learning (SoTL) research on active learning in science, technology, engineering, and math (STEM) suggests that these methods are particularly important for students marginalized because of their gender, race, and class, resulting in improved

---

1 Michael Prince (2004) characterizes active learning pedagogy as defined by a) low-stakes activities where students think about what they're learning and take responsibility for clarifying their understanding, b) collaborative/cooperative group work in which students work together on a structured learning task, and c) problem-based approaches that use a problem throughout a learning cycle to provide context and practice as students are introduced to content knowledge. These principles align closely with the process-based writing Taylor (2006) and others describe as best practices in writing pedagogy.

2 Scholarship in computers and composition and writing centers provides the most robust discussion of design and creation of writing labs/studios (see Carpenter, 2016; Charlton, 2014; Kim & Carpenter, 2017; Purdy & DeVoss, 2017). Most of this literature, however, is focused on one-off, specially-designed classrooms, studios, and centers, which are not representative of the classrooms in which most writing courses are taught. According to this study, the percentage of writing courses taught in computer classrooms ranges from 12% (advanced writing courses) to 36% (technical writing courses) and the percentage of writing courses taught in active learning classrooms ranges from 4% (basic, English Language Learning, and technical writing courses) to 18% (rhetoric/writing major courses).

self-concept (Colbeck et al., 2001) and narrowed achievement gaps (Phuong et al., 2017), especially when taught in classrooms designed specifically to facilitate active learning (Brooks, 2012). Merging writing studies' and SoTL's traditions of pedagogical research, unanswered questions emerge for WPAs: to what extent is writing being taught in classrooms designed for active learning that support process-based writing pedagogy? How do different network configurations of scheduling stakeholders and institutional ecologies affect the classrooms in which writing is taught?

NETWORK THINKING ABOUT SCHEDULING

Our field's lack of knowledge about administrative decision-making challenges our ability to translate writing studies' disciplinary knowledge into practice, especially when it comes to anticipating the impact that networks composed of policies and stakeholders will have on writing instruction. Working with institutional stakeholders in charge of enrollment, curriculum, facilities, staffing, budgets, and other infrastructural elements of writing instruction is a central feature of WPA work (Phelps, 1991, 2017; Porter et al., 2000), especially when it comes to delivering on the empowering and social justice goals our field espouses (Miller, 1998).

As Michelle Reiff et al. (2015) explained, to understand how writing programs operate and the constraints that often challenge the implementation of best practices, scholars must study writing programs as embedded in complex institutional ecologies and focus on interactions between writing programs and other institutional stakeholders, to which Bryna Siegal Finer and Jamie White-Farnham's (2017) architecture approach to WPA work adds an emphasis on transfer across institutions. While both collections take individual writing programs as the unit of analysis, our study adopts a similar focus on the networked position of writing programs within universities but shifts to a broad cross-section across institutions. Likewise, our study focuses on the interconnectedness of writing programs within institutions, linking network characteristics to scheduling outcomes that enable WPAs to a) see their own program's infrastructural position from this networked perspective and b) use our findings to argue for change based on institutional characteristics.

We also adapt the whole systems approach to WPA work developed by Michelle Cox et al. (2018) to "understand the system in order to focus on points of interactivity and change" (p. 65), breaking open what Douglas Walls and Leslie Wolcott (2017) describe as the black box constituted by a functioning writing instruction system to reveal the network's constituent actors and the connections between them to focus on network stakeholders, connections, and rules (Lin,

1999). While Cox et al. focus on understanding networks inside institutions as a diagnostic activity to support the foundation of new writing programs/initiatives, our focus on scheduling applies network analysis to processes already underway, focusing on finding relationships between different configurations of stakeholders, institutional characteristics, and course/classroom scheduling outcomes.

METHOD

We surveyed North American WPAs (N=132 respondents representing 120 schools[3]) about a) writing course and classroom scheduling procedures and b) the types of classrooms used for different courses, as well as information about their institution and program. Participants were recruited via a) an open invitation on the Writing Program Administrators listserv (WPA-L) and b) direct email invitations to WPAs/English department chairs at a representative sample of North American higher education institutions including two-year, four-year, masters-granting, and doctoral-granting institutions.[4] Participants identified themselves as serving in roles such as director of first-year composition, WAC director, writing coordinator, department chair, and dean. The sizes of the programs participants reported on (as indicated by the number of sections offered per year) varied widely, ranging from ten sections to 1250 sections annually (mean=215 sections).[5] The institutions represented in the sample were also highly varied, based on data gathered from the National Center for Education Statistics. Student body size ranged from 270 to 75,486 (mean=16,625 students). Across all schools, 83.7% of students were traditionally-aged, 55.6% of students across all institutions were female (including two women's colleges), and 60% of students were White (including one historically Black university and 21 other minority-serving institutions). Seventy-two of the universities were doctoral granting institutions, 26 were masters-granting institutions, nine were bachelors-granting institutions, and 13 were associates-granting institutions. Tuition at institutions ranged from $956 annually to over $55,000 annually (mean=$17,232).

First, survey participants described the process through which courses were scheduled at their institution. In the survey, they were asked to identify

---

3   Reconciling the number of respondents vs. number of institutions: five schools had more than one respondent complete the survey (all of these responses were kept in the data set); seven respondents completed less than 10% of the survey (these responses were dropped).

4   Direct invitation mailing list adapted from Wooten et al. (2016).

5   Many participants noted that the courses their program offered were not evenly distributed across the academic year, with many institutions prioritizing having (especially incoming) students complete English Language Learning and/or First-Year Writing courses in the fall term to serve as prerequisites for classes they would enroll in later in the year.

stakeholders and describe the scheduling process. These questions were open-ended because this work was exploratory (see Appendix A). Next, participants explained the process of room scheduling at their institutions. Two independent coders (the coauthors) identified stakeholders present in the course and classroom scheduling responses, beginning with an inductive coding approach (Miles et al., 2013) to look for patterns across responses, which we simplified to seven stakeholders: WPA, Department Chair, Office Administration, Non-Teaching Office, Upper Administration, Software, and Instructors. For a variety of reasons—because WPA was the most common stakeholder title among participants; because of the administrative-centric audience for this collection, and because our research and its implications concern those who direct writing programs, regardless of their title—we use the term WPA throughout, and invite readers to translate our terminology, findings, and recommendations into the structures and policies used at their own institutions.

We returned to the data with these seven stakeholder codes, identifying the stakeholders referenced in each response and the "decision flow" for scheduling: whether the process began inside the department/program, was a collaboration with the department/program and another university office, or began outside of the department/program (either in a non-teaching office or with an upper administrator). Both co-authors coded each response (all disagreements were reconciled via discussion and review of the data). Finally, participants indicated a) how many sections their institutions offered each year of common writing courses (first-year writing, basic writing, writing courses for English language learners, business writing, technical writing, advanced writing, digital writing, rhetoric/writing major courses, and other courses) and b) the classroom types (lecture halls, traditional classrooms, computer classrooms, active learning classrooms, online, or other) used for these courses and how many sections were offered in each type of room.

RESULTS

Note on Analyses

Coded survey data were analyzed by correlating variables with one another. Correlations (r values) and significance (p values) are reported in parentheses. The value of the correlation coefficient r can range from -1 to +1. The higher the absolute value of the coefficient (r value), the stronger the relationship (either positive or negative). Positive r values mean that as one variable increases, so does the other, showing a direct relationship. Negative r values mean that as one variable increases, the other decreases, indicating an inverse relationship.

The size of r coefficients also indicates the magnitude of an association: values of +/-.10 are considered small effects, values of +/-.30 are considered medium effects, and values of +/-.50 or greater are considered large effects. The p values indicate statistical significance. The conventional indicator of statistical significance is a p value less than or equal to .05, which suggests that there is a 5% or less chance that the relationships found are due to chance.

Who are the Stakeholders in Course Scheduling?

Responses typically discussed seven stakeholders typically involved in course scheduling (see Table 13.1 and Figure 13.1): WPA (60.00%), department chair (49.16%), office administrators (e.g., non-teaching staff working in writing program or English department, 21.67%), non-teaching offices (e.g., registrar's office, 30.00%), upper administration (typically the dean's office, 30.83%), software programs (e.g., Banner, Courseleaf, or homemade applications/databases; 9.17%,), and instructors (30.83%). The breakdown of these stakeholders across each university appeared to be fairly idiosyncratic: the only significant relationship was that if office administrators are involved in course scheduling, upper administrators are also more likely to be involved ($r=.20$, $p=.033$).

What is the Course Scheduling Process?

62.20% of respondents reported that the decision flow for course scheduling started in the program/department, 18.40% reported that the process was an equal collaboration between the department and an outside office, and 19.40% reported that the process was started outside of the department, either with a non-teaching office or an upper administrator. The greater the total number of stakeholders in course scheduling, the more likely the decision flow started outside of the department ($r=.35$, $p<.001$).

Who are the Stakeholders in Classroom Scheduling?

The same seven stakeholders emerged for classroom scheduling, although in different proportions (see Table 13.1 and Figure 13.1): WPA (17.5%), department chair (16.67%), office administrators (16.67%), non-teaching offices (50.83%), upper administrator (6.7%), software programs (10%), and instructors (62.5%). We found that the involvement of individual instructors was positively associated with WPA involvement ($r=.18$, $p=.046$) and non-teaching office involvement ($r=.24$, $p=.008$), but negatively associated with office administrator involvement ($r=-.24$, $p=.014$).

Table 13.1. Percent of Respondents with Stakeholders Involved in Course and Room Scheduling

	WPA	Department Chair	Office Admins	Non-Teaching Office	Upper Admin	Software	Instructors
Course Scheduling	60.00%	49.16%	21.67%	30.00%	30.83%	9.17%	30.83%
Room Scheduling	17.50%	16.67%	16.67%	50.83%	6.70%	10%	62.50%

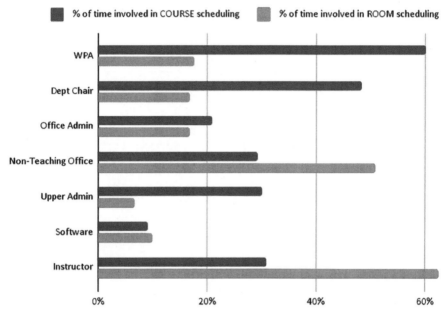

Figure 13.1. Percent of respondents with stakeholders involved in course and room scheduling.

What Types of Classrooms are Used?

Writing courses were taught in all types of classrooms (see Table 13.2 and Figure 13.2 for proportions of each writing course taught in each classroom type). Across all types of courses, traditional classrooms were the most common.

What Predicts the Kinds of Classrooms Used for First-Year Writing?

To determine what predicted the use of different types of classrooms for first-year writing (FYW) courses (the most common course offered by the programs included in this study), we ran a series of correlations between the other variables and classroom type. We describe significant predictors related to characteristics of the universities, their student bodies, and their course and room scheduling procedures.

Table 13.2. Percent of Courses Taught in Each Type of Classroom*

	Basic Writing	First-Year Writing	English Language Learning	Advanced Writing	Business Writing
	N=1377	N=12070	N=756	N=2188	N=357
Lecture Hall	0.22%	3.99%	0.26%	6.44%	0.56%
Traditional Classroom	49.82%	57.59%	65.87%	51.87%	47.06%
Computer Classroom	35.08%	19.42%	25.00%	12.25%	24.93%
Active Classroom	3.56%	6.40%	4.10%	5.07%	10.92%
Online	5.45%	10.79%	1.32%	10.19%	12.89%
Other Classroom	5.88%	1.82%	3.44%	14.17%	3.64%

	Technical Writing	Digital Writing	Rhetoric/Writing Major	Other
	N=487	N=528	N=174	N=1520
Lecture Hall	0.00%	0.00%	0.00%	0.26%
Traditional Classroom	34.29%	56.82%	58.05%	67.37%
Computer Classroom	35.52%	30.30%	16.67%	11.38%
Active Classroom	4.31%	9.85%	17.82%	5.20%
Online	20.94%	3.03%	7.47%	7.96%
Other Classroom	4.93%	0.00%	0.00%	7.83%

* While basic writing, first-year writing, and English language learning courses are lower division courses (typically taken in students' first year at the university), advanced writing, business writing, technical writing, digital writing, and rhetoric/writing major courses might be either upper or lower division courses.

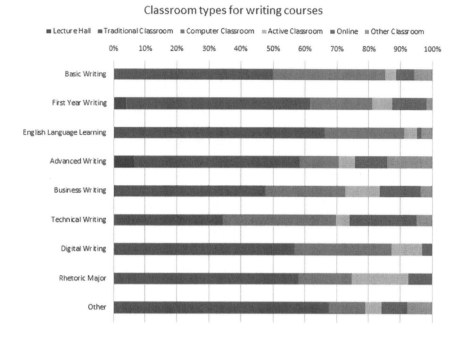

Figure 13.2. Percent of courses taught in each type of classroom.

INSTITUTIONAL CHARACTERISTICS

Interestingly, the student body size of an institution was not associated with the type of classroom used for FYW courses. However, the higher the institution's admission rate, the more likely that FYW classes are taught online ($r=.27$, $p=.02$).

Faculty appointment type also predicts classroom usage. The higher the percentage of full-time instructors at a university,[6] the more likely FYW courses are taught in traditional classrooms ($r=.36$, $p=.001$), and the less likely FYW courses are taught in computer classrooms ($r=-.24$, $p=.027$) or online ($r=-.36$, p=.001).

STUDENT CHARACTERISTICS

In general, the racial demographics of the student body seem to be related to the types of classrooms used for FYW courses. Online classes are more likely for

---

6   Faculty appointment type data was obtained from the National Center for Education Statistics for the institution as a whole; these statistics are not specific to the writing program, which categorizes faculty in terms of part-time or full-time employment, meaning that "full-time instructor" includes both tenure-track faculty and full-time non-tenure-track faculty.

schools with higher percentages of Native American ($r=.29$, $p=.006$) and Native Hawaiian students ($r=.22$, $p=.036$). A higher proportion of Black students is also associated with increased chances of teaching FYW in lecture halls ($r=.49$, $p<.001$), and lower chances of using traditional classrooms ($r=-.31$, $p=.003$). And the greater the proportion of White students, the more likely traditional classrooms are used for FYW courses ($r=.22$, $p=.004$). Taken together, these findings suggest that the more Black, Indigenous, and People of Color (BIPOC) students are enrolled at an institution, the more likely FYW courses are to be taught in rooms that challenge many best practices in writing pedagogy.

Features indicating the wealth of both universities and students are also related to the types of FYW classrooms used. For example, the higher a school's annual tuition, the more likely FYW will be taught in active classrooms (r=.31, p=.004), the less likely it will be taught online (r=.26, p=.015), and the more likely it will be taught in "other" classrooms such as seminar rooms (r=.26, p=.015). Students at institutions with larger Pell Grant-eligible populations are also marginally less likely to take FYW in active classrooms ($r=-.20$, $p=.066$). In other words, classrooms designed to promote process-based, active learning pedagogies are used more often for writing instruction at institutions with Whiter and wealthier student populations.

Course and Room Scheduling Characteristics

In general, course scheduling stakeholders were not related to the types of classrooms used for FYW courses, barring two exceptions:

- When department chairs were involved with scheduling courses, FYW was less likely to be taught in traditional classrooms (r=-.22, p=.043) and more likely to be taught in "other" classrooms (r=.37, p=.005).
- When office administrators were involved in course scheduling, FYW was less likely to be taught in lecture halls (r=.31, p=.004).

DISCUSSION

Taken together, our findings draw important parallels between the configurations of stakeholders involved in scheduling networks, showing the benefits of involving WPAs and department chairs, including a smaller number of scheduling stakeholders, and pointing to the problematic outcomes associated with involving both non-teaching stakeholders and individual instructors in making course and classroom scheduling decisions. Troublingly, our findings about the relationship between institutional/student characteristics and classroom type also illustrate how inequality manifests materially in different institutional ecologies.

IMPLICATIONS FOR COURSE SCHEDULING PROCESSES

When it comes to course scheduling, although WPAs were the most frequent stakeholders found in scheduling networks, they were involved only 60% of the time. The roles played by upper administrators and non-teaching offices (especially the registrar) were expected, as well as instructors. However, the significant role played by office administrators—administrative staff who work in writing programs, English departments, dean's offices, and other campus units—was surprising and somewhat troubling. Participants described office administrative staff playing a variety of roles in course scheduling, listed here from exerting least to most influence on the process:

- Submitting course schedule to upper admin/non-teaching office/scheduling software (schedule created by WPA/department chair).
- Assisting WPA/department chair in creating course schedule.
- Creating template adapted by WPA/department chair to build each year's course schedule.
- Creating course schedule.

While the labor involved in scheduling certainly encourages the involvement of office administrative staff, the survey results question what role these stakeholders should play, especially in light of Deborah Bickford's (2002) caution that when non-teaching staff are responsible for making decisions that impact pedagogy, their experience and job priorities may guide them to privilege efficiency and economy over student learning.

Thinking about scheduling in network terms also draws our attention to the configuration of the network as a whole. Cox et al. (2018) call on WPAs to identify and leverage the multiple stakeholders invested in writing across campus to tap into additional resources. If we read drafting the initial version of the course schedule as a sign of the writing program's authority to implement (at least some) instructional best practices, the involvement of department chairs in the scheduling process (49% of cases) makes this more likely. Conversely, if a non-teaching office (like the registrar or enrollment management office, 31% of cases) or scheduling software (9% of cases) is involved, the schedule of courses is less likely to begin inside the writing program or department. Furthermore, the more stakeholders included in the scheduling network, the more likely the initial schedule of writing courses is to be created outside of the department. Taken together, these findings suggest potential costs to expanding the network of campus writing stakeholders, an issue John Tassoni, in this collection, also considers when tracing the cross-institutional circulation of discourse about basic writing and how these competing and often problematic views have permanently relegated basic writing to marginal, invisible status. While writing programs' networked connections with other campus stakeholders may provide opportunities for advocacy and shaping policy, the location of and competing demands on these many stakeholders may impede writing instruction.

Our data are also somewhat ambivalent about the significance of writing programs developing the initial course schedule, given scheduling networks' guiding logics. Although the writing program/department drafts the initial version of the schedule for writing courses in a majority of cases (62%), many respondents explained that the scheduling choices they made were dictated by the requirements of outside stakeholders to optimize space/staff utilization rather than pedagogical best practices. Accounts like these call into question how much autonomy network-embedded writing programs have in scheduling, even when they draft the initial course schedule, given that writing programs often operate according to the enrollment-driven logics set by other network stakeholders. The amount of influence WPAs exert within the scheduling system varied widely. On the one hand, cases where WPAs play a primary role in scheduling or negotiating the schedule with other stakeholders illustrate ways WPAs can promote effective and equitable conditions for writing instruction by working with other network stakeholders and ecological resources. On the other, cases where WPAs have limited power show how their exclusion from the scheduling process impedes the kinds of writing instruction endorsed by the CCCC Position Statement on the Principles for the Postsecondary Teaching of Writing (Adler-Kassner et al., 2015).

Our findings map out the typical stakeholders included in scheduling networks, noting their impact on scheduling processes, especially the unexpected role played by office admin staff. Returning to Cox et al.'s (2018) argument for seeking out campus writing stakeholders, we found that WPAs are already connected via scheduling networks to numerous stakeholders, but that the influence of some of these stakeholders can have negative consequences for the delivery of writing instruction. This suggests that WPAs might use the work of scheduling—in addition to negotiations over funding, curriculum change, assessment, and other institutional processes—as another opportunity to educate other local stakeholders about writing studies' pedagogical knowledge and shift the campus writing culture.

IMPLICATIONS OF CLASSROOM SCHEDULING PROCESSES

Many of the same stakeholders are involved in both course and classroom scheduling, but the proportions are often reversed. Most WPAs (82% of cases) did not have a role in assigning classrooms to writing courses. The 18% of cases where WPAs did play an active role in classroom scheduling show the amount of labor some devote to this work, often because WPAs lack a formal role in the room scheduling process and rely on modifying room assignments made by other primary stakeholders:

> A staff member in our Registrar's office assigns classrooms. . . . I review their locations in an online "Class Search" utility. If I don't recognize a room, I walk over to the building and look in the classroom. If it's locked, I do my best to look in the windows. If it's open, I go in and count chairs, determine how much flexibility the instructor might have (e.g., can chairs and tables be moved for group work?), etc. If anything's unworkable or objectionable, I contact the Registar's [sic] staff member to see if we have any wiggle room. Classroom space can be surprisingly tight, which can get pretty frustrating.

This reference to the limited availability of alternate classrooms reflects a related institutional ecology issue many respondents raised about classroom shortages and their effect on writing instruction. This finding adds criteria that should be considered in campus occupancy rates: rather than focusing only on general room availability, reporting on the availability of *appropriate* classrooms would better illustrate the (unmet) spatial needs of the writing program as an ecological constraint on writing instruction. Furthermore, in cases where classroom occupancy rates are high and competition for rooms is fierce, as illustrated in the quote above, lacking a formal place in the classroom scheduling process excludes many WPAs from the (partial) agency many exert over course scheduling, forcing WPAs to forge weak, informal, or unsustainable connections to scheduling network stakeholders.

Many WPA respondents who did report working on room scheduling selected courses not based on the rooms' suitability for writing instruction, but based on their locations, prioritizing placing instructors in the same room or building to accommodate back-to-back teaching schedules. While these logistical considerations are important, this view of classrooms as an insignificant aspect of teaching was also reflected in the fact that instructors (63% of cases) and non-teaching offices (51% of cases) play a larger role in classroom scheduling than in course scheduling. These findings suggest that classroom placement is other viewed either as

- A matter of individual instructor preference, rather than a systematic programmatic effort to match pedagogy to classroom infrastructure, typically communicated by instructors directly to the room scheduler as a classroom change request (a retrofit), or

- A non-pedagogical issue appropriate to a non-teaching office (such as the Registrar) that prioritizes efficient matching of class size and room capacity, often without considering the room's material affordances for teaching and learning.

The combined effects of scheduling networks not designed to account for pedagogy are reflected in responses like the following: "Lisa our admin [handles classroom scheduling], but then there's another process where you ask Lisa to help you find a different (a "smart") room. She is good friends with Angela in scheduling" (names have been replaced with pseudonyms). This response highlights the lack of systematic attention to classroom conditions within the writing program, and how systems that downplay the importance of learning spaces place classroom scheduling decisions in the hands of instructors and office admin staff. Another response illustrates the sustainability issues created by relying on such workarounds to official systems: "The person who assigned the rooms just retired two days ago, so we don't know what's going to happen." Without a structural role in an institution's classroom scheduling network, programs will be unable to systematically advocate for classrooms that promote active, process-based writing instruction.

The effects of deferring classroom scheduling decisions to instructors' preferences helps account for one of our surprising findings: the more full-time instructors at an institution, the more likely FYW courses are to be taught in traditional classrooms. This is somewhat surprising because higher proportions of full-time instructors are typically linked with the kinds of improved teaching and faculty development opportunities described in the criteria for the Conference on College Composition and Communication (CCCC) Writing Program Certificate of Excellence (2018). Respondents suggest one reason why more full-time instructors may result in more traditional classrooms and fewer computer classrooms: some noted that instructors in their programs prefer to teach in traditional classrooms because instructors find it easier to curb digital distraction and side conversations (that is, police student behavior) in this environment, despite the obstacles these rooms can pose to active, process-based writing instruction. As more firmly situated institutional citizens, full-time instructors are more likely to have the local knowledge and capital required to request preferred classrooms. Mara Lee Grayson's chapter in this collection offers a cautionary parallel, describing how non-tenure track instructors' deficit thinking about BIPOC students circulated within a writing program, running parallel to and undermining the efforts of the network of tenure track faculty and other institutional stakeholders working to reform the program's curriculum. When WPAs concentrate on working with external stakeholders across their institutions, they ignore in-program networks at their peril. Where classroom scheduling is concerned, when WPAs don't work to connect themselves to in-program networks that circulate information among instructors, they miss opportunities to draw teachers' attention to the relationship between space and learning. In such cases, accepted practice and lore can guide instructors to select classrooms that do not facilitate social, embodied, process-based approaches to writing instruction. The local policies that determine which stakeholders populate classroom scheduling networks—especially when combined with institutional characteristics like available classroom resources and procedures like rigid performance evaluation metrics—can promote classroom placements that do not support best practices in writing instruction.

Scheduling networks that exclude the WPA defer classroom placement decisions to those without pedagogical expertise or to instructors who may be motivated by concerns that don't align with disciplinary best practices. The current composition of most scheduling networks requires writing programs to rely on workarounds and instructor preference to access effective writing classrooms, an unreliable and unsustainable tactic.

Institutional and Student Equity Concerns Relating to Access to Appropriate Writing Classrooms

Considering institutional and student body characteristics highlights the extent to which the local scheduling networks we focus on here are embedded within larger racial and economic systems that structure access to resources. Overall, our respondents reported that traditional classrooms were the most common classroom type for FYW (58% of cases), followed by computer classrooms (20% of cases). However, the absence of network logics that prioritize classrooms supporting interactive, process-based writing instruction was most strongly felt at institutions with larger proportions of Black, Indigenous, and People of Color (BIPOC) students and poor students, where lecture halls and online instruction were more common. This data points to a clear social justice issue, calling WPAs to assume more central and formal roles in classroom scheduling (see Voss, 2020 for recommendations) and that organizations like CCCC and the Council of Writing Program Administrators (CWPA) to better support these local efforts through advocacy at the disciplinary level. Our findings about the unequal distribution of active learning classrooms, lecture halls, and online instruction across institutions offer a cautionary tale of the costs to marginalized student populations when WPAs are not part of classroom scheduling networks.

Active Learning Classrooms

The use of active learning classrooms for FYW is linked to students' race and wealth: the wealthier and Whiter its population, the more likely FYW is to be taught in active learning classrooms. Although it's still rare for FYW to be taught in active learning classrooms (only 6% of cases), this finding suggests that, without the systematic intervention of WPAs, ecological conditions and the low institutional status of writing courses combine to exert considerable influence on the delivery of writing instruction, accumulating educational advantages for students already occupying positions of racial and economic privilege.

Lecture Halls

The classroom types associated with FYW taught at institutions with larger Black student populations were more problematic and show how institutionalized racism can manifest in educational infrastructure when unchecked by WPA advocacy in scheduling networks. While universities with a higher proportion of Black students were less likely to teach FYW in traditional classrooms, they were more likely to teach FYW in lecture halls, arguably the worst environment for writing instruction due to lecture halls' barriers to peer collaboration and promotion of a teacher-centered, passive mode of learning and their encouragement of extremely large class sizes.[7] Similarly, the higher the proportion of low-income students at an institution, the more likely FYW was to be taught in lecture halls. Taken together, these findings suggest that institutional context is an important factor for WPAs to consider when strategically meting out their scheduling labor: WPAs at institutions whose populations include more Black students and more low-income students may need to prioritize developing and gaining access to appropriate writing classrooms. These findings also show how familiar trends of racial and economic inequality surface when considering the physical infrastructure for writing instruction, marking this as an equity issue WPAs and the CWPA should act on. As Sehoya Cotner et al. (2013) argued, a significant body of evidence shows improved learning outcomes associated with active learning practiced within purpose-built classrooms, but due to the increased costs of building/renovating such spaces, institutions (especially the most financially-strapped ones) will require warrants to invest in active learning classrooms and allocate them to writing instruction.

---

7   This finding was driven primarily by the single historically Black university in our sample: when this was removed, this correlation disappeared. This finding suggests the need to study classroom infrastructure and scheduling at HBCUs specifically (echoing calls by Sias & Moss, 2011; Jackson et al., 2019; and others to correct the underrepresentation of HBCUs in writing studies research overall), to investigate whether the tendency to teach writing in lecture halls is characteristic of HBCUs generally or whether the institution included in our sample is an anomaly.

Online Classes[8]

While Black students and low-income students are more likely to take FYW in lecture halls, our findings about the use of online FYW instruction raise questions for other racially marginalized groups. The association we found between school selectivity and online FYW instruction runs contrary to research-based recommendations for online education: well-prepared students and White students tend to do as well or better in online classes compared to in-person classes (Cavanaugh & Jacquemin, 2015). However, we found that schools with larger Native American and Native Hawaiian student populations (which don't map onto selective institutions) offer more online FYW courses. This delivery format makes sense, given a) the "education deserts" (Hillman, 2016) found in rural areas of the US where many reservations are located and b) Hawaii's small number of colleges. These conditions may encourage Native American and Native Hawaiian students to enroll in distance learning FYW courses to compensate for the lack of higher education opportunities near home. However, while online delivery addresses the lack of local options, research on distance learning outcomes (Xu & Jaggars, 2014) suggests that BIPOC students in online courses tend to fare worse than their White peers, likely because remote instruction strips away the on-campus community support that can counter the White supremacist norms that implicitly or explicitly underpin most college curricula.

In cases where in-person FYW courses are not an option, our findings suggest that WPAs carefully attend to which students are enrolling their online FYW courses and make sure curricula are designed and instructors are trained to support marginalized student populations where they represent important populations of online students (see Davila et al., 2017). This is especially important for FYW courses, which are often the only small, interactive course first-year students take, raising the stakes for online FYW instruction even higher. In light of this information, WPAs may need to seek out new campus stakeholders, for example, working with offices of institutional research to assess the effects of different educational delivery formats on different student demographics in order to redesign curricula to support student success and with teaching centers to fund targeted faculty development. This finding illustrates how engaging substantively with one local network (scheduling) might result in WPAs becoming a central nexus point linking together multiple additional local networks of information flow and decision making.

---

8   This survey was conducted in 2017–2018, before the onset of the COVID-19 pandemic, which has dramatically changed students' exposure to online instruction and sparked an explosion of work developing online pedagogies designed for equity and inclusion.

Attending to the relationships between student/institutional characteristics and classrooms highlights several equity concerns relating to the physical environment for FYW instruction. Our findings suggest courses of specific action for WPAs, based on local data, and a larger, network-based role for WPA work within the institution to advocate for classroom space as an educational justice issue.

RECOMMENDATIONS FOR PROGRAM ADMINISTRATORS

Our data on the networks and network logistics shaping the delivery of writing instruction connects writing program management to writing studies' disciplinary knowledge and commitments, suggesting ways to implement the field's liberatory ideals in the institutional ecologies within which writing is taught. We tease out the effects of institutional policies and habits on course scheduling and go beyond anecdotal senses of the connections between student characteristics and course delivery to draw correlations to suggest courses of action to WPAs that are specific to the student populations they serve. As Louise Phelps (2017) argued, extending WPAs' work from basic management of program logistics to working across institutional levels assumes the full responsibility of administration as intellectual labor that WPA work *should* entail, positioning WPAs to occupy a central role in institutional scheduling networks. Working across these institutional levels necessitates that WPAs see themselves as significant stakeholder-nodes, and calls WPAs to attend to things like network composition, density, and logic. Furthermore, our findings about classroom scheduling underscore the importance of recognizing these decision-making networks as located within larger local, regional, and national ecologies shaped by the characteristics of institutions and their students.

Our findings recommend actions for individual WPAs and rhetoric and composition administrators to take in course and classroom scheduling and pose questions for future administrator scholars. These findings also have implications for disciplinary organizations, suggesting revisions to existing position statements and/or the drafting of new position statements to help WPAs educate scheduling stakeholders and shift local network logics. Therefore, we offer recommendations for individual WPAs, WPA researchers, and disciplinary organizations like CCCC and CWPA.

Recommendations for WPAs in Local Scheduling Networks

Stakeholders Outside the Writing Program: as one stakeholder among many, WPAs will not be able to single-handedly change problematic policies like reliance on scheduling software or enrollment-driven economizing. However, returning to Cox et al.'s (2018) network approach to WPA work, WPAs can conceive of these other actors as stakeholders in the campus writing infrastructure and work with them to embed the disciplinary knowledge and best practices of writing studies into scheduling logics. To do this, WPAs can initiate conversations—supported by local data, disciplinary guidelines, and empirical research—about the goals and competing demands of scheduling outside the fraught, hectic scheduling process, investing in such conversations in the long term to strengthen their network connections to other stakeholders in the hopes of shifting the logics that drive scheduling.

Where classroom scheduling is concerned, WPAs' work to place FYW into computer classrooms (19% of cases) is instructive, reflecting the tradition within the computers and composition subfield of working within local institutional networks to develop and maintain digital writing labs and studios (see McAllister & Selfe, 2002; Purdy & DeVoss, 2017; Selfe, 2005). Reflecting learning outcome commitments described in the computers and composition literature, survey respondents described developing scheduling policies with other network stakeholders (such as computer science departments or the registrar) to place FYW courses in computer labs in exchange for committing to digital literacy learning outcomes for FYW. This example illustrates how WPAs can—in collaboration with other stakeholders—introduce new policies into scheduling networks by enacting changes within their programs. For example, WPAs could argue for access to writing-conducive classrooms in exchange for committing to more capacious writing-related learning outcomes—such as accreditation standards related to teamwork and public speaking—facilitated by active learning classroom features.

Stakeholders Inside the Writing Program: because of the labor course scheduling entails, involving office admin staff makes sense, but—especially when they take a leading role in developing the course schedule—WPAs need to provide guidelines and background information about how to balance competing demands to ensure that things like class sizes, course loads, and teaching schedules reflect the CCCC guidelines for effective and ethical writing instruction.

The role instructors play in classroom scheduling, especially, points to the connections between larger institutional scheduling networks/logics and program-specific policies for instructor training and evaluation. At the programmatic level, the changes recommended above involve substantial infrastructural changes to the schedules, classrooms, and outcomes of writing courses. WPAs will need to support instructors throughout this process of programmatic change with transparency, professional development opportunities, changes to evaluation procedures, and other measures to help instructors buy into and thrive in the new teaching and learning conditions WPAs are working to promote.

"It's Complicated"

Recommendations for Future WPA Research

Replication Studies: while this study has mapped out typical stakeholders and procedures involved in course and classroom scheduling via open-response questions, future research can create a controlled vocabulary of scheduling network stakeholders and logics and for future research, enabling greater consistency and scope for data collection.

More Information about Writing Program Ecologies: we did not ask about campus classroom inventory/access, class size, teaching load, or instructor population, all of which shape campus writing ecologies. We also did not directly examine the relationship between institutional wealth and course or classroom scheduling. Given the high cost required to build and maintain new and existing classrooms (especially computer classrooms, active learning classrooms, and other innovative learning spaces), factoring institutional wealth measures like endowment size into analyses of course and classroom scheduling processes (especially in tandem with institution type) will add valuable theoretical and practical information to our findings here. Future research should account for these and other ecological conditions, especially to interrogate their connections to racial and economic inequality.

Linking Instructional Delivery to Student Learning: local assessment data is needed to further understand the impact of course and classroom scheduling. What impact do course and classroom scheduling procedures, classroom type, and other ecological factors have on student learning, measured in terms of FYW learning outcomes and student performance, especially when student and institutional characteristics are taken into account?

Recommendations for Future WPA Disciplinary and Policy Work

Address Course and Classroom Scheduling in Position Statements: as noted above, while existing CCCC and CWPA position statements briefly or implicitly reference the administrative and intellectual labor of scheduling, no position statement yet addresses these issues substantively. CWPA should draft a position statement or revise existing position statements to assert WPAs' centrality in institutional scheduling networks, similar to the way such documents already specify the responsibilities and authority WPAs should have within their own programs and departments. Similarly, statements like the Principles for the Postsecondary Teaching of Writing (Adler-Kassner et al., 2015) that outline best practices in writing instruction should be expanded to discuss physical classroom infrastructure as a factor affecting social, process-based writing instruction.

Bolster Position Statements with Empirical Research: scheduling-related (and other) position statements should leverage empirical research more explicitly, to strengthen them as warrants for making change in institutional scheduling networks. As McClure et al. (2017) argued, one reason for the uneven impact of existing position statements is that they don't uniformly draw on empirical data to support their assertions about best practices, enabling upper administrators and other outside stakeholders to dismiss the statements' recommendations as claims without evidence.[9] Empirical research is certainly not the only kind of valuable research, however, its absence is often used as a rationale in the 21st century university for dismissing proposals for change. The *CCCC Statement on White Language Supremacy* (Baca et al., 2021) models this integration of a reference list that includes empirical research alongside theoretical, cultural studies, and other research methodologies, offering a guide that can help fill in some of the methodological gaps around existing position statements, increasing their persuasive power.

CONCLUSION

Our findings about network stakeholders and logics can inform the kind of institutional landscape survey Cox et al. (2018) call for by documenting the variety of systems used at different institutional types to deliver writing instruction, noting more and less effective approaches to guide WPAs advocating for decision-making power and resources. The systems for course planning and classroom assignment described here articulate typical models and categories/types into which WPAs can place their programs, allowing for benchmarking with peer institutional standards when negotiating with upper administrators over scheduling questions. As this study's preliminary findings indicate, answering these questions facilitates not only best instructional practices but also the necessary first steps toward connecting equity measures like student learning outcomes and retention to administrative structures and material infrastructures. These findings also provide warrants within our own discipline for why WPAs should approach scheduling (and other administrative work) as a meaningful intellectual activity, similar to what Asao B. Inoue's (2022) race-conscious studies of grading have done for the work of writing assessment.

This chapter's data on the scheduling networks shaping the delivery of writing instruction connects program management to the kinds of disciplinary threshold concepts that Emily Isaacs (2018) argued WPAs, and rhetoric and composition administrators more broadly, should advocate for. While Isaacs points to mission

---

9   Some position statements (such as the Committee on CCCC Students' Right to Their Own Language [1975] or Elder et al.'s CWPA Position Statement on Bullying in the Workplace [2019]) do include a robust reference list of peer-reviewed research supporting the claims made in the statement. Many NCTE, CCCC, and CWPA statements, however, lack such explicit linking to their supporting research.

statements, course descriptions, and placement procedures as evidence of programmatic (mis)alignment with disciplinary values outlined in the CWPA et al.'s *Framework for Success in Postsecondary Writing* (2011) and the CWPA WPA Outcomes Statement for First-Year Composition (2014), we invite rhetoric and composition administrators to approach their scheduling work with this question: does the program's scheduling system create conditions conducive to teaching writing as a rhetorical, social, material, embodied process in ways that are inclusive of and accessible to all students? Theorizing Isaacs's recommendations in network terms, Cox et al. (2018) call rhetoric and composition administrators to "be aware of systems beyond your institution and connect those that are beneficial to the program" (p. 189–191) reminding us that we exist in three-dimensional networks where the horizontal links that constitute institutional networks are overlaid with vertical networks connecting the program and institution to outside organizations like accrediting bodies and professional organizations. We can and should mobilize these outside organizations (making changes within them as needed) to support campus-level efforts to secure effective classrooms for writing classes.

ACKNOWLEDGMENTS

Many thanks to Mira Diwan, Vincent Agredo, and Lindsay Baerg, student research assistants in the Bruchmann Lab, who enabled much of our data analysis by compiling data on participating institutions.

REFERENCES

Adler-Kassner, L., Barnhouse, S., Eodice, M., Estrem, H., Irvin, L., Kelly-Riley, D., Mitchler, S. & Palmquist, M. (2015). Principles for the postsecondary teaching of writing. *Conference on College Composition and Communication.* https://cccc.ncte.org/cccc/resources/positions/postsecondarywriting.

Baca, I., Driskill, L.-Q., Green, D. F., Inoue, A., Jackson, A., Lovejoy, K. B., Muhammad, R., Richardson, E., Smitherman, G., Troutman, D., Villanueva, V., Williams, B. & Zentella, A. C. (2021). *CCCC Statement on White language supremacy.* Conference on College Composition and Communication. https://cccc.ncte.org/cccc/white-language-supremacy.

Bickford, D. (2002). Navigating the White waters of collaborative work in shaping learning environments. In N. Van Note Chism & D. Bickford (Eds.), *The importance of physical space in creating supportive learning environments* (pp. 43–52). Jossey-Bass.

Brooks, C. D. (2012). Space and consequences: The impact of different formal learning spaces on instructor and student behavior. *Journal of Learning Spaces, 1*(2), n.p. http://libjournal.uncg.edu/jls/article/view/285/275.

Carpenter, R. (2016). Flipping the creativity class: Creating active learning environments for student innovations. In J. B. Waldrop & M. A. Bowen (Eds.), *Best practices for flipping the college classroom* (pp. 118–130). Routledge.

Cavanaugh, J. K. & Jacquemin, S. J. (2015). A large sample comparison of grade based student learning outcomes in online vs. face-to-face courses. *Online Learning, 19*(2), 25–32.

Charlton, C. (2014). The weight of curious space: Rhetorical events, hackerspace, and emergent multimodal assessment. *Computers and Composition, 31*(1), 29–42.

Colbeck, C. L., Cabrera, A. F. & Terenzini, P. T. (2001). Learning professional confidence: Linking teaching practices, students' self-perceptions, and gender. *The Review of Higher Education, 24*(2), 173–191.

Committee on CCCC Language Statement. (1975). Students' right to their own language. *College English, 36*(6), 709–726.

Conference on College Composition and Communication. (2018). CCCC writing program certificate of excellence. *Conference on College Composition and Communication.* https://cccc.ncte.org/cccc/awards/writingprogramcert.

Cotner, S., Loper, J., Walker, J. D. & Brooks, D. C. (2013). "It's not you, it's the room": Are the high-tech, active learning classrooms worth it? *Journal of College Science Teaching, 42*(6), 82–88.

Council of Writing Program Administrators. (2014). *WPA outcomes statement for first-year composition.* https://wpacouncil.org/aws/CWPA/pt/sd/news_article/243055/_PARENT/layout_details/false.

Council of Writing Program Administrators, National Council of Teachers of English, and National Writing Project. (2011). *Framework for success in postsecondary writing.* https://files.eric.ed.gov/fulltext/ED516360.pdf.

Cox, A., Dougherty, T. D., Kahn, S., LaFrance, M. & Lynch-Biniek, A. (2016). The Indianapolis Resolution: Responding to twenty-first-century exigencies/political economies of composition labor. *College Composition and Communication, 68*(1), 38–67.

Cox, M., Galin, J. R. & Melzer, D. (2018). *Sustainable WAC: A whole systems approach to launching and developing writing across the curriculum programs.* National Council of Teachers of English.

Crowley, S. (2002). How the professional lives of WPAs would change if FYC were elective. In S. C. Brown & T. J. Enos (Eds.), *The writing program administrator's resource: A guide to reflective institutional practice* (pp. 219–230). Lawrence Erlbaum.

Davila, B., Bourelle, T., Bourelle, A. & Knutson, A. V. (2017). Linguistic diversity in online writing classes. *WPA: Writing Program Administration, 41*(1), 60–81.

Elder, C., Davila, B., Perryman-Clark, S. & Rankins-Robertson, S. (2019). CWPA position statement on bullying in the workplace. *Council of Writing Program Administrators.* http://wpacouncil.org/aws/CWPA/pt/sd/news_article/256146/_PARENT/layout_details/false.

Farrell, E. J. & Jensen, J. M. (2000). Rhetoric and research on class size. In R. Indrisano & J. R. Squire (Eds.), *Perspectives on writing: Research, theory, and practice* (pp. 307–325). International Reading Association.

Finer, B. S. & White-Farnham, J. (Eds.). (2017). *Writing program architecture: Thirty cases for reference and research.* Utah State University Press.

Haswell, R. (2004). Class sizes for first-year regular and basic writing courses: Data collected from the WPA-L, 1998–1999, 2003–2004. Comp Pile. https://comppile.org/profresources/classsize.htm.

Hillman, N. W. (2016). Geography of college opportunity: The case of education deserts. *American Educational Research Journal, 53*(4), 987–1021.

Holmstein, V. (2002). This site under construction: Negotiating space for WPA work in the community college. In Brown, S. C. & Enos, T. (Eds.), *The writing program administrator's resource: A guide to reflective institutional practice* (pp. 429–438). Erlbaum.

Horning, A. (2007). The definitive article on class size. *WPA: Writing Program Administration, 31*(1–2), 11–34.

Hult, C., Joliffee, D., Kelly, K., Mead, D. & Schuster, C. (1992). The Portland Resolution. *WPA: Writing Program Administration, 16*(1–2), 88–94.

Inoue, A. B. (2022). Grading contracts: Assessing their effectiveness on different racial formations. In A. B. Inoue & M. Poe (Eds.), *Race and writing assessment* (pp. 78–93). Peter Lang.

Isaacs, E. (2018). *Writing at the State U: Instruction and administration at 106 comprehensive universities.* Utah State University Press.

Jackson, K. K., Jackson, H. & Tafari, D. N. H. (2019). We belong in the discussion: Including HBCUs in conversations about race and writing. *College Composition and Communication, 71*(2), 184–214.

Kim, M. & Carpenter, R. (Eds.). (2017). *Writing studio pedagogy: Space, place, and rhetoric in collaborative environments.* Rowman & Littlefield.

LaFrance, M. & Cox, A. (2017). Brutal(ist) meditations: Space and labor-movement in a writing program. In S. Kahn, W. B. Lalicker & A. Lynch-Biniek (Eds.), *Contingency, exploitation, and solidarity: Labor and action in English composition* (pp. 279–301). The WAC Clearinghouse; University Press of Colorado. https://doi.org/10.37514/per-b.2017.0858.

Lin, N. (1999). Building a network theory of social capital. *Connections, 22*(1), 28–51.

McAllister, K. S. & Selfe, C. L. (2002). Writing program administration and instructional computing. In S. C. Brown & T. Enos (Eds.), *The writing program administrator's resource: A guide to reflective institutional practice* (pp. 341–375). Lawrence Erlbaum.

McClure, R., Goldstein, D. V. & Pemberton, M. A. (2017). Strengthening the statement: Data on working conditions in college composition. In R. McClure, D. V. Goldstein & M. A. Pemberton (Eds.), *Labored: The state(ment) and future of work in composition* (pp. 268–284). Parlor Press.

Miles, M. B., Huberman, M. A. & Saldaña, J. (2013). *Qualitative data analysis: A methods sourcebook* (3rd ed.). SAGE.

Miller, R. E. (1998). *As if learning mattered: Reforming higher education.* Cornell University Press.

National Center for Education Statistics. (n.d.). College navigator. Institute of Education Sciences. Retrieved April 4, 2023, from https://nces.ed.gov/collegenavigator/.

Phelps, L. W. (1991). The institutional logic of writing programs: Catalyst, laboratory, and pattern for change. In R. H. Bullock, J. Trimbur & C. Schuster (Eds.), *The politics of writing instruction: Postsecondary* (pp. 155–170). Boynton/Cook.

Phelps, L. W. (2017, March 2). Administration as a design art. *Writing Program Administrators Listserv*. https://lists.asu.edu/cgi-bin/wa?A2=ind1703&L=wpa-l&P=R45240&1=wpa1&9=A&I=-3&J=on&X=C4C4A1B6F65BCF8922&Y=julia.voss%40gmail.com&d=No+Match%3BMatch%3BMatches&z=4.

Phuong, A. E., Nguyen, J. & Marie, D. (2017). Evaluating an adaptive equity-oriented pedagogy: A study of its impacts in higher education. *The Journal of Effective Teaching, 17*(2), 5–44.

Porter, J. E., Sullivan, P., Blythe, S., Grabill, J. T. & Miles, L. (2000). Institutional critique: A rhetorical methodology for change. *College Composition and Communication, 51*(4), 610–642.

Prince, M. (2004). Does active learning work? A review of the research. *Journal of Engineering Education, 93*(3), 223–232.

Purdy, J. P. & DeVoss, D. N. (Eds.). (2017). *Making space: Writing instruction, infrastructure, and multiliteracies*. University of Michigan Press. https:/.doi.org/10.3998/mpub.7820727.

Reiff, M. J., Bawarshi, A., Ballif, M. & Weisser, C. (Eds.). (2015). *Ecologies of writing programs: Program profiles in context*. Parlor Press.

Robertson, L. R., Crowley, S. & Lentricchia, F. (1987). The Wyoming conference resolution opposing unfair salaries and working conditions for post-secondary teachers of writing. *College English, 49*(3), 274–280.

Selfe, R. (2005). *Sustainable computer environments: Cultures of support for teachers of English and language arts*. Hampton Press.

Sias, R. E. & Moss, B. J. (2011). Introduction: Rewriting a master narrative: HBCUs and community literacy partnerships. *Reflections: A Journal of Community-Engaged Writing and Rhetoric, 10*(2), 1–16.

Strickland, D. (2011). *The managerial unconscious in the history of composition studies*. Southern Illinois University Press.

Taylor, T. (2006). Design, delivery, and narcolepsy. In K. Blake Yancey (Ed.), *Delivering college composition: The fifth canon* (pp. 127–140). Boynton/Cook.

Voss, J. (2020). WPAs as university learning space managers: theorizing and guiding the creation of effective writing classrooms. *WPA: Writing Program Administration, 43*(2), 109–130.

Walls, D. & Wolcott, L. (2017). The infrastructure of space: Expanding writing classroom activity into the extracurriculum. In J. P. Purdy & D. N. DeVoss (Eds.), *Making space: Writing instruction, infrastructure, and multiliteracies*, University of Michigan Press. https://www.fulcrum.org/concern/monographs/2514nn59z?locale=en.

Wooten, C. A., Ray, B. & Babb, J. (2016). WPAs reading SETs: Toward an ethical and effective use of teaching evaluations. *WPA: Writing Program Administration, 40*(1), 50–66.

Xu, D. & Jaggars, S. S. (2014). Performance gaps between online and face-to-face courses: Differences across types of students and academic subject areas. *The Journal of Higher Education, 85*(5), 633–659.

"It's Complicated"

APPENDIX A: SURVEY QUESTIONS[10]

- Name of your institution:
- Name of the program you direct:
- How many sections does the program offer each academic year?
- What types of courses does your program teach? (check all that apply; please write in any that are missing)
  - Basic/developmental writing
  - First-year writing
  - Writing for English language learners
  - Advanced writing
  - Business writing
  - Technical writing
  - Digital/multimodal writing
  - Writing/Rhetoric major courses
  - Other (please specify)
- How are courses scheduled in your program? Who is involved? What systems, metrics, etc. are used? "Scheduling" defined as
  - Determining number of courses offered
  - Distributing courses across terms of the academic year
  - Assigning meeting days/times to courses
  - Staffing courses with instructors
- How are courses assigned to classrooms? Please consider:
  - Who places courses into specific rooms?
  - Do faculty have input on the classrooms they teach in?
  - Does this vary across courses taught in the program?
  - Does this vary across types of classrooms where program courses are taught?
- What kinds of classrooms do program courses meet in? (Select all that apply by clicking on image. Sample images included to illustrate different classroom types.) [Figure 13.3 and Figure 13.4]
- Is there anything else important to know about the rooms where writing courses meet? For example:
  - Schedules in which courses meet in different rooms on different days of the week

---

10   The survey also included questions about ownership and scheduling privileges for classrooms used for writing courses (for example "Are these classrooms used exclusively for writing program courses? If not, what other courses are taught in these rooms? If users vary for different types of classrooms, please differentiate"), but because this data is not discussed in this chapter, we don't include those questions here.

319

- Pedagogical practices that effectively convert one of type of classroom into another type of classroom
- Features/affordances that are present in rooms but are broken, unreliable, or which instructors lack permission to use
- Plans to build/remodel/etc. new classrooms for writing program use

[For each writing course that respondents indicated was taught in their program, they were asked the following questions]

- How many sections of _____ are taught each year?
- How many _____ sections are taught in each type of classroom used by your program? (ignore any classroom types not used)
  - Lecture halls:
  - "Traditional" classrooms:
  - Computer classrooms:
  - Active learning classrooms:
  - Online:
  - Other (please specify): _____

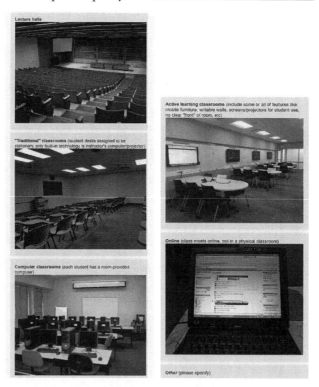

Figure 13.3 and Figure 13.4. Sample images included to illustrate different classroom types.

CHAPTER 14.
FLEXIBLE FRAMING, OPEN SPACES, AND ADAPTIVE RESOURCES: A NETWORKED APPROACH TO WRITING PROGRAM ADMINISTRATION

Jenna Morton-Aiken

Brown University

This story is the center of a Venn diagram with three very personal circles in graduate school: my desire to thrive as a pregnant and then parenting Ph.D. student;[1] my aim to elevate marginalized voices to make the world a more equitable place; and my innate drive to go faster in all things when possible. Since my current salary does not yet allow for the BMW 5 series of my dreams, going faster usually means creating more effective systems with life and work "hacks," technology, and strategic planning.

Now, reader, you might wonder what any of this has to do with archives, networks, or rhetoric and composition program administration (hereafter WPA) as the title forecast. But from my personal Venn diagram perspective, the relationships among networks, archives, and WPA work are actually very strong:

- Archives, though stereotypically presented as dusty and isolated collections of old White men's stuff, are about making things, especially documents, easily accessible to interested users. Archival theory explores how to do the organizing, with recent developments exploring the importance of names and organization in themselves to acknowledge that archives are not the neutral arrangements of neutral objects, but instead are the manifestations of rhetorically significant decisions. I'll talk more about this below.
- Networks as I discuss them here are technology-enabled ways of connecting digital objects. Moreover, networks and network theory can enable multiple names and points of access for objects, thereby

---

1   If you're interested in more on that story, see my 2019 article "Dressing for Childbearing, the Patriarchy, and Me: Auto-ethnography in Three Parts" in *The Journal of Multimodal Rhetorics*.

DOI: https://doi.org/10.37514/PER-B.2023.1848.2.14

identifying consensus and dissensus without having to move a physical file from one folder to another. It also allows for unlike things in previously unconnected places to become part of a shared ecosystem. Again, more on this below.
- WPAs are in the business of connecting people and resources, elevating voices, and putting people in touch with the right systems. Applying rhetorically informed theory to archival practice and leveraging cool tech stuff like hashtags from networks means that WPAs can do more of that work more effectively and more equitably because the resources are collaboratively named, more easily located, and accessible to a wider spectrum of users.

Part practical application, part praxis-driven research, relational architecture is the idea that institutional documents can and should be named, organized, and accessed by a lot of people, because no one person can, or should, have the power to define a closed set of keywords or applications. Recognizing the power of naming (Freire, 2001) and circulation (Graban, 2013; Gries, 2013; Yancey, 2004) and leveraging the power of digital tools, relational architecture creates a system in which all individuals are able to help decide on the nature of stuff in the archive or the documents in the Google Drive.

Though formulated separately from media artist Rafael Lozano-Hemmer's use of relational architecture (1999), my independent applications of the term seek to subvert traditional power decision and rhetorical framers. Lozano-Hemmer pushed back on how people usually move through space, deploying through art the physical relational architecture that "exposes power and privilege, and engages people in questioning our role" in public spaces (Willis, 2009, para. 1). While Lozano-Hemmer refers to the relationships among people and in relation to the space they move through, I use it here to build user-generated database points based on the relationships that users (who are distinct from archivists) contribute to expand the possible circulation of those documents or other artifacts.

Readers might note that this chapter attends to networks from a distinct perspective than those described elsewhere in the collection. While many focus on the networks and systems that affect writing program work from a systems theory perspective, this chapter focuses on the digital network possibilities, considering how a multi-authored system like relational architecture can engage with what the editors described in the introduction as the deeply personal and highly systematic nature of administrative work. Those decisions, while mundane, are in fact critical because they establish institutional memory—the resulting assemblage determines what is prioritized, seen, and inscribed versus what is buried, forgotten, or even erased. This means if the goal of the WPA director is to provide knowledge and practice for the betterment of the writing community, then current and future practitioners must be able to access, apply, and influence those resources. This shift in perspective means that archival theory, seemingly unrelated to writing programs, becomes a critical component to the program's success and longevity because archival theory focuses on the rhetorical power of the organization of resources; it is about practical ways to deal with huge amounts of stuff. Moreover, for the WPA who seeks to develop and maintain resources that provide flexible framing, open spaces, and adaptive resources on a programmatic level, the system itself must also be flexible, open, and adaptive.

THE ORIGIN STORY

I began to engage with intentional record-keeping in the second semester of my Ph.D. program. Like the editors and John Tassoni in this collection, I had to grapple with obstacles concerning locatability when I was just trying to do my job. My classmates and I were compiling a shared annotated bibliography that grew increasingly unusable by the week, as we added pages of text.

Grad student by day and parent to a darling four-month-old by night, I needed the document to perform more effectively for me, so that I could be both the student and parent I wanted to be. I proposed tagging each annotation with hashtags, so we could use the search function and skip around as needed. I built and maintained a list of the collectively generated keywords, and we all benefited with a much more user-friendly document. It wasn't yet a network, but it was a system that augmented traditional alphabetical organization and added our critical engagement into our semi-official record. My daughter started sleeping through the night, I got an A in the class, and I left the hashtags behind. Or so I thought.

Pregnant with my second daughter just over a year later,[2] I began preparing for my comprehensive exams. Our exams were four questions to be answered in a 24-hour period with later oral defense of those answers. While comps are always high stakes, the pressure to pass and keep working towards graduation (with presumed salary at the end of the rainbow) increased the mental burden on my shoulders. I didn't have the luxury of failing with a toddler at home and newborn on the way, so I turned back to hacking the organization system.

---

2   Why do I keep telling you about my private reproductive choices? Two reasons. First, I want to normalize pregnant women in professional spaces, especially in graduate school. Second, my body and my status as a parent informed my exigency and the resulting courses of action as much as my professional training. It might surprise you to hear that I am uncomfortable with situating this information in a professional chapter, but I am doing so because I believe these elements are a critical part of the story and important to share.

I created a comprehensive Word document for my notes with specific information and formatting. Figure 14.1 is a screenshot of the system, demonstrating the required elements:

1. Microsoft Word customized formatting that supporting automatic table of contents updates.
2. Prefix designation ("c" in this example) to identity categorization.
3. Recursive self-generated hashtags within the annotation summary (terms designated by # symbol) to mark specific ideas in the text with page numbers to allow for direct quote-level searching later.
4. Summarized hashtags outside the annotation (the small, right-aligned text) to identify which hashtags existed in the overall entry to support resource-level searching later.
5. Closing the entry with my own thoughts, including how this piece fits into conversation with other sources (the small, hanging indented text).

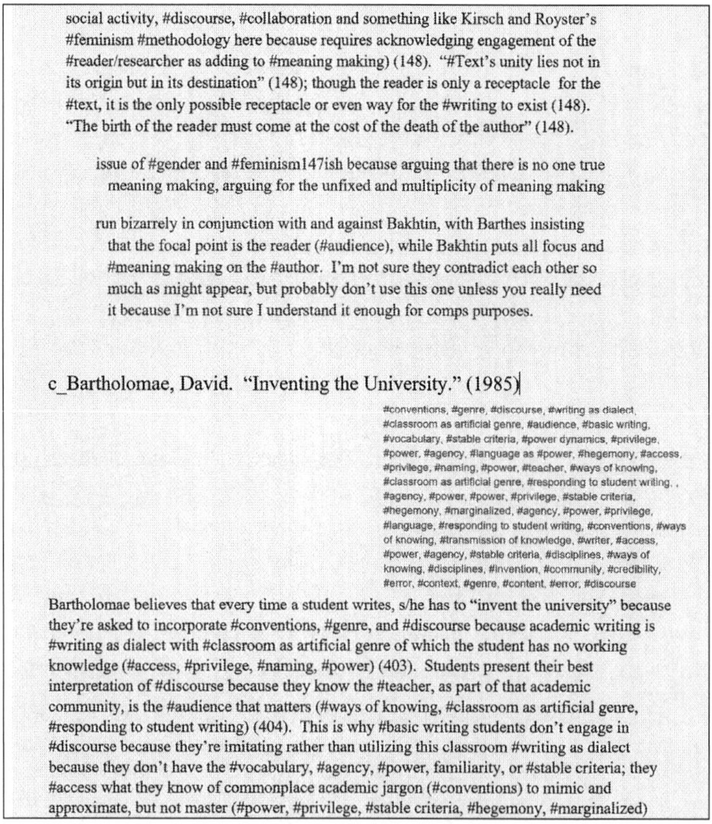
social activity, #discourse, #collaboration and something like Kirsch and Royster's #feminism #methodology here because requires acknowledging engagement of the #reader/researcher as adding to #meaning making) (148). "#Text's unity lies not in its origin but in its destination" (148); though the reader is only a receptacle for the #text, it is the only possible receptacle or even way for the #writing to exist (148). "The birth of the reader must come at the cost of the death of the author" (148).

issue of #gender and #feminism147ish because arguing that there is no one true meaning making, arguing for the unfixed and multiplicity of meaning making

run bizarrely in conjunction with and against Bakhtin, with Barthes insisting that the focal point is the reader (#audience), while Bakhtin puts all focus and #meaning making on the #author. I'm not sure they contradict each other so much as might appear, but probably don't use this one unless you really need it because I'm not sure I understand it enough for comps purposes.

c_Bartholomae, David. "Inventing the University." (1985)

#conventions, #genre, #discourse, #writing as dialect, #classroom as artificial genre, #audience, #basic writing, #vocabulary, #stable criteria, #power dynamics, #privilege, #power, #agency, #language as #power, #hegemony, #access, #privilege, #naming, #power, #teacher, #ways of knowing, #classroom as artificial genre, #responding to student writing, , #agency, #power, #power, #privilege, #stable criteria, #hegemony, #marginalized, #agency, #power, #privilege, #language, #responding to student writing, #conventions, #ways of knowing, #transmission of knowledge, #writer, #access, #power, #agency, #stable criteria, #disciplines, #ways of knowing, #disciplines, #invention, #community, #credibility, #error, #context, #genre, #content, #error, #discourse

Bartholomae believes that every time a student writes, s/he has to "invent the university" because they're asked to incorporate #conventions, #genre, and #discourse because academic writing is #writing as dialect with #classroom as artificial genre of which the student has no working knowledge (#access, #privilege, #naming, #power) (403). Students present their best interpretation of #discourse because they know the #teacher, as part of that academic community, is the #audience that matters (#ways of knowing, #classroom as artificial genre, #responding to student writing) (404). This is why #basic writing students don't engage in #discourse because they're imitating rather than utilizing this classroom #writing as dialect because they don't have the #vocabulary, #agency, #power, familiarity, or #stable criteria; they #access what they know of commonplace academic jargon (#conventions) to mimic and approximate, but not master (#power, #privilege, #stable criteria, #hegemony, #marginalized)

Figure 14.1. My comprehensive notes.

Flexible Framing, Open Spaces, and Adaptive Resources

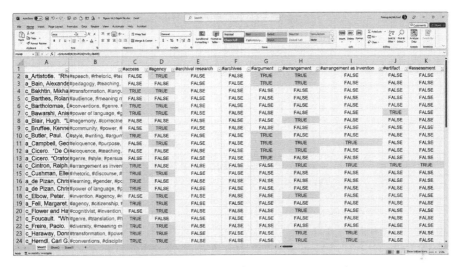

Figure 14.2. My comprehensive tags in Excel.

The formatting in that Word document had both technological and rhetorical significance. While the visual aid helped me identify the separate elements, the formatting served a much larger purpose of allowing me to "select all text with similar formatting," copy that text, and then paste into a searchable Excel document like the snapshot in Figure 14.2.

Leveraging Excel's searching capacity was a critical step. Because while the large Word document was certainly comprehensive, it was not easy to use beyond one entry at time. Copying the text out of that document and then using filters in Excel meant that I could immediately see connections among texts as well as how I had analyzed those points of conversation.[3] Using Excel's formulas to operationalize my connections technologically meant that I essentially built a network interface so that I could see non-linear connections based on my keywords.

Though I originally attributed developing my system to fear of individual failure, I realize in retrospect it was also driven by a need for accessibility in the name of equity. Being a pregnant parent in graduate school imposed non-negotiable time and energy limitations, and my notetaking system meant that I aced my written and oral exams when I might have struggled or even failed otherwise. More than that, however, I realized I could change the nature of recordkeeping itself. Though at a micro level in this situation, I could find what I needed, leave a trail of my knowledge behind, and see how everything was

---

3   That description makes it sound easy, but the process does require a decent level of comfort with Excel to get the data from the raw dump to this useable format. If folks are interested in getting step by step instructions on how to do this, I can work on it.

325

connected to everything else. If shared publicly, folks who came after me could follow my path, use my knowledge to achieve their own goals more quickly, and leave their expertise behind for yet more folks, some of whom might need that additional hand up because they're not the body that was in power when the system was built. Though I didn't know it yet, this idea of organizing stuff would evolve from personal interest to professional contribution that I hoped would contribute to accessibility well beyond my own voice.

TRADITIONAL AND CONTEMPORARY ARCHIVAL THEORY

What I would discover is that archival theory is important to folks who don't consider themselves archivists, because it's really just a thoughtful conversation about the ways that people organize stuff. Archivists spend far more time exploring records-keeping than the average person—including the way that information is recorded, the system that holds the information, and the authority of the person contributing to the official record. Looking at organization from a writing studies perspective, archival theory can interrogate how the authoring and arrangement of physical or digital records of knowledge are themselves richly rhetorical, leading to conversations about how the infrastructure of archives can dis/able the kinds of resources and information that *can* be recorded. Embedding different ways of making meaning in systems matters, because historically, traditional archival theory and record-keeping have allowed only one interpretation: the dominant interpretation.

Joanne Evans (2014) called attention to "questions of whether the plurality of archival contexts should be better represented in our international archival description standards rather than their current tendency to assume that a mono-culture is achievable and desirable" (p. 8). She's pushing back here on the traditional singular descriptive practices that date back to 1898 with the publication of the *Dutch Manual* that established that r*espect des fonds* theory and practice that has dominated archival work to the modern era (Cook, 1997). *Respect des fonds* establishes what Laura Millar (2010) referred to as the "integrity of the archive" that has historically informed archive keeping. With the specific intent of taking artifacts out of circulation, Millar wrote "artifacts must not be "intermingled with archives from another source, and that all archives within that unified whole should be preserved in the order in which they were made and used" (2010, p. 268). Most respected archival bodies offer guidelines based on the *fonds* tradition, like the United States *Library of Congress Encoded Archival Description Best Practices*, the Canadian *Rules for Archival Description*, and Margaret Proctor and Michael Cook's British manual for archival description.

These traditional approaches limit records to basic information, such as unique identifying code of number, date and source of acquisition, brief description of materials included, notes on permissions to access, and present storage location (Millar, 2010). Even as Millar lays out best (traditional) principles for the process of record creation, however, she explained the system itself is limited and potentially flawed:

> Arrangement and description demand that the archivist impose an external and artificial structure on the archival materials, usually according to hierarchical levels . . . In reality, the archivist must sometime make more arbitrary decision, categorizing material according to a logic that may never have occurred to the creator. (2010, p. 146)

Since the act of naming in itself carries significant power (Freire, 2001), Evans, along with archival scholars like Terry Cook (1997; 2001; 2002) and Sue McKemmish (1994), have begun to push back against traditional practices. They argued digital records have changed the archivists' capabilities and that records can and should be move beyond traditional information to instead include extensive metadata and be authored by multiple parties (Cook, 1997, 2001; Johnson, 2017; McKemmish, 1994; Schwartz & Cook, 2002). Marlene Manoff examines the interdisciplinary nature of modern archiving, unpacking tensions between the tradition of the historical record with and against digital tools (2004; 2010) that also manifest in conversations of folksonomies, metadata, and stable ontologies (Guy et al., 2004; Guy & Tonkin, 2006; Nicotra, 2009; Shirky, 2008; Vander Wal, 2007). In fact, while technology can present the appearance of completeness and accessibility, Marta Werner wrote, "The archive is not as outsiders imagine it—a space of order, efficiency, completeness—but a space of chance meetings between what survives and those who come to look for it without knowing it is truly there" (2016, p. 481). Cook also emphasized the appearance of neutrality, warning that "[a]rchivists inevitably will inject their own values into [archival] activities" (1997, p. 38). Arguably, even if the arrangement and description do accurately reflect the creator's logic, the record still only holds limited information about the artifact from a specific perspective.

Some organizations, such as the Australian Records Continuum Research Group, argued for more inclusive design in the record-keeping and metadata systems themselves, describing their research as "exploring the archival multiverse, identifying and addressing the needs of a participatory archival and recordkeeping paradigm, and continued extension and enhancement of continuum models" (Records Continuum Research Group, 2022, para. 3). Founding group member Sue McKemmish argued archivists must continue to expand their understanding of the information captured in the official record. She wrote that archival systems cannot fulfill their mission to preserve records in context and use if they cannot accommodate more than the physical grouping and description "to capture data about contextual and documentary relationships" (1994, p. 9). The turn towards understanding records as evolving imprints of circulation has attracted the attention of scholars in rhetoric and composition.

Liza Potts, in fact, maintained that rhetoric and composition is uniquely positioned to guide development of digital humanities projects "because of our knowledge of how to architect, manage, and improve both the process and the building of these products and services" (2015, p. 258), becoming what she referred to as "agent[s] of social change" who are able to "move on this moment and architect for experience, rather than simply archiving collections" (2015, p. 261). With attention already focused on reading and responding to existing archives as researchers (Enoch & Gold, 2013; Graban, 2013; Kirsch & Rohan, 2008; McKee & Porter, 2012; Ramsey et al., 2010; Solberg, 2012), the field has also begun to engage with the human hands at work in the processing and preserving of artifacts (Morris & Rose, 2009; Ramsey, 2010). As Tarez Graban et al. argued, "When historical metadata migrate from print to online spaces, rhetoricians must (re)define *open* and *access* so as to more ethically reach wider publics" (2015, p. 237).

Organizational principles are of note for writing program administration folks because archiving specifically, or organizing more generally, is the application and execution of coding, of a series of established conventions of making meaning through a series of agreed organizational principles. Those conventions, of course, inhabit, embody, and reproduce specific power dynamics and hegemonies, and relate directly to the widespread conversations in rhetoric and composition about the necessity of diversity and inclusion at all levels (Inoue, 2016; Lewiecki-Wilson et al., 2008; Yergeau, 2016). This means that even the writing program administrator who is just trying to keep organized runs the risk of imposing their own values and practices onto a collection of resources likely intended to support diversity and inclusion. Relational architecture, in fact, intentionally functions as a reminder that there is always a supersystem in which we function, and a network of actors who remain unconnected and unrecognized unless we invite them to author the system with us (more on that below).

Again, this matters to folks outside the archives because writing programs are all about using resources, a task easily hindered without understanding the network in which those resources exist. In this collection, for example, Mara Lee Grayson traces the history and mandates impacting development English courses at California State University, and Emily R. Johnston deploys cultural-historical activity theory to push back against oppression from within the system. Their focus on these systems, these networks of people, relationships, documents, and policies, parallel Barbara L'Eplattenier's (2009) and Katherine Tirabassi's (2010) archival infrastructure challenges of *how* to search for resources and even *what* to ask in order to affect change.

Archival theory also offers another lens through which to push for equity, with new digital tools potentially offering the chance to examine the gaps in the records, enabling what Janine Solberg (2012) described as "new habits, new ways of interacting with information, and new opportunities for serendipity as we move through texts" (p. 2013). She, like Tarez Graban (2013) and others, asserted digital technologies have the potential to enable researchers to do more than simply recover women's work, instead putting their "practices in context, and tracing them across the span of a life or career," particularly when those activities leave the academy to across genres, physical sites, or communities (Solberg, 2012, pp. 59–69).

But even these digital tools still require critical engagement. Elizabeth-Anne Johnson explained how she and her co-archivists, while working on a digitization project, might have "missed the fragments' description, improving our understanding of the fragments and their history" (2017, p. 37). As Solberg noted, "Description and indexing practices establish and perpetuate cultural and social values by allowing only certain materials to become visible to researchers, while obscuring others" (2012, p. 63). Johnson agreed, arguing that metadata (like the hashtags described throughout this piece) can and should be clearer about the decisions that the archivist makes in selecting, describing, and preserving materials:

> Whether or not archivists believe this to be true, describing archival material from a singular and authoritative point of view, as if the only way to convey the meaning of the record were to repeat how it was generated and its chain of custody, reinforces this paradigm of archival thinking. Records and their meanings are more complex than the recordkeeping paradigm allows; archival description must allow space for that complexity. (2017, p. 71)

The histories we make are knitted into our collective understanding of life; if voices and perspectives are absent from the record, they also become absent from our cultural memory.

RELATIONAL ARCHITECTURE IN AND FROM THE ARCHIVES

My interest in archival theory began in earnest when (spoiler alert) I was working in the archives. Like Tassoni and other writing practitioners, I searched and sorted through a variety of resources, none located in a central database, and none were labeled with anything remotely helpful. In my case, I was fortunate to eventually find an artifact that helped with my research questions through determination and a lot of luck. I was thrilled by the piece of the history of the Writing Across the Curriculum movement I had found, but also aware of the combination of access and luck that supported my discovery. Eager to build systems that go faster, I wondered if I could make life easier for those who followed and if I could make the records of the National Archives of Composition and Rhetoric as easy to access as my comprehensive notes had been.[4]

Motivated by the desire to make these resources accessible, to include the expertise of more than a singular archivist, and to make space for previously marginalized voices, I developed relational architecture as a records-keeping methodology that I would test in my dissertation (Morton-Aiken, 2017). I theorized that crowd sourcing contextual information from users and layering it on top of existing records would result in expanded knowledge, access, and agency. Users would be able to leave a trace in the system to augment what the archivist had already left behind, providing an opportunity for complexity and context that evolved alongside existing circulation and expanding inclusion.

Operationalizing the hashtags in my seminar and comps notes, resources in relational architecture are continually augmented by building connections with relationships identified by contributing-users. Used to its full potential, relational architecture acts as the digital string between unconnected items on a 3D corkboard, allowing users to add their own "folksonomy hashtags" (digital thumbtacks) to permanently and visibly connect these things going forward. Those "things" could be anything from actual artifacts in official archives to the filing cabinet full of stuff; as long as a digital record appears somewhere, the resulting web lets users see and use the knowledge of those who came before them.

Before the dissertation, I tested the theory in a small pilot research project, asking five faculty in rhetoric and composition to contribute their knowledge in the form of folksonomy hashtags to the artifact I had found. Figure 14.3 demonstrates the traditional archival descriptors that would have accompanied the entry without their contributions: artifact author (Elaine P. Maimon), date (1980), institution of the author (then Beaver College), and the institution of the audience (University of Maryland). Without a finding aid and with such limited knowledge in the record, that artifact would have been effectively inaccessible, especially for novices in the field. Though the document content outlined the framework for a successful WAC/WID program in 1980, the artifact

---

[4]   Bob Schwegler and I talk about the seminar I took with him in detail in "Recursion and Responsiveness" (Morton-Aiken & Schwegler, 2022) where my relationship with record-keeping formalized into something more methodological and specifically equity-driven.

would have remained valuable only to the privileged who already knew that it existed, let alone where to find it or its significance.

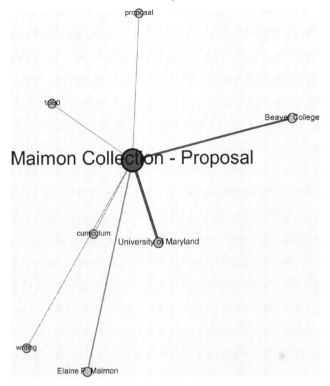

Figure 14.3. Maimon artifact with traditional archival descriptors.

Figure 14.4, however, adds faculty members' contributions, measurably increasing points of access, expanding the original record specialist knowledge from varied perspectives, and formalizing connections among previously disparate items.

Though this example specifically demonstrates relational architecture in the archives, the applications to the work of the WPA is similar—making helpful resources about writing known to more folks and accessible from more points of entry.

Relational architecture builds on scholarly work that exemplifies how researchers can and do read and respond productively (Enoch & VanHaitsma, 2015; Finnegan, 2006; Gaillet, 2012; Graban, 2013; Gries, 2013), and further develops methodologies that pushes back against the power inherent in the voices of official resources (Kirsch & Royster, 2010; Kirsch & Sullivan, 1992; Royster & Williams, 1999) to make the infrastructure itself able to support multiplicity, transparency, and evolving connectivity.

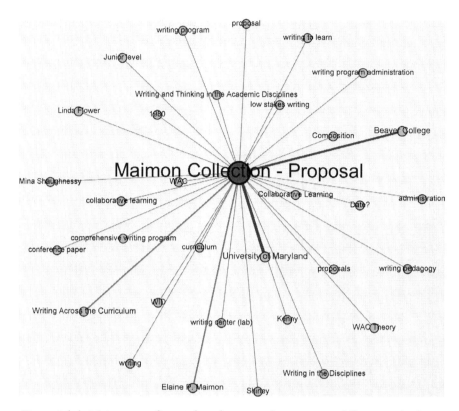

Figure 14.4. Maimon artifact with archivists and participants folksonomy hashtags.

Pulling back not only to view, but also to construct, the infrastructure of the archive as rhetorical means allows researchers to be *contributing* users who are more akin to "prosumers," blending former distinctions between experts and novices (VanHaitsma, 2015, p. 38), a markedly different approach to the suffering researcher so vividly described in the book *Dust* (Steedman, 2001). In this new position as agents of authority, all users who engage with the archives are now able to speak back to the archives rather than simply view them as powerless observers. More specifically, relational architecture changes the power dynamics of the archival infrastructure by acknowledging that multiplicities of experience, knowledge, and values already exist and should be equally represented in the official record. It illuminates archival processing work as rhetorical; recognizes the infrastructures itself as equally rhetorical to the human hands that process the collection; and records and values multiple kinds of knowledge as part of the official record and meaning-making system, all meaning making elements still at work in organization systems like writing programs or institutional bodies.

WHAT'S THE CATCH?

Unfortunately, relational architecture at this scale is still merely a theory. I used the networking software Gephi (Figure 14.5) for my project, asking contributors to submit hashtags via a Qualtrics survey. I manually cleaned and formatted the data from Qualtrics so that Gephi could build the resulting visual network. Relational architecture in its full potential would use folksonomy hashtags as digital points of origin to connect artifacts from distinct archival, institutional, or even disciplinary silos (see Morton-Aiken & Schwegler, 2017).

While some digital systems like Twitter or Imgur currently offer the ability to add keywords, they're not actually applying relational architecture, because it's not contributing rhetorically to the infrastructure, not connecting items that are outside the platform, and not identifying the weight (repetition) of contributions. Unlike Twitter's hashtags, for example, that are limited to the Twitter platform, relational architecture for archives would ideally sit outside those closed ecosystems, providing a pathway able to traverse a variety of platforms from small individual archives to the Library of Congress to sites like Twitter.

The resulting digital web would build connective tissue that is constantly cultivated by multiple users' articulations of one artifact's relationship to another, creating a trail of breadcrumbs and allowing users to see changes in data based on visualization programs.

While relational architecture originated as a rhetorically informed approach to archival practice and research, I share it in this context because it has value beyond the stacks and digital archives, also serving as a reminder that one way of naming, authoring, and contextualizing meaning-making tools is inevitably limited.

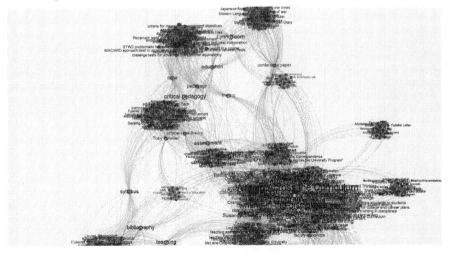

Figure 14.5. Gephi interface.

Particularly when applied to WAC/WID work as I describe later, relational architecture can remind writing program folks to purposefully include other voices and perspectives as we create and control program resources. To enact, as the editors described in the introduction collection, the understanding that writing programs are guided by ecosocial and networked systems frameworks, the stakeholder constituencies see each other not just as related entities, inorganic rooms that touch impermeable walls within buildings; but rather as vital, dynamic ecosystems within the eco-supersystem, with knowledge growing and interchanging not through rigid hierarchies but rather organically, *rhizomatically*. Therein lies the power of ecosocial systems and networks language.

Relational architecture as a lens encourages system builders to attend to multiple perspectives in all the rhetorical layers of the network and system because different perspectives can and should be articulated to the fullest context possible. As Anne Gere, et al. wrote in a recent article in *College Composition and Communication*:

> [C]ommunally revising disciplinary memory (of language history, language policy, and language discrimination) can provide powerful tools for promoting critical language awareness in the field and in the classroom . . . drawing attention to the structural nature of injustice in writing assessment and identifying structural opportunities for responding to them. (2021, p. 390)

Relational architecture offers a chance to push back against the archival habits, languages, and categories that Gere, et al. go on to write are "Privileged forms are codified and enforced as "standard," while the language varieties and discursive patterns of less privileged groups receive discrimination and ridicule" (2021, p. 385). Intentional engagement with our organizational systems, even as mundane as the filing cabinet, matters because "[w]hen we fail to think infrastructurally about our disciplinary practices and preoccupations, it becomes all too easy for us to take for granted that what we do in our classrooms is neutral. It isn't" (Gere, et al., 2021, p. 405).

BUT DOES ARCHIVAL THEORY REALLY AFFECT ME, THE ALREADY OVERBURDENED WPA?

I'm afraid so. As this collection demonstrates, the systems and supersystems we operate within inform so many of the actions we take, and recognizing those influences allows us to exert more agency and share more power when possible.

The archival principles discussed here matter, because programs are all about paperwork, and increasingly, all about assessment–potentially with assessment artifacts that live outside the organizational scope of the writing program itself.

I learned this the hard way while working on a then new scientific communication initiative at the University of Rhode Island to integrate rhetorical practice into the training of STEM graduates (Druschke et al., 2018). I helped develop robust assessment protocols that would, we hoped, validate our training of science graduate students. Though the many layers were complex, the easy one was supposed to be establishing a general baseline by scoring previously submitted dissertation and thesis proposals held in storage on campus.

That's when we discovered firsthand just how much archival arrangement affects the work that researchers can do even outside of what is generally considered archival research. In planning the process, we'd never stopped to make sure that someone was actually holding onto the documents we needed. If we had, we would have discovered that, crucially, not all proposals were archived in special collections, there was in fact no special collections archivist on staff, and changes to graduate school policies meant that proposals were no longer being stored anywhere and that hardcopies were being destroyed for space. We needed those artifacts for a key element of our argument to the National Science Foundation. Though our methodology was well designed, that portion of the methodology—the comparison of our intervention to starting data—was irrelevant without artifacts. In other words, the baseline assessment at the core of our half a million-dollar grant was at risk, because the organizational system we assumed was in place had broken down.

Whether trained archivist or harried administrator, people keep things which are of value and discard that which are not, making easily accessible the items that are more valuable and shoving into storage boxes items of lesser value. Those decisions build and transform systems that change our abilities to do our jobs, much like the institution's policy shifted from keeping hardcopies on file to destroying those hardcopies, enacting changes to unwritten policies that we could not have anticipated.

All researchers can only examine the data points they first collect; for the WPA, this means locating the artifacts that illustrate writing program work in action. Though those artifacts often come from the site of WPA work, our science communication grant is a clear example of how WPA as researchers sometimes need to engage with systems beyond their control, even for projects seemingly removed from archival work. That means updating the traditional position that values archives solely to display dusty manuscripts from another century to recognize that archives are simply systems that can prevent, limit, or expand access and progress.

BUT WAIT, THERE'S MORE...

Particularly in WAC/WID programs, participants should still have equal agency in meaning-making systems because those participants are a critical component of the program. After all, though we might be the writing experts in the room, there is no WAC program without participating faculty who bring disciplinary expertise to the table. More than simply putting worksheets, budgets, or agendas in logical filing sequence, relational architecture as a methodological lens reminds writing folks that even the decisions that undergird that sequence reflect the different ways of knowing and doing in different disciplines in different ways (Carter, 2007).

To fully value a WAC colleague's agency means examining the significance of power dynamics and understanding who and how individuals operate within systems so that not only are the facilitator's needs met, but that the system provides multiple points of connection for any users and from any discipline, to participate in and contribute to the building and organizing of resources current and historical. Instruments such as the Daly-Miller Apprehension Survey (Daly & Miller, 1975) give ways into such conversations, but the deployment of those instruments also requires attention to organizing in a way that complements the need to engage with non-writing faculty in WAC/WID programming to serve their needs as they, the participants, have defined those needs, rather than as a coordinator has dictated them (Adler-Kassner & O'Neill, 2010; Carter, 2007; David et al., 1995; Mullin, 2008; Russell, 2002; Walvoord, 1996). The key to organizing at any level is listening. As Mullin wrote:

> Those of us leading faculty toward different pedagogical understandings always have to be aware of how we are forwarding our own agendas, and we have to be flexible and open enough to reconsider our constructions of others and our definitions of their disciplines and ways of teaching. We can do this by actively listening. (2008, pp. 497–498)

Active listening requires engaging with and shifting to meet the needs of those users, and often manifests in the writing of resources such as workshop content, curriculum, or themes. But that listening should also be extended to the writing of the infrastructure of resources, to engaging with questions of system literacy as much as content, and to ensuring that user agency—allowing them to "interrupt" (Reynolds, 2009) or "talk back" (Royster, 1996)—is equitably enacted across all participants. Relational architecture is helpful, because it reminds organizers of WAC programs and activities that the organizing themselves are not neutral, and instead are a) originating-users needing contributing-users to fully deploy resources, and b) developing a system that needs to intentionally recognize and value multiple ways of knowing and doing.

This may mean opening up the physical filing cabinet for WAC faculty, perhaps with a table of contents where comments could be left or circulating documents through a Google Drive where participants have editing rights. Such collaborative leadership is risky and challenging. The results, while theoretically beneficial, might actually make the system more difficult to use. What if someone decides to literally write over the file system, or throw away documents because they don't understand their value? What if an administrator witnesses the messy, iterative process, declares it a failure because they deem it incomprehensive, and pulls all funding? What if colleagues assume that the program administrator isn't doing anything because they are delegating at best and allowing non-specialists to set the rules of engagement at worst?

Some assessment practices arguably offer a less risky method for securing feedback, but still do not necessarily position the WAC participant as contributing-user. While the participant is valued in that their feedback is requested, heard, and hopefully acted upon, authorship will remain solely with the director of those resources without the application of intentional and practical mechanisms for collaboration. This means that part of the practitioner's planning should include building in time and space to engage in conversation with those who will utilize WAC resources at the time of the writing and revising of those resources. After all, users are only able to actually use what they can find and request, and if they are not part of that naming process, they cannot be fortified with agency in the finding process.

Adopting the perspective of relational architecture reminds writing folks to recognize the layers of their work as rhetorical, as the arranger of writing resources including document, policies, and people. A networked approach specifically illuminates the habitual position of the writing program director as coder of these resources, and specifically calls for attention to the actual archive that writing coordinator develops almost accidentally as part of their day-to-day activities. As the authors of that infrastructure, they are inevitably writing personal and/or disciplinary values into the system, whether it's through the organization of the filing cabinet or the organization of the meeting to determine the new curriculum, effectively determining how (and if) other users, including future writing folks, will be able to access the resources selected to be preserved.

After all, one of the continuing challenges of WAC work is to make the faculty member, "likely to see [their] writing practices not as rhetorical devices but as business as usual or simply 'good science'" (Russell, 2002, pp. 16–17), aware of ideology reproduced within disciplinary conventions both in her own writing and in the teaching of writing to her students.

As the editors wrote in the introduction, the actors who built the system and network webs may not have designed them in ways which they function. Bringing awareness to these actors—powered and otherwise—means that the WPA is far better positioned to embed multiplicity, agency, and ease of access by working more intentionally with the guiding principles and practices of arrangement and agency in such systems. Relational architecture then becomes a powerful new lens through which to view the WPA as writer of the systems in general and writer of the archives in particular.

APPLICATIONS RIGHT HERE, RIGHT NOW

I originally developed relational architecture specifically as a feminist methodology for archives that stemmed from my desire to include and honor the perspectives of the "other" in traditional archival process and principles. I wanted to contribute to Evan's call for "thick" descriptions over traditional records because "[archival] processes and data structures need to be designed to capture and represent all rather than just part of our story in relation to the archival processing of records" (2014, pp. 8, 10). As I've demonstrated over these pages, however, the practical applications of relational architecture go much further than traditional archives.

Here's a few thoughts on how to leverage relational architecture to make writing program work a collaborative and inclusive system without breaking your brain or the budget:

- Digital applications
  - Use a shared digital repository, like Microsoft Teams or Google Drive, where all stakeholders have "edit" permission so they can augment and contribute with varied perspectives.
  - Keep meeting minutes in the shared digital files where all folks have access and can annotate as needed.
  - Use the "track changes" or "comments" function until a collaborative decision has been made on a draft so that louder voices or more aggressive contributors don't automatically drown out more vulnerable voices. (And look back through the revision file occasionally to make sure that this is actually happening.)
  - Use hashtags or other tagging system within documents (or in the metadata file information) so searching is more democratic and less reliant on simply knowing where something lives.
  - Create shortcuts to related documents within files and folders.

Flexible Framing, Open Spaces, and Adaptive Resources

- ○ Create a unit email address (like "WPA@institution.edu") so that email archives are also handed down with the position.
- ○ Create a central document or database with hyperlinks to relevant resources.
- Hard copy applications
  - ○ Make sure everyone has access to the filing cabinet. For example, don't keep it in a personal office that is often locked, and don't lock the cabinet itself unless everyone has keys.
  - ○ Keep a notebook or other record on hand where folks can leave information about what they changed, renamed, moved, added, or removed.
  - ○ Use sticky notes inside folders to leave information for others, including where else they might look for related resources.
- Digital and analog
  - ○ Create a culture of curiosity, conversation, and collaboration.
  - ○ Make space for all folks to voice their contributions and listen especially hard when folks from the margins share their thoughts.
  - ○ Talk through naming conventions for programs and terms as well as the general organizational principles. Clearly name files with specific designations and institutional abbreviations so that folks can access without specialist knowledge (Write out terms for abbreviations like WPA or WAC if those are not standard within your institution).
  - ○ Rotate through who takes notes during the meeting.
  - ○ Keep notes of meetings and file all meeting minutes in accessible and clearly designated folders.
  - ○ Make intentional organization a visible and valued part of the process by occasionally spending a few minutes talking through how you collectively want to organize stuff and distribute the labor.
  - ○ Frame record-keeping as adding value, not as grunt work.

Deployed as a tool to fight traditional and singular dominant narratives, relational architecture is a daily mindset as much as a digital tool. This means that the challenges that face archivists—issues of access, arrangement, and agency—are critical to the work of the WPA as well. Relational architecture allows users to leave a traceable path behind so that WPAs and others who follow might better understand and navigate, as the editors wrote in the introduction, the "networks and systems [that] impose agency or act like agentive beings in that they may shape how writing program administrators work, impose deficit-based pedagogies or approaches, stifle emotional and physical well-being, and/or perpetuate problematic labor practices."

CONCLUSION

This chapter focused on the potential that relational architecture offers to cultivate a more intentional, inclusive, and socially just approach to the organization, authoring, and accessing of writing program resources. Formalizing the pathways that the editors described in the battle to remove "basic" from the title of a class through multiple layers of human and non-human actors, I highlight the importance of interrogating the systems and supersystems that organize the "stuff" that makes up our writing programs. Though the methodology is most directly applicable to archival information infrastructure.

Relational architecture offers the chance to formalize what Tassoni, in another chapter of this collection, describes his efforts to trace the Basic Writing across multiple location, actors, and history, describing his work as the "story/assemblage is designed to help agents/agencies recognize their involvement in BW's interoffice, intercampus actor-network." It offers the opportunity to record and make accessible to future WPAs what Tassoni called, in an earlier draft of his chapter, the "dense network of competing and aligned interests and concerns and that, over the years, various individuals, programs, events, and offices have arisen to address and spur and squelch these interests and concerns," and to further what he credits as Jay Dolmage's (2017) legend that helped him understand where to look for information and "describe the network trajectories of the assemblage that is BW at Miami University."

Finally, however, intentional organizational frameworks like relational architecture do work in the nexus of thriving as a writing program administrator, elevating marginalized voices and making the world a more equitable place. It's about attending to our own system and keeping the rhetorical aspects of other systems in place as we negotiate differences across campus. While I realize that not every WPA or WAC director dreams of a BMW, I imagine they do dream of a paperwork world in which they can do the work they set out to do, they can better help all the people they want to help, and they can get it on by working smarter, not harder. Paying attention to where you put the stuff, what you name the stuff, who can get the stuff, and who writes the stuff will get you far. Whether it's program assessment, renaming Basic Writing, or merely challenging the hegemony, attending to organization as a rhetorical system *is* doing important rhetorical work in the world. It's not easy, but to reappropriate Home Depot's motto, it's how more doers get more done.

REFERENCES

Adler-Kassner, L. & O'Neill, P. (2010). *Reframing writing assessment to improve teaching and learning.* Utah State University Press.

British Manual for Archival Description: Procter, Margaret, and Michael Cook. *A Manual of Archival Description.* Gower, 1989.

Canadian Rules for Archival Description: Bureau of Canadian Archivists (ed.). (1990). *Rules for Archival Description Part.* Bureau of Canadian Archivists. *K10plus ISBN.* https://archivescanada.ca/wp-content/uploads/2022/08/RADComplete_July2008.pdf.

Carter, M. (2007). Ways of knowing, doing, and writing in the disciplines. *College Composition and Communication, 58*(3), 385–418.

Cook, T. (1997). What is past is prologue: A history of archival ideas since 1898, and the future paradigm shift. *Archivaria, 43.*

Cook, T. (2001). Archival science and postmodernism: New formulations for old concepts. *Archival Science, 1,* 3–24.

Daly, J. A. & Miller, M. D. (1975). The empirical development of an instrument to measure writing apprehension. *Research in the Teaching of English, 9*(3), 242–249.

David, D., Gordon, B. & Pollard, R. (1995). Seeking common ground: Guiding assumptions for writing courses. *College Composition and Communication, 46*(4), 522–532. https://doi.org/10.2307/358326.

Dolmage, J. (2017). *Academic ableism: Disability and higher education.* University of Michigan Press.

Druschke, C. G., Reynolds, N., Morton-Aiken, J., Lofgren, I., Karraker, N. & McWilliams, S. (2018). Better science through rhetoric: A new model and pilot program for training graduate student science writers. *Technical Communication Quarterly, 27*(2), 175–190.

Enoch, J. & Gold, D. (2013). Introduction: Seizing the methodological moment: The digital humanities and historiography in rhetoric and composition. *College English, 76*(2), 105–114.

Enoch, J. & VanHaitsma, P. (2015). Archival literacy: Reading the rhetoric of digital archives in the undergraduate classroom. *College Composition and Communication, 67*(2), 216–242.

Evans, J. (2014). Designing dynamic descriptive frameworks. *Archives and Manuscripts, 42*(1), 5–18. https://doi.org/10.1080/01576895.2014.890113.

Finnegan, C. A. (2006). What is this a picture of?: Some thoughts on images and archives. *Rhetoric & Public Affairs, 9*(1), 116–123.

Freire, P. (2001). *Pedagogy of the oppressed* (M. B. Ramos, Trans.; 30th Anniversary ed.). Continuum.

Gaillet, L. L. (2012). (Per)Forming archival research methodologies. *College Composition and Communication, 64*(1), 35–58.

Gere, A. R., Curzan, A., Hammond, J., Hughes, S., Li, R., Moos, A., Smith, K., Van Zanen, K., Wheeler, K. L. & Zanders, C. J. (2021). Communal justicing: Writing assessment, disciplinary infrastructure, and the case for critical language awareness. *College Composition and Communication, 72*(3), 384–412.

Graban, T. S. (2013). From location(s) to locatability: Mapping feminist recovery and archival activity through metadata. *College English, 76*(2), 171–193.

Graban, T. S., Ramsey-Tobienne, A. E. & Myers, W. (2015). In, through, and about the archive: What digitization (dis)allows. In J. Ridolfo & W. Hart-Davidson (Eds.), *Rhetoric and the digital humanities* (pp. 233–243). University of Chicago Press.

Gries, L. E. (2013). Iconographic tracking: A digital research method for visual rhetoric and circulation studies. *Computers and Composition, 30*(4), 332–348. https://doi.org/10.1016/j.compcom.2013.10.006.

Guy, M., Powell, A. & Day, M. (2004). Improving the quality of metadata in eprint archives. *Ariadne, 38*. http://www.ariadne.ac.uk/issue38/guy/.

Guy, M. & Tonkin, E. (2006). Folksonomies: Tidying up tags? *D-Lib Magazine, 12*(1). http://citeseerx.ist.psu.edu/viewdoc/download?doi=10.1.1.501.4598&rep=rep1&type=pdf/

Inoue, A. B. (2016). Friday plenary address: Racism in wri.ting programs and the CWPA. *WPA: Writing Program Administration, 40*(1), 134–154. http://associationdatabase.co/archives/40n1/40n1inoue.pdf.

Johnson, E.-A. (2017). *Toward a collaborative online framework for archival representation* [Master's thesis, The University of Manitoba]. University of Manitoba Library. https://mspace.lib.umanitoba.ca/bitstream/handle/1993/32580/johnson_elizabeth-anne.pdf?sequence=1&isAllowed=y.

Kirsch, G. E. & Rohan, L. (Eds.). (2008). *Beyond the archives: Research as a lived process*. Southern Illinois University Press.

Kirsch, G. E. & Royster, J. J. (2010). Feminist rhetorical practices: In search of excellence. *College Composition and Communication, 61*(4), 640–672.

Kirsch, G. & Sullivan, P. (Eds.). (1992). *Methods and Methodology in Composition Research*. Southern Illinois University Press.

L'Eplattenier, B. E. (2009). An argument for archival research methods: Thinking beyond methodology. *College English, 72*(1), 67–79.

Lewiecki-Wilson, C., Brueggemann, B. J. & Dolmage, J. (2008). *Disability and the teaching of Writing: A critical sourcebook*. Bedford/St. Martin's.

Library of Congress Encoded Archival Description Best Practices: "EAD: Encoded Archival Description (EAD Official Site, Library of Congress)." N.p., n.d. Web. 7 Apr. 2023. https://www.loc.gov/ead/.

Lozano-Hemmer, R. (1999). Utterance 4 relational architecture. *Performance Research, 4*(2), 52–56.

Manoff, M. (2004). Theories of the archive from across the disciplines. *Portal: Libraries and the Academy, 4*(1), 9–25.

Manoff, M. (2010). Archive and database as metaphor: Theorizing the historical record. *Portal: Libraries and the Academy, 10*(4), 385–398.

McKee, H. A. & Porter, J. E. (2012). The ethics of archival research. *College Composition and Communication, 64*(1), 59–81.

McKemmish, S. (1994). Are records ever actual. In S. McKemmish & M. Piggot (Eds.), *The records continuum: Ian Maclean and Australian Archives first fifty years* (pp. 187–203). Ancora Press Caulfield. https://figshare.com/articles/Are_records_ever_actual_/3823350.

Millar, L. (2010). *Archives: Principles and practices*. Facet.

Morris, S. L. & Rose, S. K. (2009). Invisible hands: Recognizing archivists' work to make records accessible. In A. E. Ramsey, W. B. Sharer, B. L'Eplattenier & L. S. Mastrangelo (Eds.), *Working in the archives: Practical research methods for rhetoric and composition* (pp. 51–78). Southern Illinois University Press.

Morton-Aiken, J. (2017). *Metadata and relational architecture: Advancing arrangement, agency, and access with new methodology* [Dissertation, University of Rhode Island.] University of Rhode Island Digital Commons. https://digitalcommons.uri.edu/cgi/viewcontent.cgi?article=1606&context=oa_diss.

Morton-Aiken, J. (2019). Dressing for childbearing, the patriarchy, and me: Auto-ethnography in three parts. *The Journal of Multimodal Rhetorics*, *3*(2), 197–211.

Morton-Aiken, J. & Schwegler, R. (2017). History becomes connectivity: A data network for WAC/WID practices (now and then). *Double Helix*, *5*. https://doi.org/10.37514/dbh-j.2017.5.1.04.

Morton-Aiken, J. & Schwegler, R. (2022). Recursion and responsiveness: Simultaneous dialogues in archival classroom pedagogy and archival infrastructures. In T. S. Graban & W. Hayden (Eds.), *Teaching rhetoric and composition through the archives*. Southern Illinois University Press.

Mullin, J. A. (2008). Interdisciplinary work as professional development: Changing the culture of teaching. *Pedagogy: Critical approaches to teaching literature, language, composition, and culture*, *8*(3), 495–508. https://doi.org/10.1215/15314200-2008-008.

Nicotra, J. (2009). "Folksonomy" and the restructuring of writing space. *College Composition and Communication*, *61*(1), 259–276.

Potts, L. (2015). Archive experiences: A vision for user-centered design in the digital humanities. In J. Ridolfo & W. Hart-Davidson (Eds.), *Rhetoric and the digital humanities* (pp. 255–263). University of Chicago.

Ramsey, A. E. (2010). Viewing the archives: The hidden and the digital. In A. E. Ramsey, W. B. Sharer, B. L'Eplattenier & L. S. Mastrangelo (Eds.), *Working in the archives: Practical research methods for rhetoric and composition* (pp. 79–90). Southern Illinois University Press.

Ramsey, A. E., Sharer, W. B., L'Eplattenier, B. & Mastrangelo, L. S. (Eds.). (2010). *Working in the archives: Practical research methods for rhetoric and composition*. Southern Illinois University Press.

Records Continuum Research Group. (2022). Information Technology. *Monash University*. https://www.monash.edu/it/research/research-centres-and-labs/rcrg.

Reynolds, N. (2009). Interrupting our way to agency: Feminist cultural studies and composition. In S. Miller (Ed.), *The Norton book of composition studies*. (pp. 897–910). W. W. Norton & Company.

Royster, J. J. (1996). When the first voice you hear is not your own. *College Composition and Communication*, *47*(1), 29–40. https://doi.org/10.2307/358272.

Royster, J. J. & Williams, J. C. (1999). History in the spaces left: African American presence and narratives of composition studies. *College Composition and Communication*, *50*(4), 563–584. https://doi.org/10.2307/358481.

Russell, D. (2002). *Writing in the academic disciplines, 1870–1990: A curricular history* (2nd ed.). Southern Illinois University Press.

Schwartz, J. M. & Cook, T. (2002). Archives, records, and power: The making of modern memory. *Archival Science*, *2*, 1–19.

Shirky, C. (2008). *Here comes everybody: The power of organizing without organizations*. Penguin.

Solberg, J. (2012). Googling the archive: Digital tools and the practice of history. *Advances in the History of Rhetoric*, *15*(1), 53–76. https://doi.org/10.1080/15362426.2012.657052.

Steedman, C. (2001). *Dust: The archive and cultural history*. Rutgers University Press.

Tirabassi, K. E. (2010). Journeying into the archives: Exploring the pragmatics of archival research. In A. E. Ramsey, W. B. Sharer, B. L'Eplattenier & L. S. Mastrangelo (Eds.), *Working in the archives: Practical research methods for rhetoric and composition* (pp. 169–180). Southern Illinois University Press.

Vander Wal, T. (2007, February 7). Folksonomy coinage and definition. http://www.vanderwal.net/essays/051130/folksonomy.pdf.

VanHaitsma, P. (2015). New pedagogical engagements with archives: Student inquiry and composing in digital spaces. *College English*, *78*(1), 34–55.

Walvoord, B. E. (1996). The future of WAC. *College English*, *58*(1), 58–79. https://doi.org/10.2307/378534.

Werner, M. (2016). The weather (of) documents. *ESQ: A Journal of Nineteenth-Century American Literature and Culture*, *62*(3), 480–529.

Willis, H. (2009, August 22). *Relational architecture*. KCET. https://www.kcet.org/commentary/relational-architecture.

Yancey, K. B. (2004). Made not only in words: Composition in a new key. *College Composition and Communication*, *56*(2), 297–328. https://doi.org/10.2307/4140651.

Yergeau, M. (2016). Disable all the things. *WPA: Writing Program Administration*, *40*(1), 155–165.

CONCLUSION
A TOOL KIT

Genesea M. Carter
Colorado State University

Aurora Matzke
Chapman University

Administrative work is human work. And the rhetoric and composition administrative work we do is personal: our bodies, minds, identities, positionalities, emotions, values, and experiences shape and inform our work. Because this work is human and personal, this collection makes space for contributors to bring the personal to the theoretical with real stories and practical recommendations. Unfortunately, living and working within systems and networks often have dehumanizing and disembodying effects, and we would be remiss in our efforts to create change if we ignored the human side of rhetoric and composition administrative work.

However, systems are not just disembodied machines or structures that form and force the humans working within them. Systems are ecosocial and cannot function without the human actors. Because the humans working within the system are crucial to how the system functions, our collection focuses on the (often fraught) intersection of human beings, systems, and networks. In this case, we focus on rhetoric and composition administrators because they are some of the people who can resist, reshape, and reframe the systems and networks. These administrators are critical to how higher education systems and networks will run. They are also critical to creating lasting, meaningful change within a system. Rhetoric and composition administrators—whether they are writing center directors, doctoral students who have administrative roles, non-tenure-track faculty serving on composition program committees, or writing across communities program directors, among others—are doers integrally involved in the doing. Because rhetoric and composition administrators integrally work within program, department, and university systems, they can shape and impact change work in ways that faculty, staff, and students cannot (see Lemke, 1995). Consequently, while we, the editors and contributors, use systems-based lenses to examine administrative roles within organizational structures, we equally emphasize the responsibilities of the human actors in creating meaningful change within higher education, writ large.

DOI: https://doi.org/10.37514/PER-B.2023.1848.3.1

We can become change agents who experience, listen, understand, and identify inequity and inequality within the systems and their corresponding networks. Inevitably, when we come to realize how and why higher education systems and networks are not working the way they should, it is because we have noticed a problem—a way that things should not be. As Bruno Latour (2005) wrote, "[A]ction should rather be felt as a node, a knot, and a conglomerate of many surprising sets of agencies that have to be slowly disentangled" (p. 44). This node, knot, or conglomerate is unraveled through the collection's authors' theory and practice. As bell hooks remind us, "Theory is not inherently healing, libratory, or revolutionary. It fulfills this function only when we ask that it do so and direct our theorizing toward this end" (Teaching to Transgress, 1994, p. 61). Therefore, this collection serves as a place for rhetoric and composition administrators and scholars who wish to promote practices that work to dismantle problematic systems and networks that impede change. Furthermore, we intersect systems and network theories with change making and DEIBSJ because these varying and complex efforts cannot be separate from conversations about systems and structures. We extend Lori Patton and Stephanie Bondi's (2015) work, who said

> Allies for social justice recognize the interconnectedness of oppressive structures and work in partnership with marginalized persons toward building social justice coalitions. They aspire to move beyond individual acts and direct attention to oppressive processes and systems. Their pursuit is not merely to help oppressed persons but to create a socially just world which benefits all people. (p. 489)

These oppressive structures could include, but are not limited to, short-sighted curriculum design, lack of agency for administrators and faculty, meaningless assessment methods, and biased hiring and promotion practices. With this purpose of highlighting problematic systems and networks—and inviting readers to once again examine how systems and networks stifle change-making efforts—so rhetoric and composition administrators are called to see where they can be change agents in their own systems and networks.

THE CONTEXT IN WHICH WE WRITE

With a focus on systems, networks, and change, we would like to pause, here, and acknowledge the space into which this collection has come to fruition. While, as we noted, the collection call came into being shortly after CCCC's 2018, the drafting process has taken us into the heart of some incredibly turbulent transnational times. We were deep in this collection when we continued to bear witness to atrocities enacted by figures of authority across the nation on Black folx. For many, the mass-media reckoning of White supremacist systems was too long coming and has resulted in too little, others have begun to reevaluate the roles they play in all systems and networks—from religious systems to workplace systems to family systems to political systems, among others—for the first time. As well, we wrote and researched through the 2020 COVID-19 pandemic, where we and the authors saw and experienced broken systems and networks in action. We watched and experienced the breakdown in educational systems, the isolation mount, disinformation campaigns flourish, mental health reach a breaking point, and death tolls rise. We also continue to bear witness to the atrocities and war crimes across the globe, and the fears of nuclear war once again being bandied about in the press.

It is in these contexts and lived experiences we, as editors and contributors, work, and we cannot help but reflect on the ways we contribute to broken systems and networks and where we are resisting them. And while the authors do not necessarily take up these transnational topics explicitly in their chapters, many of us recognize the harm and pain inherent in the systems and networks around us and these experiences and feelings necessarily underpin the writings found herein.

TOOL KIT: ADDITIONAL WAYS TO CREATE CHANGE IN CONVERSATION AND ACTION

While we believe it is important to acknowledge these devastating, crumbling, and broken systems that continue to shape the field's thought processes, research, and recommendations, we also are committed to providing avenues for hope and change that continue to amplify the good work taken up by collection contributors. As readers have noticed, this collection contains diverse genre conventions, and our conclusion is no different. Therefore, in line with the collection's mosaic of hybrid genre conventions, this conclusion offers readers additional ways to examine the systems, as well as care for and expand the self.

We highly recommend that all conversations about changing systems and networks include some form of recommendation, way forward, or thing to try. One feature of this collection is problem-solving, which is why we asked all contributors to offer a recommendation or strategy for readers. We have all personally experienced the demoralization that comes with talking about the systems and networks that impede our change-making administrative efforts without any accompanying naming of agency or without recommendations for ways forward. Therefore, we strongly advocate for readers, whether they are students, staff, or faculty, to be encouraged with ways to move forward, whether that includes setting workplace boundaries, collaborating on writing and research, or encouraging additional dialogue with other programs and departments. This tool kit offers readers a selection of frameworks, recommendations, and further reading to help enact change in their programs, departments, universities, and communities.

Having Conversations and Reflecting: Creating Change within Professional Communities

While there are many ways administrators can help change the landscape of administrative work within established systems and networks, the first step is to talk about how systems and networks shape and define the work program, department, and university administrators do. The more we can normalize and prioritize conversations around systems and network theory and influence, the easier it will be to find colleagues who are willing to be change agents alongside us. We draw from Sara Ahmed, bell hooks, Wonderful Faison, Frankie Condon, M. Remi Yeargeau, Lou Maraj, Carmen Kynard, and many others in the following conversation starters and action items.

These conversations and actions about systems and networks can include, but are not limited to:

- Assign decolonized, anti-hegemonic readings and work in undergraduate and graduate courses about systems and network theory alongside readings about organizational DEIBSJ and change-making writ large. Enact collaboratively built structures that exemplify these models.
- Offer regular program professional development that includes conversations about how the program can dismantle oppressive systems and support new ways to further change efforts, including teaching, hiring, promotion and tenure, tenure lines, budgets, outcomes, and strategic planning, among others.
- Start a book club with readings about the changing face of higher education, neoliberalism, systems, organizational leadership and management, or other topics that introduce participants to the ways systems and network language impede or promote change efforts. Work collaboratively to name how these theories are applied in local contexts.
- Encourage discussions about the systems and networks that shape your program, department, college, and university during committee meetings and department meetings. Collaboratively name whether these practices are inclusive or exclusionary, equitable or unjust, and plan ways forward to amplify or dismantle.

- Listen to, amplify, and center the expertise, experiences, and knowledges of BIPOC and/or historically minoritized individuals in rhetoric and composition work writ large. Assist in centering these differing knowledges and maintaining the space to amplify local and national work, from the ground up, into practices, perspectives, materials, and structures.

Education as Bridge-Building: How to Move Toward Change

As readers make decisions about what conversations to have and with whom, we offer a nowhere near exhaustive selection of readings that have shaped some of our understanding of administrative work within systems and networks. These pieces have changed our perspectives, helped us see our agency in new ways, and confirmed the personal and professional work we must continue to do. Readers may want to start here:

- Charles Bazerman and David R. Russell's *Writing Selves/Writing Societies: Research from Activity Perspectives.*
- Stuart Brown and Theresa Enos' *The Writing Program Administrator's Resource: A Guide to Reflective Institutional Practice.*
- Natalie Dorfeld's *The Invisible Professor: The Precarious Lives of the New Faculty Majority.*
- Wonderful Faison and Frankie Condon's *Counterstories from the Writing Center.*
- Kristie Fleckenstein's *Embodied Literacies: Imageword and a Poetics of Teaching.*
- Genie Nicole Giaimo's *Unwell Writing Centers: Searching for Wellness in Neoliberal Institutions and Beyond.*
- Holly Hassel and Cassandra Phillips's *Materiality and Writing Studies: Aligning Labor, Scholarship, and Teaching.*
- Mays Imad's Transcending Adversity: Trauma-informed Educational Development, published in *Educational Development in the Time of Crises.*
- Mary Helen Immordino-Yang and Antonio Damasio's We Feel, Therefore We Learn: The Relevance of Affective and Social Neuroscience to Education, published in *Mind, Brain and Education.*
- Rebecca L. Jackson and Jackie Grutsch McKinney's *Self+Culture+Writing: Autoethnography for/as Writing Studies.*
- Alexandria L. Lockett, Iris D. Ruiz, James Chase Sanchez, and Christopher Carter's *Race, Rhetoric, and Research Methods.*

- Sharon James McGee and Carolyn Handa's *Discord and Direction: The Postmodern Writing Program Administrator.*
- Staci M. Perryman-Clark and Collin Lamont Craig's *Black Perspectives in Writing Program Administration: From the Margins to the Center.*
- Rebecca Pope-Ruark's *Unraveling Faculty Burnout: Pathways to Reckoning and Renewal.*
- Bessel van der Kolk's *The Body Keeps the Score: Brain, Mind and Body in the Healing of Trauma.*
- M. Remi Yergeau's Authoring Autism: On Rhetoric and Neurological Queerness.

Readers might wish to reach out to their local communities for readings, experts, and programs designed to assist bridge-building to continue learning from and building upon the wood work local folx are already doing.

Assessing Administrative Documents: Creating Meaningful Labor and Equity Changes

As many of our contributors have written, change making starts inward with ourselves. It is incredibly difficult to create meaningful change if we are not in alignment with our professional and personal values, priorities, and needs. One way to create change for ourselves and for others is through renegotiations of our job descriptions and work allocations. As we have written elsewhere (2023), rhetoric and composition administrators can enact change by examining the documentation—job descriptions, annual evaluation materials, program budgets, tenure and promotion requirements, contracts, department bylaws, etc.—that inaccurately represents, minimizes, or undermines the realities of their work. Examining program, department, and university documentation may result in:

- A reallocation of FTE percentages, including teaching, research, service, and administration.
- An updated job description with responsibilities during the academic year and summer.
- A proposal to the dean or provost for additional funding, resources, and support.
- A revision of annual evaluation documentation and requirements.
- A memorandum of understanding (MOU) or other official renegotiations for the program administrator(s).

Listening as a Love Ethic: Listening Inward and Outward for Systematic Change

At our various institutions and communities, in our differing and layered positionalities, we believe Kyende Kinoti's (2020) work on listening is particularly poignant and offers readers a framework to learn how to listen to themselves—what they and their bodies need—and listen to others. Kinoti, ruminating on hook's (2000) *All About Love: New Visions*, wrote,

> In a colonized system we see that the love ethic breaks down when we choose not to listen to those at the center of their own lives, instead, the prevailing voices are those of experts or donors who are far removed for the truth and experiences of communities they claim to serve. Love is absent when we hold that certain groups possess a monopoly on knowledge even when that knowledge is about another's life. (2020, para. 5)

Listening with love within administrative contexts encourages us to develop relationships with and across agencies/actors from a variety of academic and administrative communities and systems. Listening changes the conversation from one that relies solely on self and existing structure to situating the rhetoric and composition administrator within an ecosocial structure of human and nonhuman actors. Listening with love to systems, networks, and people offers the administrator a tangible way to engage in identifying the gaps, the in-between, and the silences that result in broken systems and people. As Kinoti further argues, "The next time you are planning a program, or collecting feedback, or analyzing the outcomes of your work, embrace the love ethic in your process. Respect that the individuals you serve have agency and expertise within their lives. Listen to them deeply and authentically. See how your and their lives are intertwined" (2020, para. 8). Rhetoric and composition administrators may wish to apply this ethic with an emphasis on time, place, culture, and actors/agents to allow for a critical look at the micro and macro embodied practices that form sustainable change-making opportunities and practices. We also suggest readers might apply systems and network theories as an effective form of rhetorical listening to ourselves in ways that move us toward meaningful and sustainable action in our own lives.

Readers might consider journaling answers to Krista Ratcliffe's (2005) rhetorical listening questions within administrative situations and contexts to better understanding when and why they stop listening to themselves and others. Readers might start with these questions:

- In what administrative context/issue, do I stop listening to my gut desire or need and why?
- In what administrative context/issue, do I automatically react with a guilt/blame logic and why?
- In what administrative context/issue, do I start feeling excluded and why?
- In what administrative context/issue, do I focus solely on differences and why?

These reflective questions become fact gathering tasks in which we slow down and ask questions about our reactions and *why* they are happening. Once we better understand ourselves and our reactions, we can move forward to create change within ourselves, our communities, and within the systems and networks around us.

Ongoing Professional Development: Creating Change from Within

There are many online and in-person professional development venues that may help rhetoric and composition administrators align their values and ideologies with the realities of their work and work environment. Readers might explore these resources for their own personal growth which will, in turn, help them develop the skills and knowledge to work towards systematic change at the different levels of administrative influence, such as at the program, department, or college level. We recommend also seeking out resources which speak directly to the locality and experiences of the reader in order that this interaction might be best poised for success.

- The American Psychological Association's Center for Psychology and Health (https://www.apa.org/health)
- The Berkeley Well-Being Institute (https://www.berkeleywellbeing.com/about.html)
- The Bowen Center for the Study of the Family (https://www.thebowencenter.org)
- The Centre for Organization Effectiveness (https://tcfoe.com/about/)
- Happiness Studies Academy (https://www.happinessstudies.academy/abouttalbenshahar/)
- The Internal Family Systems Institute (https://ifs-institute.com)
- The Mindfulness Institute (http://www.mindfulnessinstitute.ca)
- The Trauma Research Foundation (https://traumaresearchfoundation.org)

- The University of California—San Diego Center for Mindfulness (https://cih.ucsd.edu/mindfulness)
- The University of Michigan's Program on Intergroup Relations (https://igr.umich.edu)

As this collection has explored, administrative work is often both deeply personal and highly systemic. Contributors have used storytelling, case studies, research, reflection, and theory as a way to identify, problematize, and name the administrative work they do within existing disciplinary, social, institutional, and personal systems and networks. To create lasting, meaningful change, rhetoric and composition administrators—as people and as administrators—have to examine the existing systems and networks in which they live and work. It is no easy task, as we have to pay attention and listen, ask "why" questions, discover and form connections, and allow for knowledge to move organically through the networks.

CONCLUSION

Whether you decide to have dialogue and discussion through committees, classes, meetings, professional development, or reading groups, we encourage reflection, for you and for others, on how systems and networks shape the work you do and the work you want to do. To close this collection, we offer a few final reflection questions that might shape the conversations you want to have or need to have. These reflection questions can be used to examine your own ideologies, values, beliefs, and actions, or they can be used to start or drive conversation:

- How do systems or networks inform or impede the change you want to make within your program? Who do you need to get to know or what do you need to make these changes? What changes might you need to make to further these efforts?
- How do documents, textbooks, syllabi, websites, and bylaws further the established systems and networks in your program and department? Do you and others need to examine the language in these artifacts to examine what systematic changes you can make through language?
- How do processes and protocols further the established systems and networks in your program and department that slow down or stifle change-making efforts? Do you need to form a program task force or program committee to create new processes and protocols that support social justice?

- How do program, department, and university leadership unwittingly (or wittingly) support systems and networks that impede social justice efforts, such as equitable hiring practices, clear and consistent evaluation promotion guidelines, appropriate and professional behavior, and workplace boundaries, among others. Do you need to examine your own role in furthering systems and networks? Might you bring up your concerns about existing systems and networks with colleagues, in committees, and in meetings?

If you feel stuck, such as not having colleagues who are interested in or willing to examine the existing systems and networks with you, what collaborative relationships might you develop across the institution to find like-minded faculty, staff, and graduate students? Does your campus have a teaching and learning center where you can broach these conversations? Or, perhaps, a student support office on campus would be open to your ideas. Or maybe the faculty and staff you have met in cross-campus committees would be interested in discussing the college and university's systems and networks. We encourage you to branch out and take your conversations across campus for encouragement and support, if needed.

Like the systems in which we work, this collection offers a network mosaic of *praxis*-based chapters to untangle the complex, ongoing process of building, dismantling, and existing in larger higher educational systems when one participates in change-making work. We absolutely believe we can create systemic change, and our contributors do too. Let us create that change together.

REFERENCES

Ahmed, S. (2017). *Living a feminist life*. Duke University Press.

Baker-Bell, A. (2020). *Linguistic justice: Black language literacy identity and pedagogy*. Routledge.

Bazerman, C. & Russell, D. (Eds.). (2003). *Writing selves/writing societies: Research from activity perspectives*. The WAC Clearinghouse; Mind, Culture, and Activity. https://doi.org/10.37514/PER-B.2003.2317.

Brown, S. & Enos, T. (Eds.). (2022). *The writing program administrator's resource: A guide to reflective institutional practice*. Lawrence Erlbaum.

Carter, G. M., Matzke, A. & Vidrine-Isbell, B. (2023). Navigating networks and systems: Practicing care, clarifying boundaries, and reclaiming self in higher education administration. In R. Hentschell & C. E. Thomas (Eds.), *Transforming leadership pathways for humanities professionals in higher education* (pp. 81–104). Purdue University Press.

Dorfeld, N. M. (Ed.). (2022). *The invisible professor: The precarious lives of the new faculty majority*. The WAC Clearinghouse; University Press of Colorado. https://doi.org/10.37514/pra-b.2022.1589.

Faison, W. & Condon, F. (2022). *Counterstories from the writing center*. Utah State University Press.

Fleckenstein, K. (2003). *Embodied literacies: Imageword and a poetics of teaching*. Southern Illinois University Press.

Giaimo, G. N. (2023). *Unwell writing centers: Searching for wellness in neoliberal educational institutions and beyond*. Utah State University Press.

Hassel, H. & Phillips, C. (Eds.). (2022). *Materiality and writing studies: aligning labor, scholarship, and teaching*. National Council of Teachers of English.

hooks, bell. (1994). *Teaching to transgress: Education as the practice of freedom*. Routledge.

hooks, bell. (2000). *All about love: New visions*. William Morrow.

Imad, M. (2021). Transcending adversity: Trauma-informed educational development. *Educational Development in the Time of Crises, 39*(3), n.p. https://doi.org/10.3998/tia.17063888.0039.301.

Immordino-Yang, M. H. & Damasio, A. (2007). We feel, therefore we learn: The relevance of affective and social neuroscience to education. *Mind, Brain and Education, 1*(1), 3–10. https://onlinelibrary.wiley.com/doi/pdf/10.1111/j.1751-228X.2007.00004.x.

Jackson, R. & McKinney, J. G. (Eds.). (2021). *Self+Culture+Writing: Autoethnography for/as writing studies*. Utah State University Press.

Kinoti, K. (2020). "Listening with love." *Feedback Labs*. https://feedbacklabs.org/blog/2020/12/11/listening-with-love/.

Kynard, C. (2023). *Education, liberation & black radical traditions for the 21st century*. http://carmenkynard.org/.

Latour, B. (2005). *Reassembling the social: An introduction to actor-network-theory*. Oxford University Press.

Lemke, J. L. (1995). *Textual politics: Discourse and social dynamics*. Taylor & Francis.

Lockett, A. L., Ruiz, I. D., Sanchez, J. C. & Carter, C. (Eds.). (2021). *Race, rhetoric, and research methods*. The WAC Clearinghouse; University Press of Colorado. https://doi.org/10.37514/per-b.2021.1206.

Maraj, L. (2020). *Black or right: Anti/racist campus rhetorics*. Utah State University Press.

Martinez, A. Y. (2020). *Counterstory: The rhetoric and writing of critical race theory*. Conference on College Composition and Communication; National Council of Teachers of English.

McGee, S. & Handa, C. (Eds.). (2005). *Discord and direction: The postmodern writing program administrator*. Utah State University Press.

Patton, L. D. & Bondi, S. (2015). Nice White men or social justice allies? Using critical race theory to examine how White male faculty and administrators engage in ally work. *Race Ethnicity and Education, 18*(4), 488–514.

Perryman-Clark, S. M. & Craig, C. L. (Eds.). (2019). *Black perspectives in writing program administration: From the margins to the center*. National Council of Teachers of English.

Pope-Ruark, R. (2022). *Unraveling faculty burnout: Pathways to reckoning and renewal*. Johns Hopkins University Press.

Ratcliffe, K. (2005). *Rhetorical listing: Identification, gender, Whiteness*. Southern Illinois University Press.

van der Kolk, B. (2015). *The body keeps the score: Brain, mind and body in the healing of trauma*. Penguin.

Yergeau, M. (2018). *Authoring autism: On rhetoric and neurological queerness*. Duke University Press.

AFTERWORDS

Lucien Darjeun Meadows
University of Denver

I open the door. I open the computer. We open, welcome, and invite students, learners, and, yes, *writers* into the shimmering network of academic writing. We stand with them, and we sit beside them. We move together to honor their words, their voices, their manifold identities, and the complex process of bringing themselves onto the page—within the complex assemblage of systems and networks that is *academia*. That is *writing*.

As these contributors have demonstrated, this work is energizing and vital, even as it can also be challenging and discouraging. We are all interconnected in shared networks of meaning-making. I go to the writing center. I go to the classroom. I am ready to instigate an academic writing revolution where all voices will be heard and supported! But I am aware that I, we, and the writers we serve often are navigating continual and systemic networks both of support and of oppression. The joy of uplifting one writer's process coming into bloom can be tempered by a concern that a future class or supervisor might not support this writer's unique voice. I often work—as many of this collection's authors also do—to make these systems and networks visible with the writers I serve. We need not only exist within a given system. We can make that system visible, and in so doing, we can question it, disrupt (and queer!) it, and imagine alternatives.

The editors and contributors of *Systems Shift: Creating and Navigating Change in Rhetoric and Composition Administration* help me, as an emerging researcher and professional, imagine what the future of writing centers and writing programs may hold, and these imaginations thrill me. The future is collaborative and interdisciplinary. The future is diverse. The future is on-campus and beyond-campus. The future is polyvocal at every turn; for in a network, while some tendrils might be a bit longer or thicker, they too fold into the larger pattern that we are co-creating. The future of writing centers and writing programs is far less *I* and far more *we*. And welcoming more voices to the table, to question and transform these systems, is perhaps what gives me the most hope.

In closing, to honor this emerging collaborative, polyvocal future, I offer not *my words* but *our words* in the following poem: a cento. *Cento*, coming from the Greek for *to plant slips of trees* and the Latin for *patchwork*, is a poem made of lines from other works. Here, this cento is composed entirely of lines from this collection's chapters. Voice multiplies, touches, and inspires within the system of this collection, a future system living as a seed within this present system, which we, as tutors, teachers, advocates, administrators, professionals, and writers all, may join:

> Theorize a radical rearrangement:
> our bodies, minds, identities, positionalities, emotions,
> values, and experiences shape and inform our work.)
>
> We all have stories but some are de-legitimized.
> With a broader network, broader meanings can come into play.
> (This is easier said than done, but it can be done.
>
> Theorize a radical rearrangement:
> this narrative is always evolving and always inclusive,
> driven by a need for accessibility in the name of equity.
>
> What do stories continue to teach us?
> We are learning who to be, how to act, and what to do;
> becoming the future story changing at each center.
>
> Theorize a radical rearrangement:
> here is an analysis of *how the bodies we inhabit*
> *determine the experiences we have in the world.*
>
> I hope this builds solidarity I hope this invites reflection.
> We are the future of this discipline, as we are told—
> > Let's be brave.

CONTRIBUTORS

Kelly Bradbury is Assistant Professor of English at Colorado State University, where she teaches upper-division composition courses and directs a WAC program known as the gtPathways Writing Integration Project. She is the author of *Reimagining Popular Notions of American Intellectualism: Literacy, Education, and Class* (SIUP) and has published in *Computers and Composition*, *Community Literacy Journal*, and *Journal of Teaching Writing*. Her current scholarship focuses on rhetorical empathy, critical information literacy, and linguistic justice.

Kathryn Bruchmann is Associate Professor in the Psychology Department at Santa Clara University. She earned her Ph.D. from the University of Iowa where she specialized in social psychology. Her current scholarship focuses on how factors such as implicit theories or different identities influence the use of social comparison information.

Eric C. Camarillo is Dean of the Learning Commons at Tarrant County College's Northwest campus, where he provides direction and vision for the Library and Learning Support Services. His research agenda is focused on writing centers and best practices within these spaces, antiracism in the context of writing centers, and asynchronous tutoring. His research has appeared in *WLN: A Journal of Writing Center Scholarship* and *Praxis: A Writing Center Journal*, and he has presented at numerous conferences including the International Writing Centers Association and the Conference on College Composition and Communication. He is currently Vice President of the South Central Writing Centers Association, Past President of the National Conference on Peer Tutoring in Writing, and Book Review Editor for *The Writing Center Journal*.

Genesea M. Carter is Associate Director of the University Composition Program at Colorado State University and Associate Professor of Rhetoric and Composition. Her research focuses on the intersection of systems, administration, student learning and support, and faculty mental health. Her research has appeared in *Composition Studies*, *Writers: Craft & Context*, and the *Journal of Teaching Writing*. Her first co-edited collection, *Class in the Composition Classroom: Pedagogy and the Working Class*, was published by Utah State University Press. In addition to her academic work, she has written and self-published two college student support books, *Making It Happen: A 16 Week Goal Setting Journal for Your College Success* and *How to Survive Your First Year of College: Strategies for Academic Success in a Stressed-Out World*.

Christina V. Cedillo (she/they) is Associate Professor of Writing and Rhetoric at the University of Houston-Clear Lake. Her research draws from cultural rhetorics and decolonial theory to focus on embodied rhetorics and rhetorics of embodiment at the intersections of race, gender, and disability. Her/their work has appeared in *College Composition & Communication*, *Rhetoric Society Quarterly*, the *Journal for the History of Rhetoric*, *Composition Forum*, and various other journals and edited collections. She is the lead editor of the *Journal of Multimodal Rhetorics*.

Sue Doe is Professor of English and Executive Director of The Institute for Learning and Teaching at Colorado State University (CSU). She has served as Director of Composition, as Director of the gtPathways Writing Integration, and as Chair of the Faculty Council at CSU. She co-edited (with Lisa Langstraat) *Generation Vet: Student-Veterans, Composition, and the Post-9/11 University* (Utah State P) and has published in such locations as *College English*, *WAC Journal*, *ADE-AFL Bulletin* of the Modern Language Association, *PS: Political Science and Politics*, *Feminist Formations*, *Literacy in Composition Studies*, *Teaching of Psychology*, *Composition Forum*, and numerous collections.

Matt Dowell is Associate Professor of English at Towson University, where he serves as director of first-year writing. His current research focuses on the institutional space and place of writing program administration specifically in relation to access, ableism, and disability. A recent chapter examining the sanctioned uptake of syllabus accessibility statements was published in the edited collection *Writing the Classroom: Pedagogical Documents as Rhetorical Genres*.

Bre Garrett is Associate Professor of English and Composition Program Director at the University of West Florida. She teaches classes in rhetorical theory, composition pedagogy, and public writing. Her current research trajectory intersects disability studies and rhetorics of accessibility, in which she explores topics ranging from graduate teacher training and writing program administration. She is a co-editor of *Disability, Access, and the Teaching of Writing*, coming out with NCTE's Rhetoric and Writing special series, and has an article forthcoming in *Across the Disciplines* on ePortfolios, HIPs, and wellbeing.

Mara Lee Grayson is Associate Professor of English and Faculty Coordinator of General Education Assessment at California State University, Dominguez Hills. She is the author of *Teaching Racial Literacy: Reflective Practices for Critical Writing*, *Race Talk in the Age of the Trigger Warning: Recognizing and Challenging Classroom Cultures of Silence*, and *Antisemitism and the White Supremacist Imaginary: Conflations and Contradictions in Composition and Rhetoric*, and co-editor (with Judith Chriqui Benchimol) of *Challenging Antisemitism: Lessons from Literacy Classrooms*. Her scholarship has appeared in various journals and edited collections, and she is the recipient of a CCCC Emergent Researcher Grant and the 2018 Mark Reynolds *TETYC* Best Article Award. Also a poet, her work has been nominated for Best of the Net and Pushcart prizes.

Holly Hassel earned her Ph.D. from the University of Nebraska-Lincoln and taught for two decades at the University of Wisconsin-Marathon County, one of thirteen associates-degree granting campuses that made up the University of Wisconsin Colleges. She has served as editor of *Teaching English in the Two-Year College* and as chair of the Conference on College Composition and Communication. Her research on composition pedagogy, two-year college writing programs, and college access has been published in many peer-reviewed journals and books.

Brian Hendrickson is Associate Professor of Writing Studies, Rhetoric, and Composition at Roger Williams University. His research areas include public, digital, and cultural rhetorics, writing across difference, community writing, writing in STEM, and equity-minded teaching and program administration. His work has appeared or is forthcoming in the journals *Across the Disciplines*, *Composition Forum*, *Composition Studies*, *JoSch - Journal fur Schreibwissenschaft*, *Journal of Business and Technical Communication*, *Kairos*, and *WAC Journal*, as well as several edited collections including *Best of the Journals in Rhetoric and Composition 2018*. He has been recognized by the Association of American Colleges and Universities with a K. Patricia Cross Future Leaders Award and by the Association for Writing Across the Curriculum and the WAC Clearinghouse with an Early Career Contributions to the Field Award.

Tamara Issak is Associate Professor in First-Year Writing in the Institute for Core Studies and directs the Writing Across Communities program at St. John's University. Her research focuses on cultural rhetoric, Islamophobic rhetoric, and community literacy. She is the recipient of several national fellowships and awards including an American Association of University Women Fellowship and Fulbright Fellowship in Syria. She earned her Ph.D. in Composition and Cultural Rhetoric from Syracuse University.

Janelle Jennings-Alexander is a scholar-educator focused on improving academic support structures for historically marginalized students through equity-oriented institutional change and universal design for learning. Her teaching and research explore opportunities for increasing racial literacy and engaging learners in critical discussions of African American-authored fiction. A recipient of the NCTE Early Career Educator of Color Award, she earned a Ph.D. in Literature from Florida State University and serves as the Associate Vice President for Academic Affairs at Saint Augustine's University in Raleigh, North Carolina.

Emily Rónay Johnston is Assistant Teaching Professor in Writing Studies at the University of California, Merced. Recently, she completed a five-year term as Associate Director of the Dimensions of Culture Writing Program at the University of California, San Diego. Her teaching and research focus on trauma, language, and first-year composition as a critical space for cultivating resilience. Her work appears in the journals *College Composition and Communication, Writers: Craft & Context, Rhetoric of Health and Medicine, Women's Studies in Communication,* and *Antipodes: A Global Journal of Australian and New Zealand Literature,* and in the edited collection *Composing Feminist Interventions: Activism, Engagement, Praxis.*

Trent M. Kays is Assistant Professor and Director of College Composition at Augusta University. He specializes in multimodal writing, critical pedagogy, digital rhetoric, professional writing, and Internet Studies.

Ashanka Kumari is Assistant Professor and doctoral program coordinator in the Department of Literature and Languages at Texas A&M University—Commerce. Her work centers graduate student professionalization, multimodal composition and pedagogy, and the intersections among identity studies, digital literacies, and popular culture. She is the inaugural faculty recipient of the Inclusive Excellence Champion award and a 2023 Barrus Award recipient at Texas A&M University—Commerce. Her work can be found in numerous edited collections and journals as well as her co-edited collection *Mobility Work in Composition.*

Aurora Matzke is Assistant Professor and Writing Center Director at Chapman University. She has also held positions as a Writing Program Administrator, Coordinator of General Education, and Senior Associate Provost. Her editorial work can be found in *WPA: Writing Program Administration* and is forthcoming in *Peitho.* Her publication work can be found in various collections and is focused on open-access education and feminist leadership strategies.

Lucien Darjeun Meadows is a Ph.D. candidate at University of Denver, where his research focuses on queer ecology, Indigenous studies, and poetics. His creative work has received awards from the Academy of American Poets and American Association of Geographers; and his critical work has appeared in *Excursions, John Clare Society Journal,* and *Philia.* A first-generation university graduate from Appalachia, he has worked in four writing centers and is passionate about fostering inclusive environments for all learners to be welcomed and respected.

Jenna Morton-Aiken is Senior Associate Director for Writing and English Language Support at the Sheridan Center for Teaching and Learning at Brown University, where she is also a Lecturer in the Department of English. She earned her Ph.D. from the University of Rhode Island in English specializing in rhetoric and composition. Her research has appeared in *Technical Communication Quarterly, WPA Writing Program Administration, The Journal of Multimodal Rhetorics,* and various other journals and edited collections. Jenna helped launch SciWrite@URI.

Mandy Olejnik earned her Ph.D. in Composition and Rhetoric at Miami University (Ohio) and is Assistant Director of Writing Across the Curriculum at the Howe Center for Writing Excellence. She designs and leads faculty workshops, consults with disciplinary faculty on their teaching of writing, researches and assesses WAC programming, and provides special support for graduate-level writing instruction across campus. Her work has appeared in *The WAC Journal* and *Transformative Works and Cultures*. She was a learning designer for the online Miami Writing Institute and is co-editor of the edited collection *Changing Conceptions, Changing Practices: Innovating Teaching Across Disciplines* (Utah State University Press).

Bernice Olivas teaches writing and rhetoric at Salt Lake City Community College. She specializes in first-generation students, anti-racist and inclusive pedagogy.

Lana Oweidat is Associate Professor of Rhetoric and Composition and the Director of the Writing Center at Goucher College. She teaches writing and rhetoric courses with an emphasis on border discourses and transnational narratives. Her scholarly research interests include tutor training, feminist rhetorics, anti-Islamophobia pedagogies, and multilingual composition. Her work has appeared in various journals and edited collections.

Mike Palmquist (he/him) is Professor of English and University Distinguished Teaching Scholar at Colorado State University, where he directs the University Writing Center. Prior to returning to his role as a faculty member in the 2020-'21 academic year, he served for fourteen years in various university leadership roles. His scholarly interests include writing across the curriculum, the effects of computer and network technologies on writing instruction, and new approaches to scholarly publishing.

Lynn Reid is University Director of Writing at Fairleigh Dickinson University, where she is Associate Professor of Rhetoric and Composition. Her scholarly interests include composition pedagogy, basic writing, and digital literacies. Her work has appeared in journals including *Journal of Basic Writing*, *WPA: Writing Program Administration*, *Computers and Composition*, and several edited collections. She received her Ph.D. from Indiana University of Pennsylvania, where she was awarded the Patrick Hartwell award for promising research in composition.

Caitlyn Rudolph-Schram (she/her) holds an MA in Rhetoric & Composition from Ball State University. Her research generally focuses on cultural rhetorics, Writing Centers, and the intersection of online activism and identity. Currently, she is the Writing Center Director at Indiana University Kokomo and serves as Co-Chair of the Feminist Caucus for the CCCC's.

Iris Ruiz is a Continuing Lecturer for the UC Merced Merritt Writing Program and a Lecturer with the Sacramento State University Ethnic Studies Program. Her current publications are her monograph, *Reclaiming Composition for*

Chicano/as and other Ethnic Minorities: A Critical History and Pedagogy, and a co-edited collection, *Decolonizing Rhetoric and Composition Studies: New Latinx Keywords for Theory and Pedagogy*, to which she also contributed a chapter on the keyword "Race," a co-authored caucus history, *Viva Nuestra Caucus: Rewriting the Forgotten Pages of Our Caucus*. She has also written on Decolonial Methodology in *Rhetorics Elsewhere and Otherwise*. Her 2017 co-authored article, "Race, Silence, and Writing Program Administration," deals with race and WPA history, was published in *WPA Writing Program Administration*, and received the 2019 Kenneth Bruffee award. She has written for the *Journal of Pan African Studies* about her journey toward a decolonial identity titled, "La Indigena."

Erec Smith is Associate Professor of Rhetoric at York College of Pennsylvania. His primary work focuses on the rhetorics of anti-racist activism, theory, and pedagogy. He is co-founder and President of *Free Black Thought*, a website dedicated to highlighting viewpoint diversity within the black intelligentsia. His recent writings include several op-eds as well as his books, *A Critique of Anti-Racism in Rhetoric and Composition: The Semblance of Empowerment* (2020) and *The Lure of Disempowerment* (2022). He is also a research scholar in Politics and Society for the Cato Institute.

John Paul Tassoni is Professor of English/Languages, Literatures, and Writing at Miami University. There he has served as the English Department's Director of College Composition, as Co-Coordinator for the regional campuses' Center for Teaching and Learning, and as University Director of Liberal Education. He co-founded the scholarly journal *Open Words: Access and English Studies* and is the founding editor of *Journal on Centers for Teaching and Learning*. He continues to focus the bulk of his teaching and research on basic writing programming at Miami's open-access campuses.

Julia Voss is Associate Professor of Rhetoric and Composition, former Director of Professional Writing, and current Chair in the English Department at Santa Clara University, where she researches curriculum/assessment design and equity, learning space design, and writing program administration. Her work has appeared in *Composition Studies, Computers and Composition, College Composition and Communication, Writing Program Administration*, and other venues, and she serves as associate editor for *Across the Disciplines*. Her current projects examine classroom design as a pedagogical and programmatic issue; information literacy instruction around popular sources; how diversity/equity/inclusion are represented (or not) in FYW syllabi; and frameworks-based WAC faculty development.